An Alternative to
Private Property

An Alternative to Private Property

COLLECTIVE PROPERTY

IN THE

JURIDICAL CONSCIOUSNESS

OF THE

NINETEENTH CENTURY

*

Paolo Grossi

TRANSLATED BY LYDIA G. COCHRANE

The University of Chicago Press CHICAGO AND LONDON

In memory of
GIANGASTONE BOLLA
and
SALVATORE ROMANO

PAOLO GROSSI is professor of the history of Italian law in the
Faculty of Jurisprudence of the University of Florence, where he
is also director of the Institute of the Theory and History of Law.

The University of Chicago Press, Chicago 60637
The University of Chicago Press, Ltd., London

© *by The University of Chicago* 1981
All rights reserved. Published 1981
Printed in the United States of America
88 87 86 85 84 83 82 81   5 4 3 2 1

Originally published as '*Un altro modo di possedere*': *L'emersione
di forme alternative di proprietà alla coscienza giuridica postunitaria,*
© 1977 by Giuffrè Editore, Milan.

Library of Congress Cataloging in Publication Data

Grossi, Paolo.
    An alternative to private property.

    Translation of: Un altro modo di possedere.
    Includes bibliographical references and index.
    1. Property—Italy—History.   2. Property—
Europe—History.   I. Title.
Law   346.404   81-1219
ISBN   0-226-31002-7   344.064   AACR2

Contents

Foreword

A preeminent historian of law in Europe as well as in his native Italy, Paolo Grossi is well known for his original and provocative scholarship. He is also well known for having established at the University of Florence the Center for the History of Modern Juridical Thought, of which he is the director, as an international center of legal and historical research. Transdisciplinary in its scholarship and pluralistic in its politics, the Center has become a meeting place for jurists, historians, and philosophers of various methodological and political persuasions. The research conducted by Grossi and his colleagues and students is published in the Center's series of monographs,[1] and, together with the proceedings of the Center's annual conferences, in the periodical *Quaderni Fiorentini per la storia del pensiero giuridico moderno*.[2] Founded by Grossi in 1972, *Quaderni Fiorentini* was not intended merely to settle the sparsely populated field of postmedieval legal history, but more important, to demonstrate that an understanding of the concepts, methods, and institutions associated with modern law cannot be divorced from the wider currents of European intellectual history and from historically conditioned practices. This demonstration was intended primarily for members of European faculties of jurisprudence who were and continue to be wedded to legal positivism, and who considered the history of law to be irrelevant. The object of their studies has been positive legal norms and the content of laws treated as naturally occurring phenomena to be systematically probed by means of logical operations. The aim of these logical operations has been the discovery of the fundamental principles and relationships of a legal system. What has united Grossi and his colleagues, what has given a polemical edge to their research, has been their outright rejection of these formalistic and dogmatic procedures, which attempt to reduce historical contingency to scientific certainty. The history of law and jurisprudence, they have insisted, is directly relevant to the juridical and legislative issues faced by contemporary jurists and politicians.

Besides engaging in these collective activities, Grossi has also written an impressive array of monographs under his own name. His first studies concentrated on juridical doctrines relating to monetary obligations and agrarian contracts. These were followed by studies on juridical conceptions of ownership possession and use of land in medieval and early modern Europe. The most important of these studies is the widely read *Le situazioni reali nell'esperienza giuridica medievale,* published in 1968.[3] Although not structured on explicit theoretical models, this body of work is nonetheless guided by a sustained conceptual vision. Grossi rejects both the idea that juridical texts are self-referential and self-regulating codes and that relations portrayed in juridical texts are synonymous with social practice. He insists that juridical discourse does not stand apart from the history of human consciousness. And he situates juridical discourse not in discrete economic, political, or social settings, but in a larger cultural setting, encompassing projective consciousness as well as social practice. By concentrating his analysis on the mutual interaction of juridical discourse and social practice rather than on the sterile and artificial question of their ontological priority, he has avoided the twin perils of idealist reductionism and mechanical materialism.

In his studies of the theological and juridical conceptions of ownership and property, Grossi argues that in the High Middle Ages the relationship between the individual and nature was not that of subject to external object, as it was to be in the modern world. The individual as subject and real property as external object were fixed in autonomous positions of an omnicomprehensive order. Extending the insights of the philosopher of law, Michel Villey, and the historian of "possessive individualism," C. B. Macpherson, Grossi traces the origins of the modern conception of individual ownership not to Roman law, but to three more recent historical developments: the extreme subjectivism and voluntarism of the Franciscans, the cult of individualism of Renaissance humanists, and the theology of voluntarism and economic individualism of the scholastic theologians of the sixteenth century, particularly in Spain. The triumph of voluntarism, which Grossi links to the economy of the sixteenth century, meant that the possession of things was valued more than their existence. Property became an instrument of the subject's sovereignty, an extension of his personality, liberty, dignity, and capacity to act. Liberty was conceived as an expansive and dominating force, different from the medieval conception of *libertas,* which accented independence and autonomy. To be a proprietor signified the capacity to realize one's own personality. The juridical order, according to Grossi, became an accumulation of dominative situations consecrated by natural law.

   'Un altro modo di possedere,' Grossi's most recent and remarkable book, opens with a profile of the proprietor as he was conceived by members of what he calls the official culture and juridical order of the Enlightenment. By the early nineteenth century, the moral superiority of the proprietor over the nonproprietor was a steering assumption of social, political, and juridical theory. Proprietorship was fully identified with citizenship, the capacity of proprietorship with civic virtue, and individual ownership of property as the rock upon which the state securely rested. Proprietorship was conceived as the rational and natural mode of possessing things, a mode which existed from time immemorial. Collective modes of possession and appropriation, on the other hand, were viewed as deformations of the norm and were associated with barbarians and noncivilized folk. This monocratic conception of private property, Grossi suggests, was actually reinforced rather than undermined by the pioneering investigations of the Grimm brothers, by the writings of German historians like Georg Ludwig Maurer who sought to discover collective forms of possession and primitive forms of communism in early medieval Germanic societies, and by the research of August von Haxthausen on the Russian village communities.

   This monocratic conception was effectively challenged for the first time by the great English jurist, Henry Sumner Maine. Like almost all the other protagonists in the nineteenth-century debate over collective modes of possession, Maine operated within the confines of the official culture, and neither he nor those who followed him intended to undermine the social order. "It was from a platform rigorously chosen and defined as scientific and with the calm certitude of a man of studies reorganizing the papers on his desk that Maine launched the process of demolishing the edifice of individual property as an institution of natural law. But we must note that in demolishing it, he acted not as an enemy to private property, but as one who sought to confirm the antiscientific nature of its particular theoretical construction" (p. 46). Grossi shows that Maine was critical of the metahistorical postulates supporting possessive individualism and individual ownership. Maine's challenge was indebted to Maurer and Savigny, the leader of the German Historical School of law, to contemporary theories of evolution, to reports published by amateur ethnologists, and to legislative inquests concerning the practice of associative forms of possession within and outside Europe. Maine's *Ancient Law* (1861), a synthesis of multiple discourses—history, jurisprudence, ethnology, and evolution—first put forward the revolutionary theses that the notion and institution of private property was not known in the "ancient law" and that the distinction between the law of persons and the law of things was an artifical creation of Roman jurisconsults. Extended families and groups rather than single individuals possessed things in the "ancient law." Whether historically correct or not, the significance of Maine's theses for his nineteenth-century audience was the denaturalization of the axiom that everything ought to have an owner. On the other hand, collective modes of possession were given a legitimate though problematic history, one which was to be vigorously debated by historians and jurists for the next fifty years.

Grossi's discussion of the influence of Maine's "juridical paleontology" is highly subtle. The *Ancient Law,* along with Maine's subsequent studies on the early history of institutions and village communities in the East and West, influenced an entire generation of historians, jurists, ethnologists, and political economists. One of the scholars who fell under his influence was Emile de Laveleye, a professor of political economy at Liège, a Christian socialist reformer, and the author of the widely read attack against private property, *De la propriété et de ses formes primitives* (1874). Laveleye's thesis was that collective forms of proprietorship had been the established mode of possession for most of Western history and that the modern form of possession based on individual proprietorship was an aberration of bourgeois society. The "collective property" of which Maine, Laveleye, and their Italian followers spoke, Grossi emphasizes, should not be identified with socialist and communist programs of collectivization. Nor should collective property be identified with either a thing or a specific notion. Collective property is a discourse "whose generic and basic significance is proper to a fairly broad, rather heterogeneous group of persons. Since it was originally just the historical and logical *oppositum* of ownership by a single proprietor, it is defined by a complex of alternative characteristics that emerged from that origin: the priority of the group and the subordination of individuals and their ends to the group; the priority of objective ends, of the economic nature, destination, and use of things over subjective ends; the priority within the group of subjective situations of duty over those of power or right typical of the traditional *iura in re*" (pp. 23–24).

The counterattack against Laveleye, and especially against the German historian Maurer and his disciples, was launched by Fustel de Coulanges, who employed philological methods and verbal pitch to destroy his adversaries. Grossi's admiration for the "collectivists" and his antipathy toward Fustel, whom he dubs the "Grand Inquisitor of the significance of historical forms of collective property," is expressed frankly. And his remorseless autopsy of Fustel exposes to view the great French historian's intellectual bigotry and hypocrisy.

The controversy spilled over into post-Unification Italy, where liberal legislators were attempting to abolish, in the name of reform, what remained of the collective rights of villages and agrarian associations over common lands. These collective arrangements were considered irrational vestiges of an archaic past and inimical to a maturing capitalistic economy based on private property. Parliamentary commissions were established to determine the precise nature and extent of collective landholding practices, or of what Carlo Cattaneo, the independent reformer from Lombardy, sympathetically described as "another way of possessing." And it was at this time that Maine's theses became diffused in Italy, and that their relevance to an important political problem became most evident.[4]

The heroes of Grossi's book are not only the parliamentarians— Ghino Valenti, Giovanni Zucconi, Giacomo Venezian—the historians of law—Nino Tamasia, Federico Schupfer, Filomusi Guelfi, Pasquale del Giudice—but also the administrative bureaucrats who balked at the implementation of the new laws eliminating collective landholding rights. Their investigations revealed that, contrary to official views and conventional wisdom, collective landholding arrangements had existed side by side with properties individually owned from the Middle Ages through the nineteenth century and that these collective arrangements were often economically efficient. By the 1880s, after the advent of Hegel, Spencer, and Darwin, after the discovery of Vico and after the founding of Italy's first anthropological society in Florence in 1869–70, it was no longer tenable to debate the political issue of collective property and the history of proprietorship in the Romanistic language of the official culture. In 1894 the state finally recognized the collective associations in the provinces of the former Pontifical States as juristic persons, a status hitherto reserved for individual proprietors. For Grossi, the law of 1894 represented an "enormous conquest." At the same time, he laments, this law was a unique event, a transitory triumph in a society hostile to collective landholding practices, "the price for which Italy is still paying." This price refers to the open wound inflicted upon contemporary Italy by the unresolved issues of property. Grossi's judgment of the baleful consequences of the state's failure to halt the dissolution of the old collective associations should not be translated as utopian wish-fulfillment. Nor should the failure of the "collectivists" on the practical level be interpreted as yet another missed opportunity, in which the course of Italian history might have been diverted. In Grossi's graphic phrase, "the debate opened and closed like a parenthesis."

'*Un altro modo di possedere*' has been praised by Italian historians for its pan-European vision, its wealth of detail, its robust prose, and its passionate commitment to making history relevant to contemporary problems.[5] Some Marxist historians, however, remain unimpressed with the marginal and conservative intellectuals parading through the pages of the book and are critical of Grossi's deliberate omission of the socialist and revolutionary tradition spawned by Marx and Engels. Grossi's rhetorical reply has not placated his Marxist critics. But it has underscored the paradoxical relationship between collective and private forms of possession:

> I would like to extend an invitation to our Marxist friends: Don't search for orchids in the Roman countryside, don't search the humble writings of men engaged in this nineteenth-century debate for a new vision of the world or for solicitations to revolution. I would tell them that the opposite is true: it is the conservative vision that is most prevalent. Collective property is the last expedient to save private property as the cornerstone on which society rests.[6]

Julius Kirshner

Preface

These are not abuses, they are not privileges, they are not usurpa-tions: it is another way of possessing, another system of legisla-tion, another social order, one which, unobserved, has descended to us from centuries long past.

> Carlo Cattaneo, speaking of the ves-tiges of collective landholding struc-tures in *Su la bonificazione del Piano di Magadino*

This essay is intended as a small contribution toward a fuller knowledge of that "missionary territory" represented for the historian of jurisprudence by Italian juridical science of the nineteenth century, par-ticularly that of the period immediately following unification. Specialists in positive law who have recently treated the subject deserve praise for their intention and for their efforts in attempting to unravel the tangled skein of a historiography that so far has been notably unproductive. Their writings, however, demonstrate to the responsible professional historian that his duty now lies in turning his attention to this subject in order to restore it to the richness and the complexity that characterize it, un-founded, oft-repeated, and outworn clichés notwithstanding.

The present essay constitutes the first attempt to document that richness and complexity. It belongs in the context of broader researches on the concept of property in nineteenth-century thought. Without enter-ing into the thick of the analysis of individual property that will constitute the subject of the central part of this research, it addresses a marginal problem: the emergence of alternative forms of ownership—substantially, of forms of collective appropriation—in the consciousness of men who affected the culture of a century dominated by extremely rigid canons of possessive individualism. There was an intellectual current that arose and disappeared during the second half of the nineteenth century and that ran along the edges of official doctrine somewhere between orthodoxy and "heretical" rebellion. This thought throws a different sort of light on the most hidden workings of a science of jurisprudence that was bombarded by demands for cultural renewal, tormented by basic problems of method, and deeply concerned with the rapid evolution and mutation of civil society.

The story of this current of thought is presented, then, as a noteworthy chapter in the history of the culture and the technical possibilities of the jurists. In the pages that follow, a chorus of witnesses will be examined, most particularly in terms of juridical culture and of the relation between juridical culture and other cultural dimensions. Not that one can separate culture and technical procedures: that would be absurd, since the second is an instance and expression of the first. But there is no doubt that practice has its own autonomy within and under the generic cultural problem. It is an instrument for communication among jurists and a specific and appropriate standard for the interpretation of reality. It represents a way of speaking that can elude the mediation of society, of economics, and of politics, since it involves a specifically juridical knowledge in respect to which metajuridical options come to naught.

In this first study I intend to examine the conflict between official culture—which presented a solid, compact, and unified front on the question of property—and the resumption of certain doctrinal themes relating to collective property, which was an appropriative schema far removed from philosophy and politics and extraneous to them, removed as well from the Romanistic tradition and from the sources of official culture. I intend to examine the great controversy that arose at the start of the second half of the century and dominated the whole period: the controversy that took place among historians, sociologists, and jurists about the origins and the historical forms of landholding. To be sure, the problem is much broader than this: it was expressed also in terms of juridical constructs and in terms of techniques for its elaboration and articulation. But here I intend only to touch on these aspects of the problem, to which I will return in a not too distant future.

The central argument of this volume was presented in a lecture given in Moscow in June of 1975, at the invitation of the Institute of State and Law of the Academy of Sciences of the U.S.S.R. on the occasion of a meeting between Italian and Soviet jurists. Following the interest expressed on that occasion and bowing to the flattering insistence of my Soviet colleagues, the research was pursued, enlarged, and extended. The resulting quantity of accumulated material was such that it required a more complex and more organic structuring. This is the origin of the book that I present to the reader today.

This book is dedicated to Giangastone Bolla and to Salvatore Romano, two very different personalities who are, however, joined in my affectionate memory and my sincere regret for their loss. Bolla seems to me to have been above all an eminent scholar of culture. As a research scholar, his work was often supported by felicitous insights, and on the

present subject of collective landholding structures he uttered unforgettable words. Romano had instead a more speculative mind. With remarkable skill and making his own the subtlest manipulative techniques of
juridical science of the period after the second world war, he pursued his
own original paths of investigation, leaving us a refined reflection—
unfortunately far from completion—on the great methodological problems
of private law. I recognize my own debt to certain of Romano's pages on
property, particularly on the structure of collective property, for major
conceptual clarifications.

I may be permitted to add a note: this dedication had already
been written in my mind when Giuliana D'Amelio Caracciolo left us
forever. Her first efforts as a historian of law were dedicated to the problem of customary rights and collective domains in the nineteenth century,
and both in memory of an intelligent and most cultivated colleague and as
a sign of my gratitude for the invaluable collaboration that she offered,
with the spontaneity proper to an act of friendship, to *Quaderni fiorentini
per la storia del pensiero giuridico moderno*, I wish to add her name to the
dedication.

One final consideration must be stated: it has not been easy to
locate the copious material of the nineteenth century, particularly that of
foreign origin, pertaining to the controversy. This is all the more so since
that magnificent instrument of work that once was the Biblioteca
Nazionale Centrale of Florence remains today, exactly ten years after the
disastrous flood of 1966, utilizable only with decidedly scanty results,
because of the indifference and ignorance of those in political authority
and of the central administration. In contrast, two intelligent and competent librarians sensitive to the needs of scholars have been of invaluable
and irreplaceable aid: Dr. Mario Tarini, director of the Library of the
Faculty of Jurisprudence of Florence, and Sig. Carlo Mansuino of the
Biblioteca Nazionale Centrale of Florence. I thank them most heartily. A
sincere thanks also to my friend Professor Eligio Vitale, director of the
Ufficio Studii of the Chamber of Deputies, who has been of great help in
my research in that historical archive; to colleagues and friends Paolo
Colliva and Pierluigi Falaschi, who generously aided me with research in
Bologna and Camerino; and to Corrado Zucconi of Camerino, who permitted me to work without restriction in the archive and library of his
family. Last, an affectionate thanks to my friend Pietro Costa for his
accurate reading of the manuscript and for his critical notes and sugges-
tions.

Paolo Grossi

Introduction

Individual Property and Collective Property in
Nineteenth-century Juridical Culture

About 1835, a modest French jurisconsult beguilingly named Proudhon, comfortably established among the jurists of the Bourbon and Orleanist Restoration and permeated to the marrow by the facile, rough and ready optimism of possessive individualism, was moved to write a *Traité du domaine de propriété.*[1] The work teems with technical schematization, but also contains an autonomous set-piece on the proprietor and his sociological identity which seems at first glance merely a literary flourish and a poor imitation of La Bruyère. Nearly all the jurists of this exegetic school produced stilted chromos on property, and Jean-Baptiste-Victor Proudhon's is not only among the more diligently conceived of them, but also among the more disarming in its clear revelation of the double profile, ideal and ideological, of the eighteenth-century doctrine of individual property.

But let him speak for himself:

> Who is it who fears to harm others? It is the proprietor, for he knows well that reparation for his evil will weigh on his patrimony. But, providing that the proletarian anarchist can save his skin, that is all he asks for, and it is thus that poverty comes to the aid of audacity in crime. . . . The right to property inspires in its master a feeling of security concerning his future, gives him tranquillity and makes him less turbulent: it encourages him to work to form or acquire new properties by giving him the certainty of enjoying them or disposing of them as he will; hence laborious men are always the best citizens as well as the most

1

useful ones to society. Property leads man to the conservation of his wealth through the desire to transmit it to his children, or to his relatives, or to his friends. It is for those who receive it a source of gratitude and attachment to their benefactor; it gives fathers the means to procure a good education for their children and to make them better capable to serve their country; it thus becomes one of the most powerful wellsprings of paternal love and filial piety; and even while satisfying the pious sentiments of fathers and children, is the promotive cause of public prosperity. . . . It is under the aegis of the right to property that the tranquillity of *all*[2] inhabitants of the country resides. . . . Who are the men who most dread political upheavals in the state? They are not the poor who, having nothing to lose, can only see in change a favorable occasion for their cupidity: it is therefore proprietors whom one must consider the most solidly attached to the government of the state.[3]

I have purposely cited Proudhon at such length to demonstrate the monotony but also the heterogeneity of his two recurring motifs: the proprietor is a being qualitatively different from nonproprietors and is a more complete personality endowed with a richness that transfers from the plane of goods owned to become an inner reality; the proprietor is by nature a citizen on whom the constituted powers can rely, because he is inevitably favorable to conservation of the established order. An intrinsic quality, a trait of character within a person, is blandly placed on the same level as an external circumstance, one which implies a necessarily variable relationship between proprietor and political power. The plane of validity is continually and confusingly mixed with that of practicality and opportunism.

The threads of Proudhon's argument are as meager as they are unsupported and as candid as they are approximate, but the modern historian of juridical culture will immediately recognize in them the product of themes and theories that European society had been long in constructing to support its own individualistic order. The eulogy of the proprietor as the best of all possible men spun out by our little-known nineteenth-century jurist in his province of France during the "happy" reign of Louis Philippe came along after centuries of encomiums, ranging from Locke[4] to the Physiocrats[5] and the philosopher-legislators who prepared the *Code Civil;*[6] and Proudhon's was the latest voice in a chorus completely absorbed in narcissistic contemplation of itself. Indeed, an entire society and an entire culture delighted with its own choices speaks in those voices; a society which had too hastily cast off metaphysical values and which, in the attempt to fill a void difficult to fill, constructed its own historical foundation on *having,* and indicated to its own members in individual *having* a contribution which could not substitute for the full-ness of its own being.

Medieval civilization was so extremely variegated and complex that it is difficult to interpret in its innermost nuclei, but the new absolutely simple and linear civilization, unidimensional, apparently stably fixed, perhaps paralyzed, on its single, perennial base of land, offers few problems to the interpreter. It deals only with him who *has*, and it is frantically busy, in its poverty of values, in creating new values for itself, exalting purely historical instruments in the need to make them absolute even at the cost of deforming them. Individual property thus finds a comfortable niche within the "*ordre naturel des sociétés politiques*,"[7] and the proprietor undergoes a palingenesis which separates him from common mortals and places him among the models solely through the possession of goods. The cult of *having*, in a civilization as insensitive to the sacred as individualism, abolished the former extraterrestrial vocations, constituted a new ethic, and translated itself into a theology of *having* that was singularly rife with rites and celebrants. If we add that this cultural operation was backed up by an efficient political operation that viewed the state as guarantor of the wealth of whomever held it legitimately, and as founded on the consent of the wealthy, we understand how deeply rooted was the idea of property as a natural right and that of the proprietor as ideal citizen, especially when ideological patterns profoundly corroborated these roots.[8]

Thus Proudhon speaks a language faithful to the convictions of his times. It was a language drawn from confidence in the thaumaturgic virtues of *having* and in the progress won under the banner of an economic individualism blind to the problem of the distribution of goods. It was also a language steeped in an awareness of the interests at stake and the usefulness of justifying control of those interests by natural law. Not many years after the great Napoleonic codification, which now enveloped *jurisprudentia* with all its fundamental decisions and all the majesty of its establishment, in a climate of stability and certitude reinforced among the new governing class by the July Revolution, and with the upheavals of 1848 still psychologically distant, the eulogy of the proprietor in Proudhon's pages can both be placed clearly in a specific historical context and be given a historical explanation.

When we note, however, that the pages written in 1835 are rewritten in nearly identical terms for an entire century, even after 1848 and after 1871, after so many revolutions of deeds and ideas, both the placement and the explanation must be sought instead purely on the terrain of ideology, not of history. If we open the thick volume written by a *homo novus* of Italian juridical culture, the Sicilian Giuseppe D'Aguanno,

La genesi e l'evoluzione del diritto civile secondo le risultanze delle scienze antropologiche e storico-sociali,[9] published in 1890, we shall find exactly the same conclusions and nearly the same phraseology. We will also find the reaffirmation of the close bond between property and morality that was the most evident element of Proudhon's discourse.[10]

Not only do fifty-five years separate the French jurist's *Traité* from the reexamination of the question by the Sicilian philosopher of law. The entire conception of the jurist's profession and methodology has been turned upside-down during the course of those decades. In the earlier view, the arid exegete found his only liberty in the invention of ever more refined technical instruments, working within the system proposed and imposed by the legislator and received from on high as if from metahistorical zones. The jurisconsult of the end of the century had come out of the cocoon of techniques, and he was marked in fact by an excess of extrajuridical curiosity: he read and put to use Darwin the naturalist, Mortillet the paleontologist, Spencer the philosopher, Letourneau the sociologist[11] as casually as he would an article of the Code or a fragment of the *Digesta*.

Indeed, for Proudhon's relatively conscious confidence in the validity of his observations, D'Aguanno substitutes a confidence scientifically founded on the mechanisms of evolution and on interactions between the individual and his economic and social circumstances. The affirmation that "in concert with the psychic faculties, the moral faculties also unfold with the material comforts of life [*le agiatezze della vita*]"[12] springs from a sociological interpretation of the ethic of the individual and of knowledge, no longer from an adhesion to a theory of natural law. Beyond scientific or pseudo-scientific foundations, either used critically or juxtaposed opportunistically, adherence to the notion of individual property was dominant as the prime value of a society and of a determined social order.

Whether through a post-Enlightenment and post-Code fidelity to natural law that openly reveals its conservative profile (as in the many Proudhons of the first half of the century) or in the sphere of a more gratifying scientific positivism (as in the many D'Aguannos of the end of the century), the result is always and in every case that individual property was beyond question as a social institution, as a point of arrival in historic progress from which one cannot regress, as an absolute value on an ethico-social plane. Consequently, the possibility of alternative forms or even a move toward a vigorous reexamination of the system of forms of appropriation of goods was psychologically inconceivable.

Possessive individualism, fortified by the political rise of the bourgeoisie, concretely regulated and defined by the normative support of the Codes and by the revival of Roman and Romanistic techniques, and rendered more aggressive by the frequent though inefficacious surges of antiproprietarian sentiment, was the dominant attitude throughout the entire century. The passing of time was to bring some modification of this attitude—though only in the elaboration of a theory of "limits"—when changes in socioeconomic organization and the appearance of new technologies made modification necessary.[13] But this theory still operated within the structure of individual property.

We might even say that if there is an order that the limpid, monodic nineteenth-century juristic culture found repellent, it was precisely collective property in its various forms or, more accurately, any communitarian or communistic order that might arise to corrupt the direct, immediately sovereign relationship between a subject and his goods. No example is more eloquent in this respect than the discussions of common property, and particularly of common pasturage, of which there is much evidence in the preparatory work for the civil code of the united kingdom of Italy, adopted in 1865, and especially in the authoritative and representative contribution to those discussions of Pasquale Stanislao Mancini.

To the jurist belonging to official nineteenth-century culture, educated or miseducated by two thousand years of theoretical elaboration centered solely on individual property, the dimension of collective appropriation is beyond the habitual scheme of things: on this point, in fact, the medieval revision of land rights, which had not denied the Roman tradition, could be of no help, and its place was taken by post-humanistic juridico-philosophical speculation, which stressed the "morality" of the individual bond between a subject and his objects.

Thus the official or dominant culture worked and operated—with the exception of a Germanistic school in which the problem of *Gesamteigentum* was brought into polemical relief—under and in the shelter of the postulate of individual property, which it saw as the Pillars of Hercules of its consideration of legal problems and as the limit beyond which such consideration would have been illegitimate. Even the doctrines regarding the problems of common property were developed under the shelter of these same individualistic norms and within the scope of theses reinforced by two thousand years of jurisprudential inventiveness.

Nonetheless, it is impossible to ignore a small doctrinal current that sprang into being as part of the complex panorama of the culture of the century, ran a fairly clearly defined course within the confines of the substantially unified attitude toward property, and then vanished, but that posed the historical and theoretical problem of collective appropriation for the first time in Western juridical science and, often with iconoclastic intent, proposed a dialectic between individual and collective forms hitherto unknown and unimaginable.[14]

This was a current that wound through frontier zones at the margins between official culture and heretical revolt, sometimes surfacing unexpectedly in that culture or often being banished among the more heterodox voices. It involved historians and philosophers of civic and public law, sociologists and historians, in Italy as in France and Germany, even in Russia and North America, drawing from a composite world of rather singular ideologies and cultural choices. It was a current which, far from running its course quietly amid general indifference, inspired polemics and reactions and brought to life a bitter and heated controversy that became, between the 1880s and the 1890s, the great quarrel of the moment throughout Europe.

Thus a debate opened and closed like a parenthesis, and the dominant culture—the definitive winner after an ephemeral heterodox victory—did its utmost to forget it and make others forget it. Some of the arguments and some separate portions of this debate are well known, but it has been neglected in its organic fabric, in its choral reality, in the complex structure of the cultural relationships that it brought forth and consolidated.

It is nevertheless a revealing debate, one which affronts the global problem of property—or rather of properties—in a completely new manner and from an unusual angle of vision. A study of this debate will permit us, through the interests then at stake and through its continual tendency to break through the confines of what was proper to juridical dispute, to discern the true outlines of a culture deeply engaged in great travail.

What are the problems that emerged from this debate? First, to survey the various forms of property recorded in history and to pose the question of the origin of individual landed property; then to compare, openly or not, two modes of appropriation and to attempt to limit the undivided rule of individual property. Beyond the historical documents and the philosophical dissertations, the indisputability of individual property was what was at stake. Probably, if we examine the position of these "collectivists" one by one, we will see that very few indeed presented themselves as subverters of the established order.[15] All, or almost all of them placed themselves within a scheme of things based on and articulated in forms of individual appropriation, and some of them, like Henry Sumner Maine, even professed confidence in the connection between individual property and progress. All, however, were repelled by a mythology and a theology that they wanted to destroy. They sought to deconsecrate a temple artfully constructed and to restore to history every "proprietary" instrument.

However, the problem did not break down into a simple question of method. To allow the emergence in nineteenth-century juridical consciousness of alternative forms of property—in practice, of collective forms—had two extremely serious implications. First, it threatened to provoke the cracking or even the crumbling of an edifice nearly exclusively founded on an overextended individual *having* and on its ethico-political (not its historical) overtones. Second, it could not but suggest a separation from the mainstream of a monopolistic juridical tradition, the Roman tradition, and repropose a pluralistic vision after centuries of Roman cultural imperialism. A debate could not be avoided, and it could be neither innocuous nor purely academic. It did not constitute a new, different position that reinforced the main current of thought. Rather, it constituted a clear threat to all that had been laboriously constructed since the beginning of modern times. It was a foreign body in the nineteenth-century organism that had to be absorbed or rejected.

And it was rejected. The parenthesis opened nearly miraculously in the mid-nineteenth century closed fairly rapidly toward the years in which the strains from the *Excelsior* ballet still resounded throughout Italy.[16]

In the course of this volume we will follow the itinerary of the debate from what seems to be the first real contribution to be organically and functionally tied to it, the reflections and methodological innovations of Henry Maine, up to its clamorous development on both sides of the Alps. We will follow it in its various manifestations, in its historical re-evocations as in its juridical reconstructions, until we grasp its implications at the level of technical and administrative investigations—as in the great Agrarian Inquiry directed by Stefano Jacini—or even at the level of legislative politics—as in the speeches and discussions concerning bills which involved *servitù di pascolo* [rights of pasturage] and *dominii collettivi* [common domains] presented to the national Parliament in the years following the 1880s.

There was a singular, a notable quality in our debate. It did not remain an academic affair among university professors, confined to the dazzling prose of an inaugural lecture or of an innovative scientific essay. Rather, it tended in one way or another to be translated into an operative reality. As we will see in part two, this was one of the rare instances in which a mainly doctrinal matter has the freedom of the city in the chambers of Parliament, in which it acts as a stimulant to legislators and leaves its mark on several official reports and even on several acts of legislation.

We will see in the course of this work who are the protagonists of the debate, and we will seek to determine what were their ideas and proposals. What now must be done in these introductory pages is to look at the presuppositions that underlie the debate, at the context from which it emerges and takes its strength, at the forces that permit its emergence even in a declaredly hostile climate, at the multiple configurations which it assumes. This will serve as an indispensable preliminary clarification and will make possible a better comprehension of its complex development.

The Debate on the Historical Origins and Forms of Property: Its Development and Ambivalences

The debate never set aside its cultural character. It was men of culture who carried it on and their guiding motivation was scientific. The object of debate nearly always consisted in the origin and development of the various forms of appropriation, and the field of battle was nearly always to be found in periodicals of rigorously scientific, if not outright academic, orientation. Even at the height of the controversy recorded by the violent, impassioned dialogue (this term is undoubtedly euphemistic) between Fustel de Coulanges and the "advocates of primitive communism,"[17] the discourse never ceased to be rigorously historiographic, and the participants never tired of thoroughly documenting their conclusions or of evoking correct historiographical methodology in their favor and against their adversaries.

To air the problem and debate it brought to nineteenth-century juridical doctrine a primarily and fundamentally cognitive operation; to examine origins, marked as the process was in that century by wearisome epistemological reexaminations and reforms, was to attempt to find a more solid and more critical base for the dominant literature of the social and economic sphere. The jurist, at the moment in which he becomes historian and sociologist, or the historian and the sociologist when they take over instruments typical of juridical analysis, amplify their habitual discourse, yielding to the solicitation of cultural enrichment and demonstrating a sincere and heartfelt will to be above all "producers of science."

But the dispute, as we have already hinted, has more than one dimension, and it moves on more than one level. If a cultural configuration is formally and substantially prevalent in certain currents of thought, as for example in a good part of Italian juridical thinking, elsewhere the debate draws on a more complex reality, and the historian needs more complex tools in order to observe and diagnose it.

The cultural moment is always and without exception a dependable filter by means of which the problem can be decanted and allowed to settle. It is the perennial form in which and with which the problem acquires respectability and objectivity. But we must also agree that the cultural moment is occasionally a refuge or, if one prefers, a more efficient armor for the battle. Are we really certain that we exhaust the meaning of the tedious methodological lessons of Fustel de Coulanges, of his documentarian zeal or of his spiritual exercises on the purity of the historian's craft when we read him on the simple level of what is expressed? Or is there not a discourse which runs on two levels, the visible level of formal declarations and the hidden but occasionally surfacing level of the convictions and political preferences of the interpreter?

The topic in all its incandescence was the eternal theme and problem of individual property. During the debate it was rediscussed *a fundamentis*, and each interpreter was personally committed to it. If in the social sciences the eye of the observer can never be satisfied with assertions or appearances, a similarly simplistic attitude would be a serious fault for the historian in the presence of an institution—though it certainly is not comparable, with its thousands of technical instruments scattered through juridical experience—that is by its nature tied to the essential economic structure of a society and bound to the most jealously guarded interests of each person.

Is Fustel de Coulanges reading ancient documents with detachment when he talks about the origins of landed property, or has he put on spectacles that deform the text, or rather is he not reading within himself while pretending to look with attention at historical evidence? The question must be asked, for the historian must be aware of the singular density of the controversy and of the ambivalences encountered in reading the historians and jurists of the nineteenth century. Precisely because our inquiry concerns the problem of historical forms of property only indirectly and because its immediate object is the reflections made on those forms that emerged in the second half of the nineteenth century, and precisely because we observe this reflection as a sign of an operative juridical culture, to be conscious of the composite keyboard on which wittingly or unwittingly the interpreter is playing is the one and only condition to making history of his discourse. Only in this way can we place it in its time and restore it to a culture seen not as an abstraction, but as an entity living through the solicitations that dominate it, be they scientific or methodological, political or ideological.

The perception of these outlines, of how they become isolated or mixed, of how they combine, will permit a view in perspective of an extraordinary chorus of voices. With a first word of caution: the ideological code is itself complex, individual and collective property are not in themselves symbols of opposed ideologies, but represent instruments susceptible of varying use on the part of whomever uses them,[18] and obviously political strands are woven into a clearly ideological fabric. Fustel's position is abutted in a rigidly positivistic methodology; more than just a refusal of a romantic approach, it is an obstinate and angry polemic which finds its original stimulus in an anti-German ideology matured and strengthened by the French national tragedy of 1870–71. Fustel's struggle against the *Mark* and the collectivist forms proposed by

German historicism is first of all anti-Germanic, even if programmatically it appears to be only anti-Germanistic.

With a second elementary word of caution: if what we have just said means the repudiation of facile oversimplifications uncongenial to the historian's craft, one's discourse can be effective though simple on the condition that an equally fallacious schematism not be substituted for a reading without nuances. A view of the dispute seen through lenses focused according to ideological optics would in fact be a distortion and a misunderstanding of the complexity of the debate. The latter is not carried on by two opposing ranks, the "socialists" and the "individualists," but is made up of shadings, of nuances, of gradations to which the historian must give faithful witness and which constitute the culture richness of his reflection.

Within this controversy we will find the intellectual architecture of an apparent ideological framework and we will find humors and poisons, but the prevailing sound of the great chorus seems to be found in the voice of men of culture who carry into the seclusion of their studies the preoccupations circulating in their times. A good part of the dispute finds in these preoccupations its own contingent stimulus and the reasons for its own birth, and these preoccupations are sometimes intertwined in research that is a tissue of detailed erudition and philological wisdom. The dispute is in all ways and at all times a living fabric, the faithful mirror of a doctrine questioning itself on its function, its confines, its methods, and its future—a doctrine that searches for its own identity, and not only for its cultural identity.

We will see in the next section the cultural topics that composed and dominated this controversy: they are sometimes learned gleanings, sometimes juridic romanticism, at times historicism and evolutionism harmonize and blend together, at times Germanistic rediscoveries are threaded on a now antiquated philo-Romanism; but almost always, or at least often, these themes move in a setting of which the outstanding, dominant feature is an everpresent awareness that the "social question" could not be deferred.

"The social question," "the agrarian question," "the labor question" are, depending on the specific instance, a nightmare or a challenge from which the scholar investigating the historical dialectic between individual and collective property does not easily divorce himself. We could even say that often the idea is consciously or unconsciously evoked precisely as an attempt to clarify within the interpreter's mind such a tormented and controversial point.[19]

It would be antihistorical to reconstruct the development of this small heterodox or relatively orthodox stream of thought as something that originates and can be explained in a hasty switch of sources on the scholars' work tables which would substitute Germanic, Slavic, or Indian sources for the *Digesta* and the codes consolidated by juridical tradition. This current represents instead an attitude of reexamination which operates in a particularly sensitive culture in close synchrony with a malaise fermenting in the structures of society and in the very consciousness of society. Certainly this occurs as part of the interpreter's value system and as a richness of the observer's vision, without his neglecting the obligation to produce scientifically accurate knowledge, but taking possession of the message circulating in the more impressionable currents of civil society.

We will see at times a calm dialogue between an author and his sources, at times rather an openly politicized discourse, at times either a sincere adherence to socialism or a vaguely socialistic orientation, or an obsessive concern about socialists and the subversion of society, or even the demand for a social compromise. What is certain is that the chorus of voices was varied and complex: if Francesco Schupfer seems to be totally involved in the interpretive problems of his farfensic and sublacensic monastic papers, keeping his study window shut tight against the external world, the echo of the tumults of 1848 and of the iconoclastic experiment of the Paris Commune seems to guide the pen of Emile de Laveleye in his breathless search for alternative forms of property and in his endless wanderings in space and time to note explanations and accumulate data. To choose another example, the question of the priority of the collective form of appropriation over the individual, or that of whether the Germanic tribes practiced individual landed property (the object of a famous diatribe during a session of the Académie des Sciences morales et politiques of Paris) were certainly perfectly autonomous cultural exercises in research into historical verity, but they inevitably came to be grafted onto the social awareness of the interpreters as the conscious or unconscious source of their first impulse.

Complexity, therefore, and variety, and a need to take both into account for an accurate historical reconstruction and in order to avoid humbling and debasing material which is historically multifaceted. The dispute is not a squabble between conservatives and progressives; everything in it is filtered in cultural terms. But its real significance cannot correctly be reduced to a debate between Romanists and Germanists, between advocates of natural law and historicism. The controversy we are considering is certainly all this, but it is or can also be something more.

The Debate on the Historical Origins and Forms of Property: Its Cultural "Signature"

What this dispute adds up to is a picture of great complexity, involving differing dimensions; in the course of this investigation it will be analyzed in all its complexity. The prevalent dimension of this totality is, however, the cultural, and it will repay us to linger a moment to examine the European juridical culture of the nineteenth century of which it is a faithful expression.

The first appearance of this controversy on historical forms of property can be found in mid-century, must plausibly in the thoughts of Henry Maine, as we have seen. It appears as a translation into research on concrete institutions of the broader scope, the enlargement of traditional confines that European juridical culture enjoyed in those years.

Already the juridical romanticism of the Historical School had contributed incisively to the jurists' appreciation of the non-Roman, and, with the exploitation of the Germanic tradition, had had a determining role in a first deblocking of juridic thought in certain classical or classicistic bottlenecks. But the more liberating itinerary still remained to be taken.

A taste for the positive, which had been expressed philosophically alternately in historicist and naturalistic terms, found concrete expression for the jurist and the sociologist in an incessant curiosity, a curiosity which, far from being dilettante, tended toward a purified scientific observation of the totality of surrounding phenomena.

Accompanying the establishment and consolidation of European colonies abroad, there was a discovery that was certainly more consequential on a cultural plane than that of America itself: the discovery of a terraqueous globe extremely varied in its climates, products, customs, traditions, and cultures, but exclusively and concertedly oriented toward European centers such as Madrid, Lisbon, Amsterdam, and above all, Paris and London. This meant also the discovery of a world to discover, to observe, to analyze, to understand.

No matter that this observation and this comprehension were generally just premonitory to taking possession, to a more efficient colonization of that world. These new data acted as an incredible leaven, and that is what counts for the historian of culture. The number of kinds of sources underwent a profound alteration and enlargement, and that is what counts for the historian of law.

Parallel to the organic web of mercantile traffic moving centripetally toward the English, Dutch, and French ports and company offices was an extended, uninterrupted capillary tissue of information supporting that traffic brought in by that singular personage, the nineteenth-century voyager.

If curiosity and love of truth were usually mediated in the voyager of the eighteenth century by an aestheticizing component, there was little room for aestheticism among the voyagers of the nineteenth century: quite the contrary, they seem utterly open to the absorption of data. We see a jumble of intelligent and informed observers, educated to the cult of positive facts, undoubtedly better architects of certainties than poets, strong in a consciousness that approaches scientific method, sometimes simply functionaries and merchants but often by preparation and vocation halfway to being scientists (that is, ethnologists, sociologists, historians, botanists, zoologists). The nineteenth-century English or Dutch colonial bureaucrats and merchants, like explorer-scientists, were incredibly trustworthy reporters. Although their taste for the exotic was strong, they provided more than depictions of an exotic landscape. Their information was the product rather of their professional connections and their business affairs, which stood to gain most from information founded on positive arguments of a geographical, sociological, or historical nature. Their information is rigorous because it represents authentic *instrumentum regni,* that is, it is inseparably tied to and directed to the mechanism of an increasingly finely tuned dynamic of power or of ever-increasing wealth.

In a moment when the scientist felt the need to try his talents in broader fields of knowledge and when the devotee of specialized sciences heard the call of totality, the colonial bureaucrat's report, the merchant's diary of his voyage, and the explorer's journal rose necessarily to the rank of precious instruments for the jurist and the sociologist. Even when he did not himself turn traveler or colonialist (as did Henry Maine, Frédéric Le Play, and Emile de Laveleye, to cite names which will become familiar), hitherto unknown materials landed on his work table, materials which served not only to satisfy his intellectual curiosity and the reigning taste for the positive, but which also enlarged his angle of vision enormously. This material set up a friction between the customary patrimony of sources and worn-out notions from the usual classical channels and a fresh, intact patrimony, standing often as an alternative to the commonplaces conceived throughout three thousand years of Western civilization.

The Romanistic cultural monopoly ceded before, or at least was forced to take into account, differing conceptions and explanations of the various problems inherent to associative living. As we will in fact see, the controversy began when Henry Maine chose to view Roman law in a new light, drawing support from and basing his convictions on juridical insights proper to the context of India, a realm utterly apart from the Mediterranean world. Later alternative messages originating from "vulgar" or obscure strata of the European experience or from remote Afro-Asian and American regions led Laveleye to his iconoclastic diagnosis of the history of property. The controversy thus began and developed at the moment in which a cultural pluralism permitted a previously impracticable demythicizing operation: comparison. And comparison became possible as so many zealous observers brought into French and English ports a treasure which was no less precious for not being locked in the vessels' strongboxes.

It can be seen from these few hasty notes how much the jurist's craft had been enriched and altered for those *homines novi* who wanted to take advantage of a window miraculously opened to the entire world. The participants in our dispute must be counted among just such men, and the debate arose because an enormous amount of heterogeneous and heterodox material was amassed and placed in opposition to traditional sources. Only a minimal part of this material could in fact find a counterpart in the library of proven, time-tested titles of the European man of laws, precisely because of its most singular character, often inappropriate to insertion in the rigidly formal schemes that had been elaborated to contain and condition the solemn and sclerotic notion of a legal source.

The controversy is thus characterized culturally by latitude, by a rupture with all formalism, and by a reaching beyond every privilege accorded to endojuridic sources. But the use of a patrimony of such vast and varied origin did not exhaust the possibilities of the new methodology: latitude here does not only mean a gaze which sweeps attentively from East to West, but also a conscious program in which juridic analysis takes its place in the totality of the processes and products of the other human and natural sciences. The generic taste for the positive became a vocation in an interdisciplinary encounter and a predilection for eclecticism. And here we see further identifying marks of both the culture of its participants and of the debate that was a faithful, perhaps also exasperating, mirror of the characteristics circulating in the European koine.

Eclecticism reigned, and it appeared on two levels: one extrinsic, where the eclectic means interdisciplinary; one intrinsic, in which the eclectic refers to a confused and combinatory attitude guided by diverse visions of the world and diverse methodological criteria.

Eclecticism was also, as we will note again below, a sign of a speculative poverty and, similarly, of a profound travail that the interpreter endured and was unable to dominate. The evolutionistic interpretive models which were in the air in English culture during the 1850s and which Maine adopted are always balanced and corrected by a historicism that he learned through the pages of the German scholars and that attenuated and softened the rigidity of a strictly evolutionistic interpretation. The fusing and harmonizing of evolutionism and historicism (with all the basic incoherence that that comports) was a recurrent situation, and the dialectic between evolutionary certitude and rigidity and historicist relativity and plasticity was constantly repeated, with a clear predominance on the part of the latter.

The positivism of the participants in the debate was stronger on the terrain of the natural sciences, and is here seasoned with the usual anthropological, ethnological, biological ingredients of nineteenth-century positivism. But it generally gave to history the function of freeing thought from necessary schematic systems and rules. For this reason, the mechanism of alternation between collective property and individual property, which in a purely evolutionistic view should be thought of as a clear line of development, is notably more multifaceted and complex in the interpretation of the dispute, and it appears in absolute form only in a few of the sources.

Even more singular is the fusion, fully present in Laveleye, of a central inspiration of historicist stamp, evolutionistic strands, and motifs from natural law. Laveleye was and wanted to be substantially a "relativist" but could not renounce the emergence of a religious, or more specifically, of a Christian dimension as a component of his vision of the world. By means of the instruments of historical investigation and comparatistic studies, he enriches and complicates this vision (if we may be permitted to say so) into a sheaf of heterogeneous forms, among which the ethical takes on a certain importance.

These are fleeting notations which may serve to introduce the subject of the cultural "signature" of our protagonists and of the speculative schools to which they belonged, all of which, may I repeat, are found in combination with each other. But eclecticism, as I have recalled above, reigned supreme even on a more extrinsic plane. Our protagonists put to use an enormous complex of sources—juridical, economic, purely historical, archaeological, ethnological, linguistic—almost as though they wanted to consolidate their conclusions positivistically. And they called on all the sciences to contribute to the illustration and elaboration of this socio-juridical notion. Collective property and individual property were two historical and social knots to be loosened only by multiple observation from several angles and according to several models. And the jurists, men in isolation, prepared to proclaim their fidelity to a century and their membership in a cultural koine, hoisting the standard of a positivism that is overloaded with science, open to many different applications, and weakly endowed with methodological rigor.[20]

Preliminaries to the Debate: Erudite Ground-breaking, Investigations, Collection of Data

The debate, then, began with Maine. It began with him not because the English jurist was chronologically the first in the nineteenth century to speak of the historical problem of forms of property and particularly of collective forms of appropriation, but because he was the first to approach this problem with a new consciousness, with a polemical outlook toward the official culture, with an ability to insert the problem into a dialectical relationship between the consolidated heritage of ideas and a renewed vision of those same ideas in light of new acquisitions in methodology and content.

The institution of "collective property" had already, on more than one occasion during the first half of the nineteenth century, been dealt with as an institution set in a concrete social and historical situation; it had already been liberated from the mythical and metahistorical aura that surrounded it in antiquity, in the Middle Ages, and in the natural law fables of modern times. Narrations of voyages, economic and agrarian surveys, and learned research on the part of the German Historical School had brought to attention a notable amount of material in which collective arrangements were discussed prominently. But it had always been just a question of materials, of data and information, which had not yet provoked any crisis concerning still incontrovertible methodological canons, and which had not yet surfaced to the consciousness of the interpreter or the inquirer with a specific corrosive charge. It was indeed a rich patrimony that spilled out before the eyes of all, but it was waiting for someone who could recognize it and take possession of it to construct a problem, who could place it ideally beside the traditional Western system of landholding rights and see the need for reexamining that tradition—who could give life, in other words, to the dialectical relationship of which we have been speaking.

What was achieved in the first fifty years of the century was therefore important groundbreaking, but not yet an organic debate. It was rather a sort of unrelated, completely episodic "preliminary operations," spiritually and intellectually foreign to the dispute that Maine inaugurated, detached from it by their form and their substance, and able to serve merely as premise to Maine's and Laveleye's reflections. During the better part of the debate, fresh eyes and a new consciousness were turned in fact to material accumulated diligently and intelligently during the preceding decades on the level of praxis or as scientific research. This objective platform on which the dispute would erect its own construction merits a brief glance.

The heterogeneity of this base must first be noted. This hardly concerned Maine and Laveleye: quite the contrary, it is perfectly congenial to the casual eclecticism with which they, rolling up their sleeves, produce scientific knowledge, and which permitted them to use and yoke together the learned investigations of Maurer on the German *Mark,* the information of Haxthausen on the Russian *mir,* and the results of an inquiry of the English Parliament in 1844 on the enclosure of open lands.

These examples are not chosen by chance. They are meant to call attention to the most notable "sources" that Maine found in the West and used, in 1861, to fashion his richly substantial discourse *Ancient Law.* It was with these meager and dissimilar instruments, used in comparison with the patrimony of Indian juridic culture, that our gifted Englishman achieved his lively and provocative portrayal.

Anyone searching in 1861 for a systematic picture, at once true in its details and appropriately synthetic, of the landholding situation typical of primitive Germanic society would certainly have found it in the two lengthy works published only a few years before (in two stages, in 1854 and 1856) by Georg Ludwig Maurer, and which indeed concerned the primitive *Markenverfassung*.[21]

In the Maurer's work, much more clearly than in the generalized researches of a Waitz[22] or of a Thudichum,[23] the picture emerged, notably exaggerated and heightened, as we will note later, of an organized system of landholding of collectivist character, which found its formative nucleus in a primordial community, the march or *Mark*. The *Mark*, understood as a structure which went far back in time and as the principle of origin of the Germanic constitution, was here described as a rigorously communitarian organism, supreme programmer of the economic life of the *Genossenschaft* and of the economic destination of goods, intolerant of independent economic direction within its body and of overly clear divisions concerning the possession of land.

The *Mark* was the dominion over the community's undivided property. It was exercized in full over forests and grazing lands but it made the juridical situation of the head of family on the particular piece of land allotted to him subject to terms of provisory and highly limited possession.

A clear, well-defined picture is outlined in Maurer's work that shows landed communism as a historical value of ancient Germanic civilization and presents this communism as the typifying characteristic of a Germanic realm ideally contrasted to the Roman. The vision is undoubtedly heightened and exaggerated—something which Waitz had avoided in his great sociopolitical reconstruction—and is the fruit of a unilateral Germanistic interpretation, perfectly counterposed to the apologetics of the Romanists. It is perhaps weak historically, but was undeniably functional as a support for the grandiose cultural operation for which Maine was yearning.

Since it was founded in antiindividualistic preferences and was articulated in a social, economic, and political life that led to what would soon be called the village community,[24] this Germanic realm was a precious "document" to use. In a dispute that came to have so many faces but that can certainly be grasped and characterized above all by a search for and an indication of alternatives to a theologized vision of property and land rights, that realm proposed most effectively the dimension of the "collective"; another dimension, a concrete alternative produced not by the elucubrations of a philosopher but by a society which had lived it historically. For this reason, Maurer must certainly be listed among the tutelary deities of the later debate.

For an identical reason, these deities also included several cultivated, intelligent travelers, first among them August von Haxthausen.[25] His is one of the very few names that appears in *Ancient Law*, a work miserly regarding citations; he is the voyager whose sincere eulogy Maine was moved to write, even when he was himself near death.[26] This singular personage, a typical example of the romantic cultural koine and friend of the brothers Grimm, first studied the agricultural organization of his own country on behalf of the Prussian government. Later, he traveled the expanses of Russia at the czar's invitation to study the system of landed property and the situation of proprietors and serfs, publishing several books on his voyages and experiences.[27] He thus had the merit of revealing to Western culture the age-old continuity of a Russian rural organization rich in collective forms of land management.[28]

His work, according to Maine, came as a revelation in Europe, disclosing a new order of things.[29] A community on the village level—the *mir*—sprang from Haxthausen's pages with the same pressing energy, with the same provocatory message, as the German *Mark* in Maurer's conclusions. In this case as well, there appeared a "document" of differing social life, of an alternative way of interpreting the complex relationship between community, individual, and land; there appeared an alternative indication to be picked up and on which to work.

The Slavic message now stood beside the Germanic as messages of civilizations surprised in their remoteness, in their manifestations still untouched by Mediterranean colonization. Other such messages, of equal historical veracity, would soon be received from the most far-flung corners of Asia, Africa, and the Americas, carried by dozens of explorers, merchants, and functionaries: all were of consequence for the formulation of alternative solutions and the construction of an alternative documentation.[30]

Scholars and explorers gathered together most of the materials used in the activity that prepared for our debate, inasmuch as it was they who were able to offer to it—even though from quite varied angles of observation—that opening to other cultures on which the debate itself was to be founded: cultures differing from that of official Western tradition, be they that of ancient Germans, remote in time, or of Indians, Africans, or Slavs, remote in space.

But there was also, it seems, a culture living in the West itself and in their own nineteenth century that merited comparatistic interest, a culture buried by the imperialism of official policy decisions but operating in capillary fashion in the most hidden strata of practice and custom. It was a culture that existed at a level of civilized society that rarely emerged in official history but that followed its other subterranean course parallel to the sonorous events of governments and parliaments. It was a popular culture, which the typical nineteenth-century taste for the positive, for data and statistics, brought out by means of a frequently used tool, the investigation, both technico-administrative and parliamentary, public and private. The investigation, as the positivistic probity of the century required, was always a conscientious and painstaking gathering of an enormous congeries of data. As such, and although it often also bore the intentions of the agency that produced it, it revealed a complex socioeconomic stratification covered over and stifled by the formalities of the official state, and because the dimensions of state and civil society were seen to be considerably altered, it placed them in a dialectical opposition.

It is understandable, after what we have noted above, that the investigation is by its penetrating nature an instrument most congenial to the debate which was about to open; it is equally understandable that strenuous research making use of this source was undertaken in the certainty of attaining conspicuous contributions. Worthy of mention among our preparatory tasks as one that furnished Maine with an important piece of documentation is the inquiry that was carried out in England in 1844 under parliamentary sponsorship into the knotty problem of the enclosure of the "open fields."[31] The testimony of witnesses before the Select Committee of the Chamber of Commons reveals a widespread persistence—as well as a notable amount—of the vestiges of an ancient land communism in all parts of England, but with a higher frequency in certain counties.[32] Maine made abundant use of this material and indeed he constructed his suggestive hypotheses on it.

Several inquiries later affected the course of the debate. A chapter will be specifically dedicated in the present work to the great Agrarian Inquiry in Italy.[33] Also worthy of mention is the inquiry into the conditions among crofters and cotters in the highlands and the islands of Scotland that was carried out by a Commission presided over by Lord Napier of Etterick.[34] This inquiry, dated 1884, provoked echoes even beyond the confines of the United Kingdom for the harvest of data it offered on the prospering collective arrangements still operative at the end of the century in the sylvan-pastoral regions of Scotland. On another but no less consequential plane we find the purely informative study "Systems of Land Tenure in Various Countries," promoted in the 1870s by the Cobden Club of London.[35]

Preliminaries to the Debates: The Contributions of Cattaneo and Le Play

The names of Carlo Cattaneo and Frédéric Le Play appear together at the head of this section for the simple reason that they both figure conspicuously as predecessors to the later debate and as authorities who were invoked to authenticate certain emergent basic trends.

Their testimony lent constant comfort to those who battled against the Romanistic monopoly and in favor of cultural pluralism and who invoked the need to heed the alternative voices in the historical and theoretical reconstruction of land rights. Such men identified in Le Play and Cattaneo a vigilant attention to divergent socio-juridical traditions and an understanding open to phenomena generally considered aberrant, such as collective forms of appropriation.

In spite of a profound difference in their formation and orientation, the French sociologist and the Italian polygraph shared common traits which may explain the similarity of their approaches to the problem of property.

Both of them were dominated by a marked taste for the positive, for a method which sees in observation, recognition, and subsequent classification instruments vital to knowledge. This is the reason for their common taste for the statistical survey, a device which implies both the need to exploit the single datum and to fit it into a general scheme that supercedes the particular. Verification by comparison of the disconnected data of experience thus becomes an urgent matter; and from this point a commonly shared intellectual curiosity pushed both men to look into alternative traditions. This intellectual curiosity led Le Play to conduct his investigations on a worldwide scale, and it brought Cattaneo to his researches on India and to his interest in Sardinia—in a country, that is, which remained historically and ethnically an island with respect to the surrounding European continent.

The two men shared also a marked taste for the primitive and the popular. In Cattaneo this predilection was further colored by authentically democratic accents; in both men, however, it appeared as a consciousness of the historical vitality of the popular dimension, of the nonofficial and nondominant strata of culture and society. (I am thinking in this respect of the works that were available to Cattaneo and that led him to a more precise comprehension of folklore[36] and dialects.[37])

It is difficult—as it is for many of the participants in our debate—to place the unassuming French engineer and the gifted Lombard writer within official French or Italian culture of the middle of the century. As bearers of a less than perfectly orthodox message, they placed themselves in a marginal culture destined to have little success in their time.[38] A conservative message oriented toward the past took form in Le Play's writings as he became enveloped by an overpowering vision of the past from which he could not free himself.[39] Cattaneo's message was instead infused with democratic elements.[40] Neither could be assimilated by an official culture of clear-cut connotations and equally clear inflexibility. In the heterodox eclecticism that characterizes our controversy, on the other hand, they were destined to meet with better fortune.

For Laveleye and his followers the great investigations of Le Play, *Les ouvriers européens*[41] and *Les ouvriers des deux mondes*,[42] constitute a treasury of information on communal forms of agrarian landholding in France as well as in distant countries. These works also provided the model for an experimental method of comparative history that they tried to imitate slavishly in investigations on specific forms of property-holding.

The abundant references to Cattaneo made by Agostino Bertani, Ghino Valenti, and so many other Italian participants in the debate have a specific meaning and a precise explanation. There are no apologies for collective property in Cattaneo's works, nor would they be conceivable from an economist and technician dominated by the principle of utility, accustomed to the fertile lands of the Po valley, and fully admiring of the organizational instruments of intensive cultivation. A remarkable awareness of the complex phenomenon of collective appropriation circulates in his work, however; and, even more important, it is an awareness of it as a manifestation and reinforcement of an alternative historical development, as an embodiment of demands, ideals, and interests that are *other* in respect to the familiar reality typical of nineteenth-century Italy.

His is the felicitous phrase that serves as an epigraph to this volume: it is a phrase worth reconsidering in its entirety. Cattaneo was given an assignment to write a report on agrarian conditions in the Magadino plain, the Swiss portion of the upper valley of the Ticino river, at a moment when it was being considered for a land reclamation project. Following his usual practice, he first offers meticulous and global observations of the region. He begins with an outline of its geographical and physical conditions and within them, like a constellation of interpretive elements, he then places the socioeconomic and juridical situations. We are immediately struck by an institutional reality made up of proprietary and landed corporations and lands "which come under undetermined pasturage [*il vago pascolo*] and other servitudes." "There are not abuses, they are not privileges, they are not usurpations: it is another way of possessing, another system of legislation, another social order, one which, unobserved, has descended to us from centuries long past."[43]

The cult of the positive, especially of the positive as historical fact, did not permit this observer to incorporate too much of his own feelings into his observations, but it did permit him to grasp fully the values of a position for which he did not feel particular sympathy. His observations show that he had before him a historical product that was neither ephemeral nor arbitrary but that came out of things he had observed—that is, out of nature and out of history—and was rooted in them. For that very reason this historical phenomenon merited respect and demanded to be understood, even if the observations were made from a detached vantage point. All that he noted critically was that a divergent tradition and historical movement, sustained by their own motives and their own explanations, produced this phenomenon.

Our Milanese author had made a similar analysis, come to similar conclusions, and had given proof of the same mental elasticity and undeniable intelligence several years before when he touched—albeit briefly—on a theme which later appealed to Maine: the "collectivism" of the Indian village. On that occasion as well, Cattaneo's sympathies were not involved in the object of analysis. We see only a constant effort toward intellectual tolerance, a constant coherence in the application of a positive method that imposed data both as the proper terrain for research and as a limit to the researcher's sentiments and humors.[44]

Cattaneo's cultural openness toward forms of collective appropriation stands out particularly clearly when we remember that he wrote in 1851, when the dominant officialdom viewed the phenomenon with total incomprehension or hastily and unjustly liquidated the question. It was and it remained a fixed point for the later debate, which turned to Cattaneo and relied repeatedly on the solidity of his material and his robust style.

The "collectivists" relied on the idea contained in Cattaneo's work because it was for them stronger than an apology and because it anticipated the very central concern of the dispute: reduced to essentials and beneath the inevitable redundancies, distortions, and mutations, this concern was a demand to render the notion of property more relative. This relativization was accomplished more efficaciously by avoiding ingenuous and sterile eulogies of collectivist dispositions or equally ingenuous and sterile polemics aimed at individual ownership. Rather, it was accomplished by fusing together "property" and "properties," by giving historical and social legitimacy to differing appropriative institutions. Among the "preparatory works" preceding the great debate, the views of Carlo Cattaneo thus had considerable relevance and influence.

Collective Property: Misunderstandings of a Concept

We have frequently spoken of "collective" property and will continue to do so, but we must admit that no other qualifier to the noun "property" is as equivocal or as insidious. Let us therefore eliminate possible misunderstandings.

To follow the development of ideas that exploit the socioeconomic and juridical notion of collective property during the nineteenth century, as we are doing, does not at all oblige us to review the broad movement of a socialist ideal during that century. The doctrinal current that concerns us is in fact completely removed, by its cultural formation, by the methods it chooses, and by its concrete objectives, from the context of the ideals and the programs of both utopian and scientific socialism. Certain individual socialists—Andrea Costa or Enrico Ferri, for example—eventually became aware of this current; but they did so only in its very final phases, and for their own reasons. The names and the texts of Fourier, Marx, or Engels were diligently ignored, and we say diligently because there is no objective justification for being unaware at least of Engel's rigorously historical and juridical analyses of the structure of ancient Germanic society, and of the *Mark* in particular.

To repeat once more, it was as a movement for reform in the clearly defined area of sociological and juridical culture that our doctrinal current arose. Even though it had multiple implications that must be noted, its characteristic terrain was cultural, and it was in that terrain that it chose to try out its strength.

To be sure, this movement developed on the margins of official culture; but it always, or almost always, remained within the confines of that culture, setting itself up as its critical conscience, not as its enemy. The idea of subverting an established order founded on private ownership even of the means of production was totally foreign to the program of the men who took part in this movement. Their revolt was not a program of action but a methodology, and the innovative method that they called for involved not struggle but scientific research. Their fundamental objective was to enrich traditional discourse on property in the light of newly acquired scientific knowledge, reopening discussion on a concept that had been beyond discussion. This required a critical detachment and an all-embracing, nonpartisan vision that could accept and value all of historical experience in all the wealth of its appropriative forms.

The "collective property" of which they spoke and of which we speak has nothing in common with a problem or a program of general collectivization. It is only "another way of possessing" supported by its own values and widely recurrent in history. As such, it cannot be relegated to a place among the curiosities of history or with its rubbish. Nineteenth-century individualism reacted to the uncomfortable and unwelcome realities of the rediscovery of collective appropriation by minimizing its historical importance[45] or by identifying it with a merely barbarous state, by then definitively past.[46] But those who carried the controversy forward attempted to use positive observation to reach a more comprehensive vision and to place the alternative model of collective property beside the model of individual property.

Collective property, therefore, is not a specific notion but an expression whose generic and basic significance is proper to a fairly broad, rather heterogeneous group of persons. Since it was originally just the historical and logical *oppositum* of ownership by a single proprietor, it is defined by a complex of alternative characteristics that emerged from that origin: the priority of the group and the subordination of individuals and their ends to the group; the priority of objective ends, of the economic nature, destination, and use of things, over subjective ends; the priority within the group of subjective situations of duty over those of power or right typical of the traditional *iura in re*.

In opposition to "property as belonging to," in which the message of a culture of Romanistic stamp was embodied, stood "property as function." This alternative view of property arose as a deliberate challenge to a notion of *dominium* that had become overly absolute, like a concept conceived and constructed over and above history.

The term collective property, then, refers to an appropriative *genus* contrasted to the individual. For this reason, to reduce the "property" problem here to the general and doubtless also generic dialectic between individual property and collective property means to respect the sense of the controversy, which was not particularly interested in being more specific. There was a basic problem and a basic choice to confront; the rest would follow. A problem of juridical construction undoubtedly also followed. In technical terms, the dichotomy suggested is in fact unsatisfactory, but the object of debate is primarily a problem which eludes the strictly technical. Basically, it was the excitement generated in a dialectical moment that acted as the necessary instrument to render the *unum dominium* more relative.[47]

During the course of this work we will note faithfully the clarifications of jurists and economists as they distinguish situations of public law and private law, of collective property in a strict sense and common property, of collective domain and rights of usage. But these considerations are secondary in any attempt to grasp the essential meaning of the broader debate. The important question for the historian is to know why a doctrinal movement disinterred the notion of collective property and to know how the idea was used to offer an alternative dimension to contemporary problems. It is this essential significance that we particularly want to examine.

*Part One

THE EUROPEAN CONTROVERSY

1 A Provocative Argument:

Henry Sumner Maine

The problem of historical forms of collective property had been taken up with firm determination and studied in depth by scholars of the German Historical School, and it lay stagnating in the pages of their learned works as a subject for erudite historical and juridical explications. As soon as it fell into the hands of Henry Sumner Maine, however, the problem irrupted into the public domain and, no longer containable within the restrictions proper to academic discourse, it swept through all parts of Europe to become one of the major cultural questions of the century.

To be sure, Maine's thoughts took form at the right moment: the times were ripe when the first manifesto of his overall program, *Ancient Law*, appeared in 1861. It would be an oversimplification, however, not to tie this prodigious clamor to the singular personality of the English scholar.[1]

The interest that historians of culture have shown in Maine and in his contributions to the question has never abated during the century that now separates us from his works. Although his positions were unilateral and undeniably open to question and although his reconstruction of primordial juridical orders is perhaps no longer valid,[2] his lively and provocative campaign for methodological reform has remained of interest. Icilio Vanni was acutely aware of this when, only four years after Maine's death, he felt it necessary to assess carefully Maine's contribution to the philosophy of law and to sociology, areas well beyond the confines of the history of jurisprudence.[3]

The fact that Maine broke through the conventional confines of a stagnant, traditional culture is significant in itself. It also shows us where our considerations should begin, for it offers us a reliable key to the interpretation of Maine's personality and a reason for his success as champion of a particular theory regarding primitive collective property.

There is no doubt that, professionally, Maine was, and always considered himself to be, a Romanist, or, to be more precise, a historian of law. However, it is difficult to classify professionally a man who passed imperturbed from a chair of Roman law to chairs of comparative law and international law, and who even occupied high posts in the colonial administration of his country. Still, it is certain that in everything he did he was primarily a jurist, in his specific competencies as in his angle of vision, in the set of his mind as in the intellectual procedures he brought into play. His cultural baggage was extremely varied, but the hidden core of his thinking, that which served as its base and characterized his entire "culture," was juridical. The means by which he approached reality were also substantially juridical, even when he broadened his vision to include ethnological, sociological, or purely historical interests.

Like Waitz and like Maurer, then, Maine was a jurist. But he was one whose influence on a cultural level was infinitely greater than theirs. This influence cannot be explained, as some have ingenuously sustained, by the fact that Maine wrote in a more accessible language and with an efficacious, brilliant style. The explanation lies rather in the richness and timeliness of the cultural message he bore: there, and only there lies the "secret" of Maine. That he wrote in the English language is a less relevant circumstance than his being a man of English culture—including English juridical culture—who lived in the mid-nineteenth century with his eyes and ears well open.

We have seen in the preceding pages what an invaluable vantage point was provided by the center of an empire grown to worldwide dimensions. An attentive, alert person would certainly perceive the chorus of cultural voices, and the attempt to separate them and recompose them in a sort of idealized mosaic—to compare them, in other words—must have been inevitable. That was what Maine did. Gifted with a solid Romanistic foundation, well able to handle the techniques, the language, and the systematics of the Romanists, well prepared by the remarkable patrimony of both method and content accumulated by the German Historical School,[4] Maine was not content to follow the customary itinerary of the Romanists and the historians of law. Rather, he sought to look beyond them.

All of Maine's works—and they are singularly consonant in this instance—arise from a deeply felt cultural dissatisfaction. Maine reproached the Historical School for having reduced its task to that of learned annotation of a wealth that otherwise would have been lost, without ever having infused its material with the vitality of contemporary life.[5] Although Waitz and Maurer were worthy of sincere admiration, Maine sustained, their positions had to be transcended; that is, they had to be integrated into a "total vision" and verified in light of that vision.

A basically similar sense of urgency and dissatisfaction led Savigny to write his *System of Modern Roman Law,* but Maine chose a totally different orientation. Savigny and the German scholars did their utmost to create a dogmatics, to crystallize, to systematize, to conceptualize.[6] Maine did not hesitate to extract historical data from the innermost recesses of the urn of the past, to free them from all erudite embellishments, to reduce them to essentials, to consider them within, and capable of being placed within, broad trends of development. Far from using data as an occasion for conceptualizations, he contrasted them with the infinite and varied data of present experience. Only this desacralyzing and impudent comparison could lead him to distinguish, through the long stretches of time that alone really count, a sense of history, that is, of human institutions in time.

Traces of English culture were visible and deeply rooted—indeed obvious—in Maine, both as a jurist and as a historian. As a jurist, he revealed his membership in the world of common law in every turn of his reasoning. He thus appears to be a typical product of the English juridical schools which, from the Middle Ages to the nineteenth century, consistently refused to identify their hermeneutic and didactic task in the working out of a dogmatics and of a juridical "construction" and which held the world of law to be singularly open to facts and available to influences by osmosis from the other social sciences. Maine could be classified as one of the most representative cultural products of the British juridical tradition through his sharing in certain of its constantly present and basic themes. These include an awareness of the elasticity of the law and of the historicity intrinsic to it, a diffidence toward overly rigid conceptual systems, and a demand to restore the world of law to the broader world of history. As a historian, he revealed his insularity when he reduced his argument to an evident prop for his own unwavering intuition and when, in a vision which brings to mind centuries of empiricism triumphant, he demanded of documentation, both historical and comparative, that it also concur in furnishing a solid foundation for his intuitive capacity as an observer.

Although his mind was quick and penetrating, Maine was in fact governed by intuition. His capacity to choose the right direction in a network of many paths was surprising; he knew how to grasp and follow the guiding thread through the labyrinth of scattered and complex documentation.

When he transferred his jurist's innate rigor to a historiographical terrain, his entire investigation tended to be reduced to conclusion, to become simple and linear. When we thumb through his books we see that they follow the line of the author's personal reflections, that they are developed from a base of a few fundamental assumptions and of a few but essential sources. All is reduced to its bare bones, all is spare; nothing is conceded to redundancy, rhetoric, base polemics, or even erudition. Like any conscientious historian, he had copious documentation behind him, but he generously took pity on his reader and placed his own authority as a filter between him and the huge mass of material he had gathered.

He was also extremely parsimonious with annotations. In his pages there is room only for a distilled discourse, strong in its own internal logic, impatient with diversions and additions, certainly not abstract, but—I repeat—conducted on the basis of essential data. The reader must have faith in the historian concerning both the choice of these essential data and the judgment of how essential they are. Maine insists on the reader's total faith in him: the reader is in good hands, but they are without doubt Maine's.

Maine needed few citations to other authorities to lead his reader in this manner. He could eliminate nearly all of the customary critical apparatus and rely heavily on what we might jokingly call his oral tradition. For him, the oral tradition—the conversation with a colonial bureaucrat, the news contained in a letter from a friend, direct observation *in loco*—had an objective value equal to that of a document. This was enough to make anyone who looked at this casual methodology with positivistic eyes tremble. It was also enough to make any censor who championed historiographic accuracy turn up his nose.

The term "historian's craft" must be somewhat redefined when applied to Maine. Since Maine was aware that past and present in human history are strongly woven together, he was ideally placed to throw his scholar's nets where two streams of experience—the historical and the comparative—met. These two currents were both the foundation of his experience as observer and what made his observations more complex.

To take advantage of a great variety of experiences, to observe them, to mediate between them and the future reader: this was the task that Maine set himself, and it is a program that would be misunderstood if one tried to reduce it to a purely historiographic level.[7] His procedures become clearer if we consider his predilection for those historical terrains in which a continuity from past to present was heightened by attitudes that were firmly consistent even amid the changes of whole millennia. In these situations, the historian uses his instruments as does the geologer who, probing through the surface strata, finds the laws governing the formation of those strata in others hidden deeply beneath them. His method can also be seen in his taste for the historical "fossil," the society that appears to be as inanimate as stone, but which is in its substance the sign of an uninterrupted vitality and the link between what existed in the most remote past and what today is history in the making.[8]

Thus at this point we rejoin our premises: Maine's discourse, contrary to those of Waitz and Maurer, was not and did not claim to be only historical and juridical. Indeed, it sought to avoid confinement within such disciplines. Its supporting research found its chosen terrain in the encounter and clash between dissimilar cultures, in the varied and changing play of superimposed or counterposed juridical traditions, and in their discontinuous development. All of these elements surfaced and sank according to the historical situation, and all were followed with loving attention over the largest possible spatial and temporal span. Maine was never concerned with studying the pseudo truths of local lore, not even treated with erudite techniques or trappings. Nor was he satisfied to conduct his investigations within a single historical tradition. He felt at ease only in the wide open spaces that find their historical and anthropological limits defined *naturally* in terms of broad ethnological groups.

Even his language eludes definition. Although it never abandoned its underlying juridical framework, it broadened out to include the vocabulary of sociology and history as well as jurisprudence.

His sources were atypical as well. He was just as inclined to fasten upon data of the most diversified nature as he was to read attentively legislative, consuetudinary, or doctrinal texts—the customary and time-honored baggage of juridical history. He was a formidable observer: his curiosity and his attention were perennially on the alert and his study was at the center of channels of information that put him in contact with the four corners of the globe. A note in his study, *Village-Communities in the East and West,* is emblematic: in it he put to use information gathered from the Fiji Islands, from North Africa, and even from the Rocky Mountain region of North America. His data on North America were taken from an official report on explorations published just the year before and undoubtedly no sooner received than read avidly.

We can perhaps now understand the reason for Maine's enormous success and for the extent of his influence on general culture. If his works inspired the epistemological reflections of Icilio Vanni, it was because Maine had come to speak in a universal language within a situation of a singular cultural and philosophical eclecticism, a language with which at least the sociologist, the ethnologist, and also the historian, as well as the jurist, could feel at ease. His problems were not those of a restricted circle of scholars. They were the great problems of man living in society, problems that he grasped in their intimate and ultimate roots. They were alive, burning problems: in fact, all those who identified as the first duty of a man of culture his function as a critic were to listen to Maine and to follow him. They were to find at the same time new foundations for their own work and encouragement to undertake it free from former restraints.

But there was one quality in particular perceptible throughout Maine's writings that gave them even an ethical importance: they represented a thoroughgoing methodological reform. To draw fully on the historical and comparative disciplines, as our jurist did, had a clearly definable validity on the level of method, even if he finally came to exploit these techniques for other ends. His multiple interests also represented a rupture with sclerotic approaches against which the Historical School had, for complex reasons, lost the battle that it had begun.[9]

The admiration that Maine felt for the message of the Historical School and for some of its indisputable achievements did not prevent him from lucidly noting where and particularly why they had failed. The excesses of natural law and of juridical formalism could not be combatted with a purely historical discourse that often ended up as pure erudition. If the argument was approached with these limitations it was destined to become sterile and idle or, as it turned out, to be distorted into positions that not only were far removed from the original premises but that also reinstalled *a posteriori* the formalisms that they were trying to break down.

The "comparative jurisprudence" of Maine comprised his alternative proposal. It was born of a dissatisfaction with the Baroque dogmatizations of a late rationalism based on natural law and with the torments of the analytical jurisprudence that had recently found its English spokesmen, as everyone knows, in Jeremy Bentham and John Austin. It sprang from the need to revitalize juridical science and was constructed on an indisputable certitude: the historicity of the law, of its instruments, and of its techniques, and the consequent refusal of any *a priori* reasoning.

For Maine, to be a historian and a comparatist meant to take on a demythicizing function. Nothing, on a juridical level, was definitive; nothing was free from the erosion of contingency. On the contrary, everything had to be reexamined in its relationship with everything else. The dogmas of juridical individualism were the place to begin, and first among them were private property and contracts.

Maine was a historicist more than he was a historian. This is the central core of his message and the prop that supports his entire structure, and this—reduced to the minimum—is the essential character of his method. The rest—all the rest—can be qualified as instrumental to this end.

The jurist, then, could not avoid taking on the habit of the historian and the comparatist when history and comparative studies became his most fruitful laboratory. To be sure, to write history meant for Maine to cast aside any heroic mantle and penetrate rather into his usual terrain of induction, armed with his inalienable positivism. To write history could not possibly involve for him the production of florid decoration, scholarly erudition, or amusing curiosities. It involved rather bringing into being that dimension intrinsic to the juridical universe without which its particular character could never be properly identified, hence neither understood nor correctly interpreted.

One consequence of greatest importance ensued: when historicity was positive as a dimension internal to law, historical and comparative investigation could be incorporated as an intrinsic, not just an extrinsic, part of the normal professional work of the jurist.[10] It would have been unthinkable for Maine to juxtapose a technical juridical argument and a historical argument—as though the two kinds of argument could be separated from the substance of a discourse as if they were merely specious and pleonastic ornamentation. His explorations into the history of primitive conceptions of property are first and foremost a contribution to a new theory of property.

Maine's view represented a real break and a great advance in comparison with the views on the contribution of history of "rational law" jurists or even of the leaders of the Historical School. Although historical reference is constant in the works of the proponents of natural law and even in those of the neoscholastics, it remains either a simple background without real influence or a near-fabulous metahistory. The Historical School, on the other hand, failed to incorporate historical analysis among the mechanisms used to bring unified meaning to life.

If I have lingered over Maine's place in the general culture of his age, I have not done so without reason. I believe in fact that only now can we respond adequately to the question we began with, that of the success of certain of his theories.

In the history of sociological and juridical concepts concerning property Henry Sumner Maine's work constitutes an essential step that conditioned succeeding thought in this area. If it is true that Maine did not build *ex nihilo,* that he was not the *inventor* of any theory, that probably his ultimate conclusions were largely derived from the work of preceding scholars, it is also true that with him the problem was put on the agenda of the most highly developed culture in Europe (and highly developed not only in the juridical field) and that with him it shook off its antiquarian dust and became a problem of method in the social sciences, immediately connected with social questions. One could perhaps say that Maine *invented* the problem. He invented it because in his hands, when old and new material was filtered through his complex personality and the complexity of his attitude as a scholar, what had been erudite annotations became a message that was innovative and in many ways iconoclastic.

Maine and the Demythicization of Juridical Classicism

In one of his later works, when he was looking back over his intellectual journey, Maine confessed, "When I began it, several years before 1861, the background was obscured and the route beyond a certain point obstructed, by *a priori* theories based on the hypothesis of a law and a state of Nature."[11] This is an exact identification of the enemy he sought to combat, and it signaled the launching of all of his urbane, scholarly cultural polemics. If there was one thing that irritated Maine, a generally tolerant man, it was to feel himself hemmed in by the insuperable obstacles represented by the body of generic and generically sacred institutions of *ius naturae*. He viewed them as a set of presuppositions projected theologically onto the terrain of human history, even though, by their very nature, they are foreign to its development and utterly hampering to even the most dedicated man of culture.

As a historian, Maine's quarrel was born of this insupportable condemnation to impotence and of the realization that the historicity of institutions was sacrificed in the name of illusions rooted entirely or mainly in ignorance. The struggle that occupied all of Maine's intellectual life against some of the abuses of natural law, or against using its principles as a convenient refuge, was a struggle against the *a priori* and in favor of a historicity of situations. All in the specific situation may be empirical, provisory, flexible, and relative, but the subject and the community are engaged personally in the allocation of their own liberty in time and space.

In the course of his effort to free himself and the object of his study from the dominion of myth Maine concentrated on two areas: a qualitatively new analysis of the Roman and Romanistic cultural experience, and what we can define in a formula that may be brusque but is not inexact in the context of Maine's thought as the juridical patrimony dating back to the common core of Indo-European origins. Both areas were examined and enlivened by means of the perennial counterpoint offered by comparison.

Maine singled out clearly and perceptively the profound bond between the history of Roman law and the history of the concepts related to natural law; he noted the profound interpenetration between the two, particularly in the consolidation of modern juridical culture, and the invaluable support that the former had lent to the latter. As an expert in the internal mechanisms of the system constructed by the Romans, Maine particularly appreciated its technical instruments and its rigor of terminology, a rigor that had reduced the redundancy of generic language to a sort of superfunctional juridical shorthand.[12] He also identified in that same technical and linguistic framework the instrument that had permitted the petrification of one particular nucleus of social and ethico-political doctrine and its transfer outside of the historical process as pure logical forms—as forms, that is, postulated *a priori*. The complex of notions known as natural law had crystallized thanks to the architecture within which it found itself in the Roman experience and, even more, in the modern Romanistic experience. Juridical science no longer confronted historical material that was elastic and of only relative value. Rather, it now confronted something that seemed henceforth to be identified with the objectivity of nature, to constitute the most adequate response to human exigencies, to pose, in other words, as a model and to function as a stable criterion by which the overflowing abundance of daily life could be measured.

      Maine the historicizer could not avoid feeling suffocated. Maine the historian could not avoid feeling mocked by this world of metahistorical shadows repugnant to his sense of solidity as a devotee of the "positive," as a person who realized the plenitude of his forces only in the observation of concrete experience.

      For him, Roman law had seemed utilizable in quite other terms. What he could regard with indulgence was not the construction of the system, not the conceptualization of contingent economic and cultural forces, not the metamorphosis of a historically variable rule into a *ratio scripta,* but rather the function of Roman law as mediator between ancient law and modern times. Roman law appeared to Maine to be a positive moment in Western juridical history, one which he viewed in an exclusively historical key. For him, this experience of a more than millennial continuity, which initially plucked elements out of primitive Italic law and which finally pressed forward toward the new attitudes of the High Middle Ages, assumed the value of a testimony to a colossal transfer of one age to the next, traces of which an attentive and gifted historian could perceive in the very fiber of the enormous documentation it had left behind.[13]

      This is already a noteworthy position: it is far from the usual apologetic appreciations of Roman law, all of them concerned with petrifying Roman juridical experience into purified logical categories almost wholly devoid of material contents. On the contrary, Maine's admiration of Roman law arose out of the historically verifiable references that abound in it. The rest of it—that part of the texts which had been the object of admiration during ten centuries of *scientia juris*—he considered to be too great a risk to warrant his unconditional and confident approbation.

      Maine's angle of observation was different and unique. The historicizing principles, which are never absent from his argument, transport Roman law from the limbo of a model to the reality of the mutable and the transient. They give back to it a concrete vitality, and they permit it to be judged according to the same standards as other historical phenomena. Roman law, in other words, was a great contribution to civilization and one worthy of admiration, but it was only one among many such contributions.

Maine's historicism dealt a serious blow to the monopoly of the European Romanists in juridical culture. He refused to conceive of juridical history as the history of one, unique, obligatory channel, that is, of the manifestations of Roman law alone; and he rediscovered a plurality of values to which the West at least was not accustomed. The disenchanted Englishman within him, standing open-minded at the crossroads of civilization and bearing in his nature as a juridical agent the deep-seated skepticism of seven centuries of common law jurisprudence, had the upper hand of the cultivated Romanist. Indeed, Maine the Romanist yielded more and more to Maine the comparatist. In his thought the world of history dropped its arid monocellular quality and opened up to enrichment from new sources. First came the mass of Slavic customs that travelers of the perspicacity and preparation of Haxthausen made known to the European intellectual community.[14] Then followed the arrival in British ports, along with the goods of the East India Company, of the treasure of Hindu juridical institutions.[15] Next came the complex of paleo-Irish legal texts that was made available to scholars by the publication of the ancient sources.[16] Finally, there arrived from all over the world thousands of voices great and small, from the most obscure to the most prominent, valuable to the scholar engaged in the task of demythicization for the alternative models of juridical norms they expressed.

What Maine wanted to achieve was to help human nature shake off the Roman and Romanistic incrustations that restricted the liberty of free agents when they had lost their original character and had become regarded as one with nature itself. Several years later, the greatest scholar of Celtic civilization of the century, Marie-Henry d'Arbois de Jubainville, stated, speaking of linguistic filiation, "Rome conquered us definitively. . . . What had been the sign of servitude had become an element of our very nature."[17] What was imperative for Maine as for d'Arbois was to identify the signs of servitude, to separate them from man's natural constitution, to see them as relative, and thus to render them innocuous: a vital and a liberating operation. In the name of observation and experience, that is, in practice, in the name of history understood inductively, the myth would crumble to dust and the obligatory blinders (for Maine, these were the spector of the *a priori,* of the antihistorical) would give way to a critical vision and an incommensurably augmented capacity for appropriate diagnosis.[18]

Only after he had swept the terrain clear and reacquired his entire hermeneutic freedom could the scholar move freely on the level of institutions. Once methodology had been freed, it would be possible, point by point, institution by institution, to effect changes on a cultural level.

The question of the connection between men and things remained one of the areas most central to Maine's arguments. It was also the one on which the Romans of the classical age had chosen to make a precise, decisive statement that was in perfect coherence with the politico-economic structure they had created and that notably conditioned subsequent developments in Western civilization. It was also the area, or at least one of the principal areas, in which a complex of juridical constructions had soon broken out from their historical setting and had become a suffocating model—in which one set of decisions, strongly standardized even though originally intended simply as a response to certain specific exigencies, had taken on the color of "normality" and "naturalness," relegating alternative decisions either to the dump-heap of history's castoffs or to the dour menagerie of exceptional cases. It was for just this reason that Maine's demythicizing analysis was to have such enormous influence. His investigation chose for its battleground the adversaries' favorite territory of the most purely, most essentially juridical. His weapon was the comparison of the systemizations that Romanistic juridical tradition had arrived at with conclusions from cultural orders such as the Indian or the Irish that, although they fell within the larger Indo-European family, had had an independent, parallel development without reciprocal contamination. In this way, the historicity of Romanistic systems could adequately be brought into relief.

The argument developed along three basic lines: a theory of the ways in which property was originally acquired and especially was first occupied; the great systematic tripartite division between law pertaining to persons, to things, and to actions; and the relation of private ownership to common ownership. We will soon examine how the three were linked together in Maine's thought.

Occupancy remained one of the more specious creations of the inventive capacity of the Romans for justifying the appropriation of goods by an individual through an appeal to nature. It laid the foundation for the notion of "mine" as a rightful reward for the activity of an individual who had spent more brute force, energy, volition, or zeal than others in order to isolate a thing from the undistinguished jumble of primitive chaos. The correspondence of this juridical instrument with *rerum natura* seemed evident, and the property acquired seemed to carry with it that ethical minimum proper to every natural institution to validate a previously made decision and to obtain the consensus of other members of the community, needed in order to effect the practical exclusion of all others from the exercise of powers over the thing in question. In other words, individual property had its own legitimacy in relation to the very laws of nature.

This reasoning seemed to Maine simplistic, and since he realized that it was fundamental to his adversaries' argument, he took the time to discuss it and refute it. Let us begin with a clear, indisputable definition of occupancy: "Occupancy was the process by which the 'no man's goods' of the primitive world became the private property of individuals in the world of history."[19]

Thus occupancy was the miraculous instrument by means of which the *res nullius* became *res unius* and from primitive chaos made its solemn entry into civilization, that is, into history. Maine's irony is veiled but sharp: the historical problem did not allow shades of meaning but split into a dialectic of contraries: a thing was either *res nullius* or it was the object of the *dominium unius*. And the course of history, the direction of civilization, proceeded from nonownership to private ownership.

This is the adage on which all of Western jurisprudence peacefully rested, and Maine chose Blackstone as a witness because he was particularly receptive to the dominant koine.[20] But there were urgent questions to be raised: from what historical zone had so generic an institution sprung? Within what reality did the individual operate who, in Blackstone's pages and in the similar pages of all other jurists, used his own physical force before the others, or who first settled on land to rest himself, first sat in the shade of a certain tree or shelter, and so on? For one fact was clear: occupancy was and *meant* to be the physical presence of an individual who imposed his own individuality on things. Furthermore, it also signified a respect on the part of the community for that individual effort and for the effect of that effort in the domain of things. Occupancy, then, was a product typical of a society that believed in individual affirmation and in which circulated general sentiments inspired by a strong individualism. Nothing emerges from such a society that is not characterized by the individual and that is not completely operant on the level of the individual: "It will be observed, that the acts and motives which these theories suppose are the acts and motives of Individuals."[21]

To even offer this elementary and perfectly reasonable consideration meant to begin scratching, if not shattering, the foundations of the theory Maine was seeking to refute. The principle of occupancy, which had been assigned to the moment of transition from archaic to organized society, had no temporal dimension. It belonged quite evidently to a metahistorical universe. It presupposed a consciousness concerning individual ownership, a sharply defined sentiment of what was one's own, even on the level of immovable things, an affirmation of the principle that every parcel of land had its *dominus*, all of which were inconceivable in a society more dominated by uncertainties than certainties and bound up in the basic problems of daily survival.[22] Occupancy was for this reason nothing more than a belated justification devised by the fertile imagination of the jurists in order to insert the principle of "mine" into the terrestrial paradise of the state of nature. It was testimony of the inventiveness "of a refined jurisprudence."[23]

Maine's demythicizing attack was aimed at two objectives. On the one hand it exposed the antihistorical nature of the doctrine of occupancy in its very substance. Subject and object operated within this doctrine completely disconnected from any effective reality, and the primitive world which should have been seen as historical *humus* was rather reconstructed as the decorative scenery to an arcadian performance featuring masked players or silhouettes rather than living persons. On the other hand, it pointed out that the enunciation of the doctrine of occupancy was itself obviously historical, and it made clear that the doctrine was distinctly charged with an ideological cast by the jurists who formulated it.[24]

When Maine defined the "occupying individual" culturally, he reduced that moment in which the subject theoretically becomes conscious of ownership to a purely ideological phenomenon. This was the same ideal individual as the one who, in Blackstone's alluringly tinted pages, accomplished a series of occupying activities against a background of a timeless agrarian landscape; it was the same as the individual who subscribed to the social contract in contractual theory before Rousseau. In other words, the individual that modern natural law theory perennially proposed was an abstract individual, a pure form deprived of any historical context.[25] Thus, in Maine's felicitous diagnosis, occupancy found its place beside a particular set of contractualist theories in the gallery of the inventions of natural law.

Maine knew well that the Romans had made a large contribution to the development of this doctrine, and for this reason he tied it firmly to an individualistic society and to a refined jurisprudence. But he attributed its further development above all to modern schools of natural law. It was particularly in the latter that the Romans' technical positions were colored by their own vague naturalism and assumed the odious, relentlessly *a priori* quality against which our English jurisconsult engaged such a generous battle, and it was they who passed off the defense of particular interests under the guise of the true and the just.

This was how the social contract and the occupancy theories asserted their value as an instrument in the hands of certain groups within postmedieval Western society. But these theories were utterly incapable of reproducing accurately the vital processes of a primordial social order. The primitive world, accustomed to a total lack of distinction within the community, could not conceivably develop directly into a world of proprietors without going through intermediate stages. The individual hypothesized and created by the Romanists as the subject and agent of occupancy belonged to the category of phantasms: the only individual that history could identify and who could be seen operating in the primitive world is the one who, finding solitude repugnant to him but without showing special awareness of himself, lived and operated within the group, his protective shell, his vital condition, and his necessary integration.

If one wishes to view the primitive world as a historical reality rather than to pick from it obsolete tatters by which to justify the fundamental institutions of modern society, Maine said, it is to the group and not to the individual that one must turn: "Ancient law, it must again be repeated, knows next to nothing of Individuals. It is concerned not with Individuals, but with Families, not with single human beings, but groups."[26]

It was his observation of his living fossils—of Slavic and Hindu law, as it appeared in the first full statement of his thesis, *Ancient Law,* in 1861, of paleo-Irish law in his *Lectures on the Early History of Institutions* of 1874—that brought Maine to such a clearly stated and confident affirmation. This was the first time, perhaps, that a jurist had plundered such unusual materials. It was certainly the first time that such materials had come to be used with polemical intent against the classical tradition and in the interest of an alternative cultural order.

To make my point perfectly clear: I am referring only to the course that some juridical traditions took within the sphere of what Maine called "the common basis of Aryan usage"[27] but that differed from the Roman-occidental tradition. Such traditions remained faithful to certain primitive patterns, in some places right up until the present day, in contrast to the radically innovative path embarked upon, in the sphere of economic and social organization by the civilization of the Romans.

The Hindu fossil or the Celtic fossil had the advantage of finding expression in an uncompromisingly antique language, and, far from representing merely a diverse voice in the general Indo-European chorus, they succeeded in questioning the identification of certain classical tenets with the conclusions of natural law.[28] What Maine wanted was to demythicize juridical classicism as the interpreter of a pretended state of nature—without iconoclasm and without base polemics against an undeniably admirable goal for human development. What was important to him was to reduce the classical view to one step in that development, to *one* way among many of feeling about and of conceptualizing the problems of economic and juridical organization as it took concrete historical form in historical times in Mediterranean lands.

"A new order of things"[29] came to light to render the historian's sensitivities at once more complex and more self-aware, and this new order revealed within the primitive world a protagonist different from the individual in the group and the specific relationships between individuals, the group, and the family unit.

This conclusion—elementary as it is—demonstrated the inadequacy of the theory of occupancy (at least as the banner of individualism) and introduced the second important point: the bipartite separation of the law of persons and the law of things as a category fundamental to the juridical system.[30]

Such a category is clearly discerned in the classical system. It is clearly stated by Gaius, and it is clearly repeated in Justinian's institutional manual as the sign of a *Zentralbegriff* that dominated the whole of Roman law for the entire span of its existence. It might have seemed at first glance to have been a primordial datum based on evidence, but comparative analysis showed this not to be so. The examination of his fossils brought to Maine's attention a continuous osmosis between the realm of persons and the realm of things. The two were bound together by multiple and inextricable ties in a sort of vital union, and he asserted that the concept of separation was totally incapable of rendering a correct interpretation of the reality of ancient law.[31]

Maine insisted on the historical character of this classification. He gave it an important place in his argument, and he returned to it several times during the course of his further reflections. The classification presupposed a jurisprudence—a refined jurisprudence, Maine would say—that managed to isolate the individual as a value basic to society, an individual who was a reality contained within himself and whose definition as an entity owed nothing to external reality, to the world of phenomena. He exercised his sovereignty over the field of things, the realm of undefined matter, which was separated from the human dimension by an impassable gulf. The organized world was conceivable only in a dialectic of contrasts: subjects and objects, a positive pole diametrically opposed to a negative pole, two realities qualitatively diverse, hence incommunicably separated.

This is the speculative base on which the classification was founded and it was here that it revealed its limitation. Maine insists repeatedly that an individual so conceived has no place in the primitive world. The microcosm in respect to this reality was a futurist projection. Quite the contrary, Maine continues, all documentary evidence points to a fundamental inability of primitive societies to conceive of the individual as an autonomous entity: he tends to blend in, to find the weight of his own validity elsewhere, to fit himself in with values that come *aliunde*. As far as family succession is concerned, he is only one link in an uninterrupted chain in which birth and death are mere happenings; he continues in time the life of his ancestors and finds in his descendants the prolongation of his own life in time.[32] He is unable to affirm with the arrogance of the classical individual the separation of his own person from the reality of things around him. He regards them with humility and, far from considering them as inanimate objects, he sees in them activities of moment within a complex cosmic vitality.[33]

The definition of even this essential category, therefore, was not founded in *rerum natura,* but was a solution congenial to the sociocultural order usually qualified as classical. There were, however, other historical societies with different anthropological foundations that offered alternative solutions of equal validity, at least in the eyes of an observer who had stripped his mind of archetypes and had learned to look at historical change attentively and without prejudice.

If it were important to the ends of this investigation, we could follow Maine as he dismantled the traditional classifications and systems. We could watch the disintegration of such habitual articulations of juridical knowledge in the Romanist tradition as the distinction between landed rights and rights of obligation, or between private and public law. What is important to us is that with Maine a more complex, more varied, and richer cultural panorama opened up before the jurist. Parallel to the obligatory and conditioning channel that classical culture represented, *alternative* cultures proposed *alternative* solutions, and two fixed points emerged in the new perspective. The first was that many classical verities were removed from their secure and undisputed berth in nature and set afloat on the fragile and mutable tides of history. The second was the possibility of resolving the problem of the relationship between man and goods in other than individualistic terms without doing violence to the innermost vocations of human nature. In fact, as we have noted, Maine's fossils point to the group as the one and only concrete protagonist in the constancy of historical societies that remained uncontaminated by the invasion of classicism.

His argument could and should have forged ahead, touching the innermost and most jealously guarded core of the classical citadel, the concept whose legitimization and conservation seemed to validate its entire construction: individual property. This was the *a priori* principle that juridical classicism had consigned intact to modern schools of natural law and that Maine found solidly mounted in the center of the jewel of natural law.

The Theoretical and Historical Problem of Property and the Methodological Reforms of Maine

In his "realistic evolutionism"[34] Maine had nothing against private property,[35] nor against the bourgeois society that wore its natural law as easily as a comfortable coat well suited to its needs. It was rather pseudo verities passed off dogmatically as truths that wore on his nerves.

One of these pseudo verities, perhaps the chief among them, was the theory of the origin and development of ownership by single individuals.

A continental jurist, one nurtured in the conviction that the most significant contribution to Western juridical history lay in the rediscovery of Roman law, would have found it difficult to make the cultural effort to liberate himself from this principle. Where Maine was fortunate, as we have noted, was in being born English. Unlike continental jurists, he harbored within him no Roman idol, the object of veneration and measure of the meaning in every intellectual movement. Behind him stood a juridical experience alien to metaphysics and codification, thick with incoherences, as unstructured as alluvial sediment but nevertheless fairly faithful to the facts of society. Behind him stood—to limit ourselves to the field that interests us here—the system of land rights reflected in common law, in which practical situations combined with an abundant residuum of medieval and particularly canon law to provide a perfect contrast to the rigorous Roman construction of the *dominium* and the *iura in re*. At a time when the Slav, the Hindu, and the Irish fossils were revealing a different order of things, a campaign to verify the solidity of the Roman edifice also made some headway—thanks in part to the presence of scholars able to pursue it—with the result that the edifice was gradually declassified from sacred monument to a simple historical construction.

We thus arrive at the third and most significant point in Maine's inquiry:

> There is a strong *a priori* improbability of our obtaining any clue to the early history of property, if we confine our notice to the proprietary rights of individuals. It is more than likely that joint-ownership, and not separate ownership, in the really archaic institution, and that the forms of property which will afford us instruction will be those which are associated with the rights of families and of groups of kindred. The Roman jurisprudence will not here assist in enlightening us, for it is exactly the Roman jurisprudence which, transformed by the theory of Natural Law, has bequeathed to the moderns the impression that individual ownership is the normal state of proprietary right, and that ownership in common by groups of men is only the exception to a general rule.[36]

And further:

> The mature Roman law, and modern jurisprudence following in its wake, look upon co-ownership as an exceptional and momentary condition of the rights of property. This view is clearly indicated in the maxim which obtains universally in

Western Europe, *Nemo in communione potest invitus detineri* ("No one can be kept in co-proprietorship against his will"). But in India this order of ideas is reversed, and it may be said that separate proprietorship is always on its way to become proprietorship in common.[37]

After he demonstrates that some of the most undisputed Roman juridical rules are actually the individualistic demands of a particular society, transferred to the level of jurisprudence, Maine turns to the specific question of property. Two principles enter into this framework of ideas, that is, into the designs of an individualistic society attempting to preconstitute solid theoretical foundations for itself. One is the reassertion of the principle of the historical priority of individual property over "common" property. The other is the role of private property as the model for all property, as a phenomenon that embraces and personifies the essence of the categorical notion of ownership.

But alongside individual property another historical reality became discernible. It was a reality that had played a determining role in history and that only the monopolistic arrogance of a culture of Roman stamp had placed among history's castoffs, or had at least tended to circumscribe and minimize. We refer of course to so-called collective property.

With Maine, after two thousand years of jurisprudential logorrhea, the problem was finally confronted on a doctrinal plane and as a contribution to the theory of property. Even the medieval jurists, engaged though they were in the definition of a new system of landholding situations and living as they did in a social whole rich with associative phenomena, had dodged the problem.[38] Later, after the problem had been raised, it had been seen either as a contribution to a more far-reaching, detailed knowledge of feudal relations (as in the doctrine regarding seventeenth- and eighteenth-century southern Italy), or it was absorbed by the problem—a serious one for the Romanists—of the structure of primitive society. Thus in the erudite investigations of the Historical School, usually so generously thorough, it remained marginal to the play of combinations among the various *Genossenschaften* within the total community. On Maine's pages, however, the problem was recalled from cultural exile, treated without digressions or equivocations, and made intrinsic to the problem of property presented as a genus.

The "property" problem was becoming complex and showed signs of a sacrilegious internal gemination. Two species came out of the genus property, two species assumed on a preliminary basis to be institutions of equal historical and social dignity: individual property and collective property. And Maine's argument, as was his custom, began to shift from the historical context to the theoretical—although it is never possible to separate completely the two aspects of his argument.

Maine went much further, however. It was not only the model of "individual property" that was dethroned, but also the cultural model that supported it. The credibility of Roman law came into question, or if we prefer, the law was again confined within modest historical limits. Roman documentary materials were, in the judgment of our English jurist, to be valued by the same standard as the Hindu, and testimony that arrived from Hindustan, even if it bore little or no weight of tradition, was sufficient to reduce Roman dogma to fables for the unwary.

Maine purposely and artfully cites an old legal aphorism, as if he were suggesting that such a verity was so unfounded that it could henceforth count for support only on popular adages and maxims. He quotes the adage, *Nemo in communione potest invitus detineri:* he might have added another one, of equally effective dissuasive power, that paints common property with the somber colors of *mater malorum*. That way the picture would have been a complete program of intimidation, one that praised the value of individual property and barely tolerated, as a non-value, common property.

It is implicit in the quotation of this brocard that Maine's evaluation was negative regarding an order disposed to recognize validity in every individual desire and ready to sacrifice the group for the whims of a subject the moment he becomes *invitus*. Also implicit is his insistence on retracing to the individualistic matrixes of modern Western society the entire complex of juridical constructions concerning property.

The Indian experience demonstrated that a society could choose collective property as its own bearing structure and could persist in this behavior totally unchanged to the present day, even, indeed, tending to render common whatever properties happened to be held privately. The normative quality that private property assumed within the Roman tradition had therefore to be restricted within the confines of that tradition alone. If individual property was "norm" and "model," it would be so only relative to that tradition, and its normativity ceased the moment one left those confines.

We will see in the following section how Maine pursues his argumentation. The results already obtained thus far are noteworthy: collective property was a fact that was negative, fortuitous, and exceptional only when placed in a context supported by the Roman and Romanistic cultural monopoly because only in this context did it come into conflict with the individualistic premises which sustained that monopoly. In traditions that started off from different premises, collective property could take on a function of equal importance or even become the chief element in a system. The *a priori* principle constructed by the Romans and confirmed by modern Romanists was nothing more than the result of a particular and questionable historical decision. It was a product of history, historically variable, and not a hypostasis of human nature.

We see here that Maine's analysis had important consequences for methodology. Two liberations were accomplished without bloodletting: first and foremost, historical and juridical studies were freed from an apologetic and myth-making "Romanism" or "classicism" that had previously been accepted uncritically and passed off—for complex and ideological reasons—as intimately coherent with the nature of things. Maine's implicit conclusion was merciless: to continue to carry this baggage without questioning it or verifying it was either uncritical or ideological, and so was in either event to be rejected by any scholar whose viewpoint was cultural.

One cannot emphasize enough, I believe, that the sole and characteristic dimension of Maine's investigations was cultural. When dealing with such a burning question as property, it would have been easy for him to set up a directly political argument. But this was not so. He avoided polemics: even though his argument is pitiless, one rarely is given to read pages that are more relaxed and less rancorous than those of *Ancient Law*. He avoided deliberately reformistic appeals and thus avoided the anxieties and emotional involvements that characterized Emile de Laveleye's works, as we shall soon see. It was from a platform rigorously chosen and defined as scientific and with the calm certitude of a man of studies reorganizing the papers on his desk that Maine launched the process of demolishing the edifice of individual property as an institution of natural law. But we must note that in demolishing it, he acted not as an enemy to private property, but as one who sought to confirm the antiscientific nature of its particular theoretical construction.

The chapter of *Ancient Law* that deals with the problem does not focus on individual property as a value or a nonvalue, nor on its moral or theological acceptability, but rather on how it was originally acquired and on common property. It is organized, that is, as a discourse that arises and develops on the terrain of jurisprudence, even if subsequently it was to have profound implications of an ideological character and was to be reinforced by its strong "politicality."

Maine looked at institutions with the eyes of a technician, a technician whose glasses bore lenses of that high power of technical competence that made him such a qualified observer. Furthermore, the specific observer who was Henry Maine had the invaluable quality of not being satisfied with the juridical universe from which these techniques had sprung, but of accumulating comparisons with the varied universes about which he could obtain information. It was then that institutions revealed their purely technical character and their relativity, and that Maine could with confidence and with a sense of satisfaction remove them from the sway of nature and assign to them the essential characteristic of historicity.

This was the point of arrival that the historicist in Maine sought after on a methodological level. All that had been said in Western culture regarding property was a technical invention—when it was not merely refined erudition, unbridled fantasy, or an admirable exercise in logic. If therefore all was history and nothing but history, the testimony of the Roman experience was no more and no less valid than that of the Slavic, the Celtic, or the Hindu. One could continue to hold up one institution as a model, but it would be an artificial procedure, totally separated from the nature of things and justified instead by particular political choices.

The second and more specific liberation regarded the history of the doctrine of property. When juridical classicism losts its power as a myth and when established cultural values were turned upside down, individual and collective property could be considered on the same plane. Both could be proposed as normal historical situations, as possible functional choices made by a society in relation to the demands of its own structure. The breach or perhaps the breakdown of what d'Arbois de Jubainville defined as the sign of servitude allowed a freedom hitherto unknown to the jurist concerned with the phenomenon of property. The object of his study was henceforth definitively "laicized" and more complex. Such a jurist could finally investigate it scientifically, without suffocating prejudices.

The Problem of the Origins of Collective and Individual Property: A Reexamination and Revision of the Question

Once the Romanistic cultural monopoly had been shattered by the shattering of the passive mentality that had supported it, cultures joined on an equal footing to form the patrimony of the historian of jurisprudence, and the historian of the phenomenon of property could speak of it as plural. This was already a decided acquisition in methodological terms.

But once several kinds of property were made to compete in the realm of historical becoming, once individual property lost its privilege of functioning as the voice of nature in society and hence its status as the essential moment in the transition from primordial chaos to historical order, there remained the troubling problem—one rendered all the more pressing by the void created by Maine's demythicizing—of origins, of primitive structures, perhaps also of historical precedence. There also remained an inevitable question: Did collective property perhaps deserve the privilege of priority?

Maine was intensely aware of this problem, so much so that it was the ever-present and dominating theme of his long and fulsome activity. In *Ancient Law* (1861) there is an all-important chapter, the eighth, devoted to the "Early History of Property," and the same theme soon formed the central core of *Village-Communities in the East and West,* the Oxford lectures of 1870, and the *Lectures on the Early History of Institutions* of 1875. (The latter were a continuation and deeper investigation of research already begun in the light of the rich paleo-Irish sources recently published by the government of Ireland.)

Maine, who was so faithful, so single-minded in his taste for the primitive and in his sensitivity to problems of origin, saw the question of the disposition of land, of the relation of man to land, as a primary means to understanding them. Before we continue to follow the development of his analysis, let me repeat once and for all an elementary clarification: I am not following the development of Maine's lucid diagnoses either to agree or disagree with them. Our problem is not the origin of property nor the reconstruction of how primitive societies disposed their lands. If it were, we would have to identify, call attention to, and describe the many passages in which our author is partial or strains the facts. Our aim is historiographical and our interest lies in the development of the theory of property in nineteenth-century sociological and juridical doctrine, and it is only as it applies to this aim that Maine's discourse interests us. False or true, well documented or built on air, plausible or implausible, his theories hold no interest for us in themselves—at least not on this occasion.

Our interest is kindled when his arguments become part of the play of cultural forces that led nineteenth-century juridical thought to follow certain paths rather than others and to fix on certain precise orientations, that is, when they contributed to make up the historical product that was the doctrine of property in the nineteenth century. It is not Maine as a historian of jurisprudence or as a cultural anthropologist whom we want to examine, but rather Maine as a man of culture of his time and in his time, Maine as historically important for the remarkable talent that he brought to the cultural panorama of his century of seeing through and breaking with accepted notions.

Having swept aside possible misunderstandings and reiterated our angle of vision—as if this were necessary—we can attempt to draw conclusions from Maine's analysis. Our author drew his own in a lecture that dates from his fully mature period:

> The facts collected suggest one conclusion which may be now considered as almost proved to demonstration. Property in land, as we understand it, that is, several ownership, ownership by individuals or by groups not larger than families, is a more mod-

ern institution than joint property or co-ownership, that is, ownership in common by large groups of men originally kinsmen. . . . Gradually, and probably under the influence of a great variety of causes, the institution familiar to us, individual property in land, has arisen from the dissolution of the ancient co-ownership.[39]

The "today" to which Maine refers is 1875. Our scholar could constate with satisfaction that his theses had penetrated deeply into Western culture. The works of Erwin Nasse, Paul Viollet, and Emile de Laveleye[40] had already appeared some time before, and they all extended, probed more deeply into, and documented further Maine's thought. This thought had been first stated clearly fourteen years before, when *Ancient Law* made its sensational appearance, and had also been repeated and developed further by the author himself.

Maine's basic idea was an elementary notion of one that followed almost deductively from the premises he so firmly laid down: if the primitive world was inhospitable to any individualistic attitude, if the individual dimension in this world had little opportunity to be operative and was therefore scarcely perceptible, if there was, on the other hand, a total dependence on the group as the sole vital condition of existence and survival, it followed that within that reality the interconnected relationships involving goods and on which food and the daily life of the community itself depended led to the group and only to the group, understood in its broadest sense. A fact of as much social consequence as the organization of landholding would have to be removed from particular jurisdictions and placed under the control of the center of the social totality.

Already in *Ancient Law* Maine had followed his customary method of reinforcing historical documentation with ethno-sociological observations. The structure of the Indian village as it was observed by a host of curious voyagers, merchants, and English civil servants, and the systems prevailing in Russian villages as described minutely by Haxthausen and Tegoborski (to whom Maine also acknowledged his debt) showed evidence of a body of absolutely uniform phenomena in spite of the diversity of their origins. They also showed evidence of constant behaviors persisting through time.

This primitive universe, this economic and social territory of primitive man, predominant in the zone that Maine calls "the infancy of law," continued and reemerged wherever the sociocultural or economic conditions typical of that infancy might be present.

Maine's essay, *Village-Communities in the East and West,* which marks the second important stage in his intellectual development, consists of an examination of these fragments of primitive society that had miraculously survived from a remote past and that were still partly visible in the Eastern fossil societies. We already know the date of publication of this work: 1870. It came after Maine's prolonged sojourn in India, during which he was constantly involved, as legal member of the governing council, with the problem of the relation between the law of the colonizers and that of the colonized and hence was in constant contact with Hindu juridical usages.

This essay is an excellent example of Maine's method. He makes use of Maurer's broad historical reconstruction of the *Mark* and the social order of the early Teutonic communities, and he cites Nasse's research on England, published the previous year,[41] but he draws chiefly on his own great store of direct experience. He had of course consulted documents in archives and he had read publications found *in loco;* but more important, he had seen, heard, and lived the problems of the day-to-day organization of the Hindu village.

As we have already seen, a third and extremely significant source of documentation, the Irish, would soon be added to these. Since it had come down intact, untouched by Roman or Germanic conquest, and since it had come into contact with English feudal structures only in the twelfth century, the Irish experience had the merit of being strictly autochthonous, of rising from the primordial Indo-European lineage and of speaking with a voice of particular purity.

What then was the message that this seemingly heterogeneous mass of data gave to our historian-jurist? These data spoke to him in such a completely common language and suggested such absolutely uniform solutions that it seemed foolhardy to attribute this unity to chance.[42] Quite the contrary, the Indian village, the Germanic *Mark,* the Russian *mir,* the Scottish or British township, the Celtic community all constituted the same response that in other times and places identical structural conditions required, and they therefore represented the surfacing of a reality that could be judged by unified standards. What had been thought to be particular to lands inhabited by Slavs gradually enlarged in scope to the point where, by 1870, our scholar was forced to recognize the stamp of a primordial structure: the village community, the hidden nucleus of primitive Indo-European society.[43]

If we want to pinpoint the intimate nature of this nuclear institution, we will do well to follow Maine's own words:

> The Township (I state the matter in my own way) was an organized, self-acting group of Teutonic families, exercising a common proprietorship over a definite tract of land, its Mark, cultivating its domain on a common system, and sustaining itself by the produce.[44]

If we cancel in our minds the references that limit the statement specifically to the *Mark*, drawn by Maine from his readings in Maurer, we will have a succinct and essential definition of the primitive world's cellular social unit.

Within this cell the use of land was ordered along rigidly communistic lines: near the village lay the common lands, that is, forest, pasture, and unplowed lands of absolutely common use, and the arable lands, that is, the parcels of land subjected to cultivation according to a system of lots assigned in various ways and involving an annual or triennial fallow period.[45] This scheme was not particular to the *Mark*, but was repeated in its substance in all of the communitarian aggregates cited above, all of which reflected an organizational reality that hinged on collective property.

Historical priority belonged to the collective property of the suprafamily group, then. Maine avoided the error of his adversaries and refused to compromise himself in risky affirmations of its "naturalness" (a criterion that he must after all have found incongenial), but he claimed priority for it clearly and openly.[46] Individual property was a fact that was posterior historically; it probably came from within the structure of the arable lands as a confirmation in perpetuity of a family's use of one lot of land. Its generalization would thus have been the result of an almost insensibly gradual process: it would have come from "the gradual disentanglement of the separate rights of individuals from the blended rights of a community."[47]

These are the broad architectonic lines of Maine's reconstruction of land use in primitive society. What is important for us to grasp is the one notion that is meaningful to the history of nineteenth-century juridical culture, the rediscovery and exploitation of the idea of collective property, and we can leave aside the perplexities provoked by Maine's casual juxtapositions and by his equally casual generalizations.

Maine did not need to discover anything: collective property had long been a fashionable topic.[48] As we stated at the outset, however, he created the scientific problem in proposing a considerably renewed theory of property and a considerably renewed method of approach. He created it in two senses. On the one hand, he succeeded in rendering relative a notion of individual property that had seemed to be perched at the summit of human progress, one that served as a goal, a beacon light, and an emblem. On the other hand, he showed that collective property was a historical factor of such primary importance as to merit consideration as a constant in human history and that it fitted into a unifying vision linking the primordial order of the first progenitors and the relics that had been discovered during the course of the century, not only in eastern Europe but in Germany and even in England.[49]

Maine became a traveler, an observer, and an explorer in his own country and, following the lead of foreign scholars like Nasse or technico-administrative reports like the one on the enclosure of open fields, he rediscovered for his myopic compatriots abundant evidence of situations still structured as collective property—or, if not strictly collective, that implied contamination by preceding communistic arrangements through the anomalies they presented when compared to the canons and models of traditional doctrines.[50]

Those canons and those models may not have fallen, but they had been held up to ridicule in Maine's pages. What had seemed abnormal or aberrant was just another sort of ownership deriving from different channels. It was not a barbaric monstrosity to be stored away in the cultural attic, not a historical sin to be absolved and forgotten, but a solution to a problem whose only fault was that it had not been adopted by the culture that prevailed and that it was not congenial to a society whose choices were rigidly individualistic.

2 Palingenesis of a Problem: Laveleye and Primitive Forms of Property

The Problem Addressed in a Famous Book

After Maine, the route taken by the problem of property necessarily leads us to the thought of Emile de Laveleye.[1] If we isolated our English jurisconsult from the doctrinal chorus because he furnishes a historically valid starting point for our study, we pick out the name of Laveleye not only to follow that route diligently, but also to point out the particular moment at which Maine's thought, while it was grasped in all its vitality, underwent a certain distortion. It left the purely cultural domain to be cast into other dimensions and, leaving aside the various aspects of socio-juridical organization, came to focus on the problem of appropriation of goods.

That problem was for Maine one important aspect of the entire organizational order of the village community or one example of how practice or doctrine had created or devised juridical categories. But for Laveleye it becomes *the* problem, the theme upon which he meditated for the entire span of his intellectual life.[2]

Although a prolific author, by nature a versatile writer and by personal vocation an eclectic, Laveleye nevertheless followed a guiding thread that is discernible whether he was writing a manual of political economy, an essay on agrarian economy, or the report of a voyage, and that eventually and inescapably came to be identified with the problem of historical forms of property.

Central in his works and a good example of his thinking is his *De la propriété et de ses formes primitives*. This unique work, this extraordinary event, transcends the intellectual biography of its author to find its place in the history of the problem of property in the nineteenth century.

Let us be clear from the outset: this work bears no resemblance to the many volumes and essays on the subject that are scattered through nineteenth-century juridical literature, all of which—especially those of the exegetic school—were consistently apologetic, strongly ideologically oriented, and totally lacking in disciplined speculative and cultural techniques.[3] Laveleye's book is made of another stuff. It reveals the undeniable limitations of its author, a modestly endowed person, it is not rich in theory, it has no great speculative aspirations, it is neither particularly scholarly nor founded on a base of solid erudition. However, it does reveal qualities consistent with a strong capacity for intuitive thought and a polyvalent sensitivity.

As we have said, this was a unique work. Since it was at once a scientific study and a work of popularization, it provoked the diffidence of scholars and the incomprehension of the general public. It involved history, sociology, ethnology, economy, and jurisprudence, and it revealed weaknesses in each of these areas. It was critical of capitalistic structures, but it was on the whole conservative regarding the constituted order. It was thus treated to the irony or to the scornful silence of the Marxists[4] and to the demolitionary attacks of official culture. In spite of this, it gave rise to an enormous amount of discussion and, what is more, it had a remarkable influence. Everyone felt obliged to have read the work, it was reprinted at a rapid pace,[5] and it was translated into a wide variety of languages.[6] Although the debate it inaugurated centered for the most part on the vital theme that Laveleye had treated, it found printed in the pages of his book a programmatic expression of this theme, ready to be countered or championed. During the last quarter of the century the history of socio-juridical thought concerning property was to a great extent shaped by this program.[7] Let us look closer, then, at this singular volume in an attempt to place it in historical context before we continue to discuss the point which seems to us the most pressing.

The book had been preceded by several cogent and well-received articles in the *Revue des deux mondes*,[8] and when it appeared in 1874 the time was ripe for it. The problem of property cried out to be approached with instruments different from those usually used by jurists in the age following that of the great codifications—even by a scholar who did not accept the subversive conclusions that were by then coming to the surface. A complacent bourgeois could take pleasure in the idyllic frescoes and the moralizing lessons on the function of property and on the virtues of the proprietor that were the favorite pastime of the exegetic school, though he should have sensed they were as insipid as outmoded children's tales.[9]

In 1874 the moment for weaving garlands of apologia was irremediably past, and the acrid and terrifying odor of blood remained in the Paris air along with the echoes of gunshot. The champion of the virtues of property could no longer fulfill his duties simply by sitting down at his desk and singing the praises of the institution as Adolphe Thiers had done after 1840 with such unwarranted candor (or with such lack of feeling and such sordid indifference).[10] One could no longer remain insensitive to a profoundly new historical reality that begged for innovative interpretation. It was this sensitivity, projected concretely in one clearly defined direction, that permeated Laveleye's volume, made it *readable,* and turned it into a highly historicizing work.

A professor of political economy at the University of Liège, Laveleye belonged to a well-to-do family and had the intelligence typical of the best of the agrarian entrepreneur class.[11] He was an attentive observer of his times and did not pretend not to know its urgent needs. The nearsightedness—if not the blindness—of the ruling class, the antihistorical immobilism of juridical instruments, tumults and social disorders, socialistic theorizing—all these elements stuck in his vigilant conscience like a lump in his throat; and it was they that motivated his reflections.

Maine had chipped away at monolithic dogma, and our Belgian professor was among his open admirers and followers. But Maine's discourse had the defect of being conducted on a totally theoretical level, of being a great cultural contribution and little more. Laveleye was the first to find this unsatisfying: it seemed to him that Maine's ideas should be carried further and transplanted practically in the domain of operation. Solidly at the center of a precise program of reform, they would not stand merely as the result of an inspired historiographical adventure, but would influence the very life of society in its present and in its future.

In fact, when Laveleye studied property, he did so in a dimension much more complex than the one Maine had explored. Even though it never descended to crudely empirical or coarsely practical expression, his research was always sustained by a distinct ethical ideal and by the possibility of immediate political application. If Maine's chief preoccupation was methodological, Laveleye's was operative: it was the exploitation of all that belonged to culture for the construction of a new society.

If we ask in what significant ways Maine and Laveleye differed, the immediate and most evident answer might emphasize the professional orientation of the two men. The Englishman, though for many years a colonial civil servant, was above all a historian of jurisprudence and an anthropologist; the Belgian was more particularly an economist or agrarian economist, accustomed to facts that interacted in the world of concrete reality.[12]

This distinction would be insufficient, however. Neither man is easily placed into the customary rigidly predetermined professional categories. The real mark of their separation lies perhaps in their times, in the revolutionary events of 1871 and 1872—continental events, French events—that Laveleye saw happening and that reappear continually on his pages. Between Maine and Laveleye lay the Paris Commune.

In even a casual reading of the long preface to Laveleye's *De la propriété* one is struck by the insistent, paroxysmal references to "the horrors committed in Paris in 1871,"[13] to "the ominous events that we are witnessing."[14] If we skim the equally long introduction to the later volume on contemporary socialism we note again this preoccupation, still burning in spite of the passage of time,[15] with "that hatred that once set all of Paris afire."[16]

It is undeniable that Laveleye kept his eyes wide open. The struggle of the proletariat,[17] the hatred that spiraled around the now-established conquests of the bourgeoisie,[18] an unsolved and burning social question that could not be put off:[19] these are unconcealed realities, and they were the realities that weighed on him as he formed his interpretations, orienting them and often determining them. He confesses as much honestly, without hypocrisy or pretense, revealing a complex and often ambivalent state of mind.

On the one hand, he judged democratic ideals negatively,[20] showed diffidence toward socialist theses,[21] was timid concerning struggles for social justice, and desired at all costs to avoid the subversion of the established order. On the other hand, he diagnosed this order without pity, he noted objectively and bluntly the economic monopoly of the few haves and the discomfort of the have-nots, and he genuinely desired the betterment and the social advancement of the worker.[22] These are the ambivalences and contradictions of a man placed by fate at a delicate and complicated historical and ideological crossroads and divided by tensions that were often contradictory. In him an authentically religious spirit[23] and a full, sincere adherence to the Christian principles of social renewal that he learned from François Huet and never forgot[24] coexisted with a strongly conservative impetus that was the conscious or unconscious expression of his membership in the dominant class.

Out of these contradictions came a relatively coherent if somewhat ambiguous work, solidly based in history and capable of playing an important mediating role. Its date—1874—is incontestable, not simply because it is printed on the title page, but because Laveleye, refusing the purities of the jurist or the theorist of economics, wrote his book with his study windows flung wide open, and because he noted, discussed, and suffered through the events of the society that surrounded him.[25]

For this reason, the book immediately came to constitute a sort of breviary of the bad conscience of bourgeois society. Perhaps because of the outcropping of a masochistic vein that can always be seen in periods of decline, Laveleye's self-criticism was well received. Many recognized themselves in his incoherences, in his anxieties, in his demands, and many found a grain of consolation in, or indeed were tranquillized by, his reformist proposals.

His pages bear his imprint. It is not the face of an individual that we see, but that of an idealized man, sensitive to his culture and aware of its problems, one who acts as go-between in the conflict between partisan ideals and interests. Somewhere between individualism and socialism, between models of justice and economic utility, between demands for reform and fear of chaos, Laveleye was busy defining his own view of landed property. His view was based not on a rejection of the schematic idea of property, but on a general, though shareholding, participation in ownership.[26] It was a middle-of-the-road solution and "the only one that, in conformity with natural law, also allows true democracy to last without throwing society into disorder."[27]

If this was the type of mediation destined to guarantee the book's wide circulation and its acceptance in the libraries of the most disparate readers, another mediating quality assured it a notable likelihood of influence on a cultural level. As Maine had attempted to remove the problem of the original forms of property from an exclusively academic sphere, so Laveleye, following Maine's example, inaugurated an important effort of reconciliation between an argument in cultural terms and one in operative terms and, consequently, between historical conclusions and economic programs.

Fortified by the great experiments of the Historical School of economics and by the *Kathedersozialismus* that had recently developed in Germany,[28] Laveleye gave fuller definition than Maine to the attempt to see the economic and juridical notion of property as relative, reaffirming the functional connection between historical investigation and theoretical conclusions, between historical foundation and economic and social reforms.[29] In his view, the science of economics, far from fitting rigidly into a Procrustes' bed of abstract formulas, had its own inalienable historicity, just like the other social sciences, and its instruments and structures were historically variable.

The elements of this program were certainly not new. They had already been expressed on a considerable number of occasions and in distinguished works, for example in certain essays by Wilhelm Roscher, Gustav Schmoller, and Adolph Wagner on the very subject of property. What was new was the synthetic vision in which economic data were included together with an enormous amount of historical, ethnological, and juridical materials. The style was new: Laveleye's discourse seemed to disdain the specialist reader and tended, as had Maine's, to leave out erudite embellishments, to become simplified, popularized. Economic analysis was here accompanied by appropriate historical notations and furnished with juridical diagnoses.

If Roscher's, Schmoller's, and Wagner's essays continued to be nearly unknown beyond the restricted inner circle of the usual twenty-five or so scholars—much like Maurer's and Waitz's works in juridical historiography—Laveleye's book circulated widely, irritated and inspired, touched off fierce debate, and redefined the problem of property and of its original forms.

The book's scope was a modest one and it was based on what Laveleye had absorbed from others. But this did not prevent it from taking on a more provocative role than many a work of more serious erudition or of a more solid speculative foundation. Achille Loria stated in his fulsome notice on the Belgian economist written for the *Nuova Antologia:*

> An invisible screen descended between historical studies and economic science and intercepted any attempt at a fruitful alliance. . . . This disjunction has ceased thanks to Laveleye's works, which have created the connective tissue between history and political economy.[30]

Perhaps the exuberant Loria, carried away by his evocation of Laveleye's accomplishment, gave the professor from Liège more credit than he deserved. But it is true that the mark of Laveleye's work is in his total impatience with these screens, in his reshuffling of *all* the cards relating to property, in his proposing them anew in synthesized form, in his having made available and comprehensible a documentation that was otherwise condemned to being treated as esoteric.

Although this was not the first time that a connection had been made joining history and economics, it was still the first time that an enormous amount of documentary material hitherto completely unknown or known imperfectly, was brought to the attention of the economists, the sociologists, and the jurists. For the first time, this material was arranged according to an organic structure and supported by a theoretical definition that may have been unilateral and was perhaps ingenuous, but that was clearly delineated and fully detailed.

The book brought forth an enormous reaction. Like Maine's provocative work before it, it rapidly attracted admirers and detractors. Accepted notions crumbled further under its attacks, and an image of property arose in dialectical opposition to the traditional Romanistic cul-

tural model of the *dominium*. This contrasting image was based on different values, it was found in a practice that meandered through space and
time, and it had been collected diligently from all points of the globe. For
the first time, the *dominium quiritarium* had an enemy more dangerous
than complete negation: it had encountered a vision—even if that vision
was somewhat improvised and its unhistorical configuration made it impossible to apply—that sprang nevertheless from the internal energy of
the same historical tradition and that threatened to take its place.

A Diagnosis of Capitalist Property

In order to understand the cultural impact of Laveleye's search
for a new definition of property, one must begin by examining the two
dimensions that continued to coexist in him. A source of antinomies and
contradictions, they determined the ambivalence of his position, but they
also characterized that position. They were: a vocation which, when
all was said and done, was conservative, and a profoundly religious—
indeed, a Christian—consciousness brought to bear upon the analysis of
social reality.

The first of these dimensions induced in Laveleye a profound
repugnance for solutions of destruction and a tendency to look backward
to seek for solutions to current problems in the unfolding of historical
tradition. Since he viewed the established order as relative to that tradition, the solutions he found congenial were those that avoided the overthrow of the fundamental structures of the constituted order in favor of
their more flexible adjustment. In other words, his views were of substantially historicist orientation.[31] The second dimension generated in him
a dissatisfaction with the general attitudes and theses of bourgeois society
that came into conflict with the metahistorical ideals of Christian models,
and that took the form of certain specific notions of natural law.

These concepts, arising from historicism and from natural law,
are by their nature divergent, but if they generated ambiguities and incoherences when they coexisted in Laveleye's mind, they nevertheless
converged in encouraging a fundamental attitude sharply critical of the
structures he saw around him and in feeding his feelings of increasing
frustration and dissatisfaction both as a citizen and as a scholar.

Laveleye had drunk deep of the reflections on culture of the
great German schools of the history of jurisprudence and economics[32] and
had absorbed Maine's desacralizing works, and he was annoyed by what
he defined as the "flattering illusions" of the eighteenth century.[33] They
had led to an immobile and thoroughly laicized natural law that seemed to
his spiritual nature to be without authentic foundation. The institution of
private property in its modern crystallization, which lay within that concept of law as a central and guiding construction, seemed to him un-

justified, whether he tested it by the measure of his own ethical Christianity or by the extreme mutability of historical becoming.

As a historicist, Laveleye accepted Maine's premise: individual property as nineteenth-century society proposed it—absolute, perpetual, independent, exclusive—had no functional tie with the state of nature, nor did it spring directly from nature. It was rather a product of history, the mature fruit of an individualistic society, and hence a fairly recent development in the history of human civilization. Laveleye denies the projection of the Romanist model of modern property into the paradise of archetypes; and he supports this denial on the basis both of calm, unprejudiced analysis founded in data and using comparative historical techniques, and of an analytical reconstruction of the real values—that is, the values perceived by him and in which he believed—of property. His was a singular and complex attitude in which the two analytical movements, instead of countering each other, mixed together and fused.

> Landed property took on a completely new character, without precedent in history. In primitive times, land, the collective property of the tribe, furnished each family with the means of living by its labor. During feudal times, when it was considered as belonging in principle to the sovereign, land was the recompense for functions fulfilled and implied services rendered, among others, military and judicial. Today, detached from all ties, liberated from all duties, it is no longer, for whomever possesses it, anything but a source of enjoyment. The classes who work and the classes who enjoy thus grow more and more estranged from each other and here, as in [ancient] Rome, estranged is synonymous to hostile.[34]

This passage, the eloquence of which warrants its being cited in full, is a good synthesis of these two simultaneous analytical movements. Two evaluations are joined together to aim at the same target: the historical and historicizing and the ethical. Modern property is only the deformation of an essential category of appropriation of goods. It is the aberrant choice made by the age of the bourgeoisie—as distinguished from the primitive or the feudal ages—to serve its own ends. It would thus be inappropriate to raise it to the status of an institution founded in the nature of things. Measured by natural law, it necessarily reveals the intensity of its aberration.

In this argument we see the Laveleye who had been educated in the customary criteria of the academic tradition, taught to evaluate every situation as the source of a relation and to judge in every situation the *aequalitas* within that relation. His conclusion is merciless: capitalistic property, this "privilege without obligations, without hindrances, without reservations,"[35] carried within it a macroscopic injustice. In the ideal relation that binds the proprietor to each member of the community, obliged to respect his right, the principle of *aequalitas partium* is upset. All is tipped in favor of the *dominus,* and the enjoyment of the goods does not follow from assistance given, from merit obtained, from a function fulfilled, from a duty satisfied, but is a simple position of privilege without ethical basis. Respect for such a privilege is neither spontaneous nor felt but simply submitted to, and is constituted only "by the forbearance of others."[36]

The problem of the justice of this relation was just as important as that of its historical nature, and although the two levels could be distinguished, they coexisted and tended to merge. The relation involved in property appeared to an unprejudiced observer of culture during the nineteenth century as antihistorical, antisocial, and iniquitous. It was also unilateral, that is, it was unable to divide its rights and obligations equitably among its partners. It was incapable of exercising control over the proprietor in the tangle of social relations taking form around him. It was a situation that eluded the very category of relation,[37] for it relied on two positions that were sharply separated in practice: the positive position of the *dominus* and the negative position of the general community over whom the *dominium* seemed to hover, solitary and indifferent to the ferment of everyday history.

The jurists, in their forthright technical language, qualified the subjective situation of the ninety-nine nonholders in relation to the one holder of a landed right as *pati,* and they meant by that *pati* to insist that the relation turned on the absolute passivity of the former. Laveleye the sociologist and the economist discovered a people in chains—the people of nonproprietors—beneath the detached and almost neutral term of the jurists, and he expressed his disgust for an institution that continued to exist only because it was supported by the force it had created.

But Laveleye did not limit himself to criticizing the insensitivity of modern individualism from a Christian point of view, nor to pointing out that its attitudes are only contingent ones. His study went on to analyze the deeper structural organization of capitalist society itself, as in this denunciation:

> Turned into movable goods by means of alienation, land passes from hand to hand like the fruits it bears or the animals it nourishes. By going too far in this direction, the bases of society have been shaken.[38]

It was no longer merely the justice of the property relation that Laveleye puts under accusation, but also an attitude fundamental to middle-class society. He notes that the ownership of a means of production—agricultural lands or a piece of urban property—circulates as freely as a fruit or an animal. Every *res,* even the most socially consequential, can be degraded to the level of goods, of simple objects of a transaction. It is thus significant only to the private individual involved, and its value lies in its translation into coin, that is, in its potential as an object of exchange.

As a disciple of François Huet and imbued as he was with a Christian belief in the individual person, Laveleye was naturally led to reject the rampant emphasis on things that threatened to take over all of society. We will soon discuss his predilection for certain types of common property, but let us note immediately that Laveleye sees one positive element common to these in the constant interchange that takes place between person and thing when agrarian land is not viewed as a simple commodity. The "coproprietor" in this case has no power of disposal over his property, since he holds title to an entity that can neither be separated nor removed from the greater organic unity of which it is a part.

The passage from Laveleye's work cited above closes with the expectation that collective arrangements would be seen more frequently.[39] The ownership of goods—and Laveleye, "rural to his very soul,"[40] had in mind agrarian land in particular—was neither a private fact regarding the *dominus* nor a situation that could be reduced to simple enjoyment.

It was his religious convictions that led our economist to discover the social dimension of the question and the problem of justice in the distribution of goods—two issues of which he found little trace in the history of Europe after the Middle Ages. Although his historicist's bias permitted him to relegate modern property to a place among merely historical events, stripping it of any semblance of nobility and thrusting it into the mutability of historical becoming, his latent beliefs in Christianity and natural law led him to a quite different model of property. This other model weighed on his conscience, and we will see it appearing now and then—inadvertently, fleetingly—in a work of research that was specifically intended to constitute a refutation of models. Although he rejected as a middle-class fiction the idea that individual property arose from and was a manifestation of the state of nature,[41] he still refers—infrequently but perfectly clearly—to a "rational idea of property."[42] This implies that the subject was in much more complex a situation than the one outlined in individualistic ideology. In this more complex situation the elements of duties and rights are reconciled, the reliance on duty restores to property a social dimension, and it is made to function for the benefit of the whole community.

We can go so far as to state—since Laveleye confirms this on more than one occasion—that when our professor from Liège refers to a "rational idea" he has in mind the concept of property found in the extensive meditations of the patristic and scholastic tradition and rejected only by later currents of Christian theology in response to the peculiar condition of the sixteenth and seventeenth centuries.

This situation of domination may have seemed simple, but when it was seen refracted through the prism of a "rational idea" its component elements stood clearly apart, "a social element and an individual element"[43] corresponding to the two interests involved in the institution, "the interest of the individual and the interest of society."[44]

Once it had recovered its social vocation, property could not become crystallized to accumulate only in the hands of a restricted and privileged oligarchy. Rather, it would tend to be distributed among a broad range of holders according to their needs and to the efforts they had made.

Laveleye accepted from prevailing doctrine the idea that the principle of the appropriation of goods—what we might call property without adjectives—represents a *natural* way for the subject to move out into the world of things and a complete realization of his independence and his liberty. This was to Laveleye an elementary verity, solidly anchored within his own idea of natural law. What he denied was that the product of history represented by "individual property of the Romanistic type" was able to furnish this need for every man who aspired to it. Rather, he said, it guaranteed the liberty and independence of the few and the servitude of the many.

Laveleye accepted at face value the alluring descriptions of the exegetes and of the Pandectists and agreed with their praise of property, but he drew the only conclusion logically possible for a social ethic that claims to be Christian: that property was "a right so deeply inherent to human nature that no man should be deprived of it unless he has proved unworthy of it."[45]

The message of natural law, which the jurists had formalized, must become a message of liberation for all men, he asserted. Otherwise it was a ghastly practical joke. Either society must aspire to guarantee the enjoyment of property for all or that society would be forever iniquitous, precisely because the instrument of property was congenial to human nature.[46] The argument of the jurists who strove to tie together property and liberty, property and independence, would have meaning only if everyone felt it concretely—not abstractly—addressed to him. Otherwise the message would be no more than beautiful "sonorous phrases."[47]

This reprimand, addressed to Troplong in particular, constituted a criticism of all of bourgeois jurisprudence and of the abstract nature of its libertarian framework. Under the surface, and only for an instant, Laveleye agreed with the Marxist heretics whom he disliked and was incapable of understanding.

The theories that the fertile minds of political scientists, philosophers, and jurists had invented over a two-thousand-year span to justify individual property were demolished and even held up to ridicule in Laveleye's energetic attack. What is more important, Laveleye found his instruments of destruction in the very ideals of natural law upon which those theories had been constructed. But he preferred a concrete analysis of situations to word games and the rhetoric of natural law. He respected those ideals as they affected real men of flesh and bone. And his discourse contained real substance. In light of this criticism, not only the theory of occupancy that Maine had combatted but also the much more specious theories of contract and labor could be accepted only as the intellectual games of Locke and his fellow players. They left unresolved, both as a problem and as a moral and social aberration, the very real question of the limited number of the privileged and the mass of the disinherited. For the latter it seemed offensive to good sense and to elementary equity to claim that their situation found its ethical and political justification in theories of contract or, even more, of labor.[48]

We can now define Laveleye's premises more clearly. A sense of history and spiritual inclinations led him to an interpretation that reduced modern individual property to a simple episode in the long—as long as human life—evolution of property through history. It was perhaps an episode in which raw interests had been passed off as values and in which property as an institution reached its moment of greatest separation from the bedrock of natural law. Even though its historical forms and arrangements had varied, the essential nucleus of the concept of property was rational, but the form assumed in its modern incarnation, especially in capitalist society, had betrayed this essential nucleus.

It was to remedy this betrayal that Laveleye searched so extensively in the history of the relationship of man to things and rediscovered primitive forms of appropriation. His insistence on historicity freed him from obsequious dependence on the view of property crystallized by the Romans and the Romanists. His Christianized version of natural law fixed a rational notion of property in his mind, and he searched in history, if not for a model of property, at least for a form of property that could satisfy needs that seemed to him fundamental.

All of Laveleye's historical investigation—or, more precisely, historical and comparative—found a precarious balance among intertwined and disparate themes and motivations, but they led him miraculously to the discovery of primitive property. Here was a form of appropriation in which the social element was given full importance, which reached out to permit the participation of every member of society. It was, however, a collective form of appropriation and was thus one that could well be proposed as an alternative to the one accepted by official juridical and economic science in the nineteenth century.

Alternative Forms of Property

Laveleye expressed concisely the premise central to his study:

> Quiritarian ownership, as the rigorous Roman mind bequeathed
> it to us, is not flexible enough, not human enough.... Usually
> when one speaks of property it seems that it can exist in only
> one form, the one we see in force around us. This is a profound
> and unfortunate error, and one that prevents us from reaching to
> a higher conception of the law. The application to land of exclu-
> sive, personal, and hereditary *dominium* is a relatively recent
> event, and for a very long time men knew and practiced only
> collective ownership.[49]

His dissatisfaction with how he saw ownership practiced around
him and his awareness of its extremely relative nature prompted Laveleye
to set it aside, to go beyond it, to construct a different sort of ownership.
But this took courage. He had to rid himself of Romanistic mythology and
forego the refined, time-tested technical instruments of Roman law that
had provided jurists of all the ages with protective assurance. He had to
commit himself to new cultural instruments and run the risk of breaking
with a tradition that two thousand years of acceptance and uninterrupted
application had sanctioned as indisputable.

Laveleye was well aware that Maine had opened a breach in
official unanimity, and his own analysis took swift advantage of it. Like
Maine, and even more than Maine, he realized that only an overwhelming
amount of documentation could undermine a tradition and a view of reality so deeply rooted in every jurist, and that only the historical and
comparative method could safely keep him off the shoals of nineteenth-
century juridical culture.

The history he served, however, was not that of doctrinal constructions, not that of thought tied to official culture in its triumphant
establishment. It was rather the history that was excluded from school
textbooks, that was overlooked by those who followed major political and
military turning points. Such history was marginal from the point of view
of major centers where decisions are made. It was rural rather than urban;
it was almost an underground history, found in documents reflecting daily
practice rather than in monuments of scholarship. Such history, treated
with scornful silence by Enlightenment culture, had been rescued by the
patient efforts and the romantic spirit of such scholars as Maurer, Grimm,
Waitz, and Eichhorn.

Roman law was too learned, too refined, too laden with
superstructure in its handling of relationships to be the protagonist of this
underground history. Here, relics of primitive experience merged or fitted
in with the remains of popular customs and Germanic elements to offer an
alternative image of how reality could be structured. This new image
never pretended to rival the Romanistic order, with its enormously solid

speculative categories. But now it could function as a standard to carry into battle.

When Laveleye, discussing the Germanic *Mark,* cites as authoritative testimony Grimm's affirmation that ancient German had no word equivalent to the more recent *Eigentum,* he is certainly waving a defiant banner.[50] The statement is clearly provocative to the reigning, unidirectional culture that portrayed individual property not only as a legitimate, but also as a just and innate structure.

For Laveleye, comparison went hand in hand with history, and comparison did not necessarily need to be between cultures of the same character or involving the same race. Going further in the direction indicated by Maine, Laveleye searched in the most far-flung cultures, not for heroes of human history but for the autogenous voices of autonomous cultures without ties to Romanistic tradition.[51]

Both of the sides of Laveleye's personality led him to the discovery that comparison offered the method most congenial to intellectual operations, both the Laveleye who had dedicated much of his life to extensive travels in Europe and Africa, not as a dilettante but with the serious, nearly professional objectives of the best of the nineteenth-century travelers[52] as well as the Laveleye who admired Le Play and had an equally typical nineteenth-century taste for sociological inquiries and statistical data.[53]

From Belgium Laveleye's gaze reached over the entire terraqueous globe, and he indiscriminately gathered testimony from every quarter and from sources of extremely variable quality, fitting them into contexts that were at once ethnological, sociological, economic, and juridic. With some acrimony and with open irony, but also with his customary accuracy, Fustel de Coulanges, Laveleye's greatest antagonist, defined him as the man who first undertook "universal comparison."[54] He touched a sore point, the sore point of methodology, since comparative investigation in Laveleye reached exaggerated and dubious proportions, and the mixture of such heterogeneous materials sometimes became a hodgepodge of data that were only relatively, if at all, comparable.

Laveleye was incapable of maintaining a strict respect for the subtleties of method. The quantity of material that he accumulated was directly proportional to his anti-Romanistic principles. If his material was abundant it was because his enemy was abundantly awe-inspiring. Indeed, the Roman postulates could be opposed only by a clear demonstration of an opposing koine, and Laveleye's work should be interpreted as the patient construction of the pattern of a koine like that of a mosaic whose tesserae came from every continent and every age.

His investigation bore the fruit that Laveleye had hoped for, and he now held a sort of Aladdin's lamp from which he could conjure up a vision that might be spectral and a bit vague around the edges but that served well as an alternative to the official view. Henceforth it would be unacceptable to speak of property in the singular, as the jurists and before them the philosophers had done. Their property was now *one* property, one of the many forms of appropriation that men had devised and set up as they lived through their history. Other forms had been and could still be proposed in response to differing origins and objectives:

> Another very widespread error is to speak of "property" as if it were an institution having a fixed and immutable form, whereas in reality it has taken on the most diverse forms and is still susceptible to very great and unforeseen modifications.[55]

His conclusion was the same as Maine's, but Laveleye greatly strengthened it by tying it to an impressive and burgeoning documentation. He added to this documentation as his research continued and as his information grew and in the fourth edition of 1891—not a reprinting of the text of twenty years before but *aliquid novi*—his documentation spread out in capillary fashion to form a perspective of the historical and practical importance of collective forms of appropriation that seemed to overthrow the commonplaces that underlay "orthodox" juridical science.

Even if these forms were not strikingly visible, they were a living presence right in the middle of the era of individualism. The bits and pieces collected by Maine now made a complete picture: after the signs of stress caused in the official view by the Germanic *Mark,* the mold and archetype par excellence,[56] along came the witnesses for the prosecution of bourgeois insensitivity, the Russian *mir,*[57] the Javanese *dessa,*[58] the British township,[59] the Germanic, Swiss, and Scandinavian *Allmend,*[60] and the southern Slav *zadruga.*[61] Each of these structures had characteristics particular to its historical origin, its juridical nature, its systems of organization, but all expressed a communitarian, antiindividualistic vision of landholding, and none could be reduced to the schemes of Roman dogmatics.

Referring to the common participation in the *Allmenden* in a judgment that could be generalized, Laveleye noted with satisfaction and almost with relief: "They correspond exactly neither to the *dominium* nor to the *condominium,* nor to the *universitas* of the Latin jurisconsults."[62] The technical instruments of Gaius and Tribonian were of no avail in defining them. They expressed a reality extraneous to classical concepts or Justinian's. Roman law and the Romanist tradition constituted a historical current that was born and developed absolutely parallel to them and without any significant contact with them.

This problem is an important one for the history of juridical thought, and we will return to it later when we examine more specifically the technical juridical aspects of this complex matter. For the moment, let us be satisfied with what we have noted: a "collectivist" practice managed to prosper from earliest times until 1874, in spite of the efforts of contrary practice to stifle it. This practice was not a pathological deformity, a deviation, a clouding of the limpid waters of Roman organizational schemes. It was one that had its own autonomous course and that sprang from a different cultural world. Individualism was an outcome of the times and the culture of Roman and the Romanists; collectivism was an option of other cultures that had preserved intact a pre-Roman or even a primordial organization.

Like Maine before him, Laveleye intended not only to propose an alternative view, but also to reinforce it with historical priority. "Private property came out of common property,"[63] he said, and it had taken solid form in the Roman world. But it was collective property that had lived uninterrupted from primordial times to the fourteenth century and that enjoyed the moral prestige deriving from its quality as *Urtypus*.

Individual property lost some of its status as an absolute value when these scholars related it to historical context and even judged it negatively, sometimes implicitly, sometimes explicitly. As this happened, collective ownership began to take on a degree of absolute value. It inevitably came to be seen as the form of ownership inherent to the pure structure prevailing in the society of men untouched by political struggles and ideological incrustations. Since it was tied to the state of nature, it rose to a certain extent to have the status of a model. When Laveleye got into the thick of the quarrel, it was the exponent of natural law in him that had the upper hand of the historicist, and, at least in this work, his position represents a complete reversal of the positions of the exegetic school.

Even though our Belgian economist avoided the gross error of proposing any alternative scheme as capable of being put into general practice, and although he limited his exhortations, as we have seen, to the colonial populations of America and Australia, there was nonetheless a latent invitation—occasionally a more open invitation—to multiply experiments in collective forms of ownership.

Laveleye was soon rebuked for this antihistorical ingenuity by Paul Leroy-Beaulieu,[64] among others, who dedicated his 1884 course in political economy at the Collège de France to a confutation of the Laveleye thesis in the name of the postulates of the classical school. It was an easy job for the decisive and competent Leroy-Beaulieu, once he had paid a biting but impeccably formal tribute to the "ingeniousness" of his colleague from Liège,[65] to point out by strictly technical arguments how Laveleye had idealized his vast collection of historical materials.[66]

As we noted in relation to Maine, the value of those alternative views lay elsewhere: what is relevant historically is the enrichment of the cultural discourse. It is unimportant to establish whether Laveleye or

Leroy-Beaulieu was right, or whether the construction of Laveleye's argument was fragile or erroneous. What matters is to understand the value of the book as a provocation, to examine its theses *in relation* to the uniformity that reigned in economic and juridical doctrine—in other words, to grasp its importance as an invitation to debate.

When the unanimity behind the old doctrine had been cracked, collective property certainly did not emerge to take the place of individual property like a winged Athena from the head of Zeus. The enthusiasms of our Belgian polygraph were destined to fall into an operational void, and if all had depended on him, the rich bourgeois could have continued to sleep in peace in their bed of quiritarian ownership, at the most troubled by dreams of vaguely sylvan and pastoral ghosts.

However, Laveleye's theses were not destined to fall into a cultural void. A chorus of admirers and detractors, disciples and enemies, in France and throughout Europe united during the next twenty years in a lively and vital debate that involved their culture, their methodological techniques, and their ideologies. It was a debate so important that it mirrored the features of an entire historical epoch.

Where the work of Maine and Laveleye had a specific practical influence, however, was on the fate of what Giacomo Venezian was some years later in a famous inaugural lecture at the University of Camerino to call "the relics of collective property."[67] The historical interpretation of these relics was now dramatically turned around, and it had finally become evident how tendentious and sectarian the incessant propaganda of the ruling class had been and how senseless had been the policy of indiscriminate abolition of still-existing collective practices, designed and carried out by legalized violence. What had been depicted as absurd fetters to the sacrosanct free circulation of goods, as the rotten fruit or the dross of the feudal regime, and hence as abuses that had arisen unlawfully to hinder the "liberty" of things and the "liberty" of proprietors, was revealed to be the residuum of a primitive order, of a preceding and socially legitimate form of appropriation that had been subjected to usurpations and shrinkage during the regime of lordships. Laveleye says of this situation in a Swiss canton:

> Formerly the entire canton of Unterwald formed one community whose members had usage rights over the whole territory. When the lordships and abbeys were established, they usurped little by little part of the common domain of the march.[68]

Laveleye speaks here of usurpation, but the overworked myths did not speak of swindlers who had taken possession of other people's land, taking advantage at first of the toleration and later of the indifference of the seigneur; they spoke of ancient "condominiums." However, the only traces left of the original condominium, of primitive property of which the community had been defrauded, were in certain distributive rights.

What Laveleye accomplished was not so much a moral re-habilitation of collective property or its restoration to historical dignity, but a change in the juridical situation of goods and subjects. It was this that destroyed the very premises of the policy of abolishing common rights and freeing common lands. And it was this accomplishment that led to Laveleye's name being circulated in the chambers of the Italian Parliament when that body was searching for a new perspective on the problem. But we will discuss this later, in chapter 9.

One last note, which is also a necessary clarification, on the sources of Laveleye's ideas. Considering his interests and the date of publication of his work on property, one might assume a cultural connection between Laveleye and Otto Gierke, since the first two volumes of the latter's *Das deutsche Genossenschaftsrecht* were in print when Laveleye was preparing his book in the 1870s.[69] This hypothesis does not correspond with the facts, however. When Laveleye put together the first edition of his book, his sources of inspiration were consistent. Their underlying character was shaped by the political and social thought of Le Play and Huet, and the fixed points on his horizon—culturally, historically, and juridically—were always Maine on the one hand and the German Historical School, particularly Maurer, on the other. If we open his chapter on the *Mark* we find references to Grimm, to Maurer, to Fustel de Coulanges; if we turn to the chapter on the *Allmend,* even if we expect to find ample citation of Gierke, we see that the keystone of its construction was a monograph of Andreas Heusler.[70] Laveleye turned his attention to Gierke—and to Maxim Kovalevski—with the revision of his work in 1891.[71] But even there that attention was relatively limited, and the theory of the influence of the imposing thought of the historian from Stettin on the formation of Laveleye's thought does not seem to be substantiated.[72]

3 The Forms and Substance

of a Debate

Collective Property and Historical Forms of Property: The Beginning of the Great Controversy

The great controversy over collective property kept a good many jurists, economists, and sociologists occupied with doctrinal alliances and clashes during the three decades from the 1870s to the end of the century and beyond. The origins of the controversy go back to Maine's researches and, before him, to the isolated thoughts and notes of the Historical School, but its immediate origins lay in the accumulation of "facts" made available by Emile de Laveleye.

The years between the publication of Maine's *Ancient Law* and Laveleye's *De la propriété* had already seen, however, an increasing harvest of research and reflections. They had come out of an increasing awareness of the complexity of the relations of men and goods, and they had already provided a less unilateral, less simplistic view of those relations.

In Germany, the younger economists involved in the revival of German economic science turned to the work in law of the Historical School, which by then was well established and fully developed. They learned there a double lesson: they learned a methodology that taught that all rules, all institutions must be viewed as historically relative; they discovered as subject matter the historical forms of appropriation that Grimm, Maurer, and Waitz had unearthed and that, in a certain sense, constituted a challenge to classical certitudes and to the certitudes of the reigning English economic doctrine.[1]

Erwin Nasse,[2] for example, a professor at the University of Bonn, published in 1869 a well-received study of the *Feldgemeinschaften*

71

of medieval England,[3] and in the same year Wilhelm Roscher, one of those interested in economic historicism, published a broad systemization of agrarian economy in which he did not hesitate to make central to his argument the clear historical priority of commonly held lands over individual ownership.[4] For this study he plundered a wide range of works on the subject, bending their variety to fit his unified theme. In Berlin a year later, in 1870, Adolph Wagner published a composite treatise on the theme of property under the significant title *Die Abschaffung des privaten Grundeigenthums*.[5]

Wagner was exceptionally sensitive to cultural problems. He belonged in that ambivalent cultural terrain created by the Historical School of economics as it slid rapidly toward the conferences at Eisenach and the first attempt to give an organized structure to the so-called *Kathedersozialismus*.[6] Social problems loomed behind economic theorizing, and some way out had to be found—a way that Wagner thought he could find in a greater extension of collective forms of ownership and in the abandonment of individual land ownership. He saw individual ownership as the result of historically recent developments in social organization that had been mistakenly idolized through gross historical misunderstanding.

What is important for us is that although Wagner drew his essay's explosive thrust from history and comparison, he extended his use of data to the formulation of concrete proposals, and he raised his argument to the level of economic theory.[7] Collective property had an essential role in those proposals and in that economic theory. When he wrote these pages Wagner was not just counting grains of dust on antiquarians' bookshelves, nor was he dabbling in archaeology to satisfy his curiosity. Unlike Roscher and Nasse, and unlike his sources, Wagner placed himself, with Laveleye, on a plane that was at once cultural and operative, grafting his economic thought onto the framework of real social and juridical situations, which were more evidently sensitive to historical change.[8]

There is another essay that deserves to be mentioned beside these works on economics. It followed closely on these works, was influenced by them, and, although it never enjoyed the circulation or the influence of Laveleye's work, it nevertheless represented to both supporters and detractors an obligatory benchmark for successive discussions. I refer to the volume of Paul Viollet on the collective character of the earliest forms of real property.[9]

Viollet's essay was published in 1872 by the prestigious but out-of-the-way Bibliothèque de l'Ecole des Chartes and, according to its author,[10] it was written independently of the articles by Laveleye that began to appear in the widely known *Revue des deux mondes* at just that time. It was relatively independent of Maine's writing as well, although the work was written in the cultural spirit of Maine. In fact, Viollet pushes comparative analysis to its logical limits, and his use of varied sources atypical of the customary currents of thought stands out conspicuously. By profession a historian of law,[11] Viollet enlarged his research to include travel journals,[12] colonial bureaucrats' reports,[13] works of information on the colonies,[14] sociological studies,[15] and works on the history of economics.[16] Maine and Laveleye have accustomed us to this sort of aggregation of the most disparate facts and information: Viollet uses it as the matter from which to draw an intentionally and essentially historical argument.

Laveleye intended to influence the reality of the world around him: Viollet lacks Laveleye's missionary and apologetic fervor, and he limits his analysis to a purely intellectual level. He is not interested in making concrete proposals, and he refuses the operative as largely ir- relevant to his purposes. In his mind, individual property remained a goal of the process of civilization, and it came to the surface of his ethico- social conscience as a value that he could not relinquish.[17] There was only one "truth" that he felt obliged to register and that he refused to measure by his own ideals and his own interests, and that was

> individual real property as a secondary fact in the history of
> societies, as a new idea that gradually grew out of the common,
> collective rights of all over land.[18]

This verity had lain intact in the very bosom of history until Viollet's painstaking research freed it from the sediment of history and now offered it as a contribution to knowledge.

It was not, however, an innocuous contribution. Beneath the apparent innocence of research on this objective truth there emerged *one* truth alternative to *the* truth that was currently accepted. The phenome- non was in itself a meager historical fact, distant and inoffensive, but it came to upset hierarchies and classifications that hitherto had been in- disputable.

In the beginning, property had been collective. Viollet does not permit himself to add to that statement, nor does he want to translate that ancient, primordial language into modern terms. But it was a language capable of universal translation that others with more acute senses could understand immediately, particularly when they sensed that hidden under that erudite baggage there lay a threat to their own certitudes or, still worse, to their own interests.

The campaign on behalf of collective property was about to be launched, and we will soon see combatants take up contrasting positions with varying degrees of ingenuity but with equal acrimony. With Wagner and Viollet, but even more with Laveleye, the history of the doctrine of property was enriched by a component—or by a dimension—that was not previously considered important. It was enriched, but it was also complicated. In fact, the great dispute was about to begin.

Collective property, what had been the original form of ownership, the form of appropriation practiced at different historical moments in different countries, the form practiced by the ancient Germanic tribes in particular: all of these were questions that were soon to become the object of normal, daily academic chatter and even of drawing-room conversation. In all cases, the discussion passed with extraordinary facility from the economic argument to how well founded it was in scholarship; from a juridical argument to one based on sociology or ethnology.

Do the intellectuals of those years provide us with a good example of cultural sensitivity? Was theirs a singular case of cultural eclecticism imitating the more passionate of the eighteenth-century salons? Or was it a revived Arcadia in which economists and jurists amused themselves reciting timeless poems and songs in their disarming, dry jargon? None of these hypotheses is exactly correct. To be sure, never before as in these ardent debates have we heard so many appeals to scientific objectivity, to historical verity, to the "positivity" of a document. And never again as in these diatribes will we see scholars attacking the problem of origins with such alacrity, quibbling with the candor of the obviously unprepared scholar over whether the first manifestations of property were individual or collective.

Anyone interested in tying this impassioned dialogue to history, however, would have been dissatisfied with these edifying deontological propositions and with these declarations of professional integrity. Particularly, he would have been dissatisfied with the evident detachment of these academic disputations on primitive man from all social, economic, or ideological considerations. On the other hand, such a person would have been open, as I suggested in my introductory pages, to the more complex diagnosis and the more complex answer that was there, ready to take shape as soon as he looked behind the screen of sonorous affirmations and between the lines of the erudite discourses.

Was the original form of land ownership individual or collective? It seemed like a game of pulling straws, based as it was on a dry passage from Caesar, an ambiguous text from Tacitus, an enigmatic verse from Horace.[19] We realize that beneath these scholars' exegetic rigor lay a conservative point of view and an interplay of interests that supported the structure of the society they wanted to preserve. The more that society's basic tenets were anchored in metahistorical values, the more solidly would it be consolidated; and they found one of these constant categories, impervious to temporal mutation, in nature.

The problem of the origins of forms of ownership, discussed exhaustively in this dispute, was closely tied to this need because the problem of origins was largely the problem of man untouched by his history and the distortions history brought about. It was the problem of uncontaminated human nature. Original meant—at least for them— inherent, innate, one with nature: all the rest was viewed as arbitrary, as superstructure, as later accretions.

The ingenuous naturalistic positivism that pervaded the better part of European culture of the second half of the nineteenth century was perhaps only grappling for a desperate last-ditch anchorage. Marxist and Marxian analyses were unacceptable to them, and Christian pre-suppositions were awkward. "Nature," understood in a sense that is far from the biological, seemed to be the one valid element remaining among such a poverty of values, one that could guarantee the structure of a social edifice that was the object of increasing scrutiny and iconoclastic criticisms.

In order to justify itself, that social edifice took on as its principal support the concept of the proprietary subject, and hence that of individual property as a self-serving and exclusive power. Since this was so, the only possible salvage operation consisted in holding firm to the long-established current of thought that, although it had seen different theoretical formulations through time, had always either tied individual property to individual liberty as a "capacity" of the individual, or had tied property to the nature of the subject.

This house of cards was endangered, however, by the scholars' bothersome research on primitive forms of organization and by their increasingly frequent queries as to whether primitive man took on the role of proprietor or whether he exhausted his possessive fire within a collective structure that he found even more satisfying.

It is clear that that first man was not important to the conservative camp as a chronological datum. What mattered was his position at the extreme edge of history, at the confines between history and nature. What was important was that that subject be characterized as a man of nature so that the "naturalness" and "artificiality" of human institutions could be grasped in their pure states. Such a natural man provided the opportunity to verify all the theories on the naturalness of individual ownership.

At a time when the most exaggerated of the evolutionistic interpretations continued to portray the change from collective to individual property as a progression from barbarism to civilization, from obscurantism to progress, it would have been a simple matter to accept the existence of a collective state of appropriation and to identify it with an inferior stage later belied by the conquests of social evolution. It would also have been a simple matter to draw conclusions from prevalent evolutionistic theory and to note that full and absolute individual ownership was in conformity with the *current* nature of man, and to claim that this guaranteed its conformity with nature.

This could have provided the most frontal, the most obvious way to attack the problem. But the nineteenth-century socio-juridical mind, thanks to centuries of the indoctrination of political and economic theory, had taken on individual property as the one protagonist in the human story. That mind had been so imbued with the idea of an absolutely static, immobile nature, a nature so perfectly expressive of an essential dimension of the primigenial state, that the very idea of another form of appropriation, one that changed through history, seemed necessarily repellent or even threatening. In spite of their enthusiasm for evolution, the nature to which nineteenth-century men of culture refer and which they perceive is often still the nature portrayed by the eighteenth-century Enlightenment. The philosophico-political and philosophico-juridical structure of the nineteenth century remained that of the eighteenth: a metahistorical vision of nature immune to change, immobile in the fixity of its values.

This was the meaning of the question of origins, of the priority of one or the other of forms of appropriation. The question may seem trivial. On the contrary, the problem was a serious one for the nineteenth-century juridical conscience. This is what occasioned the dispute, and it was a necessarily bitter dispute that involved men deeply and gave no quarter.

Along the Way to the Great Controversy
The interest in collective property as an organizational scheme became more and more widely diffused after the 1870s. The problem first circulated in the rather rarified atmosphere of economic and juridical thought, but it spread to an increasingly wide array of cultural groups and to intellectuals of very varied professional orientation.

In 1874 Auguste Geffroy, a historian of the best sort,[20] explicitly avowed his debt in his book on the *Germania* of Tacitus not only to the Germanistic studies of Maurer and Thudichum but also to Laveleye's articles and Viollet's essay. Furthermore, he showed that he had understood the lesson of the new theoreticians by his brief but comparative review of the various historical forms of collective property.[21]

Soon an acquaintance with those forms, particularly through his reading of Maine, Laveleye, and Nasse, became a weapon in the hands of the American Henry George[22] in his ingenuous battle against the private monopoly of the world's land.[23] George's book *Progress and Poverty* was undoubtedly debatable, and it was weakened by a scanty theoretical base; but its polemical character, aided by many translations,[24] assured it a universal circulation. It contributed to the diffusion of "collectivist" ideas among circles and persons whom the academic "inner circle" could certainly never have reached.[25]

Occasionally, the affirmation of the priority of the collective form of ownership sprang from a dispassionate examination of hitherto untouched ethnological materials. Such was the case of Lewis Henry Morgan's *Ancient Society,* published in 1877, which investigates an original corpus of data pertaining to American Indian tribes.[26]

Morgan was a scholar who stood outside the normal channels that feed general cultural movements. He is today widely known through Marx's and Engel's consideration of him,[27] but in the transatlantic isolation of his own day, he enjoyed only limited fame and appreciation in Europe. His autonomous and solitary reflections were far removed from the context of the great European polemic. An impassible ocean seemed to separate him from the disputes of the old continent: they were fundamentally alien to his thought, and a few scattered references to Maine or to Fustel de Coulanges on points not specifically related to property were not enough to modify the substance of his judgments. Morgan's book is a direct dialogue between an anthropologist and his sources, and it rejects any cumbersome mediation. He notes that the various stages of the "primitive" and "barbaric" level, in which tribal property is collective, clearly pass to a state of individual property.[28] Let me reiterate, this is not so because Morgan subscribes to this or to that interpretation, but because his sources spoke to him in this way and because he believed it evident that this is what had happened.

Whether it was because a growing number of scholars joined to lend their support to interpretations that had convinced them and that led to an influential doctrine, or whether it was because the comparative and socio-ethnological data allowed Western thought to approach a body of data that was both eloquent and fairly unambiguous, it is certain that interest in the problem grew enormously. Conclusions also circulated: that collective ownership enjoyed historical priority over individual ownership, that it was peculiarly "natural," and that it could still be endowed with the force of a value alternative to individual ownership.

It was impossible to expect that the dissemination of such a message would be totally peaceful. We must realize, as we have said before, that the doctrine regarding collective property had to be inserted into a solidly based cultural heritage. The constitutional state, laissez-faire economic structures, and a proprietarian base were not principles extrinsic to society. They were not unmotivated culturally or founded only on the *fact* that a certain ruling class held power in Europe after the French Revolution. On the contrary, these structures were set into an exceptionally learned and persuasive theoretical framework, one whose roots went deep into man's earliest philosophical and political expression. They had given form to a unified and compact construction that was extraordinarily clear and harmonious, but that was also extraordinarily intolerant of unforeseen intrusions.

The new doctrine could be characterized—to return to an image that seems to fit the case—as a foreign body inside this compact and integrated organism. Just because it was an organism justified not by practice but by a theoretical systemization of human common living, the new doctrine could not expect to be sanctioned. Faced with a foreign body, this organism could not help its reaction of rejection; faced with a poison it could not help but produce a counter poison.

The great dispute over collective property, which we propose to follow, runs in this direction. Although in appearance all may seem simple, its substance is complex. The warning that I offered in the introductory chapter must be repeated here, both as an admonition and as a canon for interpretation. There is no doubt that the cultural ground had been broken, but this complexity involved quite other dimensions beyond the cultural.

Impending social unrest stood behind every protagonist in the debate, urging him on, provoking him, be he an "advocate of communism" (as mentioned previously in our discussion of Laveleye) or a champion of quiritarian property. Complex states of mind as well as cultural acquisitions were in play, both on a conscious and on an unconscious level. An awareness of a society in turmoil, a fear of total destruction and a sense of the need to set a limit to the demolition, egalitarian sentiments, and moral aspirations were tangled together on one side, and on the other, in a more sharply defined discourse, stood the urgings of conservatism, the defense of traditional values, and a certitude regarding those values.

One conclusion cannot be denied: the dispute operated in more than one dimension. It is also certain that underlying the increase in an interest in research and in the number of investigations, a singular convergence can be discerned between the culture and the profound movements of the society of the time. Such convergences, in all their complexity, constitute a testimony precious to any historian who would like to arrive at more than a fleeting grasp of the difficult territory of ideologies through a consideration of prevailing ideas.

If we want an immediate verification of the tangle of motivations underlying the dispute that occupied the whole of the decade from 1880 to 1890 and beyond before we enter into an analysis of how it was carried on, we can find no better context, no more exemplary an event, than the debate that took place in the Académie des Sciences morales et politiques of Paris in the middle of the decade. With the promise to return later to the outcome of that debate and to show how it fits into the more general development of the question, let us limit ourselves now to a somewhat anachronistic anticipation of that discussion, picking out a few data concerning men and arguments. This will serve both to clarify some of the conclusions we have already reached and to lead us into the thick of the dialogue when we are better acquainted with the protagonists of this introductory period.

During the period that interests us, the Académie, a creation of the Revolution suppressed by Napoleon and revived by Louis Philippe, was not a showcase for bewigged sacred relics but a vital and lively center of intellectual interchange. We find as influential members during those years the men who were the most deeply involved in the dispute: first among them, Numa Denis Fustel de Coulanges,[29] followed by the economist Paul Leroy-Beaulieu,[30] Léon Aucoc, a specialist in public administration,[31] Ernest Glasson, a historian of jurisprudence,[32] and the historian Auguste Geffroy.[33] As foreign corresponding members we find the same Henry Maine and Emile de Laveleye whose names are already familiar to us. It seems singularly coincidental, but the protagonists of our dialogue had in the Académie an ideal arena for the confrontation of their opinions. The Académie, in other words, can be of great help to anyone who is less than eager to follow the entire sequence of all the various contributions to the debate through a long succession of years. It furnishes an efficient lens for focusing on the dispute at its sharpest point.

Let us open the *Compte-rendu* of the sessions and their supporting work for the years 1885 and 1886. In 1885 Fustel read before the Académie his animated "Recherches sur cette question: Les Germains connaissaient-ils la propriété des terres,"[34] and in the same year Laveleye replied with his memorandum "La propriété primitive dans les Townships écossais."[35] A year later, Fustel responded with his "Observations sur un ouvrage de M. Emile de Laveleye intitulé 'La propriété collective du sol en divers pays.' "[36]

Aside from the encounter between the two great adversaries, the question of collective property and of the origins of property came up continually. Léon Aucoc presented Belot's volume on primitive property,[37] which gave Geffroy the opportunity to make important clarifications during the formal discussion sessions. The presentation of Fustel's "Recherches" gave vent to a sharp and lively polemic: Geffroy spoke, Fustel replied, at which point Geffroy gave another speech, to which Fustel replied again; Aucoc had his say, Fustel replied to him; and finally Félix Ravaisson added his thoughts.[38] There was, in other words, a rapid and dense exchange of words aimed at unraveling a knotty problem that they all found bothersome.

But the exchange did not stop there. If one had the patience to skim the two volumes of the proceedings of 1886, he would find an ample group of essays that seem at first glance to belong to another sphere than that of the polemic over primitive man. We note, for example, a report of several academicians on Alfred Fouillée's *La propriété sociale et la démocratie;*[39] not long after, a detailed treatment by Léon Say of Lujo Brentano's *La question ouvrière;*[40] finally, in the second semester, an essay by Glasson on "Le Code civil et la question ouvrière."[41]

The duality of inspiration that seems apparent is just a duality of the manifestations of substantially the same inspiration and the same preoccupations. In this, the Académie shows that it bears out our thesis: all in these discussions was complex, nothing was of simply philological or purely historical interest, even if there were among the academicians those who so claimed.[42] On the contrary, the historians and the philologists passionately involved in studying their documents spoke with one voice and shared one passion, situated in their times and a product of those times. This is true, of course, of all things human; but these discussions were particularly strongly charged with a sense of historical import, and a hidden thread—or perhaps not so hidden—tied together the ill-concealed rage that Fustel directed at primitive communism and the whole of the broader discussion of "social ownership" and "the labor question."

The threads that made up the fabric of this debate were many, and only an awareness of this multiplicity will permit us to see the problem in its entirety and to find a sure path in tracing its development.

4 The Forms and Substance

of a Debate:

Fustel de Coulanges

**Historiographical Methodology and the History of Forms of
Property: Methodological Rigor and Philosophical "Certitudes"**

One name has come up often on the preceding pages, that of
Fustel de Coulanges.[1] We have seen him holding forth at the Académie
des Sciences morales et politiques in the context of the vicissitudes of a
discussion that originated from his decisive response to the worrisome
question: "Did the Germans practice land ownership?"[2] Fustel was in
fact the great opponent of Laveleye and the "collectivists," the scholar
who dismissed communistic solutions disdainfully in the name of a particular tradition and a particular civilization, and the man who embodied
the last defense of a particular sociopolitical ideal and, simultaneously, of
a fixed stage in human progress.

Fustel was not a political scientist, however, nor an economist,
nor even a jurist. He was a historian and, what is more, an exceptionally
gifted person. Although his aim was the ignominious defeat of what
seemed to him a hideous paradigm of the relation of men and goods and
the permanent burial of an alternative economic form, the means he used
were not, nor could they be, those of economics or political science.

Thus Fustel's discourse was complex. As it often happens in the
thick of an argument, it ran on two levels, that of explicit affirmations
aimed at an immediate objective, and that of a hidden unifying thread
tending toward a more remote goal. Fustel appears to be a professional
historian completely involved in demolishing the historical mystifications
he found in Maurer, Laveleye, and their fellow travelers, but we must
read his pages without preconceived judgments in order to grasp their real

scope and perceive their complexity. This is what we intend to do in order to see them in their full historical context.

Let us begin with a clarification of the program he set himself. Our Parisian historian took up arms specifically against the theory of the collective form of primitive landholding, not in itself, but insofar as it was a historical reconstruction of the primitive organization of goods. Similarly, he engaged battle against Laveleye's slipshod historiography, not against the man himself.[3] The problem seemed to be uniquely methodological, and the gap that separated Fustel and Laveleye seemed to be nothing but the discrepancy between rigorous historiographical method and an antihistorical approach.

For Fustel, Laveleye had committed the act most inappropriate to a historian, that of claiming real, operative power for the historical datum, thus, that of mixing past and present. It was not for the historian to advance practical proposals—this was the task of the economist and the political scientist. Laveleye's mistake, according to Fustel, was to take over materials from the historical past and treat them with the sort of attention and absence of scruples typical of an economist. For Fustel, the study of history was the observation of things past without trying to rip them from the womb of the past, without excessive recourse to the mechanisms of historical reconstruction.

He states that in general

> it would be preferable if history . . . remained a pure, completely disinterested science. We would like to see it floating in that serene region where there is neither passion, nor rancor, nor desire for vengeance. We ask of history that charm of perfect impartiality that is its chastity.[4]

This statement might seem surprising and even negligent to anyone who is familiar with Fustel's historiographical works, and particularly to anyone who had followed the many writings he dedicated to the question that interests us here. We have seen him twist texts to suit his needs, and our ears still ring with his polemical statements, personal attacks, and bitter and malevolent insinuations.

Whether he was consistent or inconsistent, Fustel's program followed the methodological intention of separating past and present into uncommunicating dimensions with no functional tie to unite them. Past and present were two objectives to be reached by differing forms of thought; they involved differing mixtures of impartiality, distance, pure ratiocination, or observation, and differing emotional states and particular interests. This separation is so carefully drawn in Fustel's thought that it reveals its absurdity only when he carries it to its logical extreme, transferring it from the objects observed and the observer's angle of vision to the observer himself. Any observer carries with him, always and everywhere, his own psychological unity, a unity that emerges, always and in all cases, with its indivisible accumulation of passion and critical attitudes. Fustel's program did not leave him in the limbo of his deodontic breviary, but carried him into the fiery regions of the debate that interests us. His rule for the writing of history is our key for reading him.

Fustel stated during the course of a denunciation of one of Laveleye's writings, delivered before the Académie:

> In the last analysis, I fail to see what interest the partisans of the collective regime could have in sustaining so hastily that that regime was the primitive and universal law of humanity. What is history doing in this affair? History is the science of the past: it does not teach the present or the future. It is a pure science, not an art. It studies the past of humanity as geology studies what is under the soil, without aiming at practical application. It has the grandeur of a disinterested and useless science. Why should we make it serve modern doctrines? Why should we risk falsifying it in order to bend it to fit those doctrines? The community of the soil in the present and in the future and the community of the soil in the past are two independent questions that must be treated separately. One is proper to the economists; the other would be better studied by historians.[5]

In this candor or tartuffery? The second seems more likely, given that the question is not very justified. If there was one assumption that was clear, unequivocal, proclaimed openly and from the outset by Laveleye and his followers, it was that the historical priority of collective property renders the very notion of individual property relative, dismantles it as a universal notion, and almost manages to create a hierarchy of values in which it is to collective property that the first place belongs.

All of this—let me repeat—may be an erroneous proposition, but it is one well integrated into Laveleye's program and fully justifies his "archaeological" researches. Why even ask a question that for an attentive and hostile reader like Fustel had an obvious and totally clear answer given in the first few lines of the work he incriminated? The interest that the advocates of collectivism had in fixing the communitarian form of property-holding among the social baggage of the first human agglomerations had the same justification as Fustel's interest in wanting at all costs to see the first men as carrying possessive individualism to the earth. The battle was fought on the same grounds, and the solution that seemed most valid to one camp could not avoid being the perfect *oppositum* of that of the other. On the one side as on the other, the image of the geological excavation pointed to an investigator whose feet were well planted in the present and who bore the weight of that complex of sensitivities and of

social and moral energies that are impossible to eradicate and that in-
eluctably make up his experience of humanity.

The theory of the "chastity" of history and, even more, of its
"uselessness" leaves one perplexed when it is checked against Fustel's
own research on property. From the *Cité antique* of 1864 to the thick
volume on the *Alleu*—his last work—the theme of property, as we will
see, is not only recurrent but dominant, if not overpowering. For Fustel,
this objective and crystalline verity, whether read in historical facts or
lent to them, lay in individual property as a fact of primordial society, as a
historical constant, and as a positive value in human history.

According to him, and in contrast to the "collectivist" dream-
ers, he had read "all" the documents, had analyzed "all" the texts, had
brought into play in considering them "all" the devices of philology; and
they "all" spoke of individual property (or at the most, of family property) and none spoke of collective property.[6] The entire life work of
Fustel showed the same urgent desire to free the space of history of an
awkward guest, collective property, to deny it where it was certain that it
existed, to reduce it in every case to familial ownership. The choices he
offered were totalitarian; his solutions bear but one meaning; his vision of
the problem is totally Manichaean. Good and evil, the good people and
the bad people, truth and error leave no room for compromise, for
nuances, or for grey areas.

Fustel the historicist appeals continually to the need for greater
investigative rigor, for sharper philological tools, for the treatment and
analysis of texts taken in isolation rather than gathered together indiscriminately in composite bundles.[7] But he presents us with a mono-
chrome reality, with one single historical language, and with a vision of
problems and solutions rendered so absolute as to make us wonder
whether his investigation has not given way to a crusade, and whether the
relativity of the patterns of history has not abdicated to the absoluteness
of morality and its convictions.

One of his many opponents, and one of the more gifted,
Rodolphe Dareste de la Chavanne,[8] reacted to Fustel's categorical denial
of collectivist forms of landholding from the sixth to the twelfth
centuries—a historical fact that seemed to Dareste self-evident—to ask a
question in perfect symmetry with Fustel's own question on the "collectivists' " interests in archaeology. With a much more evident good faith
and with much more candor toward his opponent, Dareste wondered why
Fustel should have given so much weight to a point of such minor importance to his central argument.[9] The good Dareste was undoubtedly
right, as one would have been right to note a repetition of the theme of
collective ownership so insistent that it overstepped the bounds of a given
essay or work of research. The fact is that Fustel was personally inter-

ested in that theme, and this personal interest raised to the level of scholarship became a fundamental thesis.

We will return to this point later. What is important to understand now is that few historians have been as deeply engaged in the object of their studies as Fustel. Few have poured into it as he did their humors and their passions and the full weight of the moral convictions of their particular times. Only rarely has an awareness of the present directed a historian's gaze and fixed its focus as it did in this case. The neutrality and the gratuity of historical investigation are ideas that appear to be either mere conventions or else aimed at mystifying the reader. Less openly stated than it was by the "collectivists" and used in a manner more insidious, more cunning, and hence less verifiable, the present with Fustel entered into the closed realm of the past, conditioned it, and turned it to its own purposes.

The blatant manner in which Fustel made use of the present in explaining the past will become immediately clear when one uses philological criteria to examine his philology—that is, one of the instruments, if not the primary one, with which he sought to combat the "collectivists."

It is a disarming philology, and was a source of desperation rather than of gratification for such severe critics as d'Arbois de Jubainville or Théodore Reinach,[10] whose comments we will note later. It is enough to note now that in practice Fustel's use of documents often shows an arbitrary choice of documents that suited his thesis, an artificial sectioning of single documents unwarranted by the contents, and nonchalant alterations. The result is often that the text is completely isolated from the reality that produced it, and Fustel continually runs the risk of using materials completely detached from a historical setting, and thus of becoming more the author of brilliant nominalistic exercises than of authentically historical investigations.

Nevertheless, when one reads his consistently arrogant, presumptuous prose, one has the impression of a scholar of great probity. In a polemical exchange with Viollet, who had rebuked him for an unhistorical reading of the documentation on ancient Germanic landholding, Fustel arrogantly responded:

> To each his customary procedures. I will take analysis, the study of details, the minute examination of words. He may have argumentation, logic, presumptiveness, and, above all, comparison.[11]

But what was the use of ingenious inspection of the mechanics of a text or brilliant, even genial, interpretation of one of its more obscure passages if this meticulousness did not lead to a comprehension of the text in its historical setting? Particularly if, quite the other way around, this minute attention became the *instrumentum regni* of the investigator and was aimed at shoring up his own thesis?

> I have read *all* of these documents, not once, but several times, not in extracts, but in their continuity, and from one end to the other.[12]

Fustel here makes a great public show of virtue of what is an elementary duty of any historian. He was alone, it seems, in having read *all* the documents, the only one from whom sources kept no secrets.

I am unaware of whether adequate attention has been paid up to now to the use of the adjective "all" in Fustel and to the internal function it fulfills in his style and in his relentless dialectic. It seems certain that this use was conscious. It is certainly congenial to his personality, as it identifies his own certitudes with truth and subordinates everything to this. We will soon see that collective property meant for him ownership not by a particular group but by *all*[13] and, as we have just seen, he had gone through *all* the documents, excluding none. In both cases it is the same overbearing personality that surfaces, the same *totalitarian* argument, and the same use of a deterrent, intimidating term.

The meagerness of this verbally cocksure philology was fittingly brought out by those scholars whom Fustel the sorcerer did not succeed in neutralizing. His talent was for ratiocination and dialectics; according to Giorgio Pasquali, he was a "mediocre philologist"[14] and "a sociologist rather than a historian."[15] This was an accurate and appropriate qualification if by a sociologist is meant one who endeavors to reconstruct laws and constants in societal becoming, to draw up models without excessive preoccupation with the extreme flexibility, plasticity, and mobility of historical reality.

The authentic image of Fustel can be seen in his *La cité antique*. It is intelligently constructed, it boasts several basic insights, and it is sustained on every page, on every line, by an imperious will that is little inclined to discussion or dialogue. The unmistakable mark of Fustel can be discerned emerging through the dedication to philology that he had accepted as a necessity but that was forced because it was ill adapted to his mind. It emerges in the defense of individual property and in the assertion of his great central thesis.

We know from his students—particularly from Charles Seignobos[16]—what scholarly paths took Fustel from being a robust constructor of syntheses to his rebirth as a meticulous analyst of documents and words. They were not paths that reflected the maturing process of a conviction: they were made of spiteful impulses, contrariness, and feelings of guilt.[17] Fustel's philology was always the product of a pseudo philology in which respect for the text gave way before respect for his own thesis. Behind his philology lay disguised a self-possessed, extremely willful personage who would for nothing in the world give up asserting his own line of thought.

He demolishes Maurer, stating that "once he had formed his theory in his mind, he folded up his texts."[18] He attacks Lamprecht without mercy, claiming that "he takes over the texts which are the most opposed to his theory and interprets them in his fashion."[19] He says about Viollet's procedures and conclusions that "when logic fills in the gaps in the texts, the mind can construct all the systems it wants,"[20] and he goes out of his way to note the factual inexactitudes and instances of bad faith of his opponent.[21] A conscientious observer might turn against Fustel himself all of these heavy-handed criticisms, distributed so generously to those who made the mistake of thinking differently from him.

Fustel was unconsciously autobiographical when he piled up these invectives. He was the one who took over a guiding idea and bent his texts to it, who interpreted texts with apparently obsequious respect for them but who showed more hermeneutic ability than sensitivity to history.[22] He is the one who accused the "collectivists" of impertinence and excessive zeal and who then turned on them with just such attitudes.

There is a difference in the two, however. Fustel's ideology remained underground, unexpressed; it wound its way beneath an array of documentation. His ideology was parasite to that documentation and made it speak in its stead, as if the historian were a puppeteer. But it was Fustel who drew and moved the strings; those far-off, detached, and artificial voices have the tone and timbre of his voice.

Achille Loria, a man given to images but a sincere and enthusiastic convert to the new collectivist ideas, was happy to constate a growing consensus concerning them. Writing a eulogy of Emile de Laveleye in 1892 he stated with satisfaction:

> In vain Fustel de Coulanges, from the summit of his Capitularies and his Glossaries, tried to hurl the excommunication of history at the new revelations and to reaffirm the individual character of primitive property.[23]

If we wanted to continue Loria's image and test its meaning in light of what we have said thus far, one question would come to mind. Did those capitularies and those glossaries really offer a point of observation perched high in the pure and rarefied atmosphere of historical objectivity, detached from the white heat of social reality and human ideology? Or, on the contrary, was that viewpoint rooted deep in the human soul, where ideologies founder?

I hope that I have been successful in reducing to their real dimensions the thought and the historiographical work of Fustel de Coulanges concerning the origins and historical forms of property. What

is important is not to be lulled by Fustel's expressions of scientific indignation, by his professions of philological faith, and by his cultlike
declarations in favor of "truth."

The figure of Fustel, as he appears in the context of the great
debate, is a complex one. His function as Grand Inquisitor of the
significance of historical forms of collective property cannot be explained
historically as the rebellion of science against pseudo science or of
philological certitudes against the neoterics' fabulations. It had its roots
in the profound, intricate, and multiple context in which we have situated
the controversy itself.

Individual Property as an Ethico-political Value in the Historiographical Researches of Fustel

"He called up his last reserves to defend the historical and
moral theory of individual property,"[24] declared Fustel's friend and biographer, Jean M. Tourneur-Aumont. These words were dictated by full
approval and imply no mental reservations, but we could make them our
own, for they characterize accurately not only the final years of Fustel's
intellectual life, but also the whole span of his work.

Fustel's interest in the question of property was enduring.
Already in *La cité antique* the sixth chapter of the second book was
dedicated to the right to hold property and appears as fundamental to his
thought. Beginning in 1879, when he was writing up his researches on
property-holding in Greece,[25] Fustel dedicated a good part of his attention
to this theme and to the polemics that turned around this theme. Thus in
1885 we see his communication before the Académie des Sciences on
ancient German property;[26] about the same time, his essay on the *Mark*;[27]
in 1886, his head-on confrontation with Laveleye;[28] in 1889, his general
accusation directed at all the "collectivists" that first appeared in the
Revue des questions historiques;[29] and, during the same period, his un-
finished but strongly constructed essay on alodial and agrarian landholding.[30] All of these centered around the same focal point and were governed by the same dominating interest.

Two elements stand out in all of these works. First, as was his
custom, Fustel made his historical data sing the praises of individual
property. Second, he definitively and peremptorily condemned collective
property as marginal, and he did so through a rigorously scientific examination and evaluation of his documentation. Let us limit ourselves for the
moment to the first of these aspects and look briefly at how Fustel sought
to anchor in history his "moral" notion of individual property.

In *La cité antique,* it is the connection between property and the
religious dimension that carries his argument. It was domestic religion
that had taught man to make himself master of the land and had assured

him dominion over it. That religion safeguarded this dominion made it a right of extraordinary resistence:[31]

> Religion and property were born together in the soul and formed with the family an indivisible and indistinct whole.[32]

On the foundation of this concept, which was at once juridical, economic, and moral, rose the whole of Western institutional history, and Fustel struck at its very heart when he turned to the development and the persistence of an ancient concept of property-holding.

According to Fustel, at the base of both the medieval and the modern construction lay the Roman interpretation of property. It was itself a concrete form shaped by religious motivations or by natural impulses; but in either case, it was of extremely remote origin. It was a structure that bound securely to a subject the various economic relationships that come out of things, resulting in juridical ties of rare stability and strength. Successive redefinitions of the economic and juridical organization of goods were only a continuation, a development, a realization of the classical resolution of this problem. Fustel saw everything in terms of absolute continuity.[33] History for him flowed in a clearly channeled course and was relatively untouched by inflow or contaminations from outside the main channel.

It is in this rigid and unilateral manner that Fustel presents the passage from ancient to medieval property relationships in his thick volume on the alodial estate. This work summarized his long meditations and provided the central link for joining together the entire chain of his views on historical institutions in the Middle Ages.

In this work, individual property remains for Fustel the basic institution and he finds its organization manifested in the *villa,* which he refers to as the *villa gallo-romaine.*[34] He first discovers evidence of this administrative nucleus toward the middle of the fourth century, a delicate, watershed moment between the order of the ancient world and new forms. For Fustel, there was no room in this basic cell for communitarian forms of ownership. Everything on the level of goods was the projection of a unified authority, *dominium,* conceived as the force and the vitality of an individual. Its active range was not limited to within the terrain of the *villa,* but extended to the cultivated and uncultivated lands around it, to fenced-in fields as well as to forest and pasture lands.[35]

In addition, this authoritarian right tended to develop in the direction of its more absolute aspects. Fustel notes with subtle pleasure, for example, that Roman jurisconsults, far from trying to justify private ownership through work as do modern jurists, hold it to be "an ancient and indisputable right that does not need to be justified."[36] The *villa* founded its stability on the sacred ground of this indiputable right, which bore its own historical justification, as do rights founded in the nature of things.

It would be interesting to examine exactly how Fustel portrayed this structure, but it would take our discussion too far afield. Let it suffice to note that as he painted them, any type of common property or any landholding arrangement that implied collective notions was portrayed with techniques carefully designed to minimize or camouflage them.

When the land surveyors speak of *agri communes,* Fustel hastens to treat the point *in limine* and to resolve the question unconditionally. In the section of the work on more general matters, he briefly, almost hastily, reduces explicit references to communal holdings in the sources to limited and infrequent examples of undivided property, incapable of generating any idea of commonality. They are seen as lands either held in common or by heirs in common, pasture and forest lands acquired by neighboring proprietors as adjuncts to their own agrarian enterprises and left unpartitioned, or lands that were not divided at the time of the founding of a colony and were later assigned *pro indiviso* to landholders already established within the colony:

> In these three cases as well, lands designated as common are in reality the property of determined persons; in no case are the lands common to all. The idea of agrarian communism was absent from the Roman mind.[37]

We have no intention of discussing the merits of Fustel's conclusions, nor do we seek to know and evaluate the real historical significance of the *agri communes* in later Roman society. What we seek to understand is the place that the concept of individual property held in Fustel's thought and in his works of historiography. We reserve the right to return to the question later; but our immediate interest is in pointing out, first, that his exegesis of his beloved texts is strained and his interpretation of them is one-sided. Second, we note that Fustel's use of the totalitarian language typical of him shows his constant and obsessive fear of any relationship of ownership that might apply to the general community, and of what that relationship might imply.

At any event, Fustel seemed to have fulfilled his aim, and without particular difficulty. He had placed the history of Western institutions on a rock-solid foundation. His zeal, furthermore, had cemented tight every minimal joint in this foundation so that it appeared absolutely monolithic. His task then was to continue in another direction: the entire structure of medieval landholding had to be erected on this Roman foundation, which was then asked to support successive accumulations, conditioning them decisively and, one could almost say, transfering to the sphere of social and juridical structures what was common in the context of temples and houses.

Fustel became a staunch supporter of the thesis of continuity. Even when political and juridical structures within Roman society and within the Roman state disappeared, new peoples appeared on the scene, colonial settlements came and went, Fustel saw only apparent novelty with no change in substance.[38] Systematically, as if he wanted to leave no room for doubt, he considered Roman laws adopted by barbarian peoples,[39] Germanic laws,[40] the Merovingian charters,[41] and he concluded that "the arrival of new men neither altered nor lessened the right of ownership over the soil."[42]

Fustel was not afraid of irritating repetition:

> All the documents of the Merovingian age . . . have all shown us private property. All the laws, all the charters insist on this in indisputable terms.[43]

Why this ostentatious insistence on having seen *all,* examined *all,* rummaged through *all* the documents? Why this prolixity and this insistence on the part of an author who could be succinct and eloquent, who was capable of splendid syntheses, and who was marvelously intuitive? The explanation may be offered later on in the same essay:

> I see, however, elsewhere than in the documents, that is to say, in modern works, an opinion that is much in fashion, according to which the Franks practiced a regime of "agrarian community" or at least of "village community."[44]

Once again, Fustel's reigning obsession comes to the surface, and he returns to his quarrel with his usual adversaries, the "champions of that theory":[45] scholars like Maurer, Sohm, Viollet, Laveleye, and Lamprecht. Once again Fustel makes a show of the scorn that a scientist laden with data and proofs cannot but feel for tall-tale spinners and fabulists.[46] His tone is bitter, his polemic is tightly knit, and he hits hard. The argument has a constant tendency to leave the territory of calm objectivity to become loaded with virulence and passion, but this was typical of Fustel. It was aimed more at the professional integrity and credibility of the writers he attacked than at their theses.[47] It was just this tactic that Ernest Glasson found unpardonable and that motivated his bitterest reproach of Fustel.[48]

Were these quarrels over methodology? Fustel, replying in fact to Glasson, pontificates that "nothing in history is more important than method."[49] Did this indicate an urgent desire to note verity and correct error? Fustel is eager to have his reader "know and see with his own eyes how one finds truth or how one finds error."⁵⁰ Was Fustel moved by the need to reestablish philological certainty? In his quarrel with Glasson—or, for that matter, with anyone who contradicted him—Fustel claimed that he never descended to "discuss the author's opinion" but limited himself to an attempt to "examine his citations."⁵¹

It is not my intention to deny all this, nor to limit the meaning of Fustel's harangues to this. The quarrel revolved around the testing of an axiom, to be sure; but it was not that individual property was or was not a historical verity, but rather whether it was a moral verity.

In all of this interplay of extremely learned skirmishings there was something more and something else at stake than the reestablishment of scientific truths. If that had been the case, there would have been more subtlety in the give and take between the two camps; more space in their interchanges would have been given over to doubts, to perplexities, and to indefinable areas. Instead, we see Fustel counter the "collectivists'" ingenuous, idealized, and absolute vision of the question with his own equally absolute vision.

In all probability, both camps abandoned the terrain of historical analysis, that changeable and rough terrain in which humility is the sole sure guarantee of success. What we see before us is not two versions of reality, both filtered out of history, but two metahistorical models. The participants in this quarrel no longer defended their exegesis of a text, but their conception of life and of society. Events in the past were no more than an excuse, and the problem lost its temporal dimension to be projected indifferently onto the past, the present, or the future.

Fustel's total fidelity to certain of his insights, to certain "truths" that remained intact and immutable for the entire span of his intellectual life, can undoubtedly be attributed partly to intellectual coherence; but it also undoubtedly came of his refusal of dialogue, of his inability to observe with detachment and to recognize the complexity of a phenomenon, and hence of his inability to see the validity of more than one interpretation. These were signs of an ideological fidelity that led to excess, immobility, and absolutism.

Tourneur-Aumont, who was close enough to Fustel to be a credible reporter, had this to say:

> Private property was, according to Fustel, the condition of family life, of individual morality, and of liberty, all three of which are now threatened, and with them, public order.⁵²

This is what underlay Fustel's fidelity to his basic ideas, and it was a fidelity to what were seen as the external walls of a citadel menaced by disorder. In Fustel we have the perfect parallel to the psychological complex under which the "collectivists" labored, but turned inside out.

This attitude was less open in Fustel, however, and more cloaked in scientific dignity. Rarely does the vigilant Fustel leave the safe grounds of documentation to launch an open attack, as he did eloquently on at least one occasion:

> Among the ideas that are currently masters of the human mind, there is one that J. J. Rousseau has put there, to wit, that property is contrary to nature, and that what is natural is the community. This idea rules even over learned men, who obey it without being conscious of the fact. Minds dominated by this idea will never admit that property can be a primordial fact, contemporary to the introduction of agriculture, natural to man, engendered by instinctively conceived interests in direct relation with the primitive constitution of the family.[53]

For the moment, the philologist has lowered his mask and the author's voice no longer has the monotonous pitch and the mechanical rhythms of the usual refrains on Caesar, Tacitus, or Diodorus Siculus. The passage has the authentic ring of a confession. We can easily see a complete reversal of Laveleye's premises and conclusions, particularly in the reassignment of individual property to the dimension of nature and its consequent removal from history. We do not know whether Fustel had ever read the discussions relating to the preparation of the Napoleonic *Code civil,* but his affirmations seem to repeat an entire series of prescriptions found there. These precepts can, of course, be traced back in history all the way to the famous perorations of Portalis.

Let us not forget that property and religion were for Fustel two vital ways in which the subject manifested himself, two attitudes "internal" to him, two facts of the human spirit, of the *interior homo* even more than of the *civis:* "Religion and property were born together in the soul."[54] And for Fustel, even in subsequent historical manifestations property always carried with it the mark of this tie to the sacred and to its original naturalness, demanding that historical becoming make the necessary adjustments to it, since existence cannot belie essence.

One fact colored by familiar notions from natural law emerges clearly here: it is property as a rational model removed from the wear of time and circumstances.

Fustel lets slip a significant admission of his own attitude when he discusses Emile Belot's treatment of his ideas on historical forms of property in a commemorative article dedicated to his old friend and colleague in the *Revue historique:*

> This provided him with an opportunity to fight with arguments of great vigor and *of right thinking* [*de saine raison*] the preconceived ideas that some people hold on the community of land.[55]

The italics are mine, and they are intended to underline Fustel's tendency to shift levels where property is concerned. Emile Belot's arguments against primitive communism were not only vigorous (and here we can understand: of great historiographical vigor), but they were also and especially reasonable, in conformity with a healthy rationality.

Alas, when Fustel enters the realm of the reasonable to take possession of data and methods, it is an alarming sign that he has abandoned his craft, or at least that he has shown signs of giving up the customary tools of his trade. He penetrates the domain reserved for the supreme concepts and the grandiose visions of the world that constitute the realm typical of morality. When he goes even further and qualifies this as "sane" or "healthy" or "right", he uses a term rife with ethical connotations, insidious and detestable because of the uses to which it has been put historically. By this sign we know that our author closes the question to discussion, because it is put in terms of truth or error, of good or evil. He alters the nature of the point under discussion: what had been the object of observation and evaluation and had belonged to historical reality has become a conviction based in internal reality, to be projected and tested only internally. It is a sign that what was a problem has become a certitude.

A Shadow-maker: The Requisitory against "Collectivism" and its Cultural Applications

Fustel was guided by two ideas. The first was the dominating idea of private property as an institution congenial to the intimate nature of the individual and, for that reason, as a conquest that could neither be suppressed nor abdicated. The second followed from the first and complemented it, almost as if it were a different aspect of the same basic option. It was a diffidence—indeed, an irremediable aversion—toward any collective form of the ownership or management of goods or holdings.

In his logic, if private property signified a positive value for men living in society, collective property must necessarily represent a disavowal of that value. Hence, it must represent a nonvalue.

Even before Fustel pronounced a condemnation of collective property in the public forum of the controversy on historical documents, he had already done so in the jealously guarded forum of his own convictions. This can often be divined when the data that crowd Fustel's pages give way to phrases that seem to be written with an ink of a more sympathetic sort, slipping through gaps in an argument that strives for documentary rigor to let us see moments of weakness or slackened vigilance. For example:

> What frightens me is not the theory itself—*it will not modify the* [forward] *march of human events*—but the method used in order to ensure its acceptance.[56]

May we be forgiven if we do not believe this solemn declaration? What dismays Fustel is the communistic theory, and what it could mean and bring to European society of the nineteenth century. This is demonstrated in the consoling phrase that I have underlined and that is extraneous to the logic of the sentence.

Non praevalebunt, he seems to declare. Anarchism and social disorder will not prevail over the ordered, civilized society in which individual liberty is cultivated and which finds its guarantee and its seal of authenticity in private property. We hear from the tone of Fustel's voice that he has left the sanctuary provided by the solemn debates to avow his position openly. He reveals to us the underlying explanation for so much research, so many formal replies, so many learned pages, so much relentless zeal, for a defense so desperate as to make one think that the enemy had reached the heart of the innermost bulwarks.

For Fustel, these were not unfounded and erroneous but innocuous doctrines. They represented a fatal crack in a monolithic structure, a leak in a dike. This explains why an offensive aimed at their elimination was necessary, rather than a defense against them. This explains Fustel's negations of the evidence, his clumsy alterations, his distortion of the texts, his scholastic exercises on terminology. His articles and books abound in all of these, and these were the object of his adversaries' continual salvos.

To speak of collective forms of property did not mean, in Fustel's view, to consider particular historical phenomena and, subsequently, to ask whether they might provide an alternative to current practice. Collectivism, communism, even in the mild, benevolent, and limited acception given the terms by Laveleye, Maurer, or Viollet acquire always an absolute stamp in Fustel's thought, a quality of totality. We have collectivism, he repeats ad nauseum, when the land is common to *all;* we have communism where land is the property of *all* so that it is the property of no one.[57]

The identification of collective ownership with communism is apodictic, axiomatic. It springs from an intellectual schema according to which the necessarily vague and generic terms of collectivism and communism invoke no images of particular and tranquil agrarian, forest, or pasture communities, but reflect society in general and its foundations. And this is another proof—if one is needed—of the purely ideological nature of Fustel's discourse.

When he read Laveleye, Maurer, and Viollet, Fustel was thinking of Fourier or Marx, of utopian or scientific socialism. When he read about particular community types—the *Mark,* the *mir,* the *Allmend*—he was thinking about the deeply troubled society around him. He was obsessed continually with the destruction of values that seemed destined to take place. Fustel could not manage to free his interpretation of texts and facts from this dominant preoccupation. It cast a filtering, distorting light on the objects of his study, and mistakes and misunderstandings were born of this dual vision.

Fustel's presentation of the Russian *mir* is illuminating:

> In the first place, the Russian mir is nothing but a village, even a small village, and its population rarely surpasses two hundred inhabitants. It occupies the same land constantly, so that if there is a community here, it is in any event a community within very restricted limits. This mir in no way represents a "tribal community" and even less the community of a people. One cannot conclude from the mir that the Russian people practiced the regime of agrarian communism, nor that the land belonged to the Russian people, nor, finally, that the land was common to all; and this already represents a gap with the thesis they claim to sustain.[58]

This presentation acquires a precise meaning when it is connected with Fustel's *idée fixe* that collective property was a total phenomenon implying ownership by all. We must also place it against the background of his guiding idea that options concerning the disposition of goods were not transient episodes, but drew on the essential nature of the general community. Thus they affected the community as profoundly as certain choices in religion and mores. Private or collective property, far from belonging to the surface realm of the quotidian, were for him directly connected to the ethico-social essence of a community taken as a whole. Consequently, one option seemed to him positive, the other negative, one was a value and one a nonvalue, one brought good and one brought evil. In this view, a people's choice of a form of ownership was necessarily total: it must choose one or the other of diametrically opposed forms.

We can probably surmise that for Fustel it was inconceivable or downright repugnant that a society that normally practiced private ownership should tolerate in particular communities the simultaneous practice of forms of a somewhat collectivist nature as in the *mir*. For him, the particular must be tied to the general, and the image of the global community—which landholding forms always reflect with sincerity and accuracy—must regain its unity.

Although it seems to me difficult to reproach Fustel for the ideological dimension of his discourse, when we interpret his thought in this key we note that it is carried onto a more complex terrain. On that terrain ideology is stripped of simple class interests and stretches its roots to the uttermost realm of values, where the atmosphere is less crude and more rarefied. It is an interpretive key that amplifies and elaborates the lines we have already traced. It contributes to a more convincing explanation of Fustel's Manichaeanism, of his merciless condemnations, of the incredibly harsh outbursts that constellate the space he occupied in the great debate.[59] It is also an interpretive key that shows a reason for all of the pseudo-cultural techniques—more exactly, pseudo-juridical and pseudo-philological—that he puts into operation.

There is no reason to follow Fustel's ingenious and most skillful hermeneutic exercises, nor his punctilious replies to adversaries, designed to leave absolutely nothing of their theses intact. Anyone who might be interested in investigating these errors, distortions, and alterations can do so by reading, on the one hand, Fustel's article on the origins of landed property and the volume on alodial lands, which summarize his work and his polemical positions, and, on the other hand, the responses of Viollet, d'Arbois de Jubainville, and, particularly, of Glasson in a wide-ranging and thorough essay of 1890.[60] We do not intend to do so. Our interests do not lie in deciding which camp was right about the reconstruction of the document published by Zeumer, the passage of the *Lex romana burgundionum,* or the title *De migrantibus* of the *Lex salica.* Our interest stops with a consideration of the methods Fustel employed as they relate to the conclusions he reached, with finding his place in the dispute, with identifying accurately the sound of his voice in the serried chorus of voices raised during those years.

When they are examined in this light, the array of techniques Fustel used reveals their fragility and, consequently, reveals the ends to which philological and juridical arguments were turned and by which they were shaped. Fustel's philology has been discussed in the first section of this chapter. Let it suffice to add now that often it can be reduced to simple nominalism.

The principal canon of Fustel's philology and the first procedural step in his search for the "truth" was to analyze each text in isolation so that it alone received the full attention of his scholarly research. If one felt more malevolent, he might say it was the first phase of a process that enabled Fustel to keep the text completely in his own hands. This technique was the basis, let us remember, of the polemical exchange with Viollet, in which Fustel appealed to a specific professional criterion: "Let us isolate first, and analyze; we will bring together later."[61]

It follows from such a premise that the text, the single text, was to be extracted not only from its surrounding environment, but also from the entire system of coeval indigenous texts. It came to float in its own neutral space so that the interpreter might slice into it in complete liberty.

This was how Fustel responded to his adversaries: point by point, meticulously, looking always at the detail of the documents, always responding persuasively and in such a way as to leave room for no doubt in the reader's mind.[62]

This rough and simplistic positivism satisfies at first, but shows itself to be a purely formal operation when one looks closer. Fustel hammers home each point in his minute analysis, but the great, varied, complex connective tissue in which and from which the texts take their life escapes him. To cite one example: in a document that dates from 815 there is an inconvenient adjective form, *analis,* applied to land that might lead one to conclude there was a short-term rotation of parcels of land assigned to individuals. This might thus present active evidence of a principle that was typical of all primordial collective modes of landholding.[63] Well then, with a nonchalance worthy of Tribonian,[64] Fustel proposes the substitution of *arialis,* arguing that a copyist probably had made the transcription error of an *n* for *ri.*[65] Or, to cite another example: charters and land grants speak of *vicini,* giving this term a clearly technical meaning referring quite clearly to a communitarian structure. Fustel has no hesitation in giving the term its modern sense of neighbors, which means nothing in the context, but which for him innocently expressed the simple physical proximity of one person to another.[66] One last example: there is a text of Diodorus Siculus on the collective character of the Greek community at Lipari in which the Greek verb *klērouchein* has a certain prominence. Fustel, arousing the bewilderment and the annoyance of Greek scholars,[67] distorts the sense of the word to suit his positions by making it signify only the idea of a definitive division.[68]

Fustel's preferred technique of isolating any text under consideration led him to what we might qualify as pseudo philology, and the pseudo-cultural attitude we have already qualified as nominalistic accompanies it perfectly. What we mean by nominalism is the habit of stopping short at the external manifestations of a document, seizing its formal data—particularly terminological data—without pushing hermeneutic considerations to an understanding of the world that is summed up in the document. Fustel's investigation of the Germanic *Mark* is eloquent testimony to this method. It is a veritable word hunt that for the most part makes the problem of existence and survival within an operative organizational scheme consist in the fixing of an autonomous and formal terminological representation of that scheme.[69] Thus the history of the *Mark* is also and especially the history of a name.[70]

All too often with Fustel we remain on the level of ingenious artifice, of the brilliant formula, of the exercise in artful combination. Too often, with him, the comprehension of a text is based on the identification of its logical mechanisms rather than on how that text is rooted in history. His hermeneutics remains nominalistic, and if we refuse to be dazzled by his many citations, we can see that it suffers from a particularly meager set of cultural applications. For example, the conclusion to the long and demanding work on the *alleu,* which we have discussed, is weak. Fustel stops at a superficial exploration of terms, forms, and formulas and resolves the question of continuity in a complete flattening out of the unfolding of historical process.[71]

What we have said about the philological aspect of Fustel's work must be repeated and amplified concerning its juridical aspects. In fact, Fustel goes no further than a perception of the enormous importance of the law in any attempt to understand the historical milieu.

> In this study that they claimed to have made of the most intimate character of peoples, they have in fact omitted the Law, that is to say, what was the essential. In the last analysis, this brilliant superstructure has been built on a series of confusions that they have created between the community of a people and family coproprietorship, between community of ownership and undivided tenure, between agrarian community and village commons.[72]

The appeal to methodology is exemplary. Any historian would be ill-advised to study a dimension of society as tied to profound, basic options as the relation of men to things if he deprives himself of the invaluable point of view that law offers. It is law that permits him to penetrate beyond the variability of daily life to the inner character of custom. The tragicomic aspect of Fustel's argument comes from the fact that his criticism of others appears most applicable to himself: the second part of this passage seems better designed to describe the results of his work than that of his adversaries.

Fustel's fundamental "truth"—the perfect antithesis to the collectivists' thesis—was that the phenomenon of community ownership of property could be reduced to forms of communality, that is, of coownership, condominium, or the agglomeration of individual proprietary holdings, or to family property, where family is restricted to its most limited sense. And this "truth" was founded on the very confusions and equivocal interpretations that Fustel complained of.

Fustel's work is poor in juridical notions.[73] He was largely indifferent to the complex framework of juridical organization, and for this reason he was incapable of grasping the significance and the value of a tradition, of a technical instrument, or of a legal practice. His entire knowledge of law was condensed in the clear and schematic pages of the *Précis* of Calixte Accarias.[74] But what Accarias offered to Fustel was the final result of Roman juridical digests, in their turn digested and filtered by a nineteenth-century Romanist trained in rationalizations and the virtuosities of exegesis. In other words, he offered a framework that was surely the one least well adapted to a real *understanding* and evaluation of the apparently incoherent data of high medieval and medieval practice.

The key to the classical code could not ever have served to decipher and translate all of the richness of the social language of the Middle Ages. We realize this when we see Fustel do his utmost to relegate to simple usages situations in which things were subject to the control of members of communitarian organizational structures. He makes a clear *quid iuris* of this ownership, and he fixes it in the person of the holder or holders of title to the property.

Here is an example of this: a document reflects a controversy over certain common rights of usage over a forest. Fustel teaches:

> If the word *communes* is found there, it applies to *usus,* not to *terrae.* All of the land is obviously subject to the full ownership of the abbot, the count, or the prince: not the slightest fraction is common land.[75]

The opposition of *dominium* to *usus,* applied to medieval reality, is one of the most misleading schematic notions possible.[76] It indicates a conceptual opposition between will and nature that was, for a range of reasons, totally unknown to medieval man and that instead betrays the thinking and cultural preparation of one trained in the classics.

Probably Fustel thought he had fulfilled his duty to keep up to date—in accordance with a cultural attitude widespread in the French ruling class of the nineteenth century—by having a popular manual of the Institutes of Roman Law on display on his desk. All that he would have had to do, however, to discover that a different current of thought could suggest noticeably different interpretations would have been to glance at Beseler, at Gierke, or at the Germans in general. The German jurists had the merit of pointing out communitarian structures, which they qualified conventionally, artificially, but significantly as *condominia iuris germanici.*[77] It was in this sense that the collectivists used the term condominium, although someone with Roman or Romanistic blinders might have defined these same manifestations of the relation of subject and goods as *usus.* It was these structures, moreover, that gave weight to the *effective* over the *valid* and enabled scholars to find in the effective an element that belonged to the realm of property.

Fustel lacked more than the sensitivities of a jurist, however. He lacked also the techniques that trained jurists use in the reading of a text. He was customarily incapable of perceiving superimposed layers or differences of perspective; he flattened and schematized the data before him.[78] In this way, he missed the technical sense, and therefore the historical significance, of the term *vicinus,* a notion the law had reduced from the level of the general to that of the specific. He also failed to perceive the logical gap that separates the private condominium and collective property, so that Laveleye, whose juridical training was solid, found it easy to demonstrate all of the appalling ingenuousness and lack of foundation in Fustel's arguments.[79] In the same way, Fustel did not realize that the absence of documentation on the presumed village communities, against which he builds a weighty argument *e silentio,* sprang from the very nature of these communities. This any jurist could have seen with the help of common sense alone.[80]

We cite these examples to show that the entire cultural framework of our Parisian historian, which should have been made of solid philology and juridical competence, the prerequisites of research into the concept of property, was not in reality constructed on objective foundations. It represented rather the exploitation—with a greater or lesser degree of skill—of a textual and institutional reality to serve the basic thesis of the writer. It made the "truth" of texts and institutions dependent on the "truth" of the writer.

Fustel's case is rare: seldom has a scholar so beaten his breast over other scholars' crimes of partiality and subjectivity, and seldom has one affirmed his own personality with so much arrogance[81] or shown less openness to voices other than his own.

When we analyze Fustel as a scholar, we see in him a knobby, self-enclosed construction made of thoughts, convictions, certitudes, and humors that was completely formed before he began his researches. The position that was opposed to historical forms of collective property was a "truth" to which historical fact must accommodate itself, because it was for Fustel a moral certitude impossible to abjure.

He declared, speaking of the "collectivists":

> It must be for them a conviction, an article of faith that nothing can shake, and they will always be able to bend some texts to that conviction and to that faith.[82]

Whether he was conscious of it or not, the very procedures he imputed to his adversaries were his own, and all his research was equally based on an act of faith.

It is the subterranean moral current that moves behind Fustel's impeccable citations, his prolix enumerations, his long pages of exegesis seasoned with insupportably preachy erudition, that makes them seem to us nominalistic exercises, nothing but forms, names, and shadows detached from historical experience.

René Clair, that supremely amiable film director of our own times, gave a speech on the occasion of his election to the Académie Française, as is customary. In it he expressed his surprise and his slight discomfiture in finding himself, a "creator of shadows," among so many learned persons.[83] Maker of shadows: the professional label that René Clair gave himself suits Fustel perfectly. The direction was masterly and the story line that carried the characters and their surroundings was coherent; but were these the expression of a living society, of a culture set in history, or rather a brilliant and persuasive shadow play, an intrigue filtered through the overabundant personality of the director, whose mind was taken up with the projection of his own message?

A close reading of the polemic on primitive property and on collective forms of property would make one lean toward the second hypothesis. If Fustel criticized the romantic evocations of the primitive community and of its manifestations in history as being shadows, so too was shadow the omnipresence of individual property, and perhaps it was an effective and constant presence more in the historian's will than in the multiformity of the life of society.[84] Behind his pages we sense the able hands of the director, composing the actors, the gestures, and the actions. On these pages we see a scenario in which the editing is skillful, the actors have their parts to play, and the dialogue runs freely and smoothly from beginning to end.

5 The Forms and Substance

of a Debate:

Following Fustel

*

Fustel de Coulanges was the chief spokesman for those who shared the individualist point of view in their campaign to repulse the new theories that threatened their compact historical and philosophical constructions, but he was not alone. He appears as protagonist in this drama because he was deeply and personally involved in the debate, because he dedicated many works to the subject, and because the high level and the sonority of his contributions guaranteed that his voice would be widely heard. But there are other reasons why Fustel's attitudes shaped successive contributions to the controversy. He insisted—even if on a largely formal level—on keeping his own polemical exchanges within the limits of professional historical discourse, thus parrying the objections of the new theoreticians by hitting at their cultural foundations. Furthermore, he insisted—in spite of his own passionate and idealizing temperament—on maintaining a high level of cultural integrity in his discourse. Thanks to him, the debate, although heated, remained marked by this high sense of cultural purpose.

Although the clash between opposing social and economic systems undoubtedly lay behind this controversy and provided its hidden scenario, the debate was carried on by men of culture and turned around cultural options. The participants were more likely to choose as a weapon a passage from Tacitus or a piece of archaeological evidence than notions involving libertarian economics, class struggle, the doctrine of surplus value, and so forth. The flood of interests that Laveleye, as an economist, saw no reason to limit were formally brought back to a more clearly defined channel by Fustel: into historical, historico-economic, and historico-juridical channels. This was the terrain on which Fustel chose to fight, where he thought his adversaries could be beaten and where the better part of the controversy did in fact take place, starting with the immediate and "innocent" objective of reestablishing scientific fact.

In Fustel's wake, aside from an investigation somewhat marginal to our interests by the English historian Frederic Seebohm[1] and an essay by Lothar Dargun aimed at refuting Laveleye that was more ethno-geographical than historical,[2] we first see a work by an American, Denman Waldo Ross.[3] This book, *The Early History of Land-holding among the Germans,* was the result of long years of research. It was published in Boston in 1883, and recalls Fustel at his most typical by its general outline, its methodology, and its polemical virulence.

Ross was familiar at least with the anticollectivist position found in Fustel's work on landholding in Greece, which figures prominently among his rather sparse references to the literature on the subject.[4] In fact, Ross's work could be considered a detailed development and demonstration of Fustel's premises in that book.

Ross's work is constructed as an attack on scholars who are never honored by specific mention, but always referred to contemptuously and generically in the collective, as "the advocates of the communism theory," or "the advocates of a primitive communism."[5] For Ross, they committed the gross error of mistaking cases of simple undivided property for collective ownership. According to him, the right of first occupant had pertained originally in the primitive Germanic world, and when family communities later came into being, there was not anything even resembling common ownership of land, but only undivided property that was virtually divisible, like any condominium.[6] We see here the central thesis of our capricious but talented Parisian in a bland reformulation, supported by weak argumentation and by a partial and partisan examination of the available documentation.[7]

The Little Island of Nantucket

The man and the work that best carried forward Fustel's principles, however, were Emile Belot[8] and his work on the colonization of the North American island of Nantucket.[9] This work tested Fustel's positions on strictly historical grounds, but it also displays clearly the ideology underlying their common effort on the level of culture, giving us further proof of the accuracy of our interpretation.

Nantucket entered history and Western civilization when, in 1671, a group of twenty-seven fugitives from religious persecution in Massachusetts acquired the land and began the process of establishing a settlement there. Belot's investigation follows carefully the formation of civil society on the island, and it isolates one element characteristic of their organization of landholding on which Belot dwells at some length and on which he bases the organization of his essay. The settlers established simultaneously three types of landholding, according to the nature of the terrain involved: individual ownership, common ownership, and an intermediate type combining certain elements of both.[10]

There is little to remark in this, save one thing: society was born on Nantucket as if by magic in the year of Our Lord 1671 in a setting of primordial nature. The colonists were thus the first men to project their influence over a nature of pure phenomena, both vegetable and animal. For Belot, this little Atlantic island was not just an anonymous strip of land, but a marvelous laboratory in which to discern, decipher, and test something approaching the primordial behavior of man first setting up his own social reality—and this within the reach of history, in the seventeenth century.

What interests Belot particularly is that when this "first" man, unburdened of preceding involvements and free of complexes, makes his first contact with the natural reality of the island, he should modify that nature by establishing simultaneously three types of landholding. Belot hastens to draw a conclusion:

> We might be led to believe that in ancient times, as on Nantucket two hundred years ago, this simultaneity could just as easily have occurred, and that the question of the anteriority of agrarian communism or of individual property should not be resolved but done away with.[11]

It does not occur to our good Belot that those first men may have been the first on Nantucket on that occasion, but that they had come from Massachusetts; that they had come from a continent that was by then civilized and carried within them an accumulation of principles, concepts, and prejudices that were hardly likely to be rubbed out in their fresh contact with the island's untouched hills, streams, and woods. Like the shepherds of Arcadia, these colonists came from the bewigged society of the seventeenth century. Doubtless, the island could reflect accurately the difficulties of primitive man in setting up a process of colonization, but it could not possibly reproduce the psychological isolation of primitive man. Nor was it of much relevance that, as Belot notes, the colonists set up structures in Nantucket that resembled the customs of their Scottish heritage and which, in turn, recalled even more remote structures of Germanic culture.[12] The island was and remained an artificial mirror of primitive society—even more removed from primitive times than the data put together in the ethnological and comparative researches of Emile de Laveleye.

Whether Belot's conclusion was true or false, well- or ill-founded, he used it well to serve his purposes. The presence of varied forms of landholding seemed at first to lead Belot to positions of historical relativity and detachment,[13] but during the course of his investigation, the meaning he sees and the aim he is pursuing become increasingly evident, until they negate his professed historiographical purposes.

If one reads Belot's treatise to the end, it is clear that it belongs in the realm of apologetics. Belot takes a position in deliberate contrast to Laveleye's,[14] to that of the *Kathedersozialismus* group, and to that of all those who, in his view, seek demagogically to feed the "confused aspirations of the multitude" by repeating insipid archaisms[15] or who try to "give a reasonable form to that which basically does not depend on reason."[16] For Belot, it was individual property that was rational and one with man's nature. Individual property was the supreme means by which the subject leaves his mark on external reality and, by his own efforts, ties it indissolubly to himself.[17] In Belot's logic, this was why only individual property could be identified with human progress and stand for the moment when civilization took over from crude collective forms of appropriation.[18]

What irritated Belot, as it did Fustel, was that the new theories attempted to offer a rational and historical basis to collective forms and, through them, to socialistic theories in general.[19]

> The socialists need not look, then, among recollections, nor among the debris of ancient laws for the justification of their systems. If they can believe that the future belongs to them, it is certainly not history that encourages them to such experiments. For the more society has become perfected, the more man has gained in intelligence, the more the number of proprietors has grown, and the more the forms of individual property have multiplied. The theorists of communism do not even have the option of placing the existence of their retrograde ideal at a hypothetical origin, before all the progress of modern civilization, since the first ancestors of the Indo-European race practiced complete and hereditary private property.[20]

The "discovery" that on Nantucket twenty-seven settlers brought into being a society in which several different forms of landholding were practiced did not serve, then, to enable all of those forms to be considered historically. Quite to the contrary: Belot picks out only collective property as historically motivated, and he seems to consider only individual property worthy of his attentions because original and nonartificial.

For him, the question of the anteriority of agrarian collectivism or individual property was a problem that should be done away with because it might suggest the principle that collective ownership is natural, because it might raise a question that threatened to weaken unjustifiably the position of individual property. To sweep away the problem would not mean for Belot to deny the slightest structure based in natural law in favor of any sort of real situation. It would only reconfirm the principle of the primacy of individual property, which he saw as carrying within itself sufficient vitality and rationality to suffocate any pretension to legitimacy on the part of alternative forms of property.

Even if collective ownership had been a real presence in the primordial stages of human history, Belot seems to teach, it was important to note that it did not precede individual property, that both forms were found at the frontier between history and the state of nature, both acting as a stimulus and as a rule of action for primitive man. What counted for Belot was to have discovered in that very first moment the instinct for and the act of individual appropriation of land that had never been repudiated during the successive development of history; to have declared there was an unbroken continuity between that beginning and all that evolved subsequently; and to have identified one unchanging element in associative living that reached from the dawn of time up to that very hour and on into the future.

The constancy of individual property in human history must, Belot reasons, be a sign of its inherent rationality. On the other hand, collective forms had been forgotten and had reappeared—even, he admitted, in primitive society—only when necessitated by particular, usually geographic-agronomic circumstances. Individual property represented an option congenial to the deepest nature of the subject as *socius*—or rather, a universal moment in his relation to things. Collective property represented an option that occurred occasionally and that could be changed or forgotten.

Belot's argument is a good deal less carefully developed than Fustel's. It limps along among inconsistencies and weak arguments, richer in appeals to natural law than in historical analysis. In the course of his work, however, he confesses what motivated him—a modern man deeply involved in the defense of his vision of the social world against the innovative ideas—to take up the story of a modest piece of land.

Nantucket functioned for him as a model to be opposed to another model. It was a laboratory, a workshop in which to cast a universal mold. The "sandy little isle situated on the forty-first northern latitude" that maps had often erroneously omitted took on a universal value for him and served as a living model to confute Laveleye and the socialists. Nantucket was not a historical document, subject to the contingencies of space and time: it was the glorious banner of possessive individualism, the bulwark of Western civilization in the defense of that individualism. Since it was in itself a value, it was an absolute.

Belot, who had lashed out at preconceived notions and theses based on absolutes, had created an absolute himself, raising the small, sandy island out of the changeable waters of the Atlantic to the paradise reserved for archetypes. His researches, rather than satisfying any archaeological curiosity, served as strategy for a great battle or, better, as material for a holy crusade. Nantucket was the instrument of a struggle in which the heart's reasons and political fears are poured out and mixed in equal measure.

On Belot's pages, the contrast between the particular and the general, between a most modest documentation and extremely generalized conclusions, stands out clearly as proof of the inner imbalance in the whole of his research.

Furthermore, in spite of his declared intention to remain on the neutral and impartial ground of historical documents, Belot left that terrain all too often to fly high in the skies of philosophical speculation; so high that from the height Nantucket, *"petite île"* can no longer be grasped in its geographical contours of land and ocean but assumed the vague but fixed shape of an idea.

6 The Forms and Substance

of a Debate:

Against Fustel

The "Advocates of Primitive Communism"

Schroeder has said that there were texts proving the community
of the march in the seventh century, but he did not cite a single
one of them. Then M. Kowaleski copied Schroeder; then M.
Dareste copied Kowaleski, then M. Glasson copied M.
Dareste.[1]

In this passage from his last work Fustel takes a retrospective look at his
adversaries that, as we have seen, nonchalantly reduces the entire controversy to an overworked commonplace.

Fustel's oversimplification was correct in at least one respect:
although the opinions ranged against him cannot be judged as amorphous
repetitions of one another and although each has its distinguishing marks
and particular shadings, all of the men that held them joined together to
reject Fustel's thesis, perhaps with differing motivations, but as if with
one voice.

We have already examined the contributions of the few scholars
who aligned themselves with Fustel. These scattered, sporadic, and fairly
disconnected statements were more and more submerged in an increasing
acceptance of the premises of the "collectivists." In the decade between
1880 and 1890 we see Fustel himself reinforcing the rising spiral of his bitter
attacks, while single responses emerged, interacted with one another, and
became defined in a broadly varied historiographic position, united—with
the exception of the few inevitable outbursts of individualism[2]—to reject
Fustel's approach as antihistorical.

To repeat once again, what interests us here is the general configuration of the controversy; the controversy as a means of understanding not so much the remote objects of study examined by the opposing camps as the adversaries' own patrimony of ideas. Limiting ourselves to this objective, one basic datum that should be noted is who these men who opposed Fustel were. We see in Paul Viollet,[3] Georges Platon,[4] Marcel Thévenin,[5] and Paul Fournier[6] historians of jurisprudence; Ernest Glasson[7] was a historian of jurisprudence and a trial law specialist; Rodolphe Dareste de la Chavanne[8] was a historian of jurisprudence, a comparativist, and a judge by profession; and Maxim Kovalevski[9] was a historian of jurisprudence and a sociologist. Henry-Marie d'Arbois de Jubainville,[10] "who was the most authoritative representative of Celtic studies in France" as well as being "the only French Celticist prepared in juridical studies"[11] combined great erudition in philology with solid juridical preparation. Léon Aucoc[12] was a professor of public law and a judge; and Emile de Laveleye[13] and Karl Lamprecht[14] were economists.

In other words, if we understand the situation correctly, these men were all historians of more than general preparation.[15] The additional lenses that the jurist or the economist added to the historian's vision helped them to discern dimensions and perspectives otherwise unperceived or neglected. Their key for deciphering the historical world had a richer vocabulary than Fustel's simple and simplistic one.[16] What might have appeared flattened and continuous in Fustel's works sprang into unsuspected relief in the stereoscopic vision of the jurist or the economist. What emerged was a multidimensional, infinitely more complex world, in which chronology had its modest importance, but in which structures, institutions, techniques, and systematic orders of being were thrown into high relief.

These men were not interested in the single text, the episodic datum, the formula, or the formal expression of a term. Never satisfied with the apparent or the superficial, they refused to isolate the single tessera from the complex of an entire mosaic structure, seeing that as a myopic activity that precluded global comprehension. Perhaps Fustel could reduce his research on the *Mark* to an investigation of terminology;[17] the jurist and the economist saw this as totally unsatisfactory. They demanded to deal not with a *flatus vocis* or a scriptural sign, but with a schema operating in the effective reality of the historical context.[18]

If Fustel looked to the particular and exercised all of his ingenious arrogance on it, they looked to the global, to the whole, to the comprehensive. "Let us never isolate: let us always bring things together" had been the criticism and the advice of the jurist Viollet when he reviewed the first of Fustel's major works on the subject of property. And, as we already know, Fustel's prompt reply was a categorical: "Let us isolate first, and analyze; we will bring together later."[19]

The isolation and comparison of data are not to be seen as just the innocuous subject of a noisy skirmish, nor were they just hard-hitting and brilliant witticisms to be batted back and forth. They represented the confrontation of two methodological positions, of two discernibly different modes of perceiving what it meant to write history. There was perhaps on one side a stronger effort to divide up the stuff of history to enable the researcher to exercise closer control over his material. In this way, the historian's store of moral forces and ideologies could be exploited to the profit of a historiographic line that, in spite of its positivistic appeals to sources, hinged particularly on the interpretation of the datum. On the other side, there was a greater sensitivity to effective reality, a greater taste for construction, a greater humility, and a greater detachment.

Fustel argued with virulence. The views he espoused and the conclusions he reached were clearly defined, neat, and as little open to question as articles of faith. This induces anyone analyzing his thought to look, as we have done, beyond the documents for the sources of that certitude and the reasons behind that virulence. The argumentation of the "collectivists" was calmer, more carefully shaded, and more varied.

If there was one thing the "collectivists" rejected firmly in the author of La cité antique, it was his methodological inaccuracy, his lack of constraint, and his evident manipulation of materials. These were qualities more proper to the flamboyant style of a prestidigitator than to the finely honed judgments of a man of serious study. On this point the "collectivists" were firm: they did not dispute Fustel's talent but, subjecting to their irony the array of documents that served this talent,[20] they condemned Fustel as a nominalist[21] and insisted that "his procedures are the contrary of a method."[22]

The Polemical Testimony of Ernest Glasson and Henry d'Arbois de Jubainville

Singularly enough, two polemical essays having the form and weight of a volume appeared in 1890 to confront Fustel's abundant production with a formal réponse. They were: Les communaux et le domaine rural à l'époque franque—Réponse à M. Fustel de Coulanges by Ernest Glasson,[23] and Recherches sur l'origine de la propriété foncière et des noms de lieux habités en France (Période celtique et période romaine), by Henry d'Arbois de Jubainville.[24]

Glasson's work did not arouse much surprise. He had already been involved in the controversy for some time, and his viewpoint as a professional jurist, a professor and specialist in positive law was well known. Thus it was to be expected when he denounced the "incredible travesties that the author has permitted himself,"[25] when he turned the technical and unequivocal language of jurisprudence to accuse Fustel of being a "false intellectual" and of using "false materials,"[26] and when he noted Fustel's arbitrary exegetical positions[27] and his ignorance of the law.[28]

The voice of d'Arbois de Jubainville had more significance in the context of this controversy. It was in fact remarkable that, aside from the anguished reaction of the jurist Glasson and the calmer rebuttal of the economist Laveleye, the bitterest opposition to Fustel and the toughest, most tightly constructed refutation of his theses came from a scholar of experience and erudition who, like Fustel, placed himself on a plane of rigorous historical documentation. It was the greatest expert in Celtic language and civilization who attacked the author of the *Alleu* frontally[29] and reproached him with stubbornly advancing preconceived ideas and defending them at all costs,[30] with using incorrect methodological instruments,[31] and with frankly distorting the thoughts of others and the sense of documentary sources.[32]

When d'Arbois points out Fustel's intolerance for that historically defined reality that is the text, he dismantles Fustel's credibility as a philologist. Furthermore, he claims, both the ancient text—Caesar or Tacitus—and the modern text—his own works—came through Fustel's hands in a sorry state.

In his essay of 1887 on land ownership in Gaul the great French Celticist specifically rejected Fustel's concept of a system of private land ownership that showed characteristics proper to the Roman *dominium*, criticizing the use of such a notion as substantially anachronistic. At the same time, however, he warned against espousing a notion of collective property as that term was defined by the modern consciousness, preferring to speak of a general situation of landholding marked by an intrinsic uncertainty.[33]

In a critical discussion of d'Arbois's essay on the civilization of the Gauls, Fustel accused d'Arbois of "seeing indivision of the land among them."[34] But this was a deliberate betrayal of the sense of the essay and a distortion of d'Arbois's thesis. Fustel must have read the work in the light of his own dominant preoccupation. He evidently saw in it an image of a system of landholding that could have led to an argument in favor of a "collectivist" solution and, armed with his individualistic moral bent and diffident of any conclusion that did not clearly support private property, he identified it with extreme solutions and thus condemned it without recall.

In his reading of this essay Fustel takes apart the objective texture of an adversary work—or one he took to be adversary—and recomposes its elements with subjective contributions of his own. He thus produced a version of the text whose contents seemed more pre-established by the badly focused lenses of his interpretation than established in the print of d'Arbois's text. And d'Arbois was right to object to the deceptiveness of such a historiographical method on the part of one who was a positivist, a scholar, and a philologist. This method might be comprehensible in the researches of a Montesquieu, who asked of history data to exploit in support of his own ideas. It would be unacceptable in the work of a Mabillon or of any other humble witness to the past:

> One may admire in him an heir of Montesquieu, but it is difficult to be at once the disciple of this great thinker . . . and to observe throughout a work of erudition the meticulous rules to which the Benedictines were once subjugated.[35]

What counted in Fustel—and d'Arbois knew this well and gave him credit for it[36]—was "an idea" more powerful than any critical interpretation, more vigorous than any documentation, because it touched on his moral certitudes, that is, it touched on absolutes.

Glasson noted with discomfort that the historical world of Fustel was divided in all that concerned systems of land ownership into two clear hemispheres. In one view, all—forests, pasture lands, arable lands—was the object of collective forms of appropriation. In the other view, everything was the object of exclusive, perpetual, and unquestioned full dominion.[37] There were no shades between, there was no mediation, no interchange between the two. This would have been for Fustel as inconceivable as compromise between good and evil.

The Message of the "Collectivists"
The "collectivists" one must admit, presented a very different picture from that of Fustel's idealized, openly moralizing vision. Although they tended to exploit the forms of collective appropriation that history offers, they avoided Manichaean oppositions and schematizations. Although Maurer thought he saw a structure resembling the *Mark* at every turn of the way and Laveleye fell in love with his subject to the point that his vision became one-sided, excesses in interpretation were particularly criticized by those whom Fustel condemned with the defamatory name of "collectivists."[38]

One element basic to all the "collectivists" was that they accepted the existence of landholding forms of communistic structure without prejudices and without preconceptions and showed a high degree of openness toward more flexible and varied conclusions. In this way Kovalevski did not hesitate to trace the origins and the development of primitive collective forms of ownership differently from Laveleye,[39] and

Glasson saw no difficulty in noting historical moments at which widely diverse forms of property were practiced simultaneously.[40] D'Arbois, with exquisite historicist caution, refused to use the term "collective property" regarding the Gauls previous to the time of Caesar and preferred to speak of absence of individual property.[41] Similarly, Thévenin[42] and Platon,[43] after an unconditional rejection of Fustel's thesis, qualified their own conclusion on the subject of property as much as possible, and Aucoc, after a calm discussion of Belot's essay, could not bring himself to accept the principle of collective appropriation as one that could be translated into the present.[44]

Although they occasionally colored or overemphasized one element or another, theirs was a serene and open vision of the problem, based largely in cultural considerations. They showed increasing discomfort with Fustel's unshakable guiding idea and with its ideological cast. They proclaimed this openly and they showed no hesitation in tying Fustel's systematization to the old fabulist schemes of the beginning of the age of the bourgeoisie, noting that the work of the author of La cité antique "is destined to give new luster to the old individualistic hypothesis concerning the origin of landed property"[45] and denouncing the philosophical and economic postulates in favor of individual property as a series of a priori principles.[46]

Opposition to the dense and implacable individualistic ideology that sustained Fustel did not become with the "collectivists" in the great debate, who were for the most part historians of jurisprudence or economic historians, an ideological message in the opposite direction. If there were some more than transitory socialistic strains—and there were, particularly in Laveleye—they were mixed with and lost in the preponderance of cultural criteria. The result is a historical and doctrinal context that was not only complex and varied, but that does not easily lend itself to schematic interpretations. It is worth looking at more carefully for a moment.

Even the most rapid glance at the "collectivists'" theoretical and historiographical background would have to reach beyond Laveleye and Maine—whose contributions to the discussion of alternative forms of property-holding we have perhaps treated at sufficient length—to go to the heart of the Historical School of jurisprudence. It would have to note with some degree of precision how the testimony of remote or persisting forms of collective ownership evoked, supported, and linked together, openly or not, the thought of Grimm, Waitz, Maurer, Thudichum, and Sohm.

The array of values that the Historical School had made its own, together with the cultural model expressed by Savigny, weighed on these men as they did on the greater part of juridical historiography in the second half of the nineteenth century. The methodological premises and the indications for subject-matter that originated with the *historische Rechtsschule* and with Germanistic historiography circulated freely among the jurists involved in the dispute. This interchange was facilitated by the lack of the nationalistic prejudices that were undeniably present and operating as anti-Germanism in Fustel,[47] and by the tie among those who speak a unifying language of scholarship, here juridical.[48] Furthermore, the moment in cultural history to which the economists refer—as Laveleye and Lamprecht demonstrate—does not change by virtue of the symbiotic connection that ties the Historical School of economics to the lesson of Savigny and Puchta. It is undeniable that there was a romantic attitude, or at least an antipositivistic attitude, prevalent in the complex play of ideal forces that encouraged the emergence to social consciousness of collective schemes of landholding.

Read Glasson,[49] Lamprecht,[50] and Kovalevski:[51] to the continuous, exasperating appeal that Fustel makes to the certainty, the clarity, and the precision of the documents and to the document as the *voice* of historical reality, they oppose an appeal to nonofficial history, the history that is consolidated in custom. It is signaled by the *silence* of the public document and has instead its own *voice* on the level of what effectively happened, the level on which spontaneous juridical forms circulate and the spirit of the people is incarnate.

How the law was pictured seemed to follow a dual route, running in two directions on two levels. One was marked by forms of public power and the more official aspects of life. The other was marked by that impalpable but nevertheless historically efficacious instrument that is custom and that, on the level of juridical sources, can be found being continually translated into consuetudinarian reality. Occasionally, as in the case of the Russian Kovalevski, who echoes here whole segments of the heterodox and anarchistic Russian thought of the second half of the nineteenth century,[52] this dualistic interpretation was seasoned with nationalistic and populistic elements. With Kovalevski, we see a codified, imperial law of Western, particularly of German, stamp tied to the ruling dynasty, opposed to an unwritten law tied to the Russian land, autochthonous, and more sensitive to social demands by its consuetudinarian nature.[53] This second law was the one in whose shade the *mir* flourished, that neglected but wide-branching presence in the life of the great Russian countryside. The collective modes of agrarian landholding were rooted in this terrain and in that time-honored usage, watched over by the silence of custom, they realized their popular vocation on the level of ownership.

It would be a disservice to many of these scholars, however, to try to limit their thought to an echo of Maurer and an attitude, so to speak, of juridical romanticism. Maine was there next to Maurer to invite them to practice comparison. And with Maine, Le Play, Haxthausen, Anatole Leroy-Beaulieu, and many others invited them to partake of a rich and varied banquet of disciplines: sociology, economics, ethnology, folklore, and comparative jurisprudence.[54] What we have defined as work preparatory to the debate offered the jurist and the economist a mine of data and an array of instruments designed to broaden the more traditional views and to lead them into the temptation of alternative views. One must add that Maine's stimulating ideas had freed many a mind from the subjection of Romanism.

Although the shift was the result of a complex of circumstances, of complex intellectual preparations and complex viewpoints, one can at least say with certainty that many shifted their historiographical interests from individual property as the Romanistic tradition understood it to different forms of the appropriation and organization of goods. Certainly, what motivated these scholars was as complex as Fustel's position was simple, linear, and easy to categorize in the history of ideas. If Fustel in his solipsism represents a culturally impermeable entity whose explanation must be sought deep within his moral and social beliefs, these other scholars showed a singular permeability, an openness to receive and register ideas that puts them—and this is the historian's cross and his chief delight—at the center of a tangled web of motives and data.

There is a question that must be asked: To what extent can these antiquarian pursuits be connected with the social question seething throughout Europe during those years? For Laveleye our answer was clearly that there was a close connection, and we have invoked the social background at several stages along our route as of primary importance in the understanding of this doctrinal duel.

One must keep in mind, however, that the case of the economist from Liège represents an *unicum,* that he was a personality capable of operating on two fronts. But what of those less able to cross that cultural frontier? Echoes from the external world were filtered and arranged into historiographic analyses. The choice of collective property as the protagonist in the drama of Western history—or, in any event, its preference over quiritarian property—had exclusively cultural reasons for being. It seems clear that collective forms of landholding were not put forward because of any adherence to the socialist movement or because they represented a sociopolitical model. They emerged because historiographic methods furnished with a richly varied range of investigative techniques brought scholars to discover them.

But how can one explain the attention that scholars paid to these organizational modes, the sensitivity that enabled them to note and emphasize such forms, sometimes even their movement of sympathy toward them? Here, on the level of the sociology of the thought of these intellectuals, reasoning becomes complex and arduous. First of all, the fact that these men were for the most part jurists and economists gave them a high degree of familiarity with sociological and ethnological data, encouraged them to make comparisons, and set up a friction in their minds between historical data and the patrimony of institutions and ideas that operated in the established order around them. This undoubtedly sharpened their sensitivity to social questions. And their being historians as well as jurists and economists added the sensitivities typical of the historian to their critical awareness of social problems, turning the mechanisms of comparison to what was, what had been, and what would come into being.

We have cited as typical the example of Ernest Glasson, a learned medievalist and a sensitive researcher in the field of the relation between civil codes and the labor question.[55] What moved Glasson was not at all the urgings of socialism, but an intelligently reformistic impulse. He proposed filling in gaps that in 1886 were clearly perceptible in the system of laws codified eighty years before. He also proposed the enrichment of the types of people recognized by the normative system by the addition of the worker and his family. He had no intention of reversing the ordered flow in the hourglass that bourgeois society represented, but only of bringing that flow up to date through an attentive reading and a historicist interpretation of the signs of the times.

To be conscious of the social dimension in their work meant for many of these scholars to be conscious also of the social question. But it is hardly permissible to search among the hidden mechanisms of their complex psychology to separate brutally the threads—sometimes invisible, tenuous, hardly indicated, sometimes solid and apparent—that tie, perhaps on the level of the subconscious, their penchant for the forms of appropriation practiced by the ancient Franks, say, to an awareness of a society in ebullition.

One must keep in mind the tangle of doctrines, with all of its continuity of functional, culturally motivated connections, that was interwoven among the Historical Schools in law and economics and the *Kathedersozialismus* group. One must also recall both the cultural and the political significance of the "Germanism" of someone like Laveleye, who took an active role at the Eisenach conferences,[56] or of someone like Vito Cusumano, who popularized German ideas in Italy and championed a revision of the traditional set of juridical and economic principles relative to property.[57] Just as significant on a cultural and political level was the anti-German attitude of someone like Fustel, which we have already discussed, or of someone like Francesco Ferrara, the chief Italian spokes-man for the classical school of economics and for the most inveterate liberalism.[58]

When the gap that exists in current historiography on this enor-mously important doctrinal tangle has been filled, as we would hope, with a rich group of investigations in the various sectors of the history of economic and juridical thought, we will have a clearer idea of the con-nections among culture, political consciousness, and movements for political reform during those years. As of now, it is not even enough to outline the extremely varied panorama of thought that ranges from the deep involvement of Laveleye to the detachment of d'Arbois de Jubain-ville, with attention to all of the varied and even discordant views and interpretations found there.[59] Anyone who analyzes the group of thinkers ranged against Fustel must also keep in mind the complexity of the his-torical dimension of their ideas, must refuse to be satisfied with explana-tions that are purely formal, and must not deprive himself of any technical means of interpretation.

✱ *Part Two*

THE ITALIAN EXPERIENCE

7 The Italian

Experience

The Italian "Province": Statistical Surveys and Knowledge on the Local Level

If I leave the broad reaches of Europe to direct attention to what happened within the more modest confines of Italy, isolating out of the complex story of continental happenings a line of development more familiar and closer at hand, it is not because of a pietistic respect for the affairs of my own land, and even less for any absurd desire to reserve for them a position of privilege. It comes rather from a sense of the historical record.

In fact, the Italian "province," seen from several perspectives and on various levels, echoed strongly that controversy and offered a unique "translation" of it. In Italy, the controversy not only invaded the domain of culture but also the more significant domain of practice, and it even affected the preparation of legislation in the unified state.

There is tangible evidence that the nineteenth-century Italian legislator found the problem posed by the existence of collective forms of landholding harrassing even before the advent of political unification, when political groups were drawing together. The phenomenon was so widely prevalent during that period that legislative and administrative measures on the part of the pre-Unification regimes appear at every hand.[1] We see first reference to the *vagantivo*[2] and the *pensionatico*[3] of the Veneto; then the *dominii collettivi* and the *servitù di pascolo* of the Pontifical States;[4] the *ademprivi* in Sardinia;[5] the *usi civici* and the *demanii* in the kingdom of Naples.[6] These were certainly actions that were conspicuous for their number and their possible influence. The frenzy for the redistribution of these commonly held lands and the enthusiastic ef-

121

forts to eliminate these usages had lost their original sense of mission. Still these efforts continued almost through inertia, prolonging a mistaken fideism more proper to the eighteenth century, though not tied to any precise time or place.

It was not until the decade that interests us—roughly from 1880 to 1890–that anything changed. Then, although the typical legislator remained insensitive to the question, the monolith of bourgeois culture behind him began to show zones of permeability or fracture that provided an opportunity for an unbiased and fundamental reconsideration of institutions and problems.

Utopian fervor—if there ever had been any—was miserably quenched in these years: communities were still being dissolved, lands were being released, and *demanii* were being split up, but the idea that those undertakings were useless was becoming increasingly widespread. The concrete connection between those efforts and the enormous growth of the large landed estates of the *latifondo* seemed increasingly evident, while the creation and spread of small productive holdings remained an objective that may have been real or fictive but that was completely thwarted.[7]

If the unconscious optimism of the pre- and post-Unification legislator did not diminish, at least his firm and explicit options, seemingly founded in theological belief, raised some doubts and became a problem of legislative politics. Much had been demolished, but there was much that still remained to demolish; and a dilemma arose that previously would have been unthinkable: whether to persist in such zealous undertakings or to stop short. As the policy of dissolving collective land arrangements and dividing up the land began to fail, collective property was no longer seen as a clearly deleterious survival from the past and became the object of debate. As the image of it became more complex, its structure appeared increasingly worthy of serious consideration.

Two circumstances typical of the Italian "province" worked together to this end: the extent and the broad distribution of the phenomenon as it could be seen in statistical surveys, and the increased consciousness of the phenomenon on the part of certain doctrinal tendencies.

In the years between 1870 and 1880 a laudable zeal for gathering and cataloguing information took hold of the Ministry of Agriculture. Some of the reasons for this can be seen in the nineteenth-century passion for investigation and statistics, which we have already discussed, in a reckless imitation of illustrious transalpine models, and in the desire to help legitimize the existence of the ministry itself, a recently founded and controversial institution menaced from several quarters by demands for its suppression.[8] These combined forces produced an enormous mass of useful data, sponsored and put into organic order by the efforts of the highest administrative authority; and from this data could be drawn an adequate—if not an exhaustive—picture of agrarian Italy of the time.

Thus we see in 1876 the *Relazione intorno alle condizioni dell'agricoltura in Italia;* in the following years the *Notizie e studi sulla agricoltura* published by the Bureau of Agriculture of the Ministry of Agriculture, Industry, and Commerce. In the first of these works an entire chapter of the third volume is devoted to *"Servitù e condominii,"*[9] and in the second we find a remarkable amount of information concerning the various forms of collective appropriation.[10]

All of this was not new, to be sure. But for the first time it became possible to take the measure of the phenomenon, quantitatively and qualitatively, within an organic description of the agrarian life of the nation.

Its vast scope was duly noted. Collective landholding was not restricted to rocky mountain wastes or the most desolate stretches of the southern *latifondo,* to stand as an odious vestige of former feudal tolerations. It was omnipresent in mountain lands as on the plains, in woods and pastures as in lands under cultivation, in the north and south alike, in the Alps as in the Appennines, in Lombardy, in the Veneto, and in Liguria as on the islands. The forms it took in some areas, as in Emilia and Romagna, were rationally organized and fully developed, and it represented a considerable source of wealth and an appreciable part of the nation's agricultural resources.

Its variety and complexity were also noted. Forms of common property and condominiums in private law, undivided *ab immemorabili,* stood next to joint ownerships such as the *partecipanze* and agrarian associations such as the *comunanze,* forms of collective property right and proper, other forms of the division of property involving considerable variation in the particulars of enjoyment, and customary rights, *diritti d'uso civico.* Together these all formed a jumble of particular situations in which each instance had its particular historical origin and juridical nature.

The complexity of the resulting picture was such that it generated doubts about the unequivocal, generic, and axiomatic condemnation of the phenomenon that had been pronounced up to that point. It also raised doubts about the simplistic habit generally respected in the past of lumping all instances together indiscriminately and discarding them together blindly.

The universality and the multivalence of this phenomenon could not but arouse respect, curiosity, and even a willingness to look again and more in detail at the web of historical roots and juridical configurations involved. This range and variety indicated a territory to be explored, a border land only partially known at the edges of the official nation but well within the real nation,[11] within its customs, its consuetudinary reality, and its everyday history, a territory whose reasons for being were probably so solid that they guaranteed its survival in spite of the hostility of governments and members of Parliament.

What emerged from the innocuous sheafs of statistical data, in spite of this hostility, out of reach and perhaps even against the will of the governing class in Italy, was a sense of the richness of historical forms of collective landholding in Italy and, at the same time, an appreciation of their historical and social vitality. In contrast to the indifference with which it had been viewed in the period immediately preceding, "collective property" now fully entered the realm of public consciousness, charged with a number of problems and appearing in itself as a problem that could be assessed only with criteria different from those usually applied in the age that followed the Enlightenment. Beside the image of it as antiquarian medieval bric-a-brac compromised by serfdom and feudalism, another image began to take form, that of a type of landholding situation that was outside the official Romanistic tradition and alternative to it.

This image, a vague outline of which the ministerial *Notizie* had unveiled amid arid figures and interminable lists, was soon after to be described clearly in the context of the extentive *Inchiesta agraria e sulle condizioni della classe agricola* [Agrarian Inquiry into the conditions of the agricultural class], which was initiated in 1877 under the direction of Stefano Jacini. The data thus collected were eloquently presented to the public in a discourse of notable political and cultural importance. But to this we will return more fully later.[12]

Thus it fell to the ministerial publications and to the investigative efforts of the dominant middle class to play a role they neither wanted nor welcomed and the nature of which they did not foresee. Another group of writings drawn forth by the events of the first years of national unity came to play an identical role in a different way, becoming by the 1880s a fact of quantitative importance although of very limited cultural value.

These were years during which a double sense of uneasiness developed. First, the old communitarian agrarian organizations found it difficult to recognize a place for themselves in the structures established by the new legislation, and this caused perplexities, demands for innovation, and dissention among the members of the respective communities. Second, the government authorities themselves saw in these peculiar forms of property-holding the signs of a tradition extraneous, if not contrary, to the form that had the official backing of the kingdom of Italy. For this reason, these forms were either ignored as products of a private autonomy that lay beyond the scope of ordinary statutes, or they were combatted in an attempt to eliminate them, thus giving rise to juridical controversies and doctrinal disputes.

This is exactly what happened in the much-discussed case of the *partecipanze* in Emilia. Since these existed in a region of intense economic activity, they felt the friction of contact with surrounding organizational systems more than other collective arrangements. We see examples among them of communities that drafted new regulations and of others that came to the point where they asked to be dissolved, as was the case of the *partecipanza* of Medicina in 1875.[13] In the other camp, *ex parte rei publicae,* there was no less confusion. The prefect of Bologna, a certain Capitelli, declared this openly when in 1874 he refused to continue to exercise responsibilities over the *partecipanze* that formerly had fallen to the papal legate and declared his own incompetence in the matter in an official decree.[14] Oreste Regnoli, a specialist in civil law and the accredited spokesman for the orthodox position, echoed the same perplexity when he declared himself incapable of fitting the socioeconomic schema of the *partecipanza* into the various juridical systems offered by the Codification of 1865.[15]

We see the same embarrassment in the southern provinces, although there it was born under a different sign as the result of a profoundly different socioeconomic context, a different historical process, and a consequently different juridical situation. There we see furthermore the aggravating circumstances of the outcome—disastrous rather than merely unsatisfactory—of a policy of dividing former collective holdings that had by then lasted for seventy years and that had failed both to instill a new dynamism in the economy and to promote the social redemption of the population.[16]

From these feelings of uneasiness and perplexity, from the very interplay of opposed interests bidding for the immense patrimony of common holdings in *partecipanze, comunanze,* and *demanii* arose a body of literature that was often myopic or one-sided, often blundering or capricious, but that had the historical merit of reopening, airing, and giving wider circulation to the problem. This process had still another peculiarity and had still another—even if completely fortuitous—point to its credit. Since the question often involved judicial defenses and consultive works, it became viewed as more multifaceted, even if it suffered from sharp historiographical distortions. The opposing views and proposals were far removed from historiographical interests. But their clear confrontation—perhaps too clear—brought about a recognition of the complexity of these forms of property-holding as real historical phenomena. To return to the two examples given: this is the value that we must recognize in the small-scale polemic that exploded between Giacomo Cassani and

Antonio Mangilli on the subject of the *partecipanze*[17] and in the literature on the *demanii* in the south, to which even original but sincere
and stimulating men such as Antonio Rinaldi and Luigi Lombardi
contributed.[18]

One cannot yet speak of a discourse endowed with cultural import, nor was it one that revealed a complete consciousness of the historical implications or the social importance of the problem. It was, however,
a discourse that came to be heard with increasing frequency; and among
the many contributing voices, some spoke up in favor of turning to the
question of forms of collective landholding with less hasty attention and a
more open mind.

Thus what represented for the official mind a deviation, an
"anomaly"[19] in the straight and clearly marked path of progress, and what
was therefore seen as a curiosity worthy of a sideshow or of a museum of
the horrors of the past, appeared less deformed as it reacquired complexity
and dignity. This occurred even in this body of literature that we would
like to call practical, that did not appear to belong within the great cultural
currents of Europe even when it was less practical, and that manifested all
the strength of its "vulgar" origins and of its firm ties to knowledge on the
local level.

The Italian "Province": Cultural Attitudes during the 1870s and 1880s

The two local instances we have discussed came to constitute a
concrete starting-place for the rediscovery in Italy of the authentically
historical values of "collective property." In order for Italian culture in
general to appropriate the problem much more was needed. In the years
after 1870, however, an attitude was coming to maturity in the economic
and juridical sciences that did much to prepare for the full and unequivocal theoretical statement of the question in the following decade.

Even today we know too little of the cultural consistency of the
science of jurisprudence in the post-Unification period, and what little we
know is so hastily put together, so marginal, and so superficial that it gives
us no more than a fairly flat picture. Nonetheless, from the moment Italian
juridical historiography had its full of counting the hairs in Theodoric's or
Rotarius's beard and dedicated some—though not many—studies to the
historical context that interests us here, a very varied, richly textured
image of that moment in the history of doctrine begins to take form.
Although we see a chorus obediently repeating its exegetic rosary with
absolute poverty of thought—we refrain from citing particulars on the
many jurists gifted only with good technical habits such as Domenican-
tonio Galdi, Luigi Borsari, Emidio Pacifici-Mazzoni, Francesco Ricci,

Francesco Saverio Bianchi—we also begin to hear voices of another timbre.

The new voices came from men sensitive to the positivism that permeated their cultural climate. One characteristic common to them was the consciousness that any scientific investigation was complex, and that the researcher must above all give heed to a broad spectrum of implications and connections. This consciousness took the form of a clear vocation for interdisciplinary encounters.

This was an epistemological fact that took hold in the entire network of the sciences of the period; but it was of particular importance for the thought of the jurists, who had too often felt the temptations of isolation.

This dimension of juridical science in the post-Unification period has never been sufficiently brought out, but it is the dimension that most accurately characterizes it. Although juridical theoretics stood as a last link in a chain of scientific traditions in the field of law, a chain that was authentically Italian and Roman, it was inserted into a new and relatively well-consolidated sociopolitical structure and became infused with a youthful sense of urgency. At least in its more vital currents, that of the *homines novi,* for example, juridical science was aware of the distance that separated it from the model of common law and the narrow limitations of Romanistic law; and it set out to establish itself on a lasting foundation. Some of the jurists in Italy who took an interest in juridical theory imitated and translated French terminology and French techniques congenial to the legislative constructions of the Codification. There were also legions of Romanists secure in their perennial and immobile satisfaction as compilers of inventories of the truth. But juridical science also felt its cultural solitude and the need to search elsewhere for its own reasons for being and its own meaning.

For this reason, the interdisciplinary approach was nothing but the realization of an elementary urge for survival. This explains that curiosity—occasionally an excessive curiosity—about the natural sciences that led at times to positions of an ingenuous and crude positivism. This explains the intellectual baggage that was constantly weighted with eclecticism and the avid reading of philosophers in a gamut of composite elements that ranged from Hegel and Spencer to their compatriot Vico. This explains the attention paid to economists, sociologists, and ethnologists that on more than one occasion led to an attempt at universal discourse.

What it is important to note is that the new jurist—not the exegete, who continued his fetishistic diversions with fragments of the Codes—did not hold himself aloof from the intelligentsia around him, but tended to join in with them and to find in juridical matters vital ramifications of the nonjuridical. He began to speak, as he had not previously, of Hegel and Vico, of Darwinism and Spencerian ideas, ceding to the frenzy of a Promethean adventure, to the surprising though vain temptation of a search for a new epistemological foundation for the science of jurisprudence. And he worked shoulder to shoulder with the nonjurists, associating himself with them almost as if he hoped for enrichment or rescue from them.[20]

To give a concrete example: in the fertile and compliantly positivistic climate of Hegelian regurgitations and of rediscoveries of Vico that was provided in the 1870s by Naples,[21] the meeting-place of many and varied currents,[22] the philosopher Francesco Fiorentino spoke for this confluence when he founded and directed the *Giornale napoletano di filosofia e lettere, scienze morali e politiche*. This journal had neither a wide influence nor a very long life, but its very title is significant, and even a superficial glance bears out the impression of an attempt to realize the sort of program we have indicated above.

If we open the first number, which appeared in 1875, and if we pause to note the better-known names, we see beside collaborators such as Luigi Settembrini, Giustino Fortunato, and Bartolomeo Capasso, the philosopher of law Luigi Miraglia, who summarizes the evolution of economic thought, Francesco Filomusi Guelfi, who reviews the Italian translation of Jhering's *Der Kampf um's Recht*, and the jurist Antonio Salandra, who discusses at length Laveleye's *De la propriété et de ses formes primitives*. Beginning with the second volume Salandra became a member of the editorial board and wrote a regular column, "Rassegna di studi economici," in which he reported on new developments in theory in Italy and abroad.[23] We see, in other words, a group of open-minded jurists who included exploration in different cultural dimensions in their professional tasks and who saw in a journal of broadly interdisciplinary slant a training ground where they could work and collaborate without being merely tolerated. They also found it to be an instrument congenial to their own intellectual vocations.

We have cited the example of Fiorentino's *Giornale*. But one need only run through the index of the more responsible of the law reviews to note a repudiation of isolation, a breaking of formalistic confines, and the creation of common bases for work.[24] It was indeed in one of these hospitable journals, the well-established *Archivio Giuridico*, directed with intelligence by the Romanist Filippo Serafini, that the young economist Vito Cusumano published in several installments an important essay, "Sulla condizione attuale degli studi economici in Germania" [On the current state of economic studies in Germany].[25] This essay is well known to historians of culture and of economic theory,[26] but it also merits reconsideration here in the context of the maturation of a nonjurist's methodological struggle.

This is an essay in which economic thought is placed in a context—one among many possible—of juridical thought. It is also a living proof of the interdisciplinary interchange that we have indicated, by nature of the complex argument that Cusumano treats even more than by the superficial circumstance of its appearance in this review. Beneath a penetrating analysis of the science of economics in mid-century Germany lay an awareness of its historical vitality that arose from the sense of the unity of the social sciences that providentially came into being in that country during the course of the nineteenth century.

The essay was constructed around a consciousness of the absurdity of dividing the jurist's task from the economist's, a consciousness that derived from a sense of the objective methodological unity founded "in the close connection that there is between political economy and the other political and social sciences."[27] The history of the *Volkswirtschaftslehre* thus constituted the proof of what elementary intuition declared: if it had been able to arrive at results that were universally acclaimed, it was because of the vital interchange between the Historical Schools of law and of economics,[28] between the elaboration of economic theories and the building of the systems of philosophers of law such as Mohl, Stahl, and Ahrens.[29]

When he proposed for the Italy of 1874 an interdisciplinary cultural model tested on the other side of the Alps, Cusumano was merely accentuating a tendency already operative in Italy. What is more, he introduced economic and juridic studies in Italy to an angle of vision that was immediately based on the cultural reality of Germany. The grafting operation that would soon be qualified disparagingly as "economic Germanism"[30] had begun to take form.

If we have singled Cusumano's essay out of an abundant and varied literature, it is not only because it has a specific bearing on our theme, as we will see. The essay was also emblematic of a new state of awareness circulating in economic and juridical thought in the 1880s. It was also characterized by two clear and culturally motivated positions: the vocation for working together, as we have seen, and an interest in the great seedbed of ideas that was Germany.

"Germanism" became the dominant attitude. To be sure, juridical theory in Italy had already, beginning in the first half of the century, felt the fascination of the far-reaching speculation in Germany. Similarly, the numerous—if imperfect—translations published in the 1850s of Ahrens, Stahl, Trendelenburg, or of Savigny, Puchta, and Jhering attest to the dissatisfaction of masters of doctrine on the peninsula for the small-mindedness of the French: the Italians were searching for broader horizons. But it was in the 1880s that the jurists intensified their work of diffusion and that the economists launched a massive operation of trans-lations. In these years also the *Biblioteca dell'Economista* directed by Gerolamo Boccardo placed the German masters in the place of honor, and first among them Wilhelm Roscher.[31]

What permeated the many facets of juridical science was neither a passing fashion nor an orientation chosen by chance. These importations from Germany left a permanent mark on Italian jurisprudence. They af-fected everything—from the disciplines of public[32] and private law,[33] which were markedly subservient to German thought, to the work of the historians of law[34] and of the philosophers,[35] who gained from German influence a fruitful methodology and a refreshingly new approach. The new attitudes thus engendered still showed persistent strength in the last years of the century, to judge by the famous essay of Igino Petrone on philosophical and juridical doctrine in Germany. As in the case of Cusumano twenty-two years before, a vital young man of Italian culture here offered his analysis, his summary, and his meditations to enrich a provincial culture south of the Alps that was still lacking in indigenous methods.[36]

Italian juridical culture after Unification was thus considerably well disposed toward efforts for enrichment and strengthening. It fol-lowed two paths to accomplish this: one led to nonjuridical thought and the other led to the German models. This receptivity and these chosen directions were heavy with consequences for the development of the dispute on forms of collective appropriation in Italy. Far from remaining as generalized attitudes on the level of general intellectual concepts, they drew the jurists toward particular practical applications.

To look beyond the fences that enclosed the law meant for the jurist to peek into a cultural territory freer from encumbrances than was his own. Here his path was not blocked by the immovable obstacle of the Roman model of property. It was neither removed from historicity, nor consigned to the realm of myth, nor made indisputable by a nearly univer-sal acceptance. This meant for them the possibility of seeing value not only in an official history based on legislative and doctrinal "models," but also in a history based in "facts," a popular history marked by the daily practice of operating communities.

The appearance in Italy—in this moment when it was breaking out of its isolation—of flourishing investigations of a somewhat ethnologi-cal nature, if not of juridical ethnology, constitutes more than a culturally ephemeral conquest of a slender positivism at which the historian of cul-ture can quite legitimately smile. The historian of jurisprudence cannot deny the weakness of positivism. But he also has the obligation to recognize, from his own autonomous point of view, its importance as an instrument in bringing about this rupture with, or flight from, schemes and models that had proven to be too rigid.

On the level of the infrastructure of praxis it was inevitable that comparisons, perhaps even dissension, should have arisen between official history and vulgar history, between the official nation and the real nation, between the unity found in models and the plurality found in practice. In the jealously guarded cemetery of custom, forms of collective property materialized like a sort of juridical paganism to confront the orthodoxy, the "Catholicity" of Roman and Romanistic models. And this is true even without taking into account that positivistic enthusiasm led not only to appropriating economic data and the results of sociological and ethnological investigations, but pushed the jurists' curiosity toward diverse and rival juridical systems. Experiences of utterly different temporal and geographical origin were compared and, as had been the case for Maine and Laveleye, these comparisons permitted the jurists to regain a sense of the plurality of juridical culture in opposition to the monopoly of the Romanists.

Furthermore, looking beyond the borders of Italy to the culture of Germany made the Italian jurists acquainted with the far-ranging reflections of the Historical School of law, with all of its Germanistic derivations and complications, and with the Historical School of economics and its ramifications in *Kathedersozialismus*. Consequently, the complex of values that had emerged in those movements now became available in Italy: the historical view of institutions, the understanding of institutions as internally consistent arrangements of a living social organism set in history, and the importance of the communitarian aspect of law. Even more, contact was established with an intellectual school that assigned a privileged position to the laws of the Germanic peoples—or at least it became possible to be as sensitive to these laws as to the constructions of the Romanists.

Everything, then, seemed predisposed for the reception and the appreciation of the conclusions of the great controversy, even in cultural terms. All of socio-juridical thought in Italy during those years was oriented toward finding congenial both the methodological style of Maine and the "collectivist" and relativist theses on landholding of the Germanists.

The article of Vito Cusumano has been cited above as an example of a double vocation—Germanistic and interdisciplinary—prevalent in Italy at that time. Indeed, in just this same article we can find not only the signs of a considerable sensitivity to the new currents moving in European thought, but we find in his conclusions to an argument that is at once economic, political, and juridical—like Laveleye's discourse—a clear statement of the verity that was cropping up in many places on the question of property:

> It is impossible to deny the fact that property is always and everywhere limited and that in some places it is completely rejected: this is proof that it is not an absolute; and this thesis is particularly evident in our times, in which patient historical research has proven incorrect many of the theories that were once held to be of undeniable validity.[37]

Cusumano, who wrote this essay between 1873 and 1874,[38] clung fast to Laveleye's first article in the *Revue des deux mondes* and to the researches of Maine, Nasse, and Wagner, whom we have already met.[39] The works of neither Maine nor Laveleye were available in Italian translation, but they circulated widely thanks to widespread knowledge of the French language, the language that was native to the Belgian economist and into which the entire corpus of Maine's works was translated, beginning with the translation of *Ancient Law* by Courcelle-Seneuil in 1874. A host of references and citations as well as numerous and authoritative reviews also attest to this circulation.[40]

Laveleye's discourse, with its antiquated "political" proposals, seemed perhaps to some candid souls to offer too much of a threat to the idea of progress and the certitudes of evolutionistic theory. It therefore appeared to be valid, and was in fact received, more for its diagnosis than for the therapy it prescribed.[41] Maine's discourse, which was uniquely methodological, had a particularly strong influence. In it, evolutionistic certitudes and positivistic tendencies were set in a typically English cultural experience and therefore showed strongly empirical leanings. But whether these tendencies reinforced or tempered one another, their method was comparative and historicist. Since Maine's discourse appeared as a conjunction of differing cultural orientations, many Italian intellectuals who were divided between their passion for Spencer and Darwin and their enthusiasm for Savigny were able to understand it without difficulty and to see its relevance to their own concerns. This was all the more true since the level on which Maine operated was not political but cultural and therefore removed from problems of an immediately practical nature.

It was of Maine that the Italian jurists spoke—whether to discuss him incidentally and to draw inspiration from his works, as in Pietro Bonfante,[42] or whether to make Maine's entire work the object of serious examination, as it was to be later for Silvio Perozzi[43] and Icilio Vanni.[44] His influence over Italian juristic theory was to be determinant.

The European Controversy and Its Values in Italian Translation

What we have outlined thus far can permit us a better understanding of the fortunes after the 1880s of the theory regarding collective forms of land ownership and their historical vestiges in Italy and the widespread echoes that they raised. We have further seen that this interest occurred in spite of a clearly hostile legislative and administrative practice of nearly a century's duration and an underlying attitude in juridical culture that was clearly oriented to following the late Romanistic tradition as it had been delineated in eighteenth-century theories of natural law.

Before attempting to analyze the various manifestations of these theories in Italy and the proposals that Italian culture was to make in response to the great controversy, it might be useful to arrive *in limine* at an idea of the general lines of development of the controversy in Italy and of the levels on which it came to operate.

It was an abundant literature—perhaps excessively so—that pervaded the last twenty years of the nineteenth century and overflowed into the twentieth. It moved on two clearly separate levels, the scientific and the practical. On the first level, the argument was rigorously cultural: it was chiefly concerned with method, but it never became weighed down with the ideological implications that, as we have seen, came to dominate the argument of certain factions in the dispute north of the Alps. On the second level, the argument was much more multifaceted, even if it was nearly always modest in scale and lackluster, and even if it was occasionally vitiated by perspectives that were questionable from a historiographical standpoint. Since our interest will be turned mainly to the first current, let us devote a few lines to the other before we put it aside.

This practical literature had picturesque aspects. It was the expression of an Italy of small cities, where the prestige of custom and folklore still remained intact. It came out of an Arcadia often neglected or hidden away, as attested by the unusual places of publication of the thousands of minor works trusted to the care—or to the negligence—of unsophisticated local printers. It was also the expression of a heterogeneous array of authors composed of government inspectors,[45] municipal secretaries,[46] agronomists,[47] geologists,[48] ministerial and prefectural functionaries,[49] magistrates,[50] lawyers,[51] and even teachers,[52] all of whom were moved to take an interest in the problem by many contingent circumstances in which zeal was mixed with particular interests. Their contribution could consist in a lawsuit, an administrative quarrel, an archival discovery, a report of an inspection or, more often, one or another legislative act affecting the local situation.[53]

This literature had in common with more scientific thought a reference—though it would be difficult to judge how conscious this was—to the general matrices of culture. It obviously differed from more scientific thought in its taste for the particular and for partisan distortions, since it often took the form of a defense brief or a legal opinion. But it also differed because of the "political" dimension of the problems to which it was directed. We must not forget that the copious legislative activity of the national Parliament in the decade from 1884 to 1894 gave an enormous—perhaps the strongest—impetus to this literature, and that legislation was, as we shall see, dominated by the looming "social question" and directed toward finding partial solutions to this question. It should not be surprising, then, that in some of this practical, though by no means unimportant, literature, the option for collective property-holding should be partially motivated, as it had been for Laveleye, by political and social concerns.[54]

On the other hand, this motivation was nearly totally absent from the more scientific thought in Italy. If, when we were following the thought of Fustel de Coulanges, we thought it necessary to insist upon the ideological dimension as characteristic of his thought, and if, in Laveleye, we pointed out that certain of his interpretations took on the nature of proposals, we must here make it clear that the investigations of the Italian jurists were overwhelmingly intellectual in character. These investigations were certainly not neutral: a lively consciousness of the social issues often ran through them. But they typically demonstrate a precise will to avoid being lured into the conspiracies of broader social options. By their nature, then, these investigations were above all historical and philosophical: the authors sought to bind themselves to objective reality and never to lose sight of their role as critics.

The strongest and the best-informed of the personalities involved realized that on the other side of the Alps the controversy had often become distorted and that the intellectuals' erudite arrows had often gone astray and hit other targets. They declared their express intention of avoiding this risky transfer of levels and of putting the whole of the problem back into a cultural context.

This is the preoccupation that emerges from the first pages of Giacomo Venezian's[55] knowledgeable lecture for the inauguration of his chair at the University of Camerino.[56] Echoes of the recent dispute in the Paris Académie des Sciences morales et politiques were reaching the ears of this cultivated Italian in that very year, 1887, and he noted that in this dispute the problem, originally and intrinsically a historiographical one, had been subjected to acrid dissention and distortion. Consequently, the first need was to take the "study that others have already completed with copious investigations and researches, although not with serene objectivity, to bring to it a systematic spirit as well as a consciousness of current economic and political concerns"[57] and to restore it to its natural foundation in an objectivity unburdened by the passions and interests of present-day man.

Venezian gives no footnotes and he mentions no names; but one name can be guessed at between the lines: that of Fustel de Coulanges. Who more than he brought "economic and political concerns" and "a systematic spirit" to the historiographical reconstruction of this question? Who more than he ideologized his own point of view and felt compelled to erect a clearly defined, limpid historical construction—one made of points and lines traced firmly and indelibly in india ink, without the least perplexity, doubt, or void capable of inviting curiosity or afterthoughts? That Venezian refers to Fustel is only probable; but he clearly rejects a model that he is determined to avoid.

Further down on the same page, Venezian looks at the process of liquidating and redistributing collective holdings that had taken place during the preceding half-century, and he condemns it without qualifications as "a haste-ridden mania for innovation," one spurred by "an annoyance over anything that might infringe upon what for them was the harmony of their legislative edifice."[58] From this statement and from the one previously cited there emerges spontaneously an attitude that is almost historiographic in nature of a full receptivity toward these new currents of thought. This seems to us particularly remarkable in one who was not a historian professionally, but an exponent of private and civil law, hence, one who might be expected to have been more interested in the spirit of system and the "harmonious proportions of the legislative edifice."

Instead of this, his discourse aims at being "more limited," almost descriptive, totally accessible to an accurate reading of emergent values and disvalues. To be sure, he does not eradicate his own political leanings (a virtue in any reasonable observer), but he does strive to put aside prejudgments and his particular political concerns. The thesis that results, the one that is reflected in the polemical reference to "relics of collective property" in the essay's title,[59] is the result of the gathering and analysis of information. It was added a posteriori and does not reflect a preconceived notion of a generalized basic principle to be defended at any cost.

Two other men, singular figures in Italian theoretical jurisprudence, also chose to reestablish the problem within cultural terms, each in his own singular manner. Thanks to this shared intent and identical methodological premises, an extraordinary consonance can be found in their interpretations. I refer to Giuseppe Carle and Pietro Bonfante.

Giuseppe Carle[60] arrived at his interpretation when he posed the problem of the origins of quiritarian property among the peoples of Lazio.[61] He attempted to remove himself from the political contaminations that lurked between the lines of general propositions and ways of setting up a problem, and he did so by restricting himself to the uncompromising apparatus of the laboratory of history. He too was lucidly conscious that "research on the origin of property these days has assumed the proportions of an economic and social question, in that in it diverse theories are tied together around the organization of properties;"[62] and he declared openly his strong misgivings concerning both of the opposing sets of conclusions.

Carle rejected both the "collectivist" and the "individualist" hypotheses in the totalitarian manner in which he had found them expressed[63] in the interpretations of primitive Rome by Niebuhr, Mommsen, and De Ruggiero on the one hand and by Padelletti on the other; and he rejected them in the name of a historical and sociological analysis that was more consistent and freer of the impurities of partisan humors.[64]

What in Venezian's lively lecture had come out of the very nature of the situation itself and was both motivated and documented in ways relative to that situation is here instead explicitly inserted into the ongoing controversy. The names of Maine, of Laveleye, of Fustel are met at every hand, and the animated sessions of the Paris Académie are expressly cited.[65]

What it is important to note at this point in the task we have set ourselves is the motivation behind Carle's nonalignment and his choice of a hypothesis of subtler construction. Diverse forms of both collective and individual ownership[66] seem to him as possible within the complex phenomenon of appropriation from its primordial appearance. (He speaks of "properties" in a plural that seems clearly to be the meditated choice of the writer rather than a typographer's error.[67]) This nonalignment was an attempt to get as close as possible to historical facts, humbly and without preconceptions, and to grasp their complexity, their multivalence, and their full dimensions.

Laveleye irritated the philosopher from Turin exactly because of his "political" proposals, because of his encapsulation of a historical law which did not admit that multivalence and that multidimensionality. In this way, Carle prefers "the researches of other impartial investigators, Spencer among them,"[68] only because they were, or because he felt them to be, impartial.

His was not a flight from reality: it was a refusal to use the historical dimension to suit the prejudices and the pleasures of the interpreter. Speaking of collective property in ancient Rome, Carle does not hesitate to point an accusing finger:

> There are in fact those who, like Laveleye and other authors
> more and less openly favorable to a collective structuring of

property, strive to find even among the Romans the traces of a collective property, while others, proponents instead of private and individual property, seek to take to themselves the authority of a great people to justify the form of property that is their darling.[69]

It was predilections and insufficiently critical attitudes that Carle wanted to banish: what he wanted to do was to reassign the problem and its historical formulations to the realm of culture.

Pietro Bonfante followed an identical interpretive line in his youthful study on the *res mancipi*,[70] which reveals not so much the first steps of a young man of twenty-four as the secure hand and the strength of the future master of Romanistic juridical historiography.

The work, a legitimate offspring of the school of Vittorio Scialoja,[71] has a double orientation, both historical and systematic, and is in its outline and in its working out rigorously Romanistic. It would be of no more interest to us than the many studies on the subject that flourished in those years[72] if the young author, giving proof that his ears were sensitive and his sight sharp,[73] had not allowed himself to be lured by the enchantment of a methodological argument, had not prefaced the book by a few pages of theorizing and had not inserted a chapter on the "origin and primitive evolution" of property.

It is evident even at first glance that Bonfante intended to deal with Maine. This is not only because the eighth chapter of *Ancient Law*, dedicated to property, took as a basic thesis the distinction between *res mancipi* and *res nec mancipi*. More importantly, the impatient and dissatisfied young historian of law saw around him only one possible interlocutor, only one person who, after the Germans, had attempted an intellectual adventure in historical and juridical research—however debatable it might have been—that could gratify his needs. Maine was the only one who had grafted antiquarian investigations onto a structure of living tissue, and the only one to whom Bonfante could turn, even if only to express his own dissent.

The cultural relation between Bonfante and Maine might appear contradictory to a superficial observer for it follows two concurrent trajectories: one of dependence and the other of a conscious autonomy, one of professed admiration and the other of responsible and precise criticism.[74]

Bonfante's study opens with references to the English jurist, and he takes over Maine's methodology as a presupposition to his own angle of vision and as a liberation from worn-out schemes. He sees Maine's merits as clearly methodological, and on this level "comparative jurisprudence" signified an opening up, an oxygenation, an injection of vitality.[75] Maine showed only one defect for the young Bonfante, whose solid positivism was constantly tempered by a no less solid historicism: "comparative jurisprudence" tended too often to depart from the historical nature of situations. It tended to weave general and abstract rules, to point to unhistorical universal truths, or to offer explanations that were transitory or extraneous to history, whereas the only correct procedure, in Bonfante's view, was the one that builds on facts by means of "induction," of a "historical induction."[76]

It is from this position that Bonfante reopens the question of the origins of property and gives an answer to that problem that brings him closer to Carle. He refuses both of the adversary theoretical systems, both the "collectivist" and the "individualist," insofar as they contain absolutes. He refuses logical and ethical instruments, and he consequently brings the problem and its possible solutions back to the realm of history. He shows diffidence concerning the likelihood of elaborating universal laws on the question.[77] The result is an interpretive hypothesis that is complex and fully articulated, and which it is opportune to note here.

Bonfante begins with a certainty that derives from recently elaborated theories: historical forms of property are relative; collective and individual property are equal in historical dignity. He arrives at a consequent conclusion that was important on the level of juridical science: "The rational concept of property has truly undergone an extension and a serious alteration."[78]

This last sentence is typical of the complexity and also of the ambivalence of Bonfante as a man of culture. It can be rephrased as the historicity of a "rational concept" that bore an equivocal message, that signaled, if not a contradiction, certainly a malaise. Two traditions of opposed character are at play here: first, that of Romanism and the Enlightenment, which designated one sole and archetypal property and relegated it to the limbo of concepts, and second, the more recent historicist tradition of Anglo-German derivation which had insisted on the plurality of proprietarian manifestations and on their nature as historical precipitations. Vittorio Scialoja's brilliant pupil is right there in the middle, trying to square his circle, torn by a conflict that splits the notion of property between two contraries, the rational and the historical, the absolute and the relative.

Notwithstanding conceptual hesitations attributable to his Romanistic formation, Bonfante's final conclusion is largely weighted against the archetype and it is an important one. Maine's lesson had taken hold and, what is more, had taken hold on the level of method, of the jurist's approach as a man of science. On this level there is no doubt that Bonfante belongs among the new theoreticians, even if his exclusively "historiographical" vision of the question of the origins of property led him to avoid a clear choice and to remain standing in the middle, somewhat like Carle two years before.

Like Carle, Bonfante had no hesitation in affirming that the social and the individual, "the two elements constant in property, reveal themselves at every moment."[79] In a "perpetual alternation"[80] one or the other—collective or individual property—will prevail, according to him, depending on the degree of cohesion and organization in the body of the community and on priorities among the needs to be satisfied; but in any one moment one can find traces of both forms.

For Bonfante the primordial age was marked by an atomistic view of social life, by an array of individual, fortuitous, and momentary needs that the community fails to gather together and subject to its discipline. It is individual property that triumphs in this case in a proprietary relation so tied to the single subject as to be conceived as a part of him, inherent in his very bones.[81] (Even in this first age, however, "the land is the common property of the horde and of the tribe: it is the communal hunting grounds and later grazing lands."[82]) The "collectivist" doctrine, which he qualified as dominant, triumphs instead at the second stage of human protohistory, when a more robust and conditioning social organization is substituted "for the lively independence of primitive man." And, Bonfante adds, "this is the moment of social or collective property."[83]

This may suffice: Bonfante's methodological line is clear. The rest is of secondary interest to us and to follow it would mean to set off on a path tangential to our investigation. Much remains to be said about the cultural orientation of this Italian Romanist and about how it translates into the realm of property. We could ask ourselves the meaning of such a clear refusal of comparison in the name of historical induction, and we could ask ourselves whether one can always assume to be primitive a sampling of metahistorical savagery taken by chance from the Australian desert and combined with the South African Kaffir or with the Indian from the forests of the Rocky Mountains.[84] We could ask what sense there is in refusing programmatically to point out general laws only to arrive later, after the observation of necessary and universal facts and generalized phenomena, at the formulation *a posteriori* of "universal laws."[85] We could ask what sense there is in refusing the theories of Maine and Laveleye only to arrive at the affirmation that the individual element in the primordial age was realized on the level of personal belongings consisting of household furnishings, arms, and a hut with a little fence around it, when one admits that land was the property of the community.[86] We could pose many such disquieting questions from the reading of this singular work; we could point to many unsatisfactory elements and many contradictions in it. I prefer to view it as a faithful product of its times and to be aware that the contradictions of the young and gifted author are in reality the contradictions that dominated the most responsive currents of thought in the year of grace 1888.

The discussion of the more scientific trend in Italian thought on the origins of property opened by noting that the problem would be seen in cultural terms, differentiating the Italian position from that of Fustel or Laveleye. This was characteristic of both Bonfante and Carle. In both of them, but particularly in Bonfante, who reflected more on grandiose cultural constructions and who enjoyed weaving his own research in with them, the discourse is so strongly cultural that it becomes a discourse on method.

Bonfante was so aware of the excesses and the distortions practiced by a Laveleye or by a Fustel that he set himself at a formal distance from both and tried to rediscover his craft as a historian and his instruments *a fundamentis* in the light of the exciting conquests of nineteenth-century science. He was in essence a "collectivist": the land—that is, with the exception of the straw hut and the handkerchief-sized bit of land around it—was for him the property of the collectivity in all imaginable stages of human prehistory and protohistory.

It was this and only this that interested the collectivists: it was this and this only that Fustel denied. None of Laveleye's followers ever denied to the primordial individual this insignificant form of individual appropriation, and it changed nothing in the general ordering of communitarian organization.

Bonfante, then, was substantially a collectivist, a participant in what he called the dominant doctrine.[87] And yet he tended to slip away from an excessive familiarity with the collectivists and to construct a formal doctrine on a middle ground that separated himself from them. Perhaps he—much more than the sociologist Laveleye or the ideologue Fustel—wanted to keep his research on an authentically historiographical level. Perhaps he felt a possible complicity as a historian if he participated in the melee over the origins of property, where the contribution that each person brought was more to the social and agrarian question than to the history of an economic and juridical institution.

This was what Scialoja's disciple wanted to avoid carefully. Although his discourse balances on the razor edge between ethnological data and historical information, Bonfante's investigation, thanks to his constant vigilance, does not for one instant abdicate its scientific rigor. Quite the contrary, sustained by his rigor and fully conscious that the material he was treating contained an incandescent mixture of passions and acrimonies, Bonfante permitted—almost demanded—that the argument be broadened, that it be raised to a higher level, and that an eventual epistemological dimension be accorded to that small historico-juridical point which was the distinction between *res mancipi* and *nec mancipi*.

As I stated above, Bonfante's historiographic pages become a discourse on method. It was a significant means of recapturing one's purity; a lustral experience after which the problem could be contemplated in all its objectivity.

This is the reason why we have singled out Venezian, Carle, and Bonfante, three witnesses involved in the broad discussions that took place concerning these matters in Italy between 1880 and 1890. Certainly, they were neither chronologically the first, nor the most in view. Certainly, on the other hand, they were among the most explicit in their indication of the level on which they wanted to carry on the controversy and in their differentiation of their positions from certain transalpine exaggerations. Theirs were middle-of-the-road interpretations, as the positions of the Turinese philosopher and the Roman Romanist demonstrate.

Collective Forms of Agrarian Landholding in Italian Thought: The Romanist Point of View

It is not impossible that Carle and Bonfante might have found the middle road indicated above a difficult choice, first for the reasons already cited, but also because of the influence of the Romanistic model. A long-standing familiarity with Roman sources must have led them to put a high value on the individual dimension, or at least it must have made it difficult to rid their thought of that dimension when considering the earliest ages. A passage in Carle shows clearly what a heavy encumbrance the shining and persuasive categories of Roman systemization were on the cultural liberation of a scholar at the end of the nineteenth century.[88]

They were categories that endowed the thinker with a resistance to the socioeconomic and cultural process and made the new modes of thought and the new methodological attitudes seem untouchable. The Roman system, as crystallized in its classical form by Justinian, was less a fixed point to be respected than the best of all imaginable juridical organizations, the archetype in relation to which the quality of solutions to historical problems were to be measured and approved or condemned. It is even surprising that a jurist of Romanist training like Bonfante, writing a book conceived in a manner consonant with Romanistic techniques, could, probably by dint of intellectual curiosity, have freed himself of the categories that the Romanists deemed obligatory in relation to property.

If we open instead one of the manuals that enjoyed the widest audience at the time, the *Storia del diritto romano* of Guido Padelletti, who nevertheless was accustomed to a variety of historical sources,[89] we can see how these same categories could weigh on a scholar and make it impossible for him to comprehend other juridical worlds. He declares:

> In spite of what some philosophers and economists might say, the institution of property, as it was developed from the earliest times of ancient Rome, marks the degree of greatest perfection to which the juridical rule of that same property has risen. The modern world, after having won over and risen beyond the imperfect forms of Germanic collective property and those of the feudal regime, found it *necessary* to return to the Roman conception. The tendency of one modern economic school is to insist on giving importance to the most imperfect and barbaric forms of the social jurisdiction over property . . . but the jurisconsult and the historian will not so easily let themselves be led astray by the sophisms of Laveleye and other writers, no matter how splendid or apparently based on historical studies their argument might be.[90]

This is as the text appears in the first edition of 1878 of Padelletti's *Storia* (exception made for the italics, which are mine): the modern world found it *necessary* to return to the Roman concept. The Germans and Maine had passed by in vain, and in vain had anyone protested against the Romanistic cultural monopoly. Here we see a totally impervious mind, absolutely deaf to different voices.

Roman property, in the mind of this author, was no longer an institution that was the product of historical reality. As it partook of perfect forms, which expect time to bring them nothing, it belonged more to an Olympus, to a fortified paradise of concepts and models, than to the realm of terrestrial affairs. And since this property was individual, collective forms of appropriation, if they ever existed, could not but be limited, as imperfect forms, to the barbarity of certain societies and to the aberrations of the feudal system. In other words, they could not but be the incarnation of evil on the level of socio-juridical organization.

We see here intact, directed against collective property, the wornout sideshow spiel of an entire century. It is as intact as his perfect incomprehension—or worse, his closed mind. Laveleye, the philosophers and the economists were yarn-spinners out to fool the public, and their message could be reduced to sophisms. Not one reexamination can be found here, not one hesitation, not one attempt to answer the findings of others. Here is the realm of purest orthodoxy which, like all orthodoxies, has its decalogue, its theology, its liturgies, and its celebrants. To be sure, it was a decalogue that could not stand the test of history, and the celebrants were unresponsive to historicist criteria.

If we had cited the preceding page in Padelletti's same manual, we would have seen him reject Niebuhr's and Mommsen's hypothesis of an agrarian communism in the earliest days of Rome with the axiomatic affirmation that "all information from ancient writers and the character of laws relating to land exclude this hypothesis."[91] Let us ignore the first affirmation, which interests us less but which recalls the totalitarian statements of Fustel, and let us pause to examine the second: To what character of the law, and to what historical manifestations of landholding rights was Padelletti referring? To all appearances, he had removed the very possibility of variation through time or place from what became a metahistorical pattern that imposes a single form on laws relating to land. He had hypostatized them for ever.

We know perfectly well that Padelletti was prone to exaggerate certain contrasts and that he was led by his complex ideology to give importance to the Roman model over the medieval constructions at every occasion.[92] In the area of property, however, his position was typical of an attitude common among Romanists and civilists alike. Even to someone like Biagio Brugi, who had attempted cultural adventures outside of the enclosed garden of Roman law, this monolithic tradition was a dead weight, and his very capacities for observation were distorted by it. The case of Brugi is interesting for the very reason that it enables us to see clearly the special knowledge and the historiographic apparatus that Romanists put into operation when they dealt with an institution like property.

Biagio Brugi was in fact an important personage on the scientific horizon during those years, and one could certainly not reproach him for cultural deafness or closed-mindedness. The best of his long list of works were studies that were not strictly Romanistic[93] and his youthful writings show broad cultural range and multiple interests that went far beyond the confines of juridical techniques.[94] Nevertheless, when he sat down to manipulate categories and institutions that touched on the historical dialectic between individual and collective property, we see that he was conditioned by his Romanistic training. Thus he did not hesitate to teach, Niebuhr, Puchta, and Mommsen notwithstanding, that "the primordial and continuous type of *dominium* in Rome was that of private property."[95] Nor did he hesitate to fix an institution as long-standing and as thoroughly founded in practice as common pasturage in a strict definition of condominium agreements under private law.

The essay to which we refer bears a title that is a program in itself: "Dei pascoli accessori a più fondi alienati secondo i libri degli agrimensori romani commentati col Digesto"[96] [Of pasture lands accessory to several landholdings that were alienated according to the records of the Roman land surveyors commented upon in the Digest]. The juxtaposition of fundamentally heterogeneous data is clearly visible here. Even more so is the conditioning function that one element in this data, the official doctrinal category of private *communio*, is given over another, the archaic and consuetudinarian structure of common pasturage as it was documented by the agricultural survey-takers. The fragment of Scaevola that he invokes[97] is inadequate to put into perspective a very different reality and it gives proof of the overwhelming disposition of the Romanists to identify the entire range of landholding relationships proper to the Roman historical experience in the intellectual structures of classic jurisconsults. Brugi furthermore demonstrates the most obtuse inaccessibility to any diversity of opinion, patterns, or contexts.

Francesco Schupfer's spontaneous reaction was to contest such a manifestly one-sided procedure. This reaction could have been predicted in a man trained to look at and to compare different cultures: he must have found it intolerable that nonofficial juridical experience be continually sacrificed to the official view. Schupfer protested in the name of the complexity of the phenomenon of common pasturage, a phenomenon that was crushed here by the sheer weight of the fragment from Scaevola but that had left many traces in public law as immemorial years passed by.[98]

This is all that concerns us here.[99] Whatever one might believe on the subjects of common pasturage, the contradictory texts of the agronomists, or the many interpretations of these texts,[100] all that matters to our purposes is Brugi's methodology and the cultural background that it points to—a method, a cultural intolerance, if you will, and an intellectual inertia.

Brugi was an uncommonly competent man of laws, a Romanist and a civilist. He was also an extraordinary personality amid a throng of the uninspired. Hence his insensitivity[101] has a value as a paradigm for us; and this is why we have singled him out for particular attention.

It is obvious that among those at the lowest level of this chorus of insipid voices the old privilege conferred upon Roman law, the old and constant conviction that Roman property was a supreme value to be defended at any cost, and the old scorn for different appropriative forms, continued unperturbed. We could cite Romanists and civilists by the score, but it would be senseless. The world of these jurists was immobilized in an inert tradition of which they manifested the most sclerotic features. The revitalizing ideas that Maine and the historicists had grafted onto tradition were meaningless to them. Studies on property in their hands were reduced to compendiums of axiomatic first principles, to *regulae iuris,* to brocards, to a mechanical repetition of the old exorcisms and a muttering of "rancid or distorted opinions."[102]

The consonance between those *regulae* and the legislative system of the modern state might lead one to look for an ideological tendency as the trait that best characterized this literature.

Gross generalizations should be avoided, and one should not exclude the possibility of a conscious ideology. But what we see here is above all an unconsciousness, a numbing hatred of anything new that settles within the fixed certitudes of the nineteenth-century constitutional state. In the case of a man of lively and solid intelligence like Brugi, this was due to the force of a deeply rooted and autocratic cultural tradition that tended to monism. Here we see above all the figure of a jurist removed from the great creative organizational options by the pseudo conquests of the regime of the Code, constrained to feed on crumbs from the politicians' table, apparently satisfied to work *in vitro* and to construct logical architectural models on plans proposed or imposed by others. To be sure, Brugi also contributed to the solidification of the ideology of the state on the juridical plane, but this occurred as a reflex action, as an outburst in which what was thought and desired could not be clearly separated from what was undergone, and in which there was no question of a plan lucidly carried out on a conscious level, hence on the level of science, as in Fustel or even in Laveleye.

Collective Forms of Landholding in Italian Thought: The Point of View of Juridical Historiography

When Bonfante speaks, then, of a "common doctrine" and a "dominant opinion," he is referring to a precise current in transalpine thought and to a constellation of theorists composed above all of historians and philosophers of law.

It could not have been otherwise, since the impulse to renew the problematical basis of property turned first to a revision of its historical and "rational" foundations. Furthermore, it was by necessity the historians and philosophers among the jurists who felt the influence of the new interdisciplinary studies and of the interest in the whole of European thought, both of which we have identified as important to the appropriation of the cultural values of the great controversy.

Juridical historiography in post-Unification Italy had an additional reason to take Maine's message as its own, a reason of local, Italian nature that had its concrete form in a highly visible precedent of far from negligible proportions.

We have above[103] referred to an abundant provincial literature that took form during the nineteenth century in Italy, a literature that was intrinsically modest but that had a certain historical importance. We have also referred to one particular doctrine in that context concerning the *demani* and the *usi civici* in southern Italy. It will be useful to discuss this doctrine in greater detail, not so much for its historical and juridical validity alone as for the invaluable precedent that it offered to the more purely historiographical discussion that began in Italy after the 1880s.

It should first be clarified that southern Italy showed differences from other regions of the peninsula, where contributions to the question of property had always and in all places appeared as a chance array of sparsely scattered publications that showed no interconnection other than the purely extrinsic one of taking as the object of their study the vestiges of the same primitive modes of property-holding. Within the borders of the kingdom of Naples, through historical circumstances known to all and therefore useless to expound on, the literature on state-held lands, the *demani,* followed in the wake of a plurisecular and prestigious tradition that had culminated in the works of the great "Neapolitan" jurists of the sixteenth and seventeenth centuries, Matteo d'Afflitto, Francesco d'Andrea, Giovan Francesco Capobianco, and Giambattista De Luca.[104]

In this tradition one fundamental principle—sometimes reduced to a simple intuition or to simple references—had been conserved. It was the certainty that the customary right of usage, the *uso civico,* was the last emaciated trace of an agrarian collectivism that had existed before the state, but that had been sacrificed and reduced by baronial abuses and with the connivance of the monarchy to a minimal right of use of limited extension. In other words, the Neopolitan literature showed itself to be, in the middle of the nineteenth century, the only current of thought that had carried on, systematically, continually, and from remote times, a teaching in evident contrast with official postrevolutionary doctrine.

One group of writings can be explained and understood historically only in their fidelity to this tradition: those of Antonio Rinaldi,[105] Nicola Santamaria,[106] Luigi Lombardi,[107] and Cammillo Del Greco,[108] to cite the most important names. These writings constituted, around the 1880s, a sort of nonaligned doctrine, absolutely heterodox, and scandalously alternative in relation to currently accepted views.

From the official historical and juridical point of view, the perspective of these jurists was turned upside down: it was not that the generosity of feudal lords had tolerated the existence of rights of usage on lands under the feudal system, but that their arbitrary exercise of power had not permitted the survival of communal or collective ownership. Suffocating collectively held lands, gathering them into the ever-growing large landed estates, the *latifondi,* they had left to the members of the primitive community for their subsistence an *uti-frui* reduced to the minimum. (This might have been a right to graze, to cut hay, to gather wood or faggots, and so on.) These rights or easements did not, however, represent liens on the land that had grown like parasites on private property to repress it and sap its strength: they themselves constituted a repression of a proprietary relation, reduced to only one of its multiple elements and for that reason confused with a *servitus* or a simple right to make use of land.

We can see in the works of Rinaldi and Lombardi, which appeared at a time when the mania for division of the collective lands had not yet died down, the courageous affirmation of a clear position, end product of the long history of Neapolitan reflection on demesnial lands.

Rinaldi states:

> The *usi civici* arose, at least in our parts, as a counterpoise to feudal power. . . . There arose the beneficent institution of rights of usage on the land conceded by the lord, and it was said not to be presumed that the ownership which first was of the citizens had had to be taken away from them, to the point of leaving them deprived of a modest sustenance.[109]

And Lombardi repeats:

> This right does not comport servitude, but bears intrinsic and inherent weight, so that the thing is not and can not be otherwise. [The *usi* are in fact] like absolutely inviolable primitive rights equal to any other right of nature, and thus anterior not only to the baron, but also to the king, to whom the peoples, if, as to administrators of the republic, they conceded the rights that they themselves enjoyed over the lands first occupied by them, they understood as certain fact that their right to use it, without which they could not have lived, was secure.[110]

If we had continued our citation of Rinaldi, we would have seen him reinforce his thesis by referring to an article of the noted *Istruzioni,* the royal decree giving instructions to the commissioners charged with the division of demesnial lands, dated 10 March 1810.[111] If Lombardi had cited a source, it would probably have been a *desceptatio* of Cardinal De Luca, one that was two centuries old, but that had been a constant point of reference for all of Neapolitan doctrine and jurisprudence ever since.[112] We would have looked in vain for a reference to Maine, to Laveleye, to Fustel, or to the Germans, indeed, for any reference that reached somewhat beyond the confines of the kingdom. When these two authors do become more adventuresome, it is to arrive perhaps at Andrea da Isernia and Luca da Penne, that is, to products of a current of southern jurisprudence that, while preserving its autonomy, always remained bound within a single school of thought. No connection with the great European controversy and no reflections of a methodological nature can be seen here. These writings reflect a decided and narrow cultural provincialism. They are alive with practical local instances, but they are totally unconnected to the fundamental debate that we have examined in the first part of this volume.

Even though it began with an invaluable insight, theory in southern Italy was subject to the evident and weighty limits of its provincialism, and it never succeeded in constructing a historiographically valid edifice on that base. It moved continually between two attitudes that were different in character but equally irrelevant from a cultural point of view and that, while not condemning it to sterility, did relegate it to the margins of scientific thought. Following in one direction, this theoretical school refused to put its insights into a concrete setting, and it repeated the ancient fable of *communio primaeva omnium bonorum* in which objects are in such poor focus as to give the impression not of collective forms of appropriation in a protohistorical era but rather of a nonproperty in a nonhistory. When these theorists followed in another direction, they wallowed in the practical aspects of a thousand controversies, particularizing their fundamental theses, even if with a great display of local knowledge, in the defense of the rights of one or another community examined as one atomic particle. But local knowledge—always so learned and always so unsatisfying—rarely reaches a consciousness of the unifying fabric that lies behind the particular, and consequently it never sees its problem in relation to a whole.[113]

The Neapolitan precedent was presented in these terms for nascent Italian juridical historiography. It was no more than a precedent, an accumulation of data often singularly dissonant in terms of officially received dogma, and an invitation to test the validity of its theses. It was always viewed within these limitations, as something that had already taken place and that had the value of a signal or a message. This message was perhaps somewhat crude, one that should have been translated into a richer language and extended in the form of a more complete diagnosis. But it was one that could have served as a point of departure or even as one measure that by contrast would provoke a search for another.

One theme that reappears repeatedly in those years was the need to maintain a certain distance from the methodology of this preceding tradition.[114] The subject matter itself, on the other hand, was found interesting: undeniably it had been brought up from deepest oblivion to be presented in an unusual light, in a vision different from that of the process of mystification currently developing in the traditional schools of jurisprudence.[115]

In other words, one can conclude that on the local level this new school of Italian juridical historiography did not begin its reexaminations from a *tabula rasa,* but that it was fully aware that this immense literature could be of considerable use from the historiographical point of view. Certainly, the movement for renewal drew from this literature a sense of urgency that led in the same direction as the reigning Germanism that completely dominated it.

Another fact should be emphasized, even if it is neither new nor unsuspected, after what has been said about the general attitudes of Italian juridical culture. The debt to German culture and German academia was a fact that characterized Italian juridical historiography at just the moment in which it was freeing itself from the old historical and philosophical methodology.

In the recasting of this discipline on more solid methodological bases, to draw on German sources reflected a frenzied demand for concrete data and for positive methodological criteria. The artisans of the new theories south of the Alps were bursting with an almost physical desire to conduct their own researches. I am thinking, in this connection, of Antonio Pertile, but even more of Francesco Schupfer.[116] When they searched for a training ground on which to strengthen their techniques, they found reassurance in the imposing body of nineteenth-century German learning. Here was an impressive collection of general treatises, accompanied by fecund particular investigations and by an ultrasolid documentary foundation. The consequences regarding property, the origins of landed property, and the evolution of its historical forms were the immediate and continuous transplantation to Italy of the theses of Grimm, Waitz, Sohm, Heusler, and Maurer.

Already in Pertile's first attempt at a systemization, the clear vision of a historical priority of collective appropriation over individual ownership and of the identification of collective property as the proprietary form typical of the ancient Germanic tradition came from a careful reading of the German masters, accompanied by a no less attentive examination of Italian sources.

These Italian sources were to be found with increasing frequency on the desks of the historian-jurists,[117] resting there next to Caesar, Tacitus, and Horace, the authors that Fustel and Laveleye had preferred in the launching of their challenges and diatribes, and next to the much-discussed extracts of barbarian law. The superabundant references to the Italian scene were a sure sign that the problem in Italy was beginning to be purified of its passional dross and to find an objective dimension—a dimension that was present in written form in the sources and that therefore came from things as they had been. These sources—statutory texts, public and private charters, chronicles, regional laws, and the like—served to make historical discourse more secure and more concrete, particularly in northern Italy, when, perhaps for the first time, they were used in order to corroborate systematically the lines of a general and complete picture. Pertile had within his reach the rich material particular to the mountains and valleys of his native Cadore and to the whole of the eastern Alpine chain.[118] He added it—almost as if it were a contribution from his personal experience—to an exceptionally eloquent documentation of those thriving, still operative, organized forms of common property that had survived intact to the end of the nineteenth century. These sources combined to enable Pertile to exploit fully the landholding organizations of collectivist or communistic stamp and to present them in high relief in a broad historical perspective.[119]

Pertile's *Storia del diritto italiano* was published in 1874.[120] In its wake, Giuseppe Salvioli,[121] Carlo Calisse,[122] Augusto Gaudenzi,[123] Giovanni Tamassia in his early years,[124] and Pasquale Del Giudice,[125] each working on specific themes, repeated their fidelity to the Germanistic orientation and, consequently, their full adherence to the "collectivist" hypotheses. This school of thought found its mature consolidation in the work of Francesco Schupfer.[126] Schupfer's double summary appeared, on a systematic level, in his *L'allodio* and, on the level of the particular, in his monograph on the *usi civici* in the commune of Apricena, two nearly contemporary studies.[127]

With Schupfer Italian historiography concerning the historical forms of property found its definitive systematic expression. A fortunate moment in thought, brief but intense, concluded in an interpretation that was rigorous and complete, even if rigidly unilateral. In Schupfer's study of Apricena the old "Neapolitan" models from which it took its point of departure are absorbed and resolved in a work for which the circumstances of one small locality serve only as an occasion and a stimulus for the consideration of much broader perspectives. It is an authentically historiographical work, one that permits the Italian literature on the *usi civici* to rise to the full scientific dignity that Heusler and Miaskowski had guaranteed, north of the Alps, in their investigations on the *Allmend*.[128] In the *Allodio* the fragmentary discourse of preceding theory became an admirably unified, organic argument, one developed not only out of the sources typical of the Germanic tradition—by then used and abused—but also and above all out of a rich store of Italian sources relating to landholding systems never before used systematically.

As we have seen, Schupfer puts together his plan on the basis of the documents collected by Muratori, Tiraboschi, Lupi, Giulini, Morbio, Troya, Gloria, and Porro, and on the first volumes, pertaining to the Longobard period and just published, of the *Regesto di Farfa*. He then solidifies this plan by binding it to concrete data and by freeing it from the virulence, the rancors, and the humors that had characterized the controversy in Paris. There is very little room for diatribe in this extraordinarily compact work; and there are no expressions of uncertainty, no voids, no doors left open. Polemical echoes are relegated to the admirable bibliography at the head of the essay, even though it does no more than list titles. There we see lined up, among many others, the familiar works of Fustel, Ross, Seebohm, Belot, and Dargun.

Furthermore, Schupfer's response is unique and as firm and secure as an axiomatic principle, a *degnità:*

> The element that dominates in primitive times is the social element, at least in regard to the soil; in fact individual ownership was not even known, except for mobile goods; but in regard to land, all ancient peoples began with collective property.

He continues:

> The Germans considered the soil truly as a *collective property,* which belonged to the tribe; and individuals had only temporary enjoyment of it. It is a vast community, that the sources of a more advanced period know under the name of March, Almend, or Folcland—in a word, the community of the village.[129]

When Schupfer was writing his *Allodio,* Fustel had already spoken for one form of Western culture, loudly defending its ethico-political preoccupation with individual property from his Parisian pulpit. He had already defined original Germanic property to his own satisfaction and had pronounced his anathema of the *Mark.* Of all of this only the faintest hint appears on the pages of the Italian scholar, and that faint hint is extrinsic to his argument, juxtaposed to it. There is so little of it indeed that it does not permit the author's monologue to become a dialogue, while it is not and does not intend to be an invitation for further discussion. Schupfer makes his point very clear. He is not interested in its importance either for ethics or for ideology, as was Fustel, nor is he interested in its applicability to social reform, as was Laveleye. His work remains completely faithful to the cultural current that had inspired it, that of the Germanists, and to the evaluation of the German experience as the most consequential of all historical forces.

Maurer and Laveleye—and behind them, Maine—are the most obvious participants in a discussion such as this one, which concentrates exclusively on the question of alodial estates. This was a characteristic common to all Italian juridical historiography of those years.[130] It was as eclectic as we have seen the whole of contemporary culture to be, and in its pursuit of the chimera of positivism it unperturbedly mixed the historicism it had learned from the Germans with Spencerian evolutionism and with Maine's comparative method. The linguistic data of Grimm, the economic data of Roscher, and the ethnological data of Maine and Laveleye united with Maurer's socio-juridical findings to furnish, more than a scenario or a background, the interpretive outlines into which the enormous documentation is fitted.

This methodological orientation and this cultural dimension can be grasped, even better than in the fully developed writings of an already mature Schupfer, in the investigation of the alienation of real property in

Germanic law by Giovanni Tamassia, then a novice in the discipline.[131] Tamassia's work lacks the controls proper to a mature scientific argument; but it reveals to us the hopes and convictions of a young historian of law of strong mind and keen insight in the Italy of 1885, and it shows us the base on which he intended to found his later work.

Those who know only the later scholarly career of this ex-pupil of Pasquale Del Giudice[132] might be surprised by the two most evident components of this work: an overwhelming Germanophilia and an enthusiasm for the possibilities offered by the comparative method. But it is hardly fair to ask for indications of the future master scholar of the University of Padua from this book, which was published in 1885. The book was as receptive to and as dependent upon external influences as can be expected in the work of any enthusiastic young scholar; but it is also one that offers trustworthy and accurate information about the ideas that were circulating at that time.

At that moment Germanophilia and comparative studies were parallel trends that shared a common target: the Roman and Romanistic cultural monopoly. Maurer and Maine seemed to travel the same road. The young Tamassia was irritated by the categories of official juridical tradition and by the attempt to make them coincide with what was passed off as the nature of things.[133] He saw the opposition of a perfect property, the Roman, and an imperfect property, the barbarian, as antihistorical and as a rich source of misunderstandings. It was a dead-end road and should be avoided.[134]

Maine's arguments had made a profound impression on Tamassia. They were open, not suffocated by philological or juridical jargon. They had exposed the obfuscations of natural law and had introduced voices from distant lands into the monotonous singsong of Romanistic tradition. Tamassia explicitly invoked Maine's methodological innovations to overcome the Germanists' fetishistic concentration on the sparse Germanic sources then available,[135] and he cites Maine's rediscovery of the juridical patrimony of eastern Europe as a considerable enrichment of tradition.[136]

For Tamassia as for Maine, comparison meant historicization: property would reveal its historical nature, its nature as relative in space and in time, through salutory confrontations between a range of cultures and alternative solutions—the Germanic, the Slav, and the Indian.[137] This would show that property changed as it evolved and that it eventually became consolidated in individual property, not because of any supposed conformity with reason or with nature, but in response to precise economic and social forces that underlay the juridical order.

Tamassia was typical of a culture dedicated to the interdisciplinary and the eclectic. He exploited to its fullest the dialogue with the economists, and the result was an even further shattering of the rational model.[138] No other conclusion seemed possible: "nature" was a social product like property, not outside of history but well within it.

Maine's lesson on the high risks a student of culture takes when he has recourse to natural law had found fertile terrain in which to take root, and Tamassia was in fact not the only one to heed it. A year before Augusto Gaudenzi, a man of an eccentric but also a keen mind, began research on property in the High Middle Ages. The point of departure of his methodology lay in the need to abandon at last the misleading but common "belief that the state of things which surrounds us is the most natural: whereas it is not on the nature of man, but on particular circumstances of facts operating on that nature that it depends."[139]

For Gaudenzi, this notion was best tested precisely in the history of property, particularly in the way in which individual ownership had become a theological notion and had been characterized as inherent in the most intimate structuring of man. Once again the discommodious Englishman showed his influence, for his methodology dominated these pages, shaking off the torpor of often repeated false belief and dissipating the consequent inertia of construction.

These Italian scholars had absorbed and repeated not only Maine's arguments but even his specific examples, as may be clear to anyone who has read the preceding chapter on Maine. This is the case in the work of Tamassia cited above[140] when he speaks of the questionable Roman aphorism that community ownership was necessarily temporary. Furthermore, Gaudenzi takes his argument in its entirety from a chapter of *Ancient Law*[141] when he demands the return to the historical realm, hence to the complex and the relative, of many simplistic hypotheses that stopped short—with an ineffable cultural Malthusianism—at the indisputable datum of "nature."

The ferment Maine had inspired entered through the breach opened by an ascendant Germanism. But it tended to free itself of that influence. Although Italian juridical historiography did not see substantial changes in the Germanistic outlines of this stage in its development, the English example of a reasonable empirical historicism and the familiarity with a considerable number of diverse experiences at least served to avoid a grave danger: the substitution of a Germanic model for the Roman, which would possibly have led to an arid and warped dialectic of contraries. It was thanks to Maine and to Laveleye that even in Schupfer the Italians' arguments could be couched in terms not only of the *Mark*, but also of the rather more lively *Allmend, mir,* and Indian community.[142]

Their orientation was historiographical, then, but within precise limits: theirs was a disruptive historicism, which served to deconsecrate the temple of Romanism. It had a polemical value and a polemical function. It was, however, destined to be highly conditioned by the evolutionistic vision that carried it forward: if all was history in landholding, this history nonetheless had an obligatory progression from village community ownership to family community ownership and to individual property.

In some of these works—this is the case of Guadenzi—collective property was seen as a structure typical of the infancy of the world, while individual ownership was the fruit of agrarian progress.[143] In others, as in Schupfer, who never permitted himself fully sympathetic statements regarding collective property, it was seen only as a more human form of property, as an ownership with a strong social dimension.[144] In all of them there remained, however, a belief in "that great law of gradual development that is found everywhere in history,"[145] a belief "that property evolves slowly, like any institution that is subject to natural evolution."[146]

If the reader had before his eyes the page from which this last citation from Tamassia was taken, he would see at the foot of the page a reference to Spencer's *Principles of Sociology,* recently translated by Salandra for the series under Boccardo's direction, the *Biblioteca dell'Economista.*[147] Historicism and evolutionism[148] became mixed and interwoven—as was the case with Maine. This is more a sign of plurality of sources of inspiration and of a vocation for eclecticism and synthesis than a sign of any intimate contradiction or speculative poverty.

What is important to note is that historiography, even with its differing tones and accents, permitted the emergence of notions that destroyed the mythical quality of accepted values. The first and most influential of these notions was that individual ownership of the soil was not a constant reality throughout human events. It was perhaps the last stage in an evolutionary process, appearing in history in relatively recent times. Property might thus represent a historical invention rather than an attribute of man in the state of nature, a notion that historical and comparative data lent their weight to back up, attenuating the rigidity of evolutionary theory.[149] A second new idea was that collective forms of appropriation constituted an unforgettable, indeed highly relevant, moment in human history. It was an undeniable fact in protohistorical periods; but it was vitally present also throughout the course of the progress of human experience, as exhaustively demonstrated by the rich testimony of antiquity and the Middle Ages. It was not contemptible in itself, but was simply the expression of a particular civilization, appropriate to it and functional within it.[150] The third emergent notion was that a perceptible trace of that wealth of customary landholding arrangements and of actual organizational structures had remained intact through time and was still alive at the end of the nineteenth century in a large number of social associations then undergoing demolition. Accused of desuetude and archaism, these associations gave testimony to other times and to alternative juridical cultures, to *another* way of understanding the relationship between subject and means of production. They were true and proper forms of ownership and valid alternatives to the official mode. Thanks to these conclusions, collective forms of ownership regained a more solid respectability, and at the same time their origin in the great, maternal primigenial community became understood. A new comprehension came to be substituted for the iniquitous propaganda of the reign of individual property, whose banner floated everywhere.[151]

As if by miracle, an unknown world—or, if it had been known, a completely misunderstood world—emerged. It sprang up not only as a hypothesis concerning origins, as an interpretation of Caesar, or as a result of pondering over the *lex salica,* but out of concrete investigations and the minute analysis of the most certain of historical sources: primary documents.

On the level of real and daily experience, which usually escapes those who let themselves be blinded by the grandeur of clamorous events, or on the level of the history of structures, the High and Late Middle Ages were teeming with collective arrangements. The jurist-historian of the Italian provinces satisfied both his own romantic sentiments, which made him curious concerning the "popular" and the "vulgar," and his positivistic penchants, which made him look with satisfaction upon the accumulation of textual references[152] and upon a history that sprang *ex rebus* and had been written *in rebus.*

In opposition to official history there emerged—if the expression be permitted—a kind of counterhistory; and alongside the open and highly visible vein of thought concerning individual property, there appeared a subterranean vein—one that was copious and continuous but that, when it was tapped, turned out to be completely different from the first one.

The documents—particularly the papers of the abbey of Farfa in Lombardy which, as we have seen, provided such fertile terrain to the Germanist Schupfer—spoke of marches, *communalia, vicanalia, pascua communia, fiuwaidea, silvae communes.*[153] They indicated networks of relations, responsibilities, rights, and duties within organized groups so interwoven that it is difficult if not impossible or at least inappropriate to separate the subjective situation of the single person from the comprehensive situation of the group in which he lived and within the limits of which alone he realized himself socially. An alternative reality emerges, based on an alternative social stasis, shot through with alternative lines of force, founded on alternative bases.

If today we were looking at these researches as historians of juridical historiography, we would have to note more than one forced interpretation and a singular disposition to read the sources in a "Ger-

manistic" and "collectivist" key. As historians of the notion of property
in nineteenth-century culture, on the other hand, we note the influence of
this phenomenon on that culture.

Let us take a famous example, the Pisan *charta venditionis* of
730. When two brothers sell a

> sorte de terra nostra, quem avire visi sumus de FIUVADIA in
> loco ARENA sa . . . aliis *coliverti nostri* . . . prope terra
> STAVILI

they promise the buyer:

> ut si qualive tempore forsitans ipsa terrola portionem nostra *in
> integro publicum requesierit* et ad devesionem revinerit
> cuicumque in alio homine et novis in alio locum ad vicem sorte
> redditam fuerit, si volueris tu . . . ipsa terra, nos tivi sine aliqua
> mora ipsa terra reddamus.[154]

This is a document that, because it mentions the *terra de
fiuwaida*—that is, the lot devoted to common pasturage[155]—attracted the
attention and provoked the hermeneutic exercises of many historians
after Schupfer.[156] Schupfer had Troya's reading of the text at hand,[157] but
his interpretation differed. That land had seemed to more than one scholar
as belonging to the state lands, the *latifondo regio*,[158] but for Schupfer
there was no room for hesitation:

> There is no doubt: it was a matter of a common, mutable piece
> of land. The title that had been granted to it was not to own-
> ership: it was a precarious or beneficiary title, and the *public*
> could at any time reclaim the lot that it had given. . . . Just for
> this eventuality the sellers promised to cede . . . the holding that
> might then be theirs and to take another in exchange the next
> time a division was made. . . . It seems that one is reading a page
> of Caesar or Tacitus, however, we are in 730.[159]

As a historian of the complex historical facts involved in communal lands and the *usi civici*, Giovanni Italo Cassandro later held that he
need not even take into consideration Schupfer's neat exegesis, since at a
distance of seventy years it seemed too unilateral and too dependent on
the times in which it had been written.[160] These limitations are not an
embarrassment to us, for it is not the facts themselves, but nineteenth-
century interpretations of these facts that are the object of our investigation. For us, quite the contrary, the very ties that emerge between the
interpreter and the culture that surrounded him are of primary importance; for they enable us to see the researcher, his methods, and his
results in a historical light.

Even if Schupfer's analysis was ingenuous, unilateral, and
overly Germanistic, what matters to us is that—along with the other con-

tributions to this initial moment in Italian juridical historiography—it exaggerated in a "collectivist" direction the historical view of landholding structures in Europe and, in particular, in Italy. It also insisted on a dimension different from the Roman and threw it in the face of the dominant culture. Finally, it gave wide circulation to a view of the medieval experience in which the role of forms of collective appropriation were exalted even to excess.

Collective Forms of Agrarian Landholding in Italian Thought: "Philosophers" and "Jurists"

Priority over individual property and the operative and meaningful presence of "collective property" in history: these seem to have been the conclusions that this juridical historiography reached.

Beside the historians, however, there were also philosophers of law, Romanists, and specialists in civil law just as ready to receive the message into their disciplines. Among them there ran a clearly definable although not widespread current of thought that brought contradictions into their composite cultural universe and invited them to review the prefabricated harmony of their systematic techniques.

The impression made by this current can be measured by considering men who stand out from an indistinct chorus of often anonymous voices:[161] Pietro Cogliolo and Giuseppe D'Aguanno, both philosophers of law, and Giacomo Venezian, a civilist.

Giuseppe D'Aguanno can without question be called a philosopher of law.[162] But this qualification would invite perplexity if applied to Cogliolo, who was professor of Roman law and whose work spread over the most disparate fields of juridical knowledge.[163] Still, the qualification can be justified within the limits of this book by reference to the line of thought that matured in him between 1881 and 1888—a line in which historical and juridical data were given new life by being reexamined in the light of pressing methodological problems and by being set into a broad sociological or philosophical framework.[164]

Our interest in these men, and the reason why we introduce them at just this point, lies in how they operated within their culture. It is true that they accepted the thesis that found in agrarian collectivism the mode of landholding proper to the first stage of human history. It is also true that the problem they faced was not, as it was for Schupfer, Tamassia, and Gaudenzi, to prepare a historically valid documentation of this thesis, but to provide an interpretation of it and to turn to that documentation as the occasion for a discourse on history and law. Nevertheless, it is permissible to ask ourselves how the schema of collective property would behave when seen in terms of the dominant theoretical tradition. We can anticipate the answer: in these "speculations" particularly it would reveal the ambivalence of the whole of Italian juridical culture of those years and become, as we have just shown, the sign of a profound cultural contradiction.

Both in Cogliolo and in D'Aguanno, Spencer and Maine continued to stand uncontested as models of an admirable intellectual adventure, and the influence of the real interchange between evolutionism and historicism that we have seen omnipresent among the historians continued to be true also in their case—but with the aggravating circumstance that these authors should have been better prepared in theory.

The path of historical evolutionism on which our two authors set off might appear to lead to logical suicide. Evolutionism in its strict sense necessarily involves a decisively optimistic view of history in which events are dominated by rigorous laws and by an equally rigorous internal succession in which each moment, each successive ordering of society, represents an amelioration of the preceding one in a progression from barbarism to civilization, from the imperfect to the perfect, almost from evil to good. The historicist's attitude implies a readiness to seize the values proper to and inherent in each moment in history, each ordering of society, and to see them, in all their relativity, within an overview that is impatient of laws and fixed rules. Our two authors followed the lead of more than one philosopher—perhaps even the extremely complex thought of Spencer—in which the two theoretical positions managed to be reconciled. Hence, if this path seems suicidal from a logical point of view, it nevertheless corresponded to their complicated view of culture, and it has the merit of showing clearly how eclectic and even contradictory their position was.

Let us take Cogliolo as an example. His evolutionism refused to be forced into the procrustean bed of rigid and general laws, and it is rife with varying historical circumstances, for each of which there is an appropriate counterpart on the level of law. More than an evolutionary process in a strict sense, Cogliolo wanted to show, as he says himself, an "intimate and substantial history of the law."[165]

To be sure, at one point we can read a sentence like this one:

> Every evolution therefore moves from the community to the individual, and for that reason individual property is the institution of civilized peoples.[166]

The argument here seems clear, straightforward, unambiguous. But later we note a conclusion that is significant but noticeably different, if not contrary:

> It is *indifferent* to the law whether property be collective or private: in the one case as in the other law creates the corresponding norms, and it is instead the study of the civilizations of peoples, it is economic science, it is the comparison of times and

places—it is all this, outside the law; and it can show the necessity of not turning to communism and of remaining within the institution of the individual domain.[167]

What emerges here is not only the image of an inert law, passive in respect to historical forces, to which it is indifferent. The instruments of "collective property" and "individual property" are also seen as indifferent on an ethical and social level and can—our author uses the verb of possibility—be imposed by transient historical forces that are relative—and here relativism is emphasized—to certain historical moments.

Evolutionistic ardor was not very intense in Cogliolo. An optimistic view of the iron law of progress wilted before his historicist skepticism. Perhaps his Romanistic training had the upper hand; perhaps he was influenced by the model of Maine, whom he so often invoked and whose work is so permeated by an authentic historicist sensitivity.[168] In any event, the methodological line followed by Cogliolo suffers from a profound incoherence.

Let us turn to the example of D'Aguanno, whom we have already seen at the beginning of this work as an energetic champion of individual property and of its intrinsic morality. In his thought as well, primitive communal ownership is an indisputed fact,[169] and the passage from collective village property to collective familial property and then to single ownership is equally beyond question.[170] But also in his work this evolution is not understood as a general and organic law, but is perceived in a jumble of facts that seem more like historically relative episodes than testimony to an authentically evolutive line.

When D'Aguanno reaches out to seek the reasons why the ownership of land passed from the tribe to the one-family line, and when he finds them in the chieftains' loss of power, in the diversity of cultures, in the appearance of some caste or another, and in the effects of wars,[171] it seems to me legitimate to point out that these facts, insofar as they are constants in human events and not intrinsically tied to an evolutive process (indeed, both logically and historically they are apart from this process), belong more to history than to social and juridical evolution. Furthermore, when an evolutionist is surprised collecting minute facts, intent upon the particular and the fragmentary, he has by that fact put himself somewhat out of the mainstream of evolutionism. It was a singular attitude for someone who, like D'Aguanno, had not given up the idea of individual property as a sociopolitical and juridical model, but who, on the other hand, did not show the diffidence that Cogliolo had toward the natural sciences and the methods proper to them. Indeed, a well-defined naturalism had inspired at least the first stages of his not very long intellectual career, the stages to which his essay on the genesis of the right to property belongs.[172]

To speak of historicist evolutionism signifies returning yet one more time to the problem of eclecticism, which was for this culture both a boon and a curse. Eclecticism filled the generic and empty vessels of the cultural options of our two authors with the most varied sorts of contents—however they may have been labeled. But, notwithstanding the contradictions it involved, eclecticism also enabled Cogliolo and D'Aguanno to perceive a more complex play of forces and motivations.

In them in fact we can see the reemergence of the social question that was such an important concern of the age. Still determinant north of the Alps, the social question seems to have died down in the more purely cultural expression of the debates in Italy, and its reemergence was accompanied by many manifestations of fear and perplexity.

The most rigidly evolutionistic passage in Cogliolo, the one in which he indicates in strict evolutionary terms the progress from collective to individual property, is also the one in which he declares in clear terms his fear of the wave of socialism and of a possible collectivization of goods. But, we might well ask, what in the vision of this Genoese scholar of the history of property was the result of polemics, and what reflected his view of the history of property? His praise of individual property—"the institution of civilized peoples, who have based all of their economy, their law, their progress, their morality, their agricultural science, and their industry on the *dominium unius* and not on the *dominium omnium*"—was spun out for a particular reason. It is not a scientific reflection, but a polemical dart launched against the "plebian socialists" and against their "barbarity." It is inserted into a badly composed dialectic of opposites that has the full emotional charge of ideological contrasts.[173]

D'Aguanno's essay, after running over the stages of the consolidation of individual property, concludes with a rapid but symptomatic reference to the social question. It is in the light of this question that he contemplates the problem, a problem that was still new, intact, and full of pitfalls, and that the enthusiastic revolutionary and postrevolutionary generations had left for the future to solve: "the other and more arduous problem of the right to property of all individuals."[174]

The cultural contradictions of the two Italian scholars can only be understood as a consequence of mixing the search for scientific truth with political passions. Guided by scientific objectivity, they showed their sympathy toward Maine, Laveleye, and Viollet and they rejected the propositions of Fustel[175] and Padelletti.[176] Guided by political concerns, they understood that the evolutionist argument inevitably valued individual property, and they followed this lead. This is particularly true of D'Aguanno, on whom the "truths" of possessive individualism weighed heavily, as we have seen at the beginning of this volume. From this double tendency was born the combination of attitudes that seems to us a contamination.

In their analysis taken as a whole, however, Cogliolo and D'Aguanno continued to present the image that the historians had furnished of collective forms of appropriation throughout history. It was an image of a phenomenon that was not marginal, but essential, that was universal with respect to space and time because it was laden with permanent values.[177] It had also left conspicuous vestiges even in the authors' own times, vestiges toward which they were open-minded.[178] Our interpretation can be further supported by other evidence: Cogliolo clearly rejected both Padelletti's theses and his condemnation of the theses of others, even though he had edited and annotated Padelletti's works.[179] He gave a prominent position to the unambiguous passage from Cattaneo that gives the present work its epigraph.[180] And both authors pillaged Laveleye's apologetic work on collective forms.[181]

Giacomo Venezian's inaugural lesson of 1887 on the assumption of his chair at the University of Camerino, published in 1888 and already known to us,[182] was made of quite another stuff. It constituted an unequaled contribution, a cultural event that was singular even in the many-faceted literature on civil law in Italy of the time.

The choice of a theme such as collective property was singular enough on the part of a man who, like Venezian, was professionally a specialist in civil law and, what is more, one who had strong preparation in Romanistic studies and had taught Romanistic material for some years.

More than one circumstance helps us to understand that choice, however. First of all, Venezian had been formed in the Bolognese school of Oreste Regnoli, and the problem must have been familiar to him. At just the moment that he was preparing and developing his thesis, Regnoli was much involved in the weighty questions regarding the nature, the history, and the fate of the *partecipanze* in Emilia, a task that involved political and scholarly competence and the skills of a lawyer.[183] This was the air that Venezian had breathed. To be sure, it was not an air favorable to the schemes of collective property, but it was one in which the theme circulated actively and with a sense of urgency.

Another element in Venezian's cultural formation contributed to his choice of theme: the contact that he had had from the beginning with the great works of mid-nineteenth-century German literature. This contact was neither transitory nor fortuitous: it had led him to an exhaustive knowledge of the great treatise writers of the *deutsches Privatrecht*— Stobbe, Beseler, Gierke, Heusler, and Bluntschli—whose influence on Venezian is evident in the systematic outlines of his long and weighty future work on usufruct.[184] This was a literature in which the category of *Gesamteigentum* was exploited to the fullest.

Let us add yet another element: Venezian's long postgraduate sojourn in Rome under Francesco Filomusi Guelfi, which he prepared for and planned carefully. Filomusi Guelfi was a polished and knowledgeable juridical and economic scholar. He was very close to Gierke and to the Germans in general and much at ease in his use of the Romanistic tradition; and he was soon to demonstrate his interest in the phenomenon of collective appropriation both in the *Enciclopedia giuridica* and in his ongoing courses on the law of real property.[185]

One final element is perhaps extrinsic, but it is not irrelevant. From 1885 Venezian was established permanently at Camerino, where he married into a noble local family.[186] And Camerino, located on the northernmost spurs of the Sibilline mountain chain, was an ideal vantage point from which a student of collective property could investigate a region full of the vestiges of ancient agrarian associations.[187] It was, in fact, not by chance that he found there a fellow lawyer and fellow professor at the university, Giovanni Zucconi. Zucconi, from a noble Camerino family, was a knowledgeable and intelligent observer of the history and social structure of his region and, first as a lawyer and later when he was involved in politics, he spoke out courageously on the subject of collective property, as we shall see.[188]

This formed, then, an accumulation of circumstances sufficient to invite the curiosity of the jurist from Trieste. This was all the more true as Venezian had been inculcated with a taste for the positive, for the experimental, and for concrete observation. An investigation of collective property that could take the form of research into thriving organizations operating within the agrarian-sylvan-pastoral reality that surrounded him appeared as a unique and unquestionably positive opportunity for laboratory analysis.[189]

During the whole of his intellectual career after 1887, Venezian's interest in studying these problems never flagged. This interest was one of the most deeply personal inspirations for his *opus maximum,* the weighty work on usufruct.[190] It recurred both in monographic articles[191] and in his courses in civil law and rural legislation.[192]

In his 1887 essay, Venezian's view of the problem is complex and complete. This short lecture does more than give the reader a practical and accurate synthesis of a phenomenon that was by its very nature intricate and chameleonlike. Even better, he communicates a sense of the richness of his topic; he makes his reader understand that simplistic diagnoses and solutions run the risk of being—or already are—resoundingly incorrect; that the problem has many dimensions and dimensions that run deep. A purely historical argument like Schupfer's, a methodological argument like those of Bonfante and Cogliolo, or a philosophical argument like D'Aguanno's were all simplifications of the total social, economic, and juridical complex that was collective property.

His investigation did not repudiate the advances that Italian thought had made in its discussion of property. It attempted to extend over an objective terrain, to observe the facts serenely and dispassionately; and it refused involvement in the heavy-handed political calculations or the vulgar proposals that prejudice and special interests are always quick to dictate.[193] His is the purposeful statement of a jurist of a rich cultural preparation, one who operated on a cultural level as he gave his inaugural lecture, which is, after all, still a class lecture. That is, he made it possible for himself and for his students to possess critically the object of his study. He had better means to do so than Bonfante, Schupfer, Cogliolo, and D'Aguanno had had, because he had all the dimensions of the phenomenon before him and because he drew from them a greater and more synthetic perception.

At the same time, although his argumentation remained cast in rigorously cultural terms, it was not the cold colloquium between Schupfer and his favorite sources, nor the subtle reasoning, tempered with historicism, of the philosopher D'Aguanno, that opened up, but for only an instant, to a consideration of the social movement. Behind the professor reading from his podium at Camerino lay a full consciousness of the social question and of the spread of workers' and peasants' disturbances. Rather than blocking Venezian's vision or misleading him, this consciousness was fearless, a source of inner wealth, a living force within him that made his thought even more robust.[194]

Venezian inserted the social and economic problem into the social dimension without distorting it and without losing sight of his stated objectives. It is not that he abandoned his critical viewpoint: rather, he clearly wanted to enrich his analysis in an attempt to grasp the whole of the complicated phenomenon he had chosen to examine.

Venezian's work so teems with facts that are economic, social, or even simply technical that it seems to have taken place more in some strange sort of sorcerer's den than in a laboratory. Here the vestiges of primitive landholding are subjected to an extraordinary exorcism: shielded from the spells of individualism and from partisan passions, safely sheltered by a solid observation of the facts, these vestiges acquire a configuration that not even the preceding investigations, intelligent as they were, had been able to give them. They reappear as genuine "popular rights" and as the expression of oppressed multitudes. They reemerge as signs of other traditions bearing alternative cultural values. They reconquer their character as collective property-holding arrangements with a claim to insertion in a juristic construction that fits into the cultural and socioeconomic schemes on which they rest and from which they arise.

Some features of this configuration, taken separately, were present and evident in some of the earlier investigations that we have discussed. For the first time, however, at least in the Italian literature on the subject, all of these features were to be found together and in harmony with one another in a synthetic view of the problem. Venezian considers the problem from every angle, from the angle of juristic structures as from that of historical matrixes or of social relevance—in all its complexity, as we have said before. Let us look rapidly at this presentation.

One idea is clearly fixed in Venezian's pages: that the collective forms of appropriation represented the vestiges of a popular culture that had prospered in pre-Roman times, but that had limped along under the merciless cultural imperialism of Rome, and had persisted on a provincial and municipal level in spite of the triumph of the official mode of ownership. They represented true and proper "popular rights,"[195] unwittingly or maliciously misinterpreted and violated by the class that controlled political and economic power in the unified state.

The removal of the blinders of the individualistic, Romanistic point of view that Venezian effected as he brought data and experience rather than postulates, models, biases, and prejudices to bear on this phenomenon led necessarily to a political diagnosis. By his choice of a cultural, empirical, and therefore positivist approach, our scrupulous observer raised the veil of the piteous apologies and the impossible rhetoric of the liberal intelligentsia. He denounced the odious instruments of oppression that the dominant class had used in dealing with the incommodious arrangements of collective landholding and the ideological cast of its lofty idealistic statements. He discovered in the division and dissolution of the *promiscuità* [intercommunity common pasture and gathering lands] a brilliant means of increasing the great landed estates, the *latifondi,* and a source of misery for populations accustomed for centuries to at least the decorous poverty that collective management had guaranteed them.[196]

It was a denunciation unusual for a jurist, as unusual as the piercing intellectual apparatus that Venezian used in his bold x-ray of the hidden recesses of the idea of "general interest," so frequent in the mouth of the enlightened bourgeoisie.

> When the determination of the general interest proceeds from abstract criteria and is not rigorously induced from the careful consideration of particular interests, which the general interest must summarize and reconcile; when with the pretext that society is an organism a new metaphysic is fabricated, and when activities, needs, and ends are attributed to the whole of society that are not the result of the activities, needs, and ends of the men that make it up, I become . . . afraid of the consequences of these methods that put the most legitimate of interests at the discretion of impressions, of transitory opinions, of groups of momentarily prevalent interests. . . .[197]

It is not, I believe, a distortion of the role of this study if we see in it a sign of impatience with the mystificatory character of certain supposed conquests of modern individualism, in reality more the conquests of the bourgeoisie and of interest groups than an objective realization of the demands of the community. Venezian showed courage in his indictment of the "new metaphysics" and of the general and abstract rules that, without the slightest "coordination with moral, intellectual, and economic conditions,"[198] claimed to coincide with the common good, while instead, he insisted, they hid beneath the specious and illusory guarantees of abstraction the defense of particular interests and gave "a color of liberal novelties to so many useless and harmful injustices."[199]

Venezian here took up a theme that proved to be neither sporadic nor an isolated instance in his work. To the contrary, we find it repeated in full in a brilliant course given at the University of Messina in 1898–99 on rural legislation, unfortunately left in humble and inaccessible form in mimeographed copy and nearly universally unknown. We see in these course notes confirmation of a Venezian who was certainly not a socialist, but was just as certainly antiindividualistic,[200] and who manipulated easily the categories of "class" and "dominant class" which he applied to the untouched terrain of the liberal interpretation of the state.[201]

We will examine elsewhere the Messina lectures. Let us return here to the "classism" of Venezian. Dating from the "Reliquie," we can see the outlines of an iconoclast who, irritated by the propaganda of a regime, sought to clear away the haze of a persuasive and consequently dangerous modern mythology. He refused the *a priori* argument of "the leaven of individual interest" and the illusions of the "mirages of economic transformations,"[202] and he rediscovered among factual events—in the concreteness of the interwoven and generalized conditions of men and situations in precise times and places—the sense of proportion and the basis for an accurate diagnosis that was first of all historical but that was, in consequence, also economic, social, and juridical.

In its attempt to constitute a formulation of the most accurate diagnosis possible, Venezian's lecture becomes also a discourse on method. It insists that the observer eschew facile shortsightedness and look beyond the little garden of space and time that stands around him, for that is the typical terrain of sentiments, passions, humors, and moral judgments. "The illusion of the moral perspective in which small, proximate facts grow to gigantic proportions"[203] could be overcome only when a broad range of varied experience came under observation. Then the taste for the particular, and even for that part of the particular that is the subjective contribution of the interpreter, could be blended into the richness of a material whose objectivity succeeds in conditioning any subjectivity.

Venezian makes no citations in his text—its character as a lecture seems to preclude them—but it is clear that he was talking about the distorted view of the origins of landed property that had come out of the controversy north of the Alps, particularly from the contribution of Fustel, whose historical material was totally warped by moral judgments.

Venezian's text returns repeatedly to the need for a certain distance between the interpreter and his historical material, for a return to objectivity and for a refusal of all prejudgment of the sources. The "political" condemnation of collective property formulated by nineteenth-century culture was not the fruit of calm observation and documentation of the phenomenon; it was an ideological evaluation. It did not show a contemplation of concrete materials but particular interests that those materials might tend to cast doubt on or deny. And Venezian does not mince his words in his severe condemnation of this prefabricated and irrevocable condemnation.

Venezian's judgment was also political and moral. But it emerged *a posteriori* in his conclusions, after he had summed up and evaluated the collective modes on the level that was congenial to him, that of things. Then the man of culture, the positivist scholar, the jurist, and the historian take it as a duty to make note of a betrayal and a mystification. Then the political and moral elements in his conclusions lend their weight to a critical judgment and not to prejudices or intellectual models. Such elements were born and would remain on the level of criticism as a method, on the level of a continual confrontation with the facts. In other words, they would be an inseparable and unrenounceable part of a cultural operation carried to its logical conclusion. This can occur when a scholar is receptive but vigilant, when his consciousness takes full possession of the data. Then his judgment can be well founded and motivated. This can never happen with passive compilation.

Venezian intended that his analysis be operative on a cultural level, as in fact it was. Its action extended in two directions: to reestablish collective landholding modes within a more ample and diversified set of relations among cultures, and to return them to descriptive specifications and categories that were better adapted to them than those offered by the usual canons, both interpretive and normative, of the Romans and the Romanists. More than one page of his "Reliquie" shows clear evidence of the guidance of Maine and Laveleye, who, although not cited, in accordance with Venezian's decision to cite no one, can be presumed to have been constantly present on his desk.

There are two postulates on which Venezian's argument rests. The first is that individual property "is far from being a universal fact."[204] This was proven by the collective forms of appropriation that were concretely present in history and in the real experience of a diversity of contemporary peoples: they were present in the Swiss *Allmend,* the Swedish *almaenning,* the Norwegian *almindinger,* the German *Marca,* the Scottish township, the Javanese *dessa,* the Russian *mir,* the Balkan *zadruga*.[205] The second was that after the great controversy in Europe, "the belief that individual property is a universal and necessary institution, formerly accepted as dogma, perished."[206]

All of this seems to be taken wholesale from Laveleye's work, and the tedious listing of specific collective arrangements that we have indulgently repeated above is the exact reproduction of the types studied by the Belgian economist. It thus furnishes a concrete indication of Venezian's source. What is new in the argument of Venezian—a jurist by profession and therefore a follower of the system of law in force—is that it does not wander off into economic and sociological considerations as does Laveleye's, but remains contained within the rigorous limits set by juridical culture.

Demani comunali and *usi civici* in southern Italy, collectively owned lands, *partecipanze* and so on elsewhere, were all, even in the easily ascertainable particularity of their historical and juridical situations, "vestiges of collective property." That is, they were connected to a structure in pre-Roman civilization and had arrived at the present day by means that had nothing to do with Roman analysis, systemization, and reflection.[207] For this reason, it was a historical and juridical absurdity, and it was an incorrect cultural procedure, to interpret these organizational forms by using the measure of Roman law and the Romanistic tradition or their theoretical instruments. Reversing the figure in the title of a celebrated essay of Emilio Betti, we could say that Venezian's chief care on an intellectual level lay in an attempt to avoid a false approach to the juridical question dependent on an erroneous historical diagnosis.[208]

Whether that false approach was the result of calculation or ideology, or merely of imperfect methodological instruments and of the nearsightedness of scholars, interested Venezian little at this point. What interested him was the colossal misunderstanding that a group of institutions had been subjected to, maliciously or no.

Out of these hardships came the lines of an inclusive reconstruction of collective forms, once the terrain had finally been freed of encumbrances and technical models. Until recent times, Venezian teaches, those forms had been subjected to the defamatory accusation of being in open violation of the splendid and brilliant "harmonious proportion of the legislative edifice,"[209] and they had been treated as malformed creatures, constrained by their deformity to be crushed under the harsh apparatus of juridical orthopaedia. But this had resulted more from a distortion in the minds of unreceptive observers than a deformation *in re*. It was due to procedures based on preconceived categories rather than on a pluralistic vision of an unfolding juridical process.

This attitude, courageous on the part of a young professor, was strengthened by deeply meditated reading of his beloved authors in the great German and Austrian literatures on the subject. Shaking off the problem of resolving the contradictory clichés involved, he found in this literature an alternative channel, an alternative guideline, *another* and more satisfactory juridical construction.

What had been seen by the Romanistic tradition and the harmonious but pitiless individualistic system of the nineteenth century as "concessions made by great feudal lords, lay or ecclesiastical"[210] he saw as "a way of enjoying communal goods subordinated to the tolerance of the administration."[211] Such communal modes were a complex of abnormal and heteronymous situations relegated provisorially to the refuse heap as servitudes while awaiting complete elimination. Furthermore:

> The Roman name of servitude did not place them in a category of juridical institutions, but served to stigmatize them as abuses, tolerated remedies of other abuses, which, upon the disappearance of the latter, lost their reason for being.[212]

This system unexpectedly reacquired a different dimension, a cultural dignity that permitted the canon of the eurythmy of the system to appear ridiculous. It acquired an autonomy from the spiral of Roman order, that was as intolerant of foreign bodies as are all systems of iron-clad organization. It was that *eurythmy,* that *order* that, because they were inflexible, revealed their limitations and had to be eliminated.

The central point in Venezian's juridical argument is important for the very reason that it moves within and attests to an attempt at *juristische Konstruktion.* It lies in the rediscovery of a range of institutions that resembles collective property and that he exploited by placing them carefully outside the confines of the Romanistic tradition. To continue in the error of measuring the *usi civici* with the standard of a culture that had *not* produced them, that to the contrary was structured on opposing solutions, that had always and consistently disdained and misinterpreted them, would have been for Venezian a sterile and obfuscating activity. Insights and perceptions, which we have seen as vital in many of the major figures in the great controversy, are reinforced in Venezian and are put into focus by an intelligence that saw not only the historical but also the systematic dimension of the juridical universe.

Collective ownership, then, did not involve "servitudes," that is, dependent and secondary structures necessarily attached to an original and conditioning situation. It involved "rights," rights to collective property, of which the first identifying characteristic was autonomy, both on a historical level and on a systematic level.

A completely renewed understanding of the problem thus came into being. This came about through the miracle of a genuinely historical grasp of the problem, which in turn was made possible by dislodging it from the trammels of Roman logic and from the exclusively privatistic setting into which it had always erroneously been put.[213] The logical system of the Romans was not written in the nature of things; it was a product of history. It was a framework constructed *ex post,* after a series of sociopolitical and cultural premises had already been consolidated. Without these premises it was inapplicable, forced, and threatened to compromise completely any understanding of the problem.

Intelligenza is the term that Venezian uses, and in its root sense of *intelligere,* it appears to direct all of his lively pamphlet. He tries to arrive at this understanding as *intelligere* by not neglecting any implication, any connection, any aspect of the question, putting every single thing, every datum, in its proper historical place, matrix, and trend.

Now, if that was the methodological principle that Venezian found most important, how could he possibly utilize logical and technical tools that were all designed to expunge the foreign element of collective property from the coherent and well-cemented structure of juridical order? How could he depend on an ordering that in its historical life had always aimed at mithridatizing its own organism against the poisons of that foreign body by neutralizing it and assimilating it with schemes of copropriety, collective bodies, and servitudes?[214]

But there is a great difference between collective property and these other operative schemes. When Venezian speaks of collective property, he does not in fact intend to use the term in a nontechnical sense, to use it as a vague common denominator for a group of institutions, as did many "collectivists" in the great controversy. He refers to a type of juridical phenomenon by a qualification that bears juridical significance. He had in mind particularly the communal *demanii* of the kingdom of Naples and the collective *dominii* of the ex-Pontifical States;[215] and for him collective property was that right to ownership that depends on the corporation as an expression of the general interests of the group, that is, of an indeterminate series of generations that makes up the historical reality, past, present, and future, of the group itself. This right is worked out in a complex situation of powers, rights, and duties: the unmediated power of the *universitas* over goods, but also the duty to destine the goods themselves to the direct use of the single participants, and, hence, the duty of not alienating them; the right of the single participants to the use and enjoyment of the holdings within the limits of the institutional ends of the *universitas.* These are powers, rights, and duties that presuppose the interpenetration of the subjective position of the member of the community with the ends of the corporation itself.[216]

Roman joint ownership was conceptually totally different from a structure like collective property. Its technical apparatus was thought of, in its supporting principles, as ownership involving a share for each coowner. It was seen as provisory structure, interlocutory, and abnormal in comparison to the normal proprietary situation, individual property, which was by its nature perpetual and exclusive. Collective property, on the other hand, has as its supreme guiding principle the subordination of the single positions—that of the participants but also that of the corporation—to the unrenounceable good of providing the economic support of the *universitas*. Collective property is a scheme of property as function at its highest degree, in which all seems available, in a certain teleological rigidity, to be sacrificed to the objective ends of the communitarian organization. Individual property is a scheme of property as belonging at its highest degree, in which all is the emanation of the will of the single subject.

We will return in the last chapter to the problem of the juridical construction of the collective forms of appropriation, and we will see at that time how much of this diagnosis Venezian makes use of in his volume on usufruct, which was published in 1895. Let it suffice for the moment to conclude this rapid examination of his conclusions by noting that for the first time in Italy someone had attempted and carried out a well-prepared juridical presentation of the salient features of these forms. On the level of juridical techniques as well, Venezian's work brought the impalpable material of consuetudinarian usages into a definite framework.

But Venezian's inaugural lecture remained an event nearly unique in the study of civil law in Italy. The problem of "collective property," which had forced him to undertake a stringent examination of conscience and which had posed for him so many difficult questions, generally was either not perceived in all its importance, or not perceived at all, or deliberately ignored by specialists in civil law.

Venezian's work would circulate to explosive effect in the free atmosphere of the courses that Filomusi Guelfi gave at the Sapienza in Rome and trusted humbly to the editorial zeal of his students.[217] It would circulate among the young, who understood the provocatory nature of its eloquent argument.[218] But we could search in vain in the pages of works in which we might expect to find traces of it: in the young Nicola Coviello on so-called 'irregular servitudes,'[219] in the *Istituzioni* of Giampietro Chironi,[220] or in the *Corso* of Emanuele Gianturco.[221]

Someone more attentive to sonorous titles than to the reality of the contents might be surprised not to see more than a fleeting and distracted reference to Venezian's study in Enrico Cimbali's discourse on *La proprietà e i suoi limiti*. Poor Cimbali! The rhetoric of some years later would erect a minor altar to this juristic socialist, but his intellectual development took place within a system conceived and resolved in individualistic terms. His tribute to Laveleye's "most important book"[222] is the homage of a singer to a piece that is universally applauded; it is purely external. From his conclusions, in fact, one learns only that individual property was the mature fruit of a long historical process, while the many clues that might have led to alternative forms of property are carefully avoided.

The reason for this lies in the fact that for Cimbali "the problem of property is a problem of liberty,"[223] that "real property, being the expression, or, better, the continuation of the personal property of man into the exterior world, necessarily reproduces in itself all the characteristics of that property,"[224] the first of which was that of being exclusive.

Individual property was for the jurist the last frontier, the territorial border in relation to which he measured the legitimacy of a reform or a revision. Within this area his freedom of investigation was seen as autonomous research; beyond it, it was seen as unnaturally arbitrary. The jurist's work took place within those confines, and any attempt at applications to society could run free only within the terms of the institution of individual property, which were presented as the very ends of his work and as springing from the nature of the institution itself. This was why Cimbali's thought and that of all those who worked on the question of property and its limits could not but result in an attempt to attach individual property more securely to the social context, to grasp at all possible ties with the system of the Codification and the special laws. This was why their work could advance no further.

8 The Agrarian

Inquiry: Practice

Grafted onto Theory

The Start of a Reexamination in Economic Thought

The emergence of a different and more complex image of the phenomenon of property, which occupied several schools of Italian juridical thought between the 1880s and the 1890s and forced them to a thorough reexamination of solidly established views, left more than a passing trace in economic thought as well.

The deliberations and conclusions of German doctrine, transplanted in Italy, as we have seen, beginning with Vito Cusumano's study of 1874, had already indicated new paths to discover. Soon after, Laveleye's book began to pass from hand to hand among Italian economists. His name was already familiar to them through his preceding studies in pure and applied economics, and with his work on property, those paths became more clearly defined. The classical science of economics operated with and built on the model of "property" that had been received in custody from the jurists. In philosophical terms, its configurations and its character were those of the natural right to property; in technical terms, it was the Roman and Romanistic *dominium*. When a feeling of dissatisfaction began to find its way among the jurists, the model revealed that its solidity was deceptive, and it crumbled inexorably under the attack of the corrosive new ideas.

Cusumano's and Laveleye's works advanced toward a substantially identical objective, and two years after their appearance traces of this more complex image of property can be seen in another work, the lengthy and ambitious *Economia dei popoli e degli Stati* of Fedele Lampertico, whose entire third volume is dedicated to "La proprietà."[1]

172

Although Lampertico reaffirmed traditional interpretations in this work and composed the usual mannerist chromo, depicting individual property as absolute, perpetual, and exclusive, he felt obliged to discuss Laveleye's researches fully, explicitly accepting several important points in Laveleye's argument, such as the priority of collective appropriation over private[2] and, consequently, the historical nature of the latter.[3]

He rejected firmly the Belgian scholar's sociopolitical proposals, however. Lampertico could accept the collective arrangements that were still alive and thriving at the end of the nineteenth century as "the vestige of a condition of things in other times most common and ordinary"[4] and could consider them rehabilitated to their full historical and juridical dignity; but for him they could never have any meaningful role in the future, nor could they, for that reason, be proposed as an operative scheme within contemporary society.

Lampertico remained dominated by an evolutionistic optimism. This optimism led him to understand individual property as a product of history, to be sure, but he saw it also as a reality caught up in an irresistible progress.

He was a scholar of modest resources, even if he was gifted with a sensitivity and perceptiveness concerning the new currents within the science of economics. We see in him a moment favorable for listening, a purely receptive moment, never translated into a real and personal appropriation of these ideas.

What Laveleye had to offer, Lampertico received and even exploited, but it remained external to the individualistic edifice, simply juxtaposed to it without touching its structure. This had been the case, or it was to be the case, for many jurists, for example, for the philosopher of law Giuseppe D'Aguanno and for the civilist Enrico Cimbali. They did not and did not want to think of alternative models. The result was only an individual property removed from the terrestrial paradise of the state of nature and restored to the realm of changing human affairs. Another result was that the scholar, grasping the object of his cognition on the plane of the relative, was freed from what had been up to that point a recurrent liturgy of semicultural approaches.

Lampertico's intellectual equipment permitted him no more than this; but it is already enough that a methodological reexamination of undeniable importance be included in a work that appeared in Italy as the compendium of economic thought on the subject of property up to 1876. The fruits of this reexamination were to be more evident in personalities who were more deeply involved in the great scholarly debates of those years, for example in the first organic work of Achille Loria on agrarian revenue[5] and in the essay of Salvatore Cognetti de Martiis on primitive forms in the evolution of economics.[6]

Cognetti's vision was that of sociology. He found the model for his investigations in ethnological inquiry and data gathering,[7] and he found his most congenial sources in the narratives of explorers such as Cameron, Livingstone, and Stanley,[8] in Le Play's observations, and in the data offered in the systematic overviews gathered by the Cobden Club.[9] He followed methodological canons founded in the criteria of Maine and Laveleye; and we find in the center of his volume a chapter on the economic organization of the village commune in which Laveleye's influence is determinant and in which the object of the author's study is a structure that is clearly collective.

Thus far we have seen reexaminations of method, updatings of theory, and the enrichment of cultural baggage. In these same years, however, an event of enormous consequence was coming to maturity. It was to open up, particularly for the economists, a wealth of first-hand material of incredible variety, read in the structure of their own Italian agriculture and based on a notable effort to collect minute data. It was a faithful expression of the "real nation" in all the range of its composite voices. I refer to the great *Inchiesta agraria e sulle condizioni della classe agricola* launched by Parliament with the law of 15 March 1877, and carried out, starting from 30 April of that year, by a commission presided over by Stefano Jacini.[10]

The Agrarian Inquiry and "Collective Property": The Contribution of Agostino Bertani

From the moment that the first volume of the *Acts* of the commission for the Agrarian Inquiry made its appearance, a mass of facts began to pour down on the desks of the economists and jurists.

They were for the most part facts related to an Italy of small cities, a decentralized Italy, a country profoundly rooted in its history. They were facts that offered an image of the "real nation" that lay outside the models of the official propaganda of the kingdom, but that had the merit of being concrete, of coming relatively unfiltered from the structural reality of forest, pasture, and cultivated lands and that, as such, bore the authority and authenticity inherent in things.

Some filtering there was, obviously, and some of it was the work of the commission itself. In the course of identifying, selecting, and coordinating the data and fitting it into a context, the commission aligned itself unfailingly with the programs and the positions of the dominant class and its culture. It was clearly unresponsive and uncomprehending when the subject of collective property arose, and its hostility was sometimes hidden, but sometimes openly declared. On the systematic level, the "vestiges of collective property" were identified as "encumbrances on property," almost as if to underline their nature as abuses, as superfluities, as parasitic elements accumulated through the fault of poor governance, central or local.

With such an orientation, the problem of the "proprietary" nature of those institutions was resolved implicitly and negatively. They were placed definitively at the level to which they had been forced to gravitate, a level inferior by far to that of property. It was because the members of the commission inevitably drew consequences of this sort that Stefano Jacini, its president, speaking in its name, asked in the final report to the ministry of Justice that

> the complete liberation be hastened, not only in name but also in fact, of the rural property from the ties and encumbrances that obstruct it in many ways.

He did not hesitate to list among these restraints:

> the *enfiteusi*, the *canoni*, the *censi*, the *livelli*, the *decime*, the *condominî* and *diritti promiscui*, the *servitù d'uso*, the *erbatico* and *pascolo* in the provinces of the Veneto, the *vagantivo*, and the abusive consuetudinarian servitudes to cut wood or grass, or even the right of temporary occupation and planting, etc.[11]

Jacini knew agricultural theory and was a farm proprietor himself, but he made no distinction between situations that it would have been proper and realistic to distinguish. Perhaps he was too accustomed to the fertile flood plain of his native Lombardy, for he remained dominated by a guiding idea that was ideological but also emotional and common to the new man of the postrevolutionary period: that of the liberation and the individualization of property.[12] Thus the perpetual leases under *enfiteusi* and collective holdings were unjustifiably paired with sharecropping arrangements such as the *censi* and the *decime* in a composite bundle of confused and distorted realities, as might have been the case a hundred years earlier in the discourse of some Jacobin enflamed by the fury of his passions.

Since this was not only the attitude of the president but also of the greater part of the commissioners,[13] the only result that we would have any right to expect from the enormous work of the Inquiry might be approximate and fugitive appearances of the problem of collective agrarian structures, disguised and constrained by the mechanisms that had been adopted.

But this was not so. The Inquiry was, quite the contrary, the natural channel through which collective property emerged fully and clearly and through which its importance in Italy was reaffirmed. Certainly, this was not so thanks to Jacini and to the "extremely well-off proprietors" who surrounded him[14] and seconded him in entangling in conditioning economic and juridical qualifications the entire complex of landholding structures in Italy. It was rather thanks to certain holes in that web, discovered and much discussed, that a historical and social material that was neither filtered nor distorted came to light.

There were two singular personalities who led the attack on the unified, monolithic interpretation: Agostino Bertani and Ghino Valenti. Both men worked among those who directed the Inquiry, at different levels and with a profound diversity of style, of intellectual means, and of concrete purposes; but both can be seen as forgers of an innovative analysis. Agostino Bertani was a physician, a deputy, and a man extremely sensitive to social problems who demonstrated a constant and generous sense of being a leader of the people. He was a member of the commission; in fact, its vice president.[15] Ghino Valenti was first an official in the Agricultural Administration, later a university professor. He was thoroughly prepared in theory and had read widely, he was an expert in agricultural practice and technology, and he was indeed a member of the commission as an agricultural expert.[16] Bertani directed personally the work of the Inquiry in the eighth district, the provinces of Porto Maurizio, Genoa, and Massa-Carrara. Valenti was the soul and guiding force of the researches in the fifth district in the provinces of Ascoli-Piceno, Ancona, Macerata, and Pesaro.[17] This is where the web came unraveled—in the voluminous materials from these two districts, in work directed and conceived by Bertani and Valenti and tolerated or endured by the majority of the commission. Furthermore, at the end of their labors, when the documents were there to speak for themselves, Bertani also spoke out clearly in his own voice in an accusatory appendix to Jacini's final report. This appendix was a true and proper counterreport[18] in which the evaluation of collective property constituted one of the major points of dissention and of his liveliest quarrel with the president.

For Agostino Bertani an agrarian inquiry should not have a predominantly technical and statistical character, as Jacini and his associates wanted, and as was in fact the character of the Inquiry. As he saw it, it should serve another purpose as well: it should serve to dispel confusion and should investigate the social condition of the agricultural workers. It should understand their misery and the deplorable economic and hygienic conditions in which they were constrained to live; it should examine their exploitation by many proprietors who were enlightened progressives when it came to drawing-room discussions but deafly uncomprehending when they were party to an agrarian contract.[19]

Bertani was disarmingly ingenuous but also courageous and sincere when he proposed a parliamentary inquiry into the conditions of agricultural workers in a discourse to the Chamber of Deputies on 7 June 1872. He went right to the point:

We prefer to have light shed on even the most discomforting misery, on age-long sufferings, as on the excesses of avarice and the abuses of power of some proprietors.[20]

This was a frank and honest way of speaking, stripped of special interests and preconceptions, and Bertani repeated substantially the same proposal concerning the inquiry on agriculture. His proposal met with general indifference, however, or, even worse, it clashed with a general fear of disturbing social stasis. Moral sentiments may have prevailed in the Milanese deputy to make him feel it was preferable *ut scandala eveniant;* among the other deputies political reason prevailed, and they felt it preferable to avoid the issue.

In effect, when it was possible to state in a parliamentary body that the only real needs in the area of agriculture were for "capital and security from theft in the fields" and that there was no real class dissention between proprietors and workers unless it were provoked willfully,[21] how could a program like Bertani's—and standing with Bertani there were only Pasquale Villari, Francesco Morelli, and few others—possibly be given a hearing by those who held such views and who based their arguments on the overtaxed "patience" of the poor?[22]

Evidently, Bertani's program was not put into effect, nor could it have been at that precise moment in history: Bertani could then only work in a nearly complete isolation. As has correctly been observed, his point of departure was an insight into the formation of a negative relation between the policy of the unified state and the mass of the people.[23] But to make this insight one's own and to translate it into concrete terms would mean denying the saccharine image of the liberal state supported by the enthusiasms and the energies of all citizens, an image that the political class of the 1870s still tried to preserve, although its embalming was losing its effectiveness. To challenge it would mean condemning this image as false and isolating the challenger from the political class.

This, then, was Bertani's position within the commission. This was his position in the evaluation of the collective landholding arrangements. His long familiarity with the person and the works of Carlo Cattaneo must have helped him to focus both his authentically democratic vision—threatened by the clichés of the regime—and his sensitivity to the values expressed in popular writings. The ears of Catteneo's devoted disciple must have rung with the words of his great master[24]—words of serene observation, thoroughly grounded in economics and agrarian science, rigorously pursued and purified of every pollution of the passions. This is all the more likely as Cattaneo's writings were being readied for publication by the editor Le Monnier at approximately the same time that the work on the Inquiry was taking form.

We can see Cattaneo's influence in Bertani's report on the region of Liguria and the Lunigiana. Writing of the "Promiscuità dei pascoli, gride, servitù di legnatico" [common pasture lands, rights by public proclamation, woodcutting rights], he qualified this group of institutions as the vestiges of ancient communal properties and the consequence of ancient agrarian communism, exactly as the Lombard economist had done when he wrote of the landholding arrangements of the plain of Magadino.[25]

Bertani's dissent grew in force, beginning its upward spiral in the appendix to the final report written by Jacini, the counterreport in which Bertani condensed not only his dissent but also the message of his stillborn program. Let him speak for himself:

> Likewise, I will say briefly, still in the interest of the poorest class, that one must proceed cautiously in releasing properties, nor should they all be put in the same category, for fear of offending the interests of the poor. To the eminent rapporteur it seems natural that the joint ownerships, the promiscuous rights, the servitudes regarding land should be resolved in all cases in favor of the titular proprietor, with the sacrifice of those rights of tillage, grazing, fishing, cutting cane, grass, wood, etc., that now belong to the poor. A pure and simple suppression would not be equitable.[26]

The agrarian world that Bertani evokes here does not have the same physiognomy as the unexceptionable data gathered by Jacini, which was composed of statistics, figures, data on crops and on the quality of the lands. Here was an agrarian world made of rich and poor, permeated by a pitiless dialectic between exploiters and the exploited, analyzed by means of an instrument of interpretation in wide use at the time, the notion of class.[27]

We do not know whether Bertani had read Maine or Laveleye, but we can state with certainty that his discourse drew on a limited cultural hinterland and that he carefully avoided the enticements of theoretical constructions and historical interpretations. Juridical subtleties also escaped Bertani the physician—the distinction between servitudes and autonomous rights, for instance—but it was not the problem of juridical qualification that interested him. The problem that emerges in his thought—and it is a problem that deserved a good deal less casual treatment from the commission—is the social problem. In this context, collective landholding arrangements reacquired their character of long-term instruments of survival for a population, as authentic popular rights legitimized by custom and arising out of the great stream of primitive agrarian communism.

This was little, and this was much. Bertani's declaration of sympathy for this collection of institutions was less important than the break in the homogeneous view of them as "encumbrances on property" that so often recurs in the reports of the Inquiry.

Bertani's discourse was not of a sort to have a deep influence, since it was so lacking in theoretical backing, so overbrimming with political passion, and so irritating to the Italian ruling class. It was valuable as a first sign of weakness and as a summary and approximate challenge. Included within the authoritative context of the massive Inquiry, however, and sent off to thousands of future readers, legislators, officials, and specialists, it was an invitation to reexamine the problem and to avoid taking hasty action.

The Agrarian Inquiry and "Collective Property": The Work of Ghino Valenti

Bertani, the physician, relying on his sociopolitical sensitivity, had more properly guessed at the problem than reflected on it, and he had not even tried to put it into a larger theoretical picture or to understand its historical and cultural foundations. More than an analysis, his was an instinctive and rough recognition that the problem existed. The limits of his singular personality were reflected in his writings, and they remained among the great jumble of materials of the Inquiry as a testimony that was absolutely self-contained, isolated, and sullenly polemical.

The same cannot be said for the contribution of Ghino Valenti. It was voluminous, founded in minute analysis, and carefully weighed in its every affirmation. It projected beyond the limits of the Inquiry to set up a relationship between practice—the terrain typical of the Inquiry—and scholarly reflection.

Such a program must have been particularly congenial to Valenti. His professional and cultural formation and his career give proof of a person ever inclined to mediate and to establish connections between the two dimensions of practice and scholarship.

Valenti had acquired an excellent familiarity with the law, both from his studies and from the atmosphere of his home,[28] which enabled him, as a specialist in agrarian economy, to see clearly the juridical implications of what he was saying. When he took up the study of economics he read the classical Italian authors—Romagnosi and Cattaneo first among them—and he enjoyed longstanding acquaintances with Lampertico and other well-known economists.[29] Born in Macerata, he moved easily in the world of the agrarian problems of the provinces of the Marche, where he directed a local newspaper,[30] administered his own inherited lands, and presided over the local *Comizio agrario,* one of the commissions recently instituted in every provincial capital as a consultive organ for the government and as a means of encouraging local agriculture.[31]

When Stefano Jacini called on him, as president of the *Comizio agrario* of Macerata, to participate in the work of the Inquiry,[32] it was a complex personality[33] that came to join the group. Perhaps a difficult person, but one extremely knowledgeable and eternally dissatisfied with mere data and statistics.[34]

Valenti's work was extraordinary as well. Unlike what happened in other regions, Valenti, as effective rapporteur for the Marche, far from simply gathering and then submitting the material, insisted on interpreting it in light of the history, the customs, and the complicated social and geo-agronomic reality of his native region. The result was that "unique object" within the Jacini Inquiry that was the chapter dedicated to collective holdings in the mountains of Umbria and the Marche. It was, to be sure, the work of many hands—Giovanni Zucconi's aid was significant. But above all, it bears the unmistakable imprint of the economist from Macerata.[35]

A real knowledge of agrarian techniques and of the geological structure of the region were joined in Valenti with a careful use of historical sources, a solid juridical diagnosis, and an acute sensitivity to socioeconomic phenomena. They yielded unexpected fruits. There, among the data and the figures that Jacini had asked for, the collective forms of landholding came to assume, right in the midst of the Inquiry that was to constitute a technical monument to individual property, undistorted by the class image that leaps from Bertani's pages, a reality both embarrassing and challenging for the professional politicians in Rome.

This portrait was not drawn in lines of direct and angry polemic, nor in the heightened colors of social opposition, nor in pietistic invocations. It arose from an unadorned and concrete analysis; it was drawn from objective circumstances. The reason of men—Bertani would have said the reason of the poor—remained in the background, but what was most evident was the reason of things, written in things. This time, a local boy from the Marche really winged a stone that flew all the way to Rome and created a commotion in the pigeon roost of Montecitorio![36]

An initial comparison may show the courage of the path that Valenti chose. In the material concerning the other districts, and even in that concerning the provinces of Rome, Grosseto, and Perugia in the same fifth district, the collective landholding arrangements are weakened by being placed under the heading of "encumbrances on property."[37] But the section on the provinces of Ancona, Ascoli, Macerata, and Pesaro reveals a new category right from the outset. An autonomous chapter is dedicated to these structures under the heading, "La proprietà collettiva nella zona montana,''[38] and there is, on the contrary, not the least trace of them in the succeeding chapter, "Valori e gravami della proprietà."

The heading already speaks clearly for the intention of the author. The chapter that it announced was to be, first of all, an interpretation of the data offered by the investigations into the mountainous regions of Piceno, and it was to be constructed with a coherent theoretical outline and in light of the author's scientific knowledge. It was to be, in sum, a work of a scientific nature.

The difference between this chapter and the remainder of the volume can best be seen in this additional dimension. This "unique object," to repeat a term already used, is unique because it is of another quality than the other reports. It is, to be sure, a work that came out of the data in a coherent manner and that fulfilled the institutional aims of the Inquiry. But it was also one that takes on those data as an opportunity for thoughts on the theory of property, thoughts that had matured in the author's mind and that he wanted to declare from the authoritative pulpit of the Inquiry. Seen in this light, Valenti's essay appears almost as a foreign element within a compact but rather flat body of material. It also served the invaluable purpose of connecting the Inquiry as an act of praxis to current scientific thought.

Valenti's introduction could hardly be more eloquent:

> Our civil legislation contemplates only one form of property, individual property, the *dominium quiritarium* of Roman law, susceptible to modifications, yes, but one in its essence. This is why most jurists do not admit that another form could or should exist.[39]

This sentence would have been unimaginable in the mouth of the obtuse senator Francesco Vitelleschi or of a technician competent only in his technical knowledge, and it is easy to discern its cultural derivation. We can see in it evident echoes of Maine's and Laveleye's criticism of Roman law and of the Romanistic monopoly, and we know that Valenti had read their works or was reading them during those years and was impressed by them.[40] We can see an evident and profound dissatisfaction with the one-sidedness of the legislation currently in force. We can also see familiarity with the schemes of discourse habitual to jurists: when Valenti speaks of "modifications" of property he uses a term lifted from a technical vocabulary and inserted in a systematic conceptual arsenal proper to legislation and to the doctrines of civil law after the Napoleonic Code.

The passage quoted implies that there was a knot to undo, an obstacle to remove, which was prejudicial to the understanding of the object. Like Maine and Laveleye, Valenti knew that an observer needed to rid his mind of accepted notions, and he demanded the refusal of a *prejudgment* in order to reach a *judgment* critically founded in the analysis of the "historical origin" and of the "true economic and juridical nature" that were consequent to that origin.[41]

This meant for Valenti that one must look attentively into the ways in which the different collective forms still in existence were structured and to examine minutely the various *consorzi, università, comunanze,* and *diritti d'uso.*[42] This meant that he wanted to look ever deeper into the vortex of history in an effort to locate a guiding principle that might prove not to be fictitious.[43] From this came Valenti's readiness to receive an economic and juridical thesis unspoiled by obligatory categories and the contamination of passions.[44] From here also came the need to fit the modest organizational realities of the Appennine mountains into a koine of broadest range and to measure them against the paradigm of the Germanic landholding structures, notably the *Allmend* of Laveleye, Heusler, and Miaskowski.[45]

As these local land-use arrangements became identified as manifestations of collective property, a separate historical current became delineated. It ran beside—or beneath—the great Romanistic channel, reaching prodigiously far back in time, back, as far as the situation in the Marche was concerned, to the cooperative Latin villages, to the connective tissue of pre-Roman agro-pastoral society.[46]

Valenti fixed his conclusion in four points that are worth repeating:

> (1) The *Comunanza* is an institution that rejoins the primitive and barbarian epochs of society and shows us the social community in embryo. (2) At first, the economic and the political domain are confused in the *Comunanza,* but afterwards, by the constitution of the communities, the two are differentiated, the power of eminent domain passing to the municipal agency and only the use of the primitive *Comunanza* remaining to the inhabitants that constituted it. Finally, by the expropriation of communal goods, some *comunanze* demand their complete autonomy and acquire the character of private agrarian Associations. (3) The *Comunanza* in its purest form and the simple right of usage are only modalities of the same phenomenon, one in their essence and their origins. (4) The right due to the user, whether as a member of a *Comunanza* or as a participant in what is improperly called servitudes of pasturage and woodcutting is a right that had a natural basis consisting in the primitive occupation of the land and in the long-standing and uninterrupted use of it, a fact that becomes legitimized by the need of the mountain populations and by the work undergone to satisfy that need. The right of usage, as the servitude should be called, is not a secon-

dary and accessory right that has been superimposed on that of the proprietor. Instead, considering the phenomenon historically, it seems as if the contrary happened. The right of the proprietor is feudal in origin and is founded in usurpation or in the protection that unfortunately in medieval times meant more or less the same thing.[47]

Valenti avoids the fallacious stance of an apologist for antiquated structures, but he also refuses to repeat the refrain of a propaganda that minimized and distorted these forms. He did so in the name of facts: by evaluating historical sources attentively and by gathering data concerning cooperative associations even through personal explorations *in loco*[48] or, when investigations were carried on by others, by reviewing and coordinating them personally.

We will examine in the following section how Valenti's investigation and his conclusions contributed to an accurate description of collective property and of its forms in Italy. Let us limit ourselves for the moment to its methodological implications. His investigation did not propose an antihistorical model to the society of the end of the nineteenth century. In it there becomes apparent an alternative form of proprietary structure that was coherent and responsive to determinate economic structures and that was constructed from materials coming out of a culture different from that of Rome. It was neither a model operative *sic et simpliciter* nor an ignominious effigy to be burned in the public place, but one of the many solutions to the harrassing problem of the organization of landholding. Intrinsic to it were profound reasons for being, and it could even constitute a scheme to be reproposed if the structural mechanism that underlay it were congenial to it.

The "law of evolution in landed property," in the crude sense that the orthodox evolutionists used the term, did not blind Valenti. At the end of his report, he cites Cattaneo specifically[49] and, inspired by a common-sense empiricism, he asks this law to cede its rigidity to the variability of economic facts, by which it must be measured. In other words, when the rules of evolution were read in the light of the most elementary good sense, they bowed before a largely historical orientation, and we see here again the complex web of cultural promptings that we have seen guiding many of the jurists.

Valenti's pages invited the student of economics to verify the facts, and they thus have strictly methodological implications. He argued that the fact of the sylvan-pastoral setting, a constant in these landholding structures, had such a *reality* of structure, and that such pressing necessities were born of that *reality,* that this must necessarily modify the abstract pronouncements that had been compiled and were applied to all situations. The technical and economic problems of the forest industry and of open pasturage were "particulars" that demanded particular rules. These realities had to be distorted to make them fit into the scheme of individual property, while it was evident—yesterday, then, and in the future—that collective ownership was an institution congenial to them.[50]

This was a line of thought that did not intend to influence practice but methodology, and on this level was its undoubted importance. Valenti was not attacking the practices of landholding in Italy; he was aiming at the theory of property. His study of the sylvan and pastoral modes of production and organization was modest in its scope, but it freed the structure of collective property from the limitations of protohistory and "barbarity" and placed them next to the ruling mode, individual property, thus cutting into the latter's absolute monopoly by forcing it to be seen as relative.

There existed, then, more than one sort of agricultural landholding in 1884. It was not true that one sort was the deformation and corruption of the other; not true that the second worked through history to purify what were contaminations and excrescences to remain as the unique model, whose only eventual variation lay in its application. There were two schemes of appropriation, each furnished with its own historical and cultural legitimacy and, particularly, each autonomous, the one as the other tied to the extrinsic circumstances of historical reality and economic organization, and not bound into an inexorable progression in which one scheme evolved absolutely in favor of the other and thus became absolutely preferable.

To be sure, the economist from Macerata had gone far beyond the limits of his task of coordinating materials from the region of Piceno. Valenti's coordination arrived always at an interpretation. This was his only concern, and he reduced the Inquiry to a laboratory for his experiments, to little more than an occasion for what he wanted to say.

The Work of Ghino Valenti: The Joining of Practice and Theory

That the theoretical and programmatical conclusions that Valenti inserted into the reports of the Inquiry, discussed above, were already present in substance in his first brief remarks published in 1880 in the *Rassegna* of Macerata[51] proves that our diagnosis is accurate. More important, they were also transcribed in their entirety in the highly technical essay on reforestation, *Il rimboschimento e la proprietà collettiva nell'Appennino marchigiano,* published in 1887.[52] The first work, which dates from a period that coincides with the work of the Inquiry, can be assessed as an expression of those efforts and as a simple extrapolation of the process of investigation. The second, however, was published when all the volumes of the *Acts* of the Jacini Inquiry had been offered to their readers and were remembered largely only in the disputes raised by the essay. This study bears witness to Valenti's sensitivity to theoretical questions, and it attempts to pursue the reexamination of the notion of property. The Inquiry had furnished an opportunity to test this notion,[53] but here its reexamination fits into research to which Valenti remained faithful up to the appearance of his most ambitious volume, *Le forme primitive e la teoria economica della proprietà,* the central chapter of which sketches the outlines of an economic theory of property.[54]

Valenti's reflections, then, had already taken form in 1880, and they reached full development in 1892. For this reason we can state that Valenti was among the first in Italy to follow the lead of Laveleye and to meditate on these problems with an open mind. Without doubt, his thought preceded that of Cogliolo, of Venezian, of Bonfante, and of the greater part of the scholars we have examined in the preceding chapter.

This apparently incongruent chronology does not have to be justified. Historical moments, especially on the level of history of doctrine, almost never follow in a causal succession of detached persons and events, but can be identified and put into order only when one can look at the uneven interplay of relations and rhythms that operate above and beyond the episodic to guide experience as a whole.

In this perspective, while Venezian and the others reestablished ties with a preceding discourse in juridical science and joined in the great European debate, Valenti stood apart in his little corner of the Marche. He relied on his data from the Appennines and on Laveleye's book, which he recognized as his theoretical breviary, and he divided his interests between the technical and structural "particulars" of agriculture in his own circumscribed province and the "universal" represented by a new vision of property, fixed in theory but drawing its motivation empirically from practice. His thought was separate from the great European controversy, both by its formation and by its geographical concentration.[55] It was, however, tied more than any other, partially through the Inquiry, to the work concerning collective property that would soon occupy the national legislature.[56]

His thought cannot be paired with that of men like Cusumano or Venezian because of its increasingly composite character and because it was more projected toward the future development of the problem than it was the most recent stage in the history of doctrine. Thanks to his deep involvement in the Jacini Inquiry, which meant an involvement with agrarian practice and with the organizational apparatus of the state, Valenti's thought represents an obligatory step in a progression of events that led to the activities in Parliament of men like Zucconi and Tittoni, and it would be to underestimate him simply to fit him into a chronological survey of opinion.

On the other hand, it would not make much sense to interpret Valenti as essentially a professional economist. For one thing, this would be belied by the references given in our last section. But also, even though

Valenti's writings rested on agrarian statistics, and even though he was ever conscious of the results of economic diagnosis and prognosis, as we will soon have occasion to point out, he was always dominated by a finely tuned consciousness of the juridical, and his methodological approach to reality was intrinsically juridical. It would make no more sense to incorporate his major contribution up to 1887 into the melting pot of the *Acts* of the commission for the Inquiry, since we already know the part that he played in that initiative.

Let us turn to the salient points in this singular body of thought and attempt to understand its internal development.

Valenti's point of departure, even in the essay of 1887, is the reality of the local situation. It seems as though he needed to anchor his thought in the world of things, and of tangible things. In fact, this work arose from the context of an assembly of farmers from the Marche.[57] It is dedicated to Giovanni Zucconi, the deputy from Camerino to the national Parliament and for some time chief support of the "communists" of the mountains of Piceno in a lively parliamentary battle.[58] The work sets out to be an investigation of the "reality" that was the Appennines of Umbria and the Marche, to understand the "real" needs of a forest region and a forest economy, of a society whose survival hinged on woods and pastures. But, as was Valenti's custom, his discourse soon takes flight and, leaving the terrain of the observation and contemplation of the practical, it becomes a theoretical construct.

Collective ownership seemed to him a basic and urgent "reality." It was a form congenial to and without counterindications for a world, like that of the mountains, which refuses the excesses of individualism and is founded on the supremacy of things and of the community, a world, that is, of an order that surpassed the individual. For forests and pastures, collective property was a natural institution; it was furthermore an organizational scheme demanded from below, not one imposed by the arbitrary will of someone or by the caprice of history.[59]

This was not the first time that Valenti had expressed such an idea, drawn from his thorough knowledge of the way forestal social structure and economy operate. Speaking of these same structures in a short juvenile study rich in insights, he declares in a moment of transport:

> Human institutions, when they are determined by natural conditions, have in themselves such a force of resistence that the arrogance, the prejudices, and the will of majorities and the dispositions of laws are not always able to annihilate them.[60]

Arrogance, prejudice, will of the majority, dispositions of the laws: this was not a rhetorical listing. Rather, these were the elements of an accusation levied against official culture and its law. Valenti was to develop this critical attitude during the course of his intellectual career, but it was present *in nuce,* already felt and stated, in the few immature pages that the author later did not even think to include among his works[61] but that are important to reconstruct his thought, which from the outset was extraordinarily compact and coherent.

Valenti saw the question of property in a mountainous terrain not as a philosophical or cultural problem, but as an economic one. His knowledge of concrete things—the minimum requisites for economically feasible management of a parcel of woodlot or pasture, the long-term rhythms of rotation needed for timbering and the utilization of grazing land—suggested and molded a particular image of property. The image was verified and realized in just those organizational modes that had existed in the Appennines *ab immemorabili.* They were there in all their intrinsic "naturalness," justified by their multisecular existence and their effective resistence to a political and ideological climate hostile to them.

From this specific point of departure, Valenti's argument widens, and so does the problem. In a world made up of individual holdings and dominated by hallowed declarations of their rationality, declarations that were accepted and defined in the tables of the law, common and general, the existence of the collective forms of ownership in the Marche forced Valenti to raise questions, to posit relationships, and to look to a broader range of causes for these forms. It was no longer a question only of economic management of the terrain, but of a clash between different cultures, between different ideologies.[62] Perhaps it was thanks to the effervescent air of the mountains of the Marche, perhaps to the stimulating contact with an impressive historical and juridical patrimony, but the miracle that we observed in Venezian in Camerino was repeated in Valenti: he perceived the complexity of the phenomenon. Not only that: he also perceived the complexity of the definitions on which that phenomenon had a shaping influence and by means of which it had to be examined. We have seen that there were many ways of explaining this miracle in Venezian, a jurist of a particularly broad cultural background. In the agrarian economist Ghino Valenti, who traveled through his mountains with Laveleye's book tucked under his arm like a breviary and who in the 1880s had no major predecessors in economic doctrine to liberate his thought, the fact is even more singular.

It was in his first independent studies that Valenti's vision was more completely manifested. In his contribution to the Agrarian Inquiry, he found his thoughts channeled both by the technical character of the task and by the presence of personalities who hampered him, first among them the official rapporteur and signer, Senator Nobili Vitelleschi.

Valenti did not consider the *comunanze* and the other collective forms of association in isolation. Their affirmed "naturalness" within the socioeconomic context to which they were related evoked another "naturalness,'' proclaimed in much more general and absolute terms: that of individual property. Any writer of some preparation would be led spontaneously to compare two concepts formed by history, two answers in conformity with "nature," two juridical traditions. But the result was one: both schemes of organization became relative.

Penetrating observation of the local scene led Valenti to challenge a fortress of certitudes. He questioned a system that had been accepted supinely as the best possible and perhaps the only imaginable one, and had been accepted with all of its trappings of philosophical and pseudo-philosophical explanations. The modest group of collectively held sylvan-pastoral lands in the Marche had become the example of a cultural patrimony alternative to the official one, a patrimony that furthermore appeared to our scholar from Macerata as the victim of arrogance, prejudice, and legislative abuses, as the patrimony of an oppressed minority.

This doctrinal prejudice bore the stamp of the Romanist tradition and consisted in having elevated to the status of model that property which the Romans had defined and imperiously applied within their span of historical events and which had been carried into the succeeding experience of Western jurisprudence. On this model *the* theory of property had been constructed, and on the theory a concordant legislation had been erected. What did not seem to fit within the logical terms offered by the model was either forced to fit or was ridiculed and, by implication, condemned as an aberration.

This had been the fate of multisubject proprietary situations. In the juridical regime of Italy after unification, they were the only proprietary situation that in fact received the privilege of autonomous legislation. But communality was disfavored. It was tolerated as a temporary and transitional situation and reduced to a complex of individual holdings in copropriety.[63] Valenti was right to call this a simple "modification" of individual property, for all intents and purposes embraced by the one accepted model even if it was placed in the system of the laws in an autonomous position immediately following the heading on the "modifications of property."[64] There was no trace of the multisubject proprietary situations as logically and historically separate from the *dominium quiritarium*. The legislature was silent on the subject except when its attitude toward the doctrine changed to one of explicit disdain. We are forced to conclude with Valenti that "against the collective form of ownership there subsists a doctrinal prejudice."[65]

It is evident that the line of argumentation that we have summarized recalls Maine's hammered attacks—already familiar to us—on the Roman incomprehension of forms different from individual property.[66] Valenti also attempted to free himself from the coils of a suffocating and obligatory discourse and to outline a more open theory of property, born not of human prejudice but of the richness and variety of history. Here the lesson of Laveleye bore its fruit. The concordance in the materials that he had gathered gave them universal application, and they permitted the modest documentation from the Appennines to be removed from the catch-all closet of local curiosities and to become a specific manifestation of a universally recurrent alternative mode of conceiving and resolving the relationship between man and goods.[67] When the data that Valenti had gathered in the Marche were inserted into the great picture traced by Laveleye, tested by it and interpreted in its terms, they no longer represented a limited message of communities lost in the mountains. They gave a sign of alternative voices among a chorus of others, coming to complete the expression of a counterhistory lived for centuries at the edges of official history. At this point Valenti could attempt to construct an innovative theory of property.

We will not follow him through the details of this theory, and we will not go into considerations of its range and its influence. What we have attempted to bring out is how Valenti achieved his cultural liberation; how a mute and dull raw material was understood as belonging to a different culture and came to be evaluated without prejudices in its own evident historical logic.

Valenti was capable of achieving this without showing prejudices of any kind, either those that derive from a one-sided juridical preparation, or those that spring from the determination to conserve and protect a certain political and social order. As we have said, like Venezian, Valenti was ready to perceive the ideological and political implications of the arguments on collective property and to face a complex problem. This problem was that

> the almost invincible aversion that some have for collective property finds no explanation if not in a doctrinal preconception against it that . . . many carry with them from their *school* and from the *fear*, let us say it clearly, of making a concession of which socialism could in the future take advantage in order to realize its boundless ideals.[68]

I have emphasized the words *school* and *fear* because they indicate clearly the two obstacles that the notion of collective property encountered as it emerged to the consciousness of the nineteenth century. The first of these was property as a scholastic category that relied on the wretched fear of novelty that gripped the schools to support its claim to be immutable and indisputable. The second was the fear of a breach in the fortified walls of the bourgeois citadel, in its foundations in natural law, or in its cult of the individual.

Valenti may have been perched up in his mountain vantage point far above these anxieties, but the telescope of his cultural and technical interests was focused on all of their complexities and their implications.[69]

His work of 1887 undeniably succeeded in giving new value to the collectivist phenomenon, as seen in certain particular structures, but as seen in
their economic and social dimension as well.[70] The agrarian world of the
mountains appeared to him as unpropitious for any implantation of small
landholdings,[71] so the choice offered there was between large private
estates and collective ownership. But collective ownership was not only
economically feasible: it also involved so many positive moral and social
values that an attempt to conserve and promote it was imperative.

The *comunanza*, Valenti argued, was a reality that deserved to
survive and that should not be dissolved in the name of a misunderstood
sense of individual liberty. It would only be "individualized" by raising it
to the status of a juridical person, which could be accomplished only if
this instrument, which seemed so menacing to postrevolutionary culture,
came to inspire less hatred.[72] In fact, the *comunanza*, if it were given a
juridical personality, if it held direct title to its agrarian patrimony, if it
were internally organized as a certain number of rights of usage limited in
their application just as the corporate property was limited in its ends,
seemed a scheme particularly indicated for the economy of the mountains.

It was not collective property that was economically damaging
in a mountainous zone—Valenti had already stated this in the *Acts* of the
Inquiry[73]—it was the division of the domain as it was realized, for example, in the so-called *servitù di pascolo*.[74] In this instance even Valenti was
in favor of disfranchisement, but his choice went to release in favor of the
user-laborer rather than in favor of the proprietor-capitalist.

Different sorts of evaluations underlay this choice: Valenti's
habitual vision was indeed always backed up by considerations of a social
character of the relation between capital and labor.[75] But there was also in
it the scholar's awareness that those so-called servitudes were nothing but
what remained of a remote collective ownership, that direct dominium
over those lands was the result of an abuse that had taken place in the
course of history, that the user was in juridical and moral terms the heir of
the primitive community member.

Valenti and the Economic Theory of Property

The picture that we have traced thus far of the orientation of
Valenti's monograph of 1887 is not contradicted in his volume of 1892 on
primitive proprietary forms and the economic theory of property. Indeed,
the basic themes of this work, *Le forme primitive e la teoria economica
della proprietà*, the culminating point in Valenti's intellectual development, have an even stronger cultural orientation.

The essay is dedicated to Emile de Laveleye and, as the author
takes the trouble to tell us, it originated in an invitation from the Belgian

economist to his Italian colleague to speak to the Italian public of the fourth and revised edition of Laveleye's celebrated and highly successful book.[76] Thus Valenti underscored the reliance on this work that he had always recognized, and he felt encouraged to use, adapt, and develop Laveleye's thoughts.

When Valenti wrote this essay in 1891,[77] Fustel had already been dead for two years and the collectivist movement was gaining ground. The great controversy had ended, and victory seemed to belong to Laveleye. With the detached air of one who establishes an objective evalution, but in reality with an ill-concealed sense of satisfaction, Valenti reviews the most authoritative opinions, noting and emphasizing their agreement.[78] What we have said in regard to his *Rimboschimento* concerning the isolation of his position was not to be repeated concerning the volume on *Le forme primitive*. This volume presupposes and adopts the values of the European debate, and it can rightfully be considered a corollary of the debate and a full exposition of it on the theoretical as well as on the practical level.

Its central argument concentrates on the logical and historical opposition of the economic and the political constitution of property. If the economic constitution of property was that organization dictated by needs emerging spontaneously from the structures of the agrarian situation, thanks to which it could be considered as perfectly based in factual events and thus very approximately as "natural," no institution filled that definition on the level of ownership better than the primordial form of collective appropriation. It was a world still without history, in which the demands of the real situation appeared to predominate over perversions, exploitations, and artifices.

These latter interpolations, which were the result of the historical process, would instead tend to give substance to the political definition of property, that is, to the concrete image that property had attained in its varied historical reality and that, in spite of theoretical explanations, was justified for the most part in choices that were basically political and not in options that partook of the economic nature of things. One could not explain "with only economic reasons" quiritarian dominium, the feudal landholding system, and bourgeois property, which privileged one subject with respect to another[79] and broke the egalitarianism that was the "natural" vocation of man and that was respected in primordial proprietary forms.[80]

Valenti's argument is clear, but the risk he took in methodology was great: what result does one arrive at from an opposition between the economic and the political constitution of property, between primitive property and historical and individual property? Perhaps that of upsetting the individualistic model of property and holding as just and opportune that nineteenth-century society return to the scheme of its origins? The reader might well ask these questions, and Valenti himself offers them as possible objections. Nor does he, while pursuing the thread of his tightly constructed attack on individualism, have the unpardonable ingenuity to yield to the illusion of an impossible and ludicrous total reversal of roles.

To suggest a return to origins, a notion that occupied a notable body of sociologists, economists, and jurists, was an enrichment of theory, not the transplantation of an operative scheme.[81] For them, and particularly for Valenti, primitive collective property had a purely dialectical function as a moment that served to reestablish in its real proportions the individual property that succeeded it. To exalt the one as a possibility not necessarily tied to the protohistorical phase meant to take the other out of the realm of myth and to see it in more relative terms.

It was all too obvious that primitive collective property, devised in a society of a sylvan-pastoral survival economy, could not be proposed to a more evolved agrarian and industrial society, unless in extremely limited, particular, and marginal zones, and that it could not properly be applied universally. What could be universal, however, was the truth that emerged from the relationship of a remote scheme to the modern one, and from a comparison between the various forms that had followed each other through history: historical property was a good deal more an answer or a solution given by the political power to pressing sociopolitical problems than it was an objective necessity of production and distribution.

The primitive and egalitarian proprietary form—that pure distillation of the laboratory of nature—was valuable not as a model but as a denunciation of successive abuses, as an invitation to search for new forms in which the working man might finally be freed from an economic subjection that neither the French Revolution nor the legislation that followed it and that translated it into normative terms had wanted to free him.[82]

This critical reflection provided Valenti with a starting place for the theoretical elaboration of an authentically economic theory of property, founded in a differentiation between the objects of appropriation that he calls "natural goods" and "natural elements of production" and those that he calls "produced goods."[83] This distinction allowed the relationship of property and liberty, which had been completely distorted and misconstrued by modern individualism, to return to its natural setting[84] and to establish the equality of producers of labor with respect to goods.

As we have noted, it is not our task to follow Valenti onto a terrain that lies outside the concerns of this study and on which we are neither able nor willing to express an opinion. It is enough for us to note clearly that this nonsocialist scholar[85] underwent the influence of the lessons of the great German economists of the nineteenth century. What interests us even more is his social reading of every form of collective property, seeing it as a structure that efficiently guaranteed the situation of the laborer-user as a member of the group, backed up by the group,[86] and the interpretation of it in a purely economic key as a "cooperative form."[87] Valenti later elaborated on these insights in a broad systemization that would make him—together with Ugo Rabbeno—the most highly accredited Italian theoretician and proponent of cooperation in agriculture.[88]

In the twelve years that separated Valenti's first approach to the subject of collective property from his summarizing work on primitive forms, the world of economics saw a great increase in the number of works on the subject, whereas they had been infrequent and disconnected before the 1880s. Valenti's own diligent listing of the preceding literature demonstrates this fully.

In France the problem of property, of its origins and its historical forms, continued to be confounded with and joined directly with the social question, to the point where it was seen only as one facet of that question. Economists there argued in directly political terms, often even in the political arena, and their arguments tended to be highly colored and personal.

The economist Charles Gide troubled the waters in 1883 with a discussion of Henry George's *Progress and Poverty*,[89] published in the authoritative *Journal des économistes*, and the following year the philosopher and sociologist Alfred Fouillée took the occasion of a discussion of several more or less recent works to try bringing the problem up to date, writing in the prestigious *Revue des deux mondes*.[90] It was not by chance that in that same year Paul Leroy-Beaulieu dedicated his third course at the Collège de France to the theme of collectivism[91] and that both the *Journal des économistes* and the *Économiste français*, understanding perfectly well the sense and the importance of the bitter debate between Fustel and his adversaries,[92] devoted a good deal of attention and space to the debates in the Académie des Sciences morales et politiques.

The picture was somewhat confused. There were those who, like Fouillée, showed themselves to be sympathetic toward the attack on reigning myths that was already under way.[93] Others, like Leroy-Beaulieu, reaffirmed their firm adherence to the classical certitudes.[94] Still others, as Charles Letourneau was soon to do, accepted Laveleye's theses without too many reservations.[95]

In Italy the picture concerning the economic and sociological literature on the subject was also somewhat confused. The work of Napoleone Colajanni on collective property as a doctrinal problem—a work that fully adhered to the collectivist theses—was greeted with expressions of perplexity in the *Giornale degli economisti,* to judge from the introductory explanation that the directors of the review felt obliged to add, stating that the article was being published "only to fulfill a duty of impartiality," since the opinion of the editors was favorable to the total liquidation of what remained of forms of collective property.[96]

We are in 1887, and the world of the economists appears dominated by a great and basic uncertainty. To be sure, Loria was correct in stating that the Agrarian Inquiry had condemned "to the abyss of venerable antiquities" "the mellifluous doctrines of Ferrara";[97] but those who agreed with Valenti's presentation—as demonstrated by Colajanni's summary of it—were heard only rarely and sporadically. Following in the wake of the Inquiry and agreeing with Valenti were Carlo Bertagnolli, a competent student of applied economics,[98] Napoleone Colajanni, a sociologist sensitive to the message of socialism,[99] or economists of primarily theoretical interests like Giacomo Luzzatti[100] and Eugenio Masé-Dari.[101] At the same time, more than one ambivalent element can be seen in the thought of Ugo Rabbeno,[102] a cooperatist, and of Francesco Coletti, a singular and courageous personality and a follower of Loria, who had also heeded and followed the lessons of Marxism,[103] and who showed his clear dissatisfaction with the narrow and conservative limits within which the problem had been confined almost universally up to that point.

The old polemic now seemed set on a precisely fixed course: on one side, the side of official culture, there was a revived and excessive fear of the collective at whatever level and in whatever form it might be found. On the other side, the side of a more heterodox culture, there was dissatisfaction with the reproposal of schemes that were revolutionary in theory but conservative in their operation and that made these men turn toward a collectivism of a quite different quality, tied to the options of scientific socialism.[104]

This stalemate of contrary and antagonistic positions was the product of two radically different visions of the social world. The mediation attempted by Laveleye and Valenti appears ludicrous and remains suspended like a parenthesis between the 1870s and the 1890s, as if it were a pastime for learned children. It was impossible to translate it into the heat of a reality where the only debate was over whether to conserve or destroy collective structures. Primitive agrarian communism and its vestiges had lost their appeal; they had lost that power to provoke debate that they had undeniably enjoyed in the culture of the later nineteenth century.

But the episode was only apparently over. The disputes on the primitive collective organizations had contributed much to force open a forbidden zone in jurisprudence, that of individual property as an institution of natural law. One solid acquisition of the entire debate was the historical nature of property, its replacement among historical phenomena, set in among a patrimony of available things. This acquisition was permanent and durable.

In Italy those disputes were to ring out in the national Parliament, where, in a perhaps unique example of symbiosis and harmonious cooperation between scientific thought and legislative process, they had an incisive influence on several legislative measures.

9 A Difficult Visitor

in Parliament: Juridical

History at Montecitorio

A Tortuous Legislative Itinerary: From the Grimaldi Bill to the Law of 24 June 1888

The brilliant new minister of agriculture, industry, and commerce, Bernardino Grimaldi,[1] probably thought that the government would have little trouble obtaining assent to the bill he presented to the Chamber of Deputies on 29 November 1884, on the "Abolition of the servitudes of pasturage, selling grasses, and leasing lands in the Provinces of Rome, Perugia, Ascoli Piceno, Ancona, Forlì, Macerata, Ravenna, Pesaro and Urbino, Bologna, and Ferrara."[2] Up to that point, the Chamber had always been acquiescent and ready to confirm its long-standing preference for abolition, and he undoubtedly did not expect the resistance, criticism, and opposition that awaited the bill and that forced him to change many aspects of his policy.

One cannot blame the minister for having proposed this bill without second thoughts since the proposal was the last link in a long chain of legislative and administrative provisions that had expressed the convictions, hence the socioeconomic values, of the class dominant since the French Revolution. In spite of political upheavals, this chain had run uninterrupted through the passage from the government of the princes before Unification to the national state, and the proposal was designed to fill a void in the general picture of regions within the post-Unification state.

In 1865 the *ademprivi* had been abolished in Sardinia,[3] as had the *usi civici* in the former principality of Piombino in 1867[4] and the rights of pasturage and haying in the provinces of Belluno, Udine, and Vicenza in 1882.[5] It seemed just and fitting, in 1884, to continue to dismantle in

196

other regions[6] those antiquated social constructions in which the Italian ruling class—educated by the economists and the jurists to the cult of the individual—did not, could not, and did not want to believe.

That this was Minister Grimaldi's understanding is clear in his unequivocal presentation of the bill to the Chamber: the "so-called servitudes of pasturage, of selling hay and leasing others' landed holdings . . . go back to the barbaric and the feudal eras. . . . They were introduced with the feudal system," and they resulted from the "tolerance" of the proprietors.[7] They were the source of "immense losses" to agriculture,[8] and for that reason they should be totally and immediately abolished, in accordance with "that principle which now directs our legislation: reconciling the respect due to property with the supreme interest of agriculture and the economy."[9]

This is obviously a mumbo-jumbo of antiquated and outmoded refrains, an uncritical repetition of the usual historical misinterpretations and the usual one-sided vision proper to the reigning culture,[10] cast once again in the form of proposed legislation, that is, of an instrument capable of operating with rare incisiveness. Whether true or false, the principles on which this interpretation was founded were uncomplicated, lucid, and rigorous, as befitted their unyielding Enlightenment character. They could be translated into a normative proposal that was neatly defined and extremely coherent: collective rights "in whatsoever form and denomination and with or without reciprocation are abolished in the extension and measure of the last de facto possessor" (article 1); "The proprietors of the holdings subject to servitudes . . . are obliged to pay to the interested commune an annual canon corresponding to the value of the grass destined to pasturage" (article 2); "The annual canon . . . is assured with a special encumbrance" and is "disfranchisable" (article 3); "When the right to pasturage is exercised by the generality of the inhabitants or by associations of citizens, the interested Commune can, in recompense for the dissolution of the servitude, ask the proprietor to cede a part of the holding or of the land encumbered with that right" (article 4); "For the recognition and identification of the holdings subject to servitudes, . . . for the liquidation and assignment of the recompense to those holding rights, and for the resolution of whatsoever question relative to these, there is established in the provincial capital of each of the above-mentioned provinces a Commission of Arbitration" (article 9).

Reduced to essentials, the scope of the bill was this: the minister, in an operation that was designed to be all-inclusive, brought these complex and ambivalent juridical situations within the clear and carefully defined limits of the structures and subjects provided for and regulated by the state. Two privileged interlocutors remained to interact: the proprietor of the holding and the minicipal entity, endowed with the quality of subject. Two patrimonies absorbed the economic problem to themselves: the proprietor and the commune; and both of them were destined to undergo a qualitative alteration and, in fact, to wax rich. There was no trace of the users, the beneficial owners, of their associations, of their structures and consuetudinary norms, all of which were buried in the cemetery of the feudal system with a sigh of relief.

More than in reproposing for legislation ideas that up to that moment had been accepted without discussion by the legislature, the Grimaldi bill was objectively at fault in reproposing them at the close of 1884, at a moment in which economists and jurists began to exchange, as we have seen, their reflections and perplexities concerning the origins and the history of the forms of landed appropriation. Furthermore, a far-reaching inquiry into Italian agriculture had one year before posed the problem of the forms of collective appropriation still in existence in an analysis and in a perspective that turned upside down the previously accepted view of them.

The tortuous progress of the bill through the Chamber—and also, to a lesser degree, through the Senate—for almost four years before it became law of the Italian state, the gulf that separated the final law from the original proposal, the polemics and skirmishes that filled those four years of parliamentary debate, the renewed presentations of the bill and the full reports of the commissions following each presentation—all of this activity attests that the time for abolitionistic enthusiasms was by then past. There was a malaise that wound its way even within the walls of the national Parliament, crowded with members of the great agrarian land-holder class. Something had broken the solidarity of a class of society joined compactly in the defense of its own interests.

I do not intend to follow this revealing parliamentary affair in all of its complicated development, nor the checkered process of shaping the legislative text. The pages that follow will disappoint anyone seeking this.[11] For me, both the parliamentary discussion and the drafting process serve as a verification. They testify to the influence and the wide diffusion of the so-called collectivist theories. They show how deeply alternative models of individual and collective property had penetrated the mechanism for the fashioning of the norms of the unified state. In my opinion, the events in Parliament represent a fortunate moment of meeting between practice, legislative history, and a doctrinal problem treated to extraordinarily penetrating and scientific thought. Thus they fall within the history of the notion of property in the nineteenth century as part of that current of ideas that we have followed step by step in the course of this volume, to be interpreted as a significant and important episode in that movement.

From this viewpoint, then, let us examine the complicated working out of the Grimaldi bill, limiting ourselves for the moment to noting the various positions as they confronted and adjusted to one another, reserving for the next section of the current chapter an attempt to reconstruct the principles and the causes underlying the resistance of the Commission charged with examining and reporting on the bill.

When the bill was presented on 29 November 1884, as we know, it was submitted to examination by a commission composed of the deputies Luigi Alfonso Miceli (president), Giustino Fortunato (secretary), Carlo Buttini, Rafaello Giovagnoli, Filippo Mariotti, Giuseppe Merzario, Francesco Spirito, Pietro Venturi, and Giovanni Zucconi. In their meeting of 22 May 1885, Zucconi was named rapporteur, in recognition of his particular competence in the matter.[12] Zucconi worked in perfect agreement with the other commissioners, and from his careful studies as rapporteur came not only a learned and well-organized report, but also a true and proper counterproposal to the Grimaldi bill, dated 30 March 1886.[13]

The conclusions of the Commission, as summed up in Zucconi's thickly written pages and in the twenty-two articles of the new bill, can be resumed for our purposes in the following terms: the abolition of the collectives was to be neither radical nor total. To the contrary, after the general program stated in article 1, article 2 established explicitly that "the rights to pasturage and to planting on the mountains and on lands that by their condition are not susceptible to better cultivation are to be preserved." In order to avoid proprietors' contestation of the situations enjoyed by users *ab immemorabili* but lacking in supportive documentation, article 3 clarified that "the rights mentioned in the two preceding articles are to be considered by the present law to have been derived from an express or presumed title and having the nature of negative or prohibitive servitudes." They provided that aside from the commune, the "associations or *università* of users" could also act as valid destinatories and administrators of the indemnity in money or in corresponding terrains received from the proprietors whose title to lands subject to servitudes was abolished (article 3). They provided that "when the enjoyment of the servitudes on the part of the users is exercised to the absolute exclusion of the proprietor from all of the products that the land in question is capable of bringing forth, with the payment of a canon the communities, *università*, or associations of citizens will have the right to free the entire holding" (article 4). Rules were established capable of facilitating the founding of true and proper collective domains on the lands freed to the users or received as recompense from the proprietors whose title was abolished (particularly articles 13, 14, and 15).

I still reserve the right to return soon to the complex cultural and political motives that brought the Hon. Zucconi and the Commission to such singular results. For the moment, let us limit ourselves to saying that it is easy to see that the rapporteur and the Commission were dominated by a very different attitude toward collective structures than was the minister. Indeed, we can see a view decidedly favorable to the users, who for the first time are named as released of their obligations toward the proprietor. We can also see a notable reduction of the historical, moral, and juridical importance of the proprietor and an understanding of the role of collective property in particular agro-sylvan-pastoral conditions that lent it increased importance.

The end of the parliamentary session prevented the two bills from being discussed in the Chamber. It was instead Minister Grimaldi who, on 18 January 1887, presented to the new Chamber a second bill,[14] in which the positions and the conclusions of his first bill were largely confirmed.[15] The minister firmly rejected the possibility of continuing life for the collectives, any consideration of associations of users on the same level as the communes, and the dissolution of servitudes legitimizing the users' claims. In other words, he rejected the three points that characterized the Zucconi "counterproposal." The reasons for this rejection seem to consist principally in the difficulty of making the proposed provisions coherent within the Italian legislative system, and in a preoccupation that their singularly innovative character might be perilously deviant from established social structures.[16] As far as our interests are concerned, the only modifications introduced by the Commission and judged not to disturb the harmony of the bill were the power conferred on the minister in particular and exceptional circumstances to "permit the continuation of the exercise of the servitudes for that period of time that will be seen as indispensible" (article 2) and the acceptance of their article 3 governing expressed or presumed title to the rights of usage.

Once again Zucconi was a member of the new Commission[17] and was chosen rapporteur. During the session of 18 June 1887,[18] he expressed to the Chamber his regret at seeing the government refuse the principal demands urged by the first Commission. In a counter bill he further reaffirmed his and the other commissioners' intention to insist on two qualifying principles: the conservation of the rights to pasturage and to tillage in mountain terrains and on lands inappropriate to better cultivation (article 2) and the consideration of users' associations as bodies authentically representative of the interests of the users (article 3). However, since he judged the minister to be totally unreceptive at that time to his proposal, he gave up trying to use the occasion of legislation governing the servitudes of pasturage for drawing up an organic regulation for all collective domains.[19] The report closed with an "agenda" that obliged the government first of all to undertake a specific administrative investigation and, following that, to present a bill offering "general norms for the existence, exercise, and, where it shall be indicated, the dissolution" of the collective domains operative in the regions of the former Pontifical States and in Emilia.[20]

The minister's response was not long in coming. In the session of 19 November 1887, he proposed a third bill[21] not dissimilar in its substance from the previous one and, in a scanty presentation preceding the text, once again but more abruptly rejected the principles that the Commission had tried to confirm. In particular, the minister took care to make it quite explicit that he was not in favor of "undivided property," contrary to the positive assessment of the rapporteur and the commissioners, and that he was suspicious about the creation of anomalous associations (like that proposed of the "generality of the users") which, in the light of Grimaldi's juristic training, did not seem to have "any counterpart in our traditions."[22]

The cord was now strung too tight. There remained only two possibilities: either a direct challenge or a more or less honorable compromise between the two "parties." That this was the path the Commission took, after such obstinate defense of their ideas, can be seen in the bland and extremely brief report with which the Hon. Zucconi, making the best of a bad job, gave notice to the Chamber on 5 December 1887, of the Commission's decision to surrender on two points that it had defended for three long years.[23] This was a conditional surrender, however, as became clear several days later upon the appearance of a text of the bill agreed to by both the minister and the Commission.[24] The Commission had given up much, and the conclusion that the minister had won the match seemed legitimate. But the compromise text held a surprise: deliberately confined well within article 9, purposely buried deep in the workings of the law, but no less dramatic for all that, we find the affirmation of the principle that in the presence of certain circumstances the Arbitration Commission could allow the entire parcel in question to be left to the users, in the case of the abolition of an encumbrance, in exchange for a yearly payment to the proprietor.[25] The minister had thus paid his price for the compromise.

After this moment, our interest in following the continuing itinerary of the law flags. Only unimportant variations came out of the general discussions in the Chamber and from the Senate's examination of the bill.[26] As far as the affirmation of a disagreement in principles was concerned, the compromise text of the bill was faithfully mirrored in the law of 24 June 1888.

If one compares this normative complex with the commission's original counterproposal, the difference is great. Nevertheless, the 1888 law remains an extraordinary event in the context of Italian legislation regarding the collective structures. For the first time a crack appeared in a monolithic attitude that without the slightest sign of sympathy had uprooted and destroyed these constructions in the name of the superior model of individual property. If this law can and in fact must be numbered among the laws that abolished collective forms of appropriation in Italy, there was within it a recognition of the users and of their capacity for benefiting from disfranchisement that deserves to be emphasized.

I have used the term "capacity" deliberately: in general, in the continual dialectic between proprietors and users—except for the one case of the holder of an emphyteusis or perpetual lease, which tradition had for centuries qualified as *dominus utilis*—the subject recognized as actively capable of being released from obligation was the capitalistic proprietor. The user, who spent his life and his labors on the land, was judged incompetent by his nature. On the level of the juridical constructions evolved by modern formalism, he found himself in an inferior position, as often happened in this juridical culture when situations of exercise are in confrontation with situations of title.

The principle involved was undoubtedly not in harmony with the system of the laws, and it was also undoubtedly a principle born of compromise. Its historical importance lies in just this fact. For the first time there was considerable discussion of a government proposal for abolition; for the first time such a proposal was countered by representatives of the ruling class itself. Whether little or much of that debate remained in the eventual law, the debate did take place—broadly ranging, far-reaching, bitter, made of contrary convictions and of opposed political programs—and that is a historical fact of importance. A historian of jurisprudence is perhaps more interested in the debate than in the legislation that came out of it, because in it more than in the text of the law, which is a static witness to the efficacy of power, is found the living sign of a society in movement, of a culture that circulates and penetrates even the halls of Parliament, of new ideas that reoxygenate the stagnant waters of established tradition—a tradition particularly dear to Minister Grimaldi.

This is why we have gone into the detail of the dialogue and its protagonists in an account that seemingly contained only barren data. Now let me try to offer some idea of the meaning and content of those data.

The debate occurred; but what were the moving forces behind it? What were the ideas, and who were the men that carried it on? We will discover among that mass of dates and personalities, reports, speeches, and proposals the presence of something not usually seen in the Palazzo di Montecitorio: the great intellectual debate on the historical forms of property. This debate had been actively present, as we have seen in the details of the Jacini Agrarian Inquiry, and it had played an important role in the formation of such a determined resistance to the project of the minister of agriculture. The law of 1888, whose making we have followed, and the law of 1894, which we will soon examine, were motivated—perhaps primarily—by a culture that was clearly historical and juridical. This too should be emphasized as exceptional.

A Connection between Historical and Juridical Culture and Parliamentary Practice: The Work of Giovanni Zucconi

I have conscientiously listed the names of the members of the parliamentary commissions that examined the first and second Grimaldi bills, guided less by a mania for informing my reader than by an interest in the meaning that some of these names have. They characterize for us the climate in which the commissions worked and explain their headstrong opposition to the initiatives of the minister. It is far from irrelevant to note that Giustino Fortunato was secretary of the first commission and that Leopoldo Franchetti was an active member of the second. These two were among the men in the Italian political world most attentive to the so-called southern question and in particular to the knotty problem at its center that was the "demesnial question."

When the commission began its work, Fortunato's carefully written article on the *demani* in southern Italy[27] and the realistic report of a fact-finding trip through Sicily by Franchetti and Sidney Sonnino[28] had already appeared some time before. Both the Tuscan observer and the Lucanian denounced as if with one voice the ignorance of the dominant class in Italy and its insensitivity to the juridical and social problems of the countryside and toward the agrarian proletariat of the kingdom. In 1885, when the commission had begun its labors, there appeared the *Atti della Commissione reale pei demani comunali nelle provincie del Mezzogiorno*, in which one of the two economic reports bore the signature of Franchetti and was nothing other than a long and well-documented act of accusation against the conduct and results of the policy of liquidation and dissolution.[29]

The reports of the parliamentary commissions relied heavily on those studies and those acts, taking them over as their corroborating documentation and reinforcing them[30] with the *Lettere meridionali* of Pasquale Villari of 1875. The latter remain in the literature on southern Italy as perhaps the first conscious and lucid attempt to shake off stubborn commonplaces.[31]

Thanks to the presence of Fortunato and Franchetti, the shadow of the many errors committed in the past in other regions loomed over the Commission, creating a climate of vigilant attention, a determination to avoid inured, habitual reactions, an attitude of caution and of critical reflection, and a readiness to look again, reformulate, correct, and innovate.

The spokesman for this orientation—and more than its spokesman, its goad, consultant, and chief drafter—was Zucconi, who reigned over the commission as rapporteur. Zucconi[32] had represented the constituency of Camerino since the autumn of 1878, when the seat remained vacant at the death of the Hon. Cesare Bruschetti, and he was a key personality in the complicated parliamentary affairs outlined in the preceding section. It was to him that the Commission owed the greater part of its heterodox direction and the innovations that were inserted in the legislative text of 1888.

From our point of view, Zucconi had the further and not irrelevant merit of having served as intermediary between a parliamentary chamber potentially deaf to the urgings of culture and a historical, economic, and juridical culture which he reflected and to which he had devoted heartfelt meditation, particularly on the problem of the relationship between property and civilization. As with Ghino Valenti in the context of the Agrarian Inquiry, we recognize in him a man of extraordinary personal merit. Zucconi, however, encountered much greater difficulty. He acted in a closed world, isolated from the reality of civil society, conditioned by political options and dominated by people directly interested in those choices, whereas Valenti had worked within a team of technicians who enjoyed considerable autonomy in their consideration of objective informational and interpretive data.

A brief characterization of the man will permit us to understand better the reasons for his "heretical" beliefs. Aside from his social status as the proprietor of a considerable landed estate, Zucconi had an anthropological and a professional status that was, if not dominant in him, at least conditioning.

First of all, Zucconi was from the Marche, indeed, from Camerino.[33] That is, he was native to the most authentic part of the Piceno mountain region, where social customs and economic structures had been conserved intact for centuries in a complex of values different from and even counter to those in wide circulation in nineteenth-century society. He was a man who noted those values scrupulously and clung to them tenaciously.[34] He was something more than a provincial enamoured of his place of origin: he was a well-prepared observer of the local scene, one sociologically attuned to the inconspicuous level of custom[35] on which the multiform collective structures flourished, and one intent on understanding and evaluating them rather than on rejecting or disdaining them.

A specific sort of knowledge and understanding—gained not by chance but through his profession—was juxtaposed in him to this generic acquaintance with collective structures and understanding of them. Zucconi was a lawyer, and a large part of his activity lay in giving opinions and judicial assistance to communities and users' associations in their perennial litigations with landed proprietors and the communes.[36] He was also, as we have noted, president of the subcommittee for Camerino charged with the collection of local data for the Agrarian Inquiry.[37]

All of these circumstances, however, are not enough to circumscribe him. It would diminish Zucconi's stature to confine him to a provincial society and a provincial zone of activity. He was a man of varied culture,[38] professor of economics and statistics at the University of Camerino,[39] and he counted interesting colleagues—Pietro Cogliolo, for example—among his friends. As a student of economic theory he heeded the lesson of evolutionistic theory and tended to apply it in his specific field.[40] He was on close terms with Giacomo Cassani,[41] Ghino Valenti (also through their work for the Agrarian Inquiry),[42] Maffeo Pantaleoni, Giustino Fortunato,[43] and many others, particularly among the economists who brought into Italy the new theories of the German school.[44] He followed the currents of intellectual thought on a European level, and he had read Maine and Laveleye.[45]

This deputy from the mountains had throughout his life studied the orderly and thriving collective structures that functioned in the mountain zones of his native Marche. He had defended them as their legal counsel, and he had examined and sifted through their particulars as an important part of his work with the Agrarian Inquiry. Following the interpretations of his favorite heterodox economists, Valenti, Laveleye, and Maine, his portrayal of those structures was unfettered by the brutalizing propaganda of the official view, and he was able to place them in a broader and more satisfactory horizon. One can perhaps understand better how this deputy from the mountains arrived in Rome with a more complete consciousness of the phenomenon than was normal to the usual local politician and speaking in more varied terms than one might expect from a man who belonged to a particular segment of the dominant class and the official culture. Signs of alternative ideas and agreement with the criticisms of the regime expressed by Fortunato and Franchetti were to be expected from his experience and his personality.

However, Zucconi never limited his message to a specific defense of Camerino or of the many community structures and associations of his native Piceno mountains, although he was fully familiar with all of them. He never restricted this phenomenon to local occurrences. Rather, he carefully spoke in terms that were essentially cultural; in other words, he turned the problem into one that could accurately be called scientific, that was historical, juridical, and economic, even though based on local facts.

When the question of the *servitù di pascere* in the territories of the former Pontifical States arose, it was the intention of the government to prepare hurriedly one of the many local provisions that served it in canceling out the composite image of the Italy of municipalities and in substituting for it a compact image of a unified state. It was Zucconi's intention to carry into Parliament the echo of the European debate, a debate that regarded the entire world, with all its diversity of peoples, and universal history. It was his intention to weigh carefully the scientific foundations of the legislative proposal and to help the legislators arrive at a higher level of awareness and at a less narrow and more up-to-date idea of the realities involved.[46]

Zucconi's lesson—and this should come as no surprise—was methodological. It was a contribution to the battle against an "axiom."[47] The controversy that was born in Maine's study in Cambridge and Laveleye's study in Liège found here its last offshoots. That vein of alternative culture and, consequently, the vein of alternative options that we have seen running through and characterizing all of the dispute, continues in this complex political figure.

There is a published legal opinion written by Zucconi in 1884—thus earlier than his work in Parliament on the subject—that is among the best products of this consultatory literature, a genre halfway between the scientific and the practical. In it he affirms:

> I am persuaded with Laveleye . . . that one can only judge badly
> of these customary rights if one is guided solely by the *jus
> quiritarium* and does not inquire into their intrinsic nature and
> origin. . . . Thorough research on the customs of peoples has
> now demonstrated as erroneous the concept held by some
> jurists who regard private property as the primitive form of stable
> property and the communist as a form derived from it by force
> of contracts or associations among private proprietors or in vir-
> tue of concessions of princes and of prescription. Thanks to the
> studies of Maurer and Nasse in Germany, of Emile de Laveleye
> in Belgium, of Gabriele Rosa[48] in Italy, and especially of the
> Englishman Henry Maine in his book, *Ancient Law,* it has been
> demonstrated that the primitive form of landed property among
> all people is the collective or communal.[49]

The quarrel with Roman law, which occupied so much space in the juridical literature of the end of the century and which too often was embodied in empty stylistic exercises, takes here—as in Maine and Laveleye and in many of those who participated in the controversy—the only direction that was historically concrete and efficacious: that of a refusal of Roman law as an omnivalent interpretative instrument, of reliance on alternative cultural values and techniques, of the comparison of ideas, and of a limitation of the Roman monocracy by a decisively pluralistic vision.

The liberating movement that Maine had achieved years before by means of comparison is still alive here. It remained alive in the rest of Zucconi's works, appearing evidently and concretely in the reports and discussions in Parliament, which for a man who wrote as little as Zucconi constituted his most extensive writings. In fact, we find the principle repeated again and again in the full report of 30 March 1886,[50] and we see it change into a denunciation of the juridical miseducation of the Italian ruling class, one stated with decision but punctuated by the interruptions of his honorable colleagues during a parliamentary discussion in 1891.[51]

The problem was a scientific one, as Zucconi did not hesitate to declare to the legislators gathered in the Chamber.[52] From the controversy and from recent research in economic and juridical history he had formed a new view of the phenomenon of collective structures, which he sought to affirm in order to combat the distortions of the Romanistic tradition. Collective structures did not represent abuses or inordinate liberties; they were not a residue of feudalism, but "vestiges of the primitive agrarian regime, in which enjoyment of the land and the exercise of the right of ownership over it was exercised in collective form by the components of the tribe or by the inhabitants of the villages."[53] They represented "popular rights,"[54] "possessions of the plebe"[55] now reduced to mere semblances in the rights to graze, sow, and cut wood more "by violent usurpations of the barons or the governments" than by the free choice of the joint owners.[56]

This argument springs from the alternative cultural apparatus that is well known to us. We find it intact in the notes to the *Acts* of Parliament: there we find cited Maine, Laveleye, Nasse, Roscher, Heusler's article on the *Allmend*, the *Report* on the townships of the English Commission of Inquiry, the writings of Cattaneo, an essay by Cencelli Perti and one by Cassani, the older southern juridical literature (De Luca) and recent southern literature (Fortunato, Villari, Racioppi, Franchetti), to which the hefty volume 11 of the Jacini Inquiry was added, practically fresh off the presses.[57]

Zucconi's conclusions were also in the alternative vein. There is no sign of the repugnance toward collective property and toward the juridical person that in individualistic juridical culture had been the result of prejudicial attitudes. Zucconi viewed collective property as intrinsically neither good nor bad: it was another form of property with its own reasons for being and its own place in the history of civilization. What was bad was the unsatisfactory dualism between proprietor and user in the form that had developed in the so-called customary servitudes.[58] Rather than the abolition pure and simple of the *servitù*, the government and the national Parliament ought to occupy themselves with the suppression of the ambiguous dualistic situation that was articulated in the servitudes and the recreation of the collective domains, furnished, it was hoped, with juridical personality.[59]

In Zucconi's vision, there would no longer be one proprietor and many users scowling at each other, powerless in the procrustean bed of their respective inflexible juridical positions, but associations of economically active and socially useful cooperants.[60] Ghino Valenti's analysis of the economic validity of collective forms in particular geo-agronomic situations was here taken over by Zucconi, as he took over the pairing—typical of Valenti and original in him—of collective property and agrarian cooperation.

It is here that the second step in the validation of the scheme of collective property, the economic and social aspect, enters Zucconi's argument, following after the cultural premises that always oriented and determined it. Collective property should be examined with one's mind free of cultural models and must be reestablished within a cultural pluralism where it can be understood and valued; but this process should continue until collective ownership reaches a technical, economic, and social status that will establish a harmony in its complex characteristics.

We have little to say of the technical and economic aspects of Zucconi's argument. He limited himself to repeating once again Valenti's analysis of the particular exigencies of the mountain lands, of the negative aspects of small or large properties in those lands, of the particular congeniality of collective property to them.[61]

The social definition of collective property, on the contrary, deserves further clarification. Zucconi's great mentor always remained Laveleye, and not a few of Laveleye's concerns enter into Zucconi's pages, as one can note from an attentive reading of his parliamentary reports. Thus we see an obsession with the social question,[62] an insistence on taking into account the needs of the deprived classes, a vision of collective property as an instrument for the social elevation of the agricultural laborers, for cooperation among them,[63] and for peaceful compromise between an immobile conservatism and a complete overthrow of the political order.[64]

Some questions come immediately to mind. Are these ideas simply a repetition of Laveleye's? Do we see a reaffirmation of principles that are beginning to become commonplaces? Is this the abstract program of an enlightened proprietor? Or is it shaped by fears of social disorders and the demands of the proletariat? Undoubtedly there is a little of all of this behind Zucconi's proposals, but we would do him an injustice if we did not look to further documentation capable of illuminating his complex personality.

Zucconi's brisk activity on the local scene can help us in making a more complete assessment. He was president of a multitude of more or less beneficent institutions and an authoritative member of hundreds of boards of directors of others, scholastic, agrarian, and assistential,[65] to the point where our image of him runs the risk of incorrectly picturing him as a generous provincial patron. But Zucconi did more: he rolled up his sleeves and entered into the heat of the first workers' organization in the province of Macerata, giving them loyal and concrete support.

In 1880, as president of its promotional committee, he spoke to a convention of workers' associations of the province of Macerata in a speech that was not the usual paternalistic discourse of a city father, in which rhetoric and presumptuousness shine through broad generalities.[66] If the affirmation that "the emancipation and the rising up of this [working] class . . . is the problem of our age" is in itself too generic to be fully credible, the statement changes in value when he turns to a pitiless historical analysis of the so-called bourgeois revolution. Zucconi says:

> The elevation of this class [the bourgeoisie], formerly itself oppressed, . . . rendered even more perceptible the abjection in which another and even more numerous mass of people remained: those who from daily and manual labor draw the support of their lives. The ease in which the capitalist lives confronts the privation of the workers, who have become a servant class for the former.[67]

This is raw speech that expresses clearly its impatience with the usual popular image of the French Revolution and of the society that it produced. The optimistic portrait of a society ransomed by the Revolution. with liberty and juridical equality for all of its members, is banished. Zucconi's unusual point of departure was liberty and social equality, and these ideals led him to point out inequalities that were even less excusable than before and to qualify as servitude the pretended liberty of those whom the Revolution had claimed to liberate on the level of the law.

There was no room for rhetoric in this historical analysis, this comparative assessment of the *ancien régime* and of the conquests of the bourgeoisie. There was no room for demagoguery either, easy as that would have been on that particular occasion. Nor does his speech take on the tones of nostalgia for the past that would have been chosen by Le Play.

Our enlightened conservative from provincial Piceno had above all two undeniable merits: lucidity and concreteness. Without writing an apologia of this unknown discourse at Camerino, these merits must be acknowledged. They help us to compose a more coherent image of Zucconi four years later, when he could be seen deeply involved in the legislative problem of the servitudes of pasturage, standing up to the king's minister—at least in the first and second report of the Commission— fighting for the users rather than for the proprietors, and managing to propose for the first time in the chambers of Montecitorio the legitimization of the users' and not of the proprietors' claims under disfranchisement.[68]

Although it is certainly vain and ingenuous to try attacking the enormous problem of the social question by beginning with the minor details of the servitudes of pasturage in the former Pontifical States, it was nevertheless that occasion which the "legislator" Zucconi took in order to turn his words into concrete action, to begin scratching at the surface of an impenetrable insensitivity, to begin building into fact a substantial equality between the agricultural worker and the capitalistic proprietor.

That finally the learned deputy from Camerino had to yield to the minister, that he suffered a not-too-honorable compromise, and that he perpetrated a "betrayal" of the premises set up and defined in his intelligent first report is another question. These were signs of the isolation and the indifference in the midst of which Zucconi operated and of the massive opposition that the government brought to bear on an intrusion into the general order of a principle that from their viewpoint seemed a first breach in the inviolate walls of their fortress.[69]

Discussions in Parliament

The general debate that took place in the Chamber of Deputies toward the end of 1887, after this bill had lived through many vicissitudes, contained a wealth of ideas and themes. It confirmed that the government's bill was badly aimed and that it hit only partially—very partially—the target the government had intended and had coolly selected.

As we have seen, Minister Grimaldi had to employ all of his resources to save the substance of his project when he unexpectedly found himself faced with the "scientific" and sociopolitical dissent of the Commission, and particularly of Zucconi. He also had to "compromise" with the Commission and swallow the bitter pill of article 9 of the compromise bill. The minister's speech became singularly frank when he found himself in general debate, where spontaneous reaction was more possible than in the formal and studied presentations of his various proposals to the deputies, and he avowed indirectly the government's disappointment in the partial failure of his initiative.[70]

He reminded the heterodox deputies—who, as we will soon see, were to try to make further inroads into the compromise text—that the proposal on the servitudes of pasturage "cannot be looked at in isolation from the rest of our legislation." On the contrary, it "is a part of a program, of a complex of bills, some of which have been approved and have become the laws of the state, some of which have been presented to Parliament, and some of which are still to be presented."[71] In saying this, he seems to be warning the deputies indirectly that he had already conceded too much and that, in any case, the concessions he had made represented a limit beyond which he would not go.

When he had presented his original proposal, the minister did not foresee any problems. Indeed, he had stated his unhesitating support and the bill's consistency with the established policy of abolition. Complications had arisen when Zucconi had brought in names and problems the minister thought to be peripheral to the question and had spoken in incomprehensible and irritating terms of "primitive communism" and "original condominiums." The minister either did not understand very well the theoretical importance of the affair and its possible social repercussions, or had understood them all too well and feigned incomprehension. To the Hon. Penserini, a judge who was a member of the Commission of Referral and who pressed him regarding the central point of the juridical qualifications of the collective structures, Grimaldi answered impetuously and frankly, without his usual prudence:

> With this law I intend to liberate property from all of its encumbrances under any form or name. . . . Whatever the origin of the right might be, whether it is born of servitudes or *iure dominii,* it is a right included in article 1, and the Chamber, if it wishes to follow my direction, will vote that all these rights of whatsoever nature will be abolished.[72]

This was a rough and generic way of speaking that reveals a political preoccupation to safeguard a fundamental principle at any cost. It also reveals a total insensitivity toward the emergence and affirmation of other and opposing principles; indeed, it shows a precise determination to block them.

There was for the minister a supreme value before which all juridical situations objectively worthy of some protection fell to the level of situations that are contingent and only relatively protected. If this is true, Grimaldi was right to define as a question of "form and name" the juridical nature of the position of the users and in considering them coproprietors and objective participants in property or titular holders of rights over things belonging to others. The logical *prius* that is presupposed here is the postulate that property is only that kind held by the capitalist proprietor. Consequently, that property and only that property was held by the general juridical order to be an *a priori* principle and, according to a famous expression of Pisanelli,[73] "the fundamental idea that molds the whole of the civil code." The problem that the Hon. Penserini had posed was an authentic problem bearing on the substance, on the essence of things, if only one were open-minded enough to look without prejudice. However, posing such a problem became a purely formal pastime if the substance of property had already been attributed to a subject and if the only remaining question was whether or not to concede one more embroidery, one more epithet to a different subject.

The curt response of the minister showed that he had no interest in clarifying the intricate tangle of relationships between proprietors and users. This stands out even more clearly when one considers the study and the cultural curiosity that inspired the Commission and led it on its autonomous path. His answer showed that article 9, without doubt an important article, constituted an innovation that he endured and that the exact historical and juridical place of the users was a problem to which he was indifferent. Article 9 was not an attempt better and more justly to adjust the law to concrete situations; it was imposed by the rules of the game. The minister's desires for justice seem all to be absorbed by his affirmation of the supreme value of "individual property" and its liberation from every obligation. The rest was pure form, or an amusement that could be left to the jurists. The far-reaching work of the commissions, the speeches—which we will soon examine—of Leopoldo Franchetti, Emilio Campi, Carlo Luzi, Francesco Penserini, Edoardo Pantano, Menotti Garibaldi, all intent upon looking at the various situations in light of delicate historical, juridical, and economic analyses and upon discovering and applying in legislation the principles of justice contained in the property relationship, encountered in Grimaldi the closed mind of one who held to a single verity, one founded in morality and ideology, a verity which he respected and expected others to respect.

The same reasoning by axioms, the same procedure by *a priori* arguments, can be seen in the speech of the Hon. Giacomo Balestra, the voice of the conservative majority in the Chamber and a man whose mind was even more closed than the minister's.[74] The succession of so many reports and so many bills on the same theme and the conflict that had occupied the Chamber for three years of exhaustive debate had not left the least trace on this obstinate defender of the dominant political line.

For Balestra, all was conditioned by an unquestioned postulate: property was and was *only* individual property as defined in the codes of modern legislation. If the aim of the bill was to liberate property from antieconomic encumbrances, this goal could *only* be reached by legitimizing the claims of the formal proprietor and conceding disfranchisement in his favor, as he was the *only* party who could claim to be proprietor. To consent, as article 9 of the compromise bill stipulated, to a possible dissolution of the obligations in favor of the users would have implied the identification of a negative element not in the rights of the users but in property itself. This was unthinkable, not even to be suggested. "Property as such," said Balestra, "cannot be an obstacle to the development of agriculture."[75] That the individual proprietary scheme was good was once again offered as axiomatic truth.

It did not occur to the Hon. Balestra that there might be a grain of another truth in one of the many opinions so eruditely listed by Zucconi or in all of the data-crammed history that emerged from his lively pages. It did not matter to Balestra that the investigation of the historical origins of property had imposed a redefinition of the connection between proprietors and users, and that it had come close to upsetting this connection and making the users participants in the scheme of property. All had to be resolved according to the system and to the typology of the Civil Code, in which was expressed a law that apparently derived more from nature than from history. We see again in Balestra's words a horror of "abnormalities,"[76] of anything irregular that violated the limpid and established general rule sanctioned by the official juridical system. (As we have seen, many men of doctrinaire leanings shared this horror of the formless monster of collective property.) Despite a climate that was still profoundly anticlerical and antipapal, Balestra went as far as to sing the praises of the "liberality" of the pontifical *Notificazione* of 1849 because it was totally abolitionist and, hence, authentically "liberal."[77]

In the other camp, that of the "heterodox" and the "collectivists," we will not bother to follow the activities of the Hon. Zucconi. Zucconi's zeal for innovation was completely spent after his "compromise" with the minister and we find him busying himself with the defense of his work on the bill and of its relative coherence. Neither will we trace the meager, insipid, and largely distracted contributions of the socialists, Andrea Costa among them, to the question.[78] There are, however, three points worth bringing out.

The first, which relates to the history of juridical thought, is the point made, as we have mentioned, by the Hon. Francesco Penserini, member of the second Commission of Referral.[79] Relying on certain ideas taken from the first Zucconi report and aligning himself with the sense of the Commission's work and the debate in the Chamber, Penserini insisted that the inappropriate though convenient term of *servitù di pascere* be abandoned and that the situation of the users be defined within the scheme of condominium in accordance with the findings of recent scholarship.[80] When the minister swept away his objection by nonchalantly reducing the problem to one of nomenclature, Penserini replied that something more than an epithet was in question, and that was the juridical nature of the institution and, consequently, the general capacity of the users, conceived of as joint owners, to benefit from disfranchisement.[81]

The Hon. Edoardo Pantano, a physician who had nevertheless dedicated himself to the study of economics and sociology,[82] reproached the Chamber for continuing in its confused notions and unfounded fears of collective property, notwithstanding the recent efforts of scholars to redefine it.[83] More important, however, this nonjurist offered arguments of a purely technical and juridical nature in favor of the users. Holding the collective nature of the *servitù* as it was practiced in the provinces of the former Pontifical States to be in most cases "true and proper condominium," "the last residue of an ancient, truly popular property,"[84] he invoked by analogy and in the interest of the users the favorable treatment that the Italian juridical system reserved to the holders of the lease with respect to the holder of title to the land in the system of emphyteusis.[85]

The Hon. Leopoldo Franchetti[86] analyzed the question in greater detail.[87] He arrived at the same result as the one in Zucconi's report: he proposed the creation of agencies to represent the interests of the "class" of the users. He reached this conclusion by two paths. The first of these was the information made available in recent scholarly investigations.[88] The second source was his own disheartening experience as a traveler and inspector in the south, where the communes—according to the minister the natural representatives of the collectivity—had legally stripped the users of their rights with the connivance of the entire administrative apparatus of the state.[89]

Thus far, this seems to be a repetition of the discourse that we have heard many times before and that stood out only because the deputy from Tuscany continued to proclaim his position even after an agreement had been reached between the majority of the Commission and the minister, at one point shouting to the entire Chamber his negative opinion of the compromise and his intention to vote against the bill.[90] What is remarkable in his position is the keen and penetrating sociopolitical analysis that accompanied it, in which he laid bare the most hidden motive for the government's and Parliament's hostility to the creation of the suggested representative bodies.

In Franchetti's analysis, beyond the purely formal explanations, the one obstacle—the obstacle that was really insuperable—was the recognition of collective rights,[91] the admission to organization and protection of a category of persons who drew their reason for being, their cohesion, and their vitality from the collective labor force that they represented. The bourgeois state thus felt an invincible aversion for collective structures and, Franchetti adds, this was understandable, since the state could not be asked to harm its own interests. As long as it assumed an abstract individual as its interlocutor and the object of its care, the nineteenth-century state carried on an activity that was formally egalitarian and impartial. In reality, however, since it represented a caste identified by its wealth, the state sought to defend its own interests and thus promoted in fact a clear distinction between the haves and the have-nots. It continued to exist by an accord with the rich, who recognized their own image in the complex rules dictated to fit their particular measurements and who succeeded in pushing the poor into a faceless mass deprived of individual qualifications and thus by this very fact incapable of establishing a functional connection with the decisional apparatus of the state.

In reality, the myth of the value of the abstract individual, Franchetti argued, was translated into an option in favor of the individual holding concrete possessions. It was an instrument that precluded making others—all of the others—coresponsible, for they would never constitute an influential presence as long as they remained a shapeless, unorganized mass. This was, in the last analysis, a supreme act of social selection, impalpable but pitiless, expressed in no written laws so that its macroscopic injustice was protected from eventual opposition. Rather, it was written in a sympathetic language that hid it behind the seductive fiction of political conquest valid for all the people. This was what explained the constant need for keeping control of the workings of the juridical system, for limiting the elaboration of new juridical schemata, types, and categories.[92] This was what brought on a juridical absolutism so in contrast with the political liberalism that was constantly proclaimed—an absolutism aimed at not permitting any escape from the rules of the game.

Franchetti explains his thoughts eloquently:

> The direction that now prevails in our legislation, inspired by the theories of the classical school of economics, certainly has advantages, but it also has one great defect. The classical economic school refuses to recognize any juridical or social relationship that does not correspond to its definitions, that is not included in one of the categories it has determined. . . . Classical economics is fond of the distinctions between capitalists and laborers, and it feels an instinctive antipathy for hybrid entities like the *università* of users in which the individual disappears and the aim of which is to assure the well-being of a category of persons as such. Thus the government bill does not want to recognize the users' associations and thus it destroys and throws into confusion a category of persons who, although in conditions of poverty, have a connection with public affairs and with the organs of justice. It destroys them and rejects them, throwing the users into the great inorganic mass of an agricultural proletariat. A policy that encourages the formation or the growth of proletarian classes that have no connection with public affairs is not liberal; is not conservative in the true and healthy sense of the word. This law creates an even greater separation than the one that exists today of an entire class of persons who have few interests in common with the general order of society. . . . You are separating them out, you are disinheriting them, and you do not care how you do it. You are stripping them of all they have. . . . You can certainly find a way to indemnify the single users as individuals, but as a class they remain dispossessed. . . . You will have created for future generations a class of proletarians that now does not exist.[93]

This diagnosis may seem obvious, but it became a strong denunciation in the mouth of a man who possessed conspicuous wealth and

was a member of the politically dominant class of Italy in the year of grace
1887. Seen through this iconoclastic attack upon it, the misoneism of the
legislature, its love of juridical tradition and the classical cast of the Code,
and its attachment to the schemata of Roman constructions reveal causes
that reach well beyond a love of system and a demand for linear simplic-
ity. The roots reach to the inexpressed and inexpressible program of the
Italian establishment.

Following the Law of 1888

The law of 1888 was the result of an agreement into which both
parties had been forced. As such, it was a combination of diverse principles, sometimes of opposite inspiration. In its composite nature as a law
to abolish the *servitù,* it was dominated by a preference for individual
property; but it also contained an affirmation of points of view favorable
to the maintenance of collective holdings. Hence it seemed constructed so
as to satisfy no one and to create, when it came to be applied, difficult
problems of interpretation.[94]

The minister, still smarting from the section of article 9 that
conceded to arbitrational commissions the power to effect' disfranchisements to the favor of the users, moved immediately to restrict
this power. Making use of the vague wording of the last section of the
article, concerning recourse to the minister of agriculture against the decisions of the Arbitration Commissions,[95] he interpreted this recourse as a
safeguard conceded only to the proprietor, and he held such appeals from
users' associations as inadmissible.[96] For him, only decisions unfavorable
to the proprietor were to be blocked, not those unfavorable to the user,
and this stance shows an evident attempt to take back surreptitiously any
possibility that the Commissions might open up to the users on the local
level by an appeal to the supreme administrative authority in every case of
the creation of a new collective domain.[97] The enabling legislation was
written in this sense[98] and both the minister of grace and justice[99] and the
Council of State[100] pronounced their agreement with this reading. The
central administration of the state presented a unified front to the danger
represented by article 9 in its directional and consultive branches, and it
tried to reduce the vitality of the "foreign body" in its organism with
every means in its power.

But the "collectivists" were waiting for just this. They also
were unsatisfied with the law of 1888[101] and they took it as an occasion to
launch a new debate, to show that the old principles and the old solutions
could be disputed, to create fissures where all seemed to be inviolable,
and to introduce innovative ideas into the most rigorous immobilism. They
were aware of the extreme difficulty they faced in trying to bring about a
change of direction in the short term; the law, in their eyes, was like a

stone flung out that had not yet hit its target. Let us not forget that the law was intended to cover a socio-juridical situation in the so-called *diritti promiscui* that was even for them of secondary and of doubtful value, and that it did not touch the structures that were more important to them, those organized into true collective ownership. They had seized the opportunity offered by the law to launch an alternative line of argument and to reflect on collective forms more than had been possible, almost always and consistently considering them for their historical origins and their exotic juridical nature. They had hoped to reshuffle the cards that had seemed definitively and indisputably dealt out. Their interest was projected toward the future, toward what they intended to do after the law was passed. This gives a plausible explanation even of the abdication of Zucconi and the Commission over the compromise text and explains why their interest and their attention was concentrated instead on the agenda that obliged the government to work for a reorganization of the collective domains.

For that reason it is understandable that the government's attempt at "restoration" gave them a welcome pretext for taking up again the argument that had hardly begun and that the passage of the law had threatened to stop. On 12 June 1889, taking as a point of departure the government's failure to published the administrative decrees (which appeared only in August of 1889), the deputies Tittoni, Zucconi, and Menotti Garibaldi presented a query on the matter to the minister of agriculture. They insisted on "a wide and liberal application of section 3 of article 9 of the law concerning the admission of the users to disfranchisement of the servitudes against the proprietors" and "a thorough regulation of the collective holdings already existent or created by these disfranchisements."[102] On 1 May 1890, on the occasion of the general discussion of the budget for agriculture and commerce, the Hon. Tommaso Tittoni posed clearly to the minister the problem of the right of the users to present appeals of the decisions of the Arbitration Commissions and forced the minister, Miceli, to commit himself to present a bill that was technically a modification of article 9, but that was essentially an interpretation of it.[103] This bill, presented and represented to the Chamber,[104] offered the rapporteur—who was inevitably Zucconi—another chance to ask the government to go beyond the fragmentary provisions proposed and to "complete the job, filling in the voids . . . and finding the proper place for collective property";[105] and it gave the Hon. Tittoni a chance to present a dry and decisive ultimatum.[106]

The government's delays enabled the Hon. Tittoni and a large group of deputies (among them Giovanni Zucconi, Edoardo Pantano, and Napoleone Colajanni)[107] to present a bill of parliamentary initiative which was discussed by the Chamber in its session of 4 March 1892. The object of the proposal was the organization of the collective domains in the provinces of the former Pontifical State.[108]

The fetters imposed by abolitionistic legislation seemed to be broken, and the mania for destruction seemed to have given way to a task of putting into order and, implicitly, of encouraging a phenomenon until then unknown or scorned. The few seeds sown in the unfertile ground of the law of 1888 were producing their first fruits. Accordingly, the tone of parliamentary debate changed in quality: there was no longer question of servitudes, rights of usage, or common rights, but of the reorganization of another form of property, one that was not and could not be regulated by the civil Code. It seemed an invitation to leave the law of 1888 behind as a last stage in a negative understanding of the problem in order at last to attack it positively, to pass a series of laws governing collective property that would stand beside those regulating individual property.

And something did happen. It was not perhaps a flying start, but only a fixed point that failed to be extended into a functional line. It was destined to remain a unique event, while proposals, bills, plans, and projects again piled up on one another amid a nearly general indifference to the problem. In order to see something translated into legislative reality, one must wait, alas, for the law of 1927, the price of which Italy is still paying.

The Report and Work of Tommaso Tittoni

The fixed point, the unique event, was the law of 4 August 1894, n. 397, regarding the organization of the collective domains in the provinces of the former Pontifical State. It had originated in the legislative proposal formulated in 1892 by the Hon. Tittoni and other deputies. This law established that "in the provinces of the former Pontifical States and Emilia the agrarian *università, comunanze, participanze,* and the associations instituted to the profit of the generality of the inhabitants of a commune, or of a fraction of a commune, or of a determined class of citizens, for the cultivation or the collective enjoyment of landed holdings or the social administration of troops of animals, are considered juridical persons" (article 1) and they were bound to draw up regulatory statutes within a year (articles 2 ff.).

Reduced to its essentials, this is all there was in the law. But it represented an enormous conquest. The normative void in which the old collective structures had operated was in part filled. The old associations that had prospered *extra legem* came, so to speak, to be assimilated into the organization of the state which, for the first time, gave direct relevance to collective property as a scheme of agrarian reality, estimated it positively for what it was, for its intrinsic values, and left off its centuries-old attitude of obstinate hostility.[109]

Given the nature and the limitations of the present work, we have nothing further to add on the subject of this law, even though there would be much to say about its significance to the history of agrarian legislation in Italy after unification. We would like instead to turn our attention to how it came to be formulated and to the extent to which it represented a noteworthy convergence of cultural forces and cultural connections.

There is no doubt that the law of 1894 was a product of the work and the debates on the problem of collective property relating to the Grimaldi bill, like a last stage in a process of distillation. Equally evidently it was born with the encouragement of those forces that we have called heterodox and that we have seen actively present in the Italian Parliament of the 1880s. The continuity of Zucconi's presence is symptomatic of an ideological continuity between the work of the old parliamentary commissions that had fought against Grimaldi and the legislative action of the group that proposed the new project. The same cultural influences that had shaped Zucconi's thought also continued to weigh on others, and the connection that we have emphasized as a trait characteristic of this singular legislative experience between parliamentary initiative and scholarly conclusions was fully and clearly confirmed.

This conclusion deserves to be elaborated more fully for two reasons, first, in order to have a final and yet more clearly defined confirmation of our assumptions, but even more because these cultural forces and this scholarly reflection were revealed, in this second moment of the events in Parliament that we have been investigating, in attitudes particular to it and reflective of the particular personality of the men who were their spokesmen in the great hall of Montecitorio.

Indeed, new men emerged among the older ones, and more than one was prepared by his specific experience to treat the difficult theme with competence.[110] There is one personality that stands out from the others, however, one who incited the group to action and served capably and intelligently as its guide and organizer. This was Tommaso Tittoni.

Since 1886 Tittoni had served as a deputy from the electoral district of Viterbo and Civitavecchia, and his name came up with increasing frequency in the parliamentary debate on the law of 1888 and on its subsequent modifications. We have seen him first leading the protests against the minister's partiality and failure to act. Then we have seen him supplanting Zucconi as leading actor in the process of preparing the way for a new law specifically dedicated to collective property.

But who was Tommaso Tittoni? Such a question posed of such a well-known name might appear to be rhetorical or ingenuous, but it has a precise meaning. Nearly all Italians have heard of Tittoni as prefect of Perugia and of Naples (1898–1903), as minister of foreign affairs (1903–9), as head of the Italian delegation to the League of Nations (1920–22), as president of the Senate (1919–28), and as president of the Reale Accademia d'Italia (1929–30). We know much, in other words, of the politician in his mature years, whom a multitude of apologetic writings have done their best to present for veneration, but we know nearly nothing of the young deputy who showed a surprising knowledge and interest in the problem of collective structures. Quite the contrary, it is evident that part of his public life has been kept in the dark despite the remarkable results he undeniably achieved; for the law of 1894 is largely his work. Perhaps it was overshadowed by the more striking events of his future life. Perhaps it was considered unworthy of consideration by the official culture—first bourgeois, then fascist—precisely because it was closely connected with an attempt to encourage collective property.[111]

We will attempt a fuller presentation of the man which will serve to reach a better understanding of many aspects of the parliamentary career of the notion of collective property and that otherwise would be difficult to explain.

Tittoni was born into a wealthy family of large landholders with estates in Lazio; but he was a proprietor accustomed to spend a good part of the year on his land, and he showed not detachment but familiarity with the things, men, and customs connected with the land.[112] This permitted him to keep alive within him a positive, realistic view of the problems of the land and with it a strong sympathy for tradition, conservation, and order.[113]

Even more than in the case of Zucconi, we must insist upon these ties with the land. They were realistic, not sentimental, idyllic, or Arcadian; and they tied him to the structural problems of agrarian society. Also, like Zucconi, Tittoni was a serious and sensitive observer of the rural world, and his approach to it was positive and almost scientific. One clue to understanding him, or at least one detail that throws light on this attitude, is the discovery in the young Tittoni, who completed his academic studies of law, sociology, and economics at Rome, Oxford, and Liège, of a fairly serious student of geology with enough technical knowledge to be listened to by professional geologists.[114] This complex cultural background, which singularly enough included the more recondite area of the natural sciences, undoubtedly had its effects. It must have contributed to cementing Tittoni's positive ties with the land by increasing his familiarity with it and to enabling him to read it in two dimensions, one of strata and fossils and one of customs and history, all of which were joined together as integral parts of that rich reality that is the land.

In 1924, in his later days, Tittoni returned to his geological studies and, speaking as a geologist before a meeting of geographers and geologists, he looked back with complacency on his many activities. He proclaimed with conviction that the study of the physical sciences "is a good preparation for the understanding of political, economic, and social phenomena,"[115] a declaration that may refer to the avoidance of the emotive or the subjective typical of research on physical phenomena, or that may refer to the need to anchor the evolution of socioeconomic phenomena to an evolutive order that included things and men. We are reminded of Maine, of his "juridical fossils" and his "juridical paleontology," of his comparison of the professions of the historian and the geologist; and we know that certainly Maine—like Darwin, McLennan, and Lubbock—figured among the reading of the young student in Rome.[116]

The man who had walked the length and breadth of his own land to investigate its long-past history, who had bent down humbly to pick up a mineral sample or a fossil finding in order to penetrate the objective structure hidden deeply within it, had a better reason to add historical fossils to his collection of natural fossils and to weave prehistory and protohistory into one unified fabric. He needed to push his curiosity to the observation of the depths of the physical as well as the historical in order to grasp the total organism in all its multiple aspects. In this total vision, the historical fossil, just like the rock sample, enjoyed the objective assessment of the researcher and the same respect for its genesis, its formation, and its location.

Even when it was juridical and economic reality that he was looking at, Tittoni maintained the geologist's gaze, positive, detached, inquiring. His attitude was positive, but also positivist;[117] and while still a student he promoted and directed a university journal of positivistic cultural leanings entitled L'Ateneo.[118] In this journal the young Tittoni did not mince words when he proclaimed his impatience with metaphysics and with "the abuse . . . of nebulous abstractions, like natural law"[119] or his enthusiasm for the critical revisions of Bentham and the iconoclastic investigations of the English, Maine among them, who had turned a fixed but unprejudiced attention to the moment of society's origins.[120] Although up to that moment Tittoni was diffident toward economics, he was attracted by the lessons of the Kathersozialisten, and was an alert student of economics in a general sense. He was even more sympathetic with the methodological precepts of the Historical School of jurisprudence and economics in their call for a refusal of dogmatic abstractions and in their appeal to that relative and positive complex which is history.[121]

The sense of the positive proper to a man of the land and the natural scientist was transferred to the scholar as a sense of coherence. This sense would always bring Tittoni to reject the house of cards built by classical economics, particularly its liberalistic metaphysics that had so little connection with reality. His empirical turn of mind made him a bitter critic of theoretical systems that were polished within the confines of someone's study and that could not be checked continually against changing experience. For him, principles needed to be placed in continual friction with the facts.

When in 1878 and 1888 the *Comizio agrario* of Rome asked him to serve as rapporteur on important regional problems, we see in his reports the same talent for careful observation, positive analysis, and thorough technical information, turned this time to the problems of the Rome-Viterbo railroad line,[122] the regulation of the forests of the province of Rome,[123] the reclamation of the Roman countryside,[124] or a bill regulating hunting and birding.[125] When these talents were joined to a broad cultural background, provincial problems ceased to be disarticulated and atomized and became a living part of great national and European problems. Even more extraordinary, these same talents, supported by a careful attempt to avoid every form of facile rhetoric, can be found as well in his speeches to the voters of Lazio.[126]

These are the terms in which Tittoni saw the problem of the collective structures of the Italian agricultural experience. As was true in the case of Zucconi, he knew them thoroughly, since agrarian *università* were widespread in the Tolfi mountains of the part of northern Lazio in which he lived.[127] He knew them, that is, not through books as feudal residues but as organizational forms of daily life in rural areas. He knew that they had their positive aspects, that they contained "something rational, logical, natural," and that at least they were structures rooted in custom and in the spirit of the people, emanations of a spirit that fitted as coherently into a landscape and into a geo-agronomic structure as did the flora and fauna. He knew them, above all, as forms of his personal experience, for he had involved himself in them and had observed them from the base and from within, not from on high or from afar with the arrogance and inaccuracy that comes from lack of direct experience.[128] Furthermore, he spoke of them to his electorate as of a problem that was familiar to them because it was closely interwoven with local agrarian affairs. He made them a specific plank of his platform and focus of his activities as deputy. He criticized the abolitionist attitude as all too often an homage paid to an empty principle, a generic formula, a political commitment, and nothing more[129]—paid, in sum, to what he did not hesitate to call "an outdated and perilous prejudice."[130]

Nevertheless, Tittoni never takes refuge in the shadow of the local church tower or the town hall: the problem never becomes one of petty details of practice. His strong cultural preparation and his thorough knowledge of the debate among European economists[131] saved him from any tendency to make the question trivial. The problem was complex, richly articulated, and far-reaching. It arrived to the shadow of the church tower, to be sure, but it spread out over the universal territory of the history of forms of property. The problem, for him, called always for a universal projection, and it was connected with the broad interpretations of human protohistory and with the great controversy over the original forms of landed appropriation.

Tittoni's voyages of study abroad, after he had taken his *laurea* in Rome, helped him to establish the problem in cultural terms. He went to Oxford, where we do not know whether he was able to meet Maine, but where certainly he must have heard echoes of Maine's recent and highly applauded Oxford lectures on village communities and primitive institutions in Ireland. He then went to Liège where, thanks to letters of recommendation from Marco Minghetti and Quintino Sella, he attended Laveleye's courses and, as he later was fond of recalling, he had scholarly conversations with the Belgian economist on the theme so typical of his thought, the history of the forms of property and the historical dialectic between individual property and collective property.[132]

Tittoni's studies at Liège must have served to fix the collective structures of his native Lazio onto an unlimited geographical horizon, and they must have left an indelible mark on him, strengthening his interest in the phenomenon of "collective property." We can even say without qualification that Tittoni posed the problem in Laveleye's terms and that it was a vision shaped by Laveleye that he would later try to introduce into the parliamentary events that interest us. All of his many and carefully fashioned contributions to the discussion of the law of 1894 attest fully to this.

There were many points of agreement between the young Tittoni and Laveleye. They shared a decidedly anti-Enlightenment temperament; they were both firm in their refusal of every form of radicalism and hostile toward modern individualism and toward the values of the nineteenth century. We can recognize attitudes common to both of them: a conviction that social formations had an ethical dimension, a perennial insistence on mediation between the political and the religious spheres,[133] a respect for tradition and the order that history has left behind that was substantially conservative, but open-minded and strongly sensitive to the call for justice, and a constant give and take between rigorous cultural research and the necessity for social action, the constant presence of the "social question" and the constant priority of order, to be reached at any cost by using all possible techniques of mediation.

Tittoni's position was born of the conjuncture of these singular experiences and his personality. It enabled him to be receptive to the reorganization and strengthening of collective property. It brought the alternative values of the great controversy into the work of the Italian

Parliament. And it carried on the movement initiated by Zucconi, developing it and providing its natural completion, although with variations that it will be necessary to point out.

An attentive reading of Tittoni's speeches in Parliament after 1889, most particularly the admirable report of 20 February 1893, in which he elaborates his thoughts at greater length, brings out recurrent examples of criticism of the principles that were acclaimed and in wide circulation in nineteenth-century society. From Tittoni's different perspective, these principles—the cult of the individual, the education to egoism, and the incomprehension of values other than those based on wealth—were charged with negative values. He saw these principles as negative, not only for their insensitivity to essential dimensions like the religious and the social, but above all because they were themselves imposed as absolute values and accepted as such.

As Tittoni saw it, a new metaphysic of immanence had been created after the eighteenth century. It was separated from facts and their positive nature, immobilized in a sort of dogmatics, and supported by complacent formulas written in economic terms by the classical school and in terms of jurisprudence by the Romanists.[134] But our devotee of the positive, our geologist accustomed to deducing laws and identifying formative processes by scrutinizing the wrinkles of the earth and examining rocks, was equally unable to accept a pure science made of concepts and logical propositions when it had to govern different men and things, different epochs and places.

There was, however, another element in Tittoni's personality: his repugnance toward the pseudo conquests of bourgeois society was a repugnance toward a society that had no history, that had been constituted in recent times with many an improvisation, and that furthermore had presumptuously claimed to cut the umbilical cord that bound it to the past and that might have been the vehicle of its enrichment. For him, this was a society that had stupidly thought to be able to ignore the traditions and the spirit of the people and that had unnaturally cut itself off from history.[135] Laveleye's disciple used a subtle and devious polemical technique that was nevertheless deadly and pitiless. Deliberately mixing the good with the bad, he likened the barbarian "feudalism"—in the eyes of the nineteenth-century bourgeois the quintessence of the worst that human history had produced—to "revolution" and "the doctrinarianism of modern constitutions" in that they were equally closed to collective structures.[136] That this comparison was charged with a contempt for that doctrinaire attitude should be evident.

But since it was Tittoni who made these accusations, let him speak for himself:

Reiterated attacks are today being made on the *third estate,* reproached for having taken literally the dictum of Sieyès—to want to be all. It is certain that the people have much to complain of in individualism and in the unconscious egoism that derives from individualism. And it was an act of unconscious egoism to extinguish every religious sentiment in the masses; it was an act of unconscious egoism to call them to the right to vote without having given them education and independence; it was an act of egoism in the old laws to have destroyed not only that which held the people in subjection, but also that which constituted for the people protection and help; it was an act of egoism to constitute the economic world on the base of an unlimited competition, because unlimited competition means the prevalence of the strong and the rich over the weak and the poor.[137]

This bitter criticism of the postrevolutionary regime is mixed with a *laudatio temporis acti,* with an infinite nostalgia for the *ancien régime.* Tittoni's polemic against the capitalistic order has paleoconservative and passistic nuances and seems dominated by a call for return, by a backflow that leads beyond the recent past to the rediscovery of the remote past.[138] In the prerevolutionary regime, Tittoni seems to teach us, even amid glaring inequalities, priority was given to the corporation; it did not tolerate in the single person rights without duties, powers without ethical or religious legitimizations, or inferiority without protections. It was, in other words, a world whose macrostructures more resembled Tittoni's ideal of order than did the fragmentary fabric of the modern world, concentrated as it was on the microstructures of the individual and subjected for that reason to an array of disorganized and uncontrollable stimuli. These stimuli could allow the prevalence of the rich, the strong, and the astute in de facto situations, but not the prevalence of the values proper to the social body. This argument immediately recalls the passage in Laveleye in which he opposes the subjective right to property as it sprang unopposed and in all its fullness out of the Code and brought privilege for the title holder, with the property of the *ancien droit* that defined the proprietor within the spiral of the social system in which it was included. Tittoni must certainly have had this passage in his mind as a model.

In Tittoni's argument, when the usual individualistic preconceptions had been cleared away to leave a *tabula rasa,* when the path was free of misleading commonplaces, all the alternative cultural techniques and the ample information collected in the preceding decade could be exploited to face the problem of collective property with serenity and certainty. With his usual taste for the positive, Tittoni was anxious first to demonstrate the extraordinary quantity of instances of the phenomenon in the former Pontifical States.[139] Then, with the accumulated data to back him up, he went on to analyze its quality in historical and juridical terms.

Here again we continue to sense the shadow of Laveleye—and of Roscher and Schäffle, Valenti and Colajanni—and Tittoni's conclusions are those that we have encountered before in alternative currents of thought, though he states them with a rigorous accuracy of language and concepts. This, like the enormous mass of bibliographical information that follows the report, is a sign that Tittoni's proposal was as carefully worked out as had been Maine's insights long before. Not only does he repeat that collective property represented the first form of landed appropriation,[140] but he goes on to clarify that "collectivity can always be found as a capacity inherent to property."[141]

This clarification is useful as an indication of the refinement of Tittoni's technico-juridical methods: property was a complex situation that was worked out in the perennial dialectic between a social moment and an individual moment. The social moment, an integral part of the most deeply hidden nature of property, had its historical form and its most typical manifestation in collective property, which was therefore an authentic expression of property, a *species* of a broader *genus*.[142] As such, it was also a constant of human civilization from protohistorical times, with a core of continuity that united the distant Germanic *Mark* documented for us by Caesar and Tacitus to the structures that still existed throughout Europe and the entire world at the end of the nineteenth century.[143] What Tittoni saw as important was to bring new life and relevance to the old trunk with appropriate graftings, perhaps to insert the budding slips of cooperation into the old static structures. Thus would "tradition" be harmonized with "progress."[144]

Tittoni's report of 1893 did not contradict the meaning of the whole of the movement in Parliament: it was a movement that transplanted cultural forces into the experimental situation of the legislature and that recognized in those forces a determining if not dominant motive for action. The bibliography that follows Tittoni's pages provided a proud display of erudition, even if it was somewhat singular in its setting among the parliamentary acts. It was also perhaps the most complete and the most impressive listing that we have seen of the scholarly research throughout the whole of Europe dedicated to the problem of the history of forms of property.[145] Although we cannot be sure whether it indicates reading that Tittoni had done or reading that he intended to do, it certainly proves him well informed on the subject, and it shows the scholarly level on which he meant to place his report. Even if the debate took place in a chamber of Montecitorio and had as its goal the passage of an act of legislation, it could not avoid being inspired by scientific rigor, and it seemed to translate the very most recent research on the question into terms congenial to the legislator, since the nucleus of the problem was the revision of an erroneous notion of property and only subsequently the appropriate adjustment of the laws.

And this was the fact of the matter. Tittoni, who had from his early days with *L'Ateneo* always prided himself on his studies in economic doctrine and who had always dealt with competence with the messages that arrived from Manchester or Eisenach, asked of the doctrine of collective property that it provide an aid "to understanding economic theory and explaining the historical fact of property."[146] He thus inserted the schema of collective property into the prismatic array of theories of property of the classicists, the socialists, and the *Kathedersozialisten*. We are reminded once again of Laveleye, in particular of the concluding chapter of his book on primitive forms, in which he draws together the meaning of all of the research accomplished in order to attempt the construction of a renewed doctrine of property.

When Tittoni speaks, then, we hear a dedication to culture and to theory, even though he was a politician speaking in a hall that was by definition dedicated to political debate. But Tittoni's fidelity to Laveleye did not permit him to leave these motives in isolation, but mixed them with a tangle of concerns which, while they render his thought more complex, also give it a far more historical cast.

The social question was overwhelmingly present in Tittoni's thought even more than in Zucconi's, although it was constantly in the background of all of the events in Parliament that we have been examining, and the idea of making even a minimal contribution to its solution was shared by many others. To the image of Tittoni as a man dedicated to positive reconstruction, a man of broad cultural interests, and a man who confidently held to alternative socio-juridical principles, must be added the image of the landed proprietor who looked with satisfaction at the "social peace" of his native Lazio. He saw that peace as connected with the existence of a considerable group of collective landholding arrangements in the region, and he identified in them a compromise solution that might serve to guarantee the maintenance of socioeconomic order.[147]

In Tittoni's parliamentary speeches there is in fact always a precise echo of the growing social unrest in the Italian countryside following the agrarian crisis of the 1880s and particularly after 1887.[148] There is a note of insistence in his reference in one place to the "agrarian troubles,"[149] in another to "the agitations that have disturbed our country"[150] and in his recognition that "the agricultural masses are in tumult everywhere."[151] And always, as in Laveleye, there crops up the belief—

accompanied by the harmonious but somewhat artificial picture postcard image of the Swiss *Allmend*—that collective property could serve as a means of reconciling opposed interests.[152] For Tittoni it was not only a question of freeing oneself of prejudices and errors and thus reestablishing historical truth and an accurate juridical diagnosis. It was also—and this was perfectly consonant with his function as a deputy and with the seat of the debate—a matter of launching an operative proposal that might in part resolve the enormous social problems that troubled agriculture.

We must note, however, that Tittoni was not innocent enough to have believed that he had found a sort of philosopher's stone in collective property capable of changing every potentially explosive situation in the rural areas into social peace. It is certain, however, that he believed in the "social character" of "his" legislative proposal.[153] When forms of cooperation and participation in the ownership of the soil were constituted,[154] ever greater numbers of workers would be taken away from the masses of the migrant workers and day laborers[155] and two objectives were satisfied: one practiced "practical socialism,"[156] aiming at the concrete betterment of the moral and economic condition of shepherds and peasants, and one guaranteed public tranquillity and, consequently, supported the established order.

A "proposal of evolution, not of revolution"[157] Tittoni took pains to repeat in an effort to reassure the many coarse landholders who sat in alarm on their benches at Montecitorio and listened unwillingly to his various speeches and to his disquieting conclusions. In a moment of sincerity, almost of confession, after he had proclaimed his endorsement of the proposal of an "avowed socialist" that had appeared that year on the pages of *Critica sociale*,[158] Tittoni quickly added:

> What seems to him purely agrarian socialism seems to me above all a measure of social conservation, and so I believe that it should appear to anyone who succeeds in divesting himself of antiquated prejudices and preconceptions. With the adherence of the ruling classes, conservative by nature and by interest, to the principle of collectivity, the prediction of Schäffle will come true: "Not violence from the base, but the experience of the perils that menace capital in the system of capitalistic competition will win over those who today hold large possessions to the cause of the reforms that are historically mature.[159]

An operation of social conservation was taking form beside the cultural operation. A reformism arose that was without doubt immediately favorable to the interests of certain categories of agricultural workers, but indirectly its effect would be to avoid total reform and to allow the old social framework to hold together and to continue to survive.

If we had turned to the next page in Tittoni's report of 20 February, we would have found, accented by italics, two indicative references, to class struggle and to the *fasci* [a socialist movement organized into local cells] and we would have grasped the orator's dismay concerning these disruptive manifestations that had taken shape in the turbulent Italy of those years. In his eyes, they aspired to the destruction of order, and their position was in deliberate opposition to the principle of the law. They were not the result of the normal workings of the evolution of institutions but were completely innocent of any tie with the past and with tradition, symbols of a violent and improvised present with no yesterday.[160]

The Tittoni who was interested in reestablishing popular traditions, who was aware of the enormous controlling force that a connection with tradition exercised, who played the card of tradition like a saved-up ace, was repelled by movements like class struggle and associations like the *fasci*. They fell outside of his categories; they eluded any attempt at regimentation; they put themselves programmatically outside of the order of the state. He felt for them not only repugnance but fear, and he found in them reasons to reinforce his own thesis in favor of compromise and to urge the Parliament of the unified state to move toward the realization, encouragement, and regulation of collective landholding structures. Collective property, "that which even Canon Law calls *dulcissima rerum possessio communis,*"[161] the *Gesamteigentumsrecht* of Germanic tradition,[162] as it had been filtered by custom and passed on by history, inspired a good deal more confidence.

The testimony of Tommaso Tittoni suffers from the same ambiguities as that of Laveleye: it is almost as though the young and brilliant Italian student had absorbed his master's concerns and anxieties along with his general orientation in their many contacts in Liège. Laveleye, as we know, wrote his volume on property when the echo of the gunfire of the Paris Commune had hardly died down. Tittoni joined this parliamentary debate on the collective domains between 1887 and 1894, a span of years that saw for the first time a valid and organically structured organization of workers and peasants, united in strikes, in agitations, and in struggles that were increasingly openly and frankly proletarian. This was the background inherent to his accomplishments.

Tittoni's contribution, then, was ambivalent and complex, and it is undeniable that his mentality was conservative. He had the merit of not relegating scholarly research, historical and juridical investigation, and problems of method and methodological correctness, to a merely ancillary or instrumental position as he studied the forms of property and their history. If anything, he maximized their importance. Scientific investigation and the need for sociopolitical action moved in concert toward the same goals, but it would misrepresent the formidable cultural apparatus of Tittoni's contributions to reduce them to a set of useless decorations or to a screen of forms behind which the real play of interests was taking place. Not only would it be a distortion, but it would be to deny all that has been said in the preceding pages. For Tittoni, as for Laveleye, we must stop at the affirmation of a complexity of discourse. What he represented was in the final analysis not self-contradictory, but it certainly was neither unequivocal nor simple.

Tittoni's report of 20 February 1893 concludes with an invitation to the government to "be inspired by the principle of collective property to resolve with all expedition the question of the rights of usage and of the communal domains in all of the other provinces of Italy."[163] Drowned in the impenetrable silence of official juridical science, lost in the unreceptive, closed-minded misoneism of the Parliament, Tittoni's was a solitary voice destined to disappear into the void. But it was a voice of sincere and limpidly clear dissonance with the cultural premises of the official juridical orders and it offered alternative cultural values. Even if he proposed indifferently both scientific truth and political opportunity as reasons for the revision of the old options, even if his thought was shot through with veins of conservatism with more than one instance of indulgence toward the past, Tittoni's contribution remains an important event in cultural terms.

In fact, it still represented a liberation from old predicaments, a refusal to accept some of the best established clichés, a critical awareness confirmed by the mirage of the interests at stake rather than obfuscated by it. Knowledge was completely autonomous of ideology in Tittoni. His point of departure was the reestablishment of a positive truth and the consciousness of a value to be won back to civilization—which, to be sure, would promptly mitigate the more relative values tied to political opportunism. But if we want to evaluate Tittoni's ambivalence objectively, we must not forget that he was a politician and that he spoke in a political setting in which the cult of individual property had always been a guiding force. Here even a minimal skill with a notion of tactics would have advised him to offer his unaccustomed and unpalatable material in an acceptable manner.

What is extraordinary is that, thanks to Zucconi's lead and Tittoni's efforts, collective property as *one* sort of property captured the attention of the Italian legislature in a positive manner for the first time. In the terms of the history of juridical thought in modern times, the cultural pluralism that Henry Maine had invoked became law in one state, thanks to an uninterrupted current of thought that flowed, even though with many meanderings, from the brilliant Englishman to the Italian geologist-jurist.

There is no doubt, in fact, that the events that took place in the Italian Parliament presupposed the great controversy and can be directly connected to it and that the Italian laws of 1888 and 1894 had among the several causes that contributed to their definitive .formulation one— perhaps the determining one—that was inherently cultural.

The current of thought in Italy that reflected the great European controversy became more cohesive and more clearly defined, and the old but valid seed that Maine had sowed gave isolated but remarkable fruit in Italian soil. This problem had hardly begun to be resolved, however, and the subsequent legislation that in 1895 these deputies called for and expected was unfortunately not to come into being. But the cultural and political work accumulated during the formulation of the law of 4 August 1894 would leave perceptible marks on the fulsome discussion and the many several proposals that would follow.[164]

10 Problems of

Juridical Construction

Property "In the Singular" and Its Model

The protagonists of the controversy were almost all historians: historians *tout court,* historians of jurisprudence, Romanists, and economic historians, or at least jurists or sociologists with a particular sensitivity to vertical comparison. As such, they posed themselves a typically historical problem and tried to resolve it from that point of view.

Historically, both the question of the origins of property and that of its evolution had a certain linearity and could correctly be reduced to the simple but distinct antithesis between collective property and individual property. From the genetic point of view, in fact, the notion of collective property as a common denominator indicative of true and proper collective domains (whether they were communal or collective) and of rights of usage (civic customs and, as they were improperly called,[1] servitudes of pasturage, woodcutting, tillage) was *historically* correct. This is because it understood all of these landholding structures in their consituent aspect, in their origin, indeed, in their genesis, and proposed them as historical forms all deriving from a single protohistorical phenomenon, as various offshoots of the same socio-juridical matrix: primitive landholding communism. One could correctly speak of remnants—more or less conspicuous, more or less distorted—of ancient "condominium." Nor could such a reduction of the problem appear incorrect in terms of the unfolding of history, since it seemed to consist in a dialectic between two perfectly opposed basic options, between antithetical modes of conceiving and living the relationship of man to the earth, identified summarily in collective property on the one hand and individual property on the other.

232

In this dialectic of contraries, the various distinctions that came to be drawn within the two polarized constructions tended to be lost, and arguments about them, exaggerating the opposition of one to the other, were soon reduced to a simple and limpidly clear give-and-take between two appropriative genres. Collective property, in itself a profoundly imprecise generalization, assumed greater precision as a *relative* notion—that is, when it was thought of in relation to individual property and when it was made to refer to an organizational structure opposed on the socioeconomic and the juridical level to the structure of dominium in severalty, almost as if it were its logical *oppositum*.

It was in this *relative* sense that the notion was always used in the great controversy, and in this sense it assumed a *relative* precision. What was important to the participants in the controversy was a dialectic between two landholding structures that were not only structurally remote from each other but that had substantially different functions and ends. One structure was dedicated to guaranteeing that a holding belonged to a single person, the other to its conservation for an entire generational line. One was subjective to the point of being confounded with the volitional sphere of the subject and it was therefore the source of as many powers over the thing held as could be recognized in the will of the single subject; the other was objectified to the point of being articulated internally as a structure of truly collective dimensions, with the consequence of disallowing to the "condominium" members not only powers of disposition but also of administration of the holding if that administration distorted its normal destination. One was a situation of privilege for the title holder that became an aspect of his very individuality and that was projected onto the thing held, regardless of the realities of the situation; the other was so conditioned by economic facts—one could almost say it emanated from them—that it was elaborated more in duties for the participants than in their rights as subjects.

If one aimed at a historical dialectic composed of a positive and a negative, the unified notion of "collective property" was an appropriate and adequate instrument for understanding the clash between different cultures. It was portrayed in the course of the great dispute as an eminently dialectical moment, as an instrument for the relativization of individual property; and I have portrayed it in these terms in the preceding pages. As I said in the introduction, collective property was in this context a message on method, the battle flag of a struggle, and a means to a cultural liberation; it was only secondarily a juridical institution. And the objective in this struggle, more than individual property as such, was the cultural and socioeconomic model in which that property was embodied. Collective property functioned efficiently against this model as a call to action, a rallying cry, and a strategy.

With all of this, however, collective property remained a generic instrument, valid on the historico-cultural plane, but unsatisfactory and vague for anyone who viewed the question in the light of a specific and technical competence. This was the case of those few jurists who did not let themselves be dominated by the general repugnance toward an institution that to so great an extent sacrificed the individual and exalted the group. These few found that they had before them a historical object that expressed itself in extremely varied forms, ranging from collective domains to rights of pasturage or, as they usually said, from "condominium" to "servitudes," and that led them to an *extraordinary, irregular, abnormal* structure outside the order, the rule, or the norm that inspired the *sensible* institutions of bourgeois law.

How to qualify this collective property that seemed, on the level of juridical organization, not to want to take human egoism into account, when the edifice of individual property had so *wisely* been constructed on that egoism? That did not encourage the accumulation of a patrimony, and that protected not ownership but survival? That was a fact not derived from the political and economic plane but one that was rife with ethical, religious, and biological implications? That was aimed at satisfying not the individual, but the group and a chain of successive generations? The *sensible* jurists tied to official culture generally ignored the aberrant institution or if, through a desire for thoroughness, they were induced to speak of it, they placed it among curiosities or referred to it incidentally as they spoke of the so-called irregular servitudes.

There were jurists who, in their studies of closely related subjects, encountered the phenomenon and were forced to raise the question of its juridical nature in terms of construction. Using only the deductive force of their own conceptual instruments, they succeeded in denying to it the least proprietary dignity. Gustavo Bonelli is a good example of this. His keen mind, always confined within the logical armor of his high skill, was responsible for a passage that, although written at the beginning of the century, is worthy of attention today for the methodological orientation it expresses. Bonelli does not hesitate to state:

> When one speaks of collective property, this term is used in an inexact sense, namely, to indicate a completely different relationship, historically anterior to the very genesis of true property.[2]

We see here a principle enunciated in the lapidary style of one who restores a basic truth that has been attacked. The only question here is correctness or incorrectness, truth or error. The great controversy, to which Bonelli seems to allude indirectly, has not done him the slightest good. If undoubtedly collective property preceded individual property, this was for him a circumstance of no significance, since the former was only a rough and primitive approach to the possession of goods for which such an august name and such a rigorous concept were not suitable. The history of property, no matter what came before it, began only with the appearance of individual property as marked with its essential dimension of exclusiveness.[3]

One should not conclude that this intelligent specialist in commercial law was insensitive. Rather, his was a distorting mentality that was common in civil law in Italy and that the passage of time has not succeeded in assuaging. We find substantially the same mentality in more recent reflection on the subject in a man who most seemed destined to liberate himself from scholastic orientations. When in the 1960s Salvatore Romano attempted a reconstruction of the question, he repeated that:

> What is necessary, and at the same time sufficient, in order to have a concept of property, is autonomy in the sense of dispositive power. . . . The "collective" aspects . . . do not invest power directly in its due place, but attain moments or elements of a functional exercise.[4]

Even though indirectly, the old misunderstanding is perpetuated, the old Romanistic mental category is reproposed; we see the old juridical education that both the older and the more recent civilists have not managed to shake off in spite of changes in legislation and mutations in society and culture.

The central knot of the question is still the one that Maine and Laveleye identified: one model of property and one alone, the Romanistic, measure and canon of truth and error. It is a model that has penetrated the Italian jurist to his very bones. It rises irresistibly to the surface even between the lines of a courageous methodological adventure like that of Romano, and it is so commanding that it condemns the jurist to a rigid monism.[5]

It is a model based on at least two fixed principles. The first: property is a situation that is by its nature exclusively individual. The second: it is an attribute characterizing the subject and conferring on him a moral and political supremacy over the object held. Only the disfranchisement from these canons could have led to the crumbling of the model, and that liberation could be achieved only if two dimensions could be returned to the notion of property: collectivity and factuality. It would have been necessary, in other words, to rescue the notion of property from the quicksands of dominium in severalty and of a pure juridical relationship.[6] But doctrine could not and did not want to take this direction.

The old theory of property as a *facultas moralis,* a situation typically intrasubjective in both its genesis and its essence, a situation that found in its projection toward external reality a simple added power,[7] continued in these more or less conscious repetitions of a reassuring reliance on natural law. The repugnance toward considering property a need that stemmed from reality, that was conditioned by reality, continued as well. In the passage cited above, Bonelli points to the purity of juridical science and of its conceptual arsenal as an end to be attained at any cost.[8] This purity has here its concrete translation in the moment in which he refuses to consign to facts the elaboration of an extremely important institution and continues to think of it as a dehistoricized entity that belongs rather to the universe of ethics. It would be necessary to wait until 1922 to hear, in the inaugural lecture in Florence by a pupil of Venezian, Enrico Finzi, a clear and open denunciation of the pretended purity of the proprietary relationship and also, although less openly, of its ideological implications.[9]

In a similar manner, *fin de siècle* doctrine persisted in its refusal of any possible tie between "collectivity" and the holding of title—the proprietary position in all its fullness. Such an idea was considered unnatural and therefore unsustainable. To tie the idea of "collectivity" to the *true* notion of appropriation seemed to do violence to a notion that appeared bound to the idea of the individual and of the unique individual, bound by its essence rather than by accident.

Any historian who might wish to take stock of the influence of this model on the *scientia iuris* even of the later nineteenth century would have only to retrace the path of two heated and strongly related controversies that took place in those years. Their specific grounds were the juridical nature of condominium and the juridical personality of commercial societies. Given the nature of the present work, we can do no more than refer to these two questions, reserving the right to return to them more fully at another occasion. It is certain, however, that they provide an invaluable opportunity to verify the arguments outlined here.

The malaise that winds through the most competent literature on the subject of condominium is born of a critical realization that the traditional schema of *dominium* cannot fit into a communitarian structure. While most writers were content to reduce the *communio* of an ideal entity like the *quota* to the sum of tenancies in severalty, a solid thinker like Silvio Perozzi—though he was not alone[10]—resolved this difficulty in a carefully meditated refusal to restrict "the common concept of property." Perozzi further insisted on "finding in the right of the coproprietor the characteristics of such a right to property."[11] He limited himself to carrying on a corrosive but painless destruction of the limping old hypotheses. He did not construct a proposal of his own, but was content to have eliminated certain hermeneutical and conceptual ambiguities. The only truly positive indication that springs from his study of 1890 is the invitation to "a revision of the idea of property" as the only and ultimate means for avoiding the predicament of Byzantine constructions.[12]

There was another doctrinal current that showed a courage equal to Perozzi's and that broke out of the jurists' usual fear of novelty. When it was faced with creations like the commercial societies—institutions that were born of practice and consolidated in a tradition of non-Romanistic stamp—it found itself dissatisfied with the categories of simple community and of the juridical person and took as its standard of measurement historical inventions from diverse traditions—like the Germanic, which had among its characteristics the flexible notions of *Gesamteigentum* and *Gesamtehand*. But although this current is not difficult to identify in cultural terms, it is one that soon vanished and that went no further than providing a singular and interesting contribution to juridical science.[13]

Attempts at a Juridical Construction

The jurists in the doctrinal currents that were more sensitive to new ideas and that were searching for new paths certainly felt this malaise, and there were several attempts—few, meager, but significant—at a juridical construction of the phenomenon of "collective property" that appeared in the last decade of the century. They came in the wake of the great controversy on historical forms of property, and they appear to us to represent, on the level of juridical procedures, both the chronological and the logical consequences of the work accomplished in the 1880s.

Filomusi Guelfi and Venezian and their pupils in private law,[14] and Oreste Ranelletti in public law, the strongest representatives of this group, presupposed a knowledge of the previous history of the controversy. Filomusi's courses on landholding rights—at least after 1888–89, but perhaps also from the time of his first course in 1885–86—the Venezian Camerino inaugural lecture of 1887 and his volume on usufruct of 1895, and the study of Ranelletti on the public domain published in 1898,[15] can be imagined only after the great liberation from Romanistic scholastic positions that the debate had accomplished, and they constituted a continuation of the general debate in procedural terms.

One senses in these scholars a double and urgent interrogative: to what extent was it legitimate to speak of collective property as a notion that comprehends both "condominiums" and "servitudes"? And what was the internal structure of a condominium so removed from the commonly accepted Roman and civilistic notion? They felt the vital need for a juridical construction, but they were persuaded that the usual schemata were incapable of furnishing the instruments to carry it out. They were determined not to be blinded by prefabricated notions, and they sought the help of a freer consciousness and a freer vision.

Undoubtedly, the generalized philo-Germanism of Italian juridical culture filtered down into these doctrinal manifestations to operate within the closed sanctuary of the technical representation of landed rights. It led to the recovery of two lost dimensions: the collective and the factual. The jurists' connection with the Germanic and Germanistic tradition was a precise and concrete expression of their dissatisfaction with the wornout schemata of the Italian tradition, and at the same time it prefigured still other schemata. They spoke of this German influence as an opportunity to break out of the limitations of the old Roman authority and to construct something in the free, unoccupied, but extremely unstable territory of the non-Roman.

Gierke introduced these jurists to new technical procedures and new communitarian structures, and their discovery of his work was an important event. The formal citation of times past disappears, to give way to an effective use of materials destined to fill in the void left by the abandonment of the old frontier.[16] They discovered the complex architectonic lines that had for decades remained hidden in the disarmingly gothic pages of treatises by Bluntschli, Beseler, and Stobbe, where the ignorance, the neglect, or the deliberate intention of Italian jurists had left them buried.[17] Philo-Germanism became a discourse that enjoyed technical validity for analysis because it claimed to be an orientation and an argumentation that could be opposed to the discourse that had for centuries enjoyed enormous validity.

Once embarked on this path, the jurist who intended to focus his attention on the problem of collective property—seemingly a Gordian knot—by bringing to it his specific knowledge found in the Germanists the elements necessary to do so. Constructive values then emerged from collective property. One such value was the group as an organic entity that protected and integrated the scattered energies of individuals on the socio-juridical level. The concept of the entire organism—a legacy from the Historical School—was omnipresent. It focused attention more on the organic complex than on the single components, more on the community than on the individual member. The second such value was concrete fact as an inalienable source of that order, making it impossible to conceive of that order in the abstract.

The entire realm of landholding rights seemed shaken by these values. Far from representing a *facultas moralis* guaranteed by the will of the state, far from being an ontological intrapersonal reality preceding in its perfection the powers that become realized in history and in society, property was joined to facts and was born of those facts, whether they were facts of blood, of residence, of enjoyment, or of work. Inasmuch as property was bound to facts and not to the inseparable unity of a legal personality, inasmuch as it originated from the base, from things themselves, it put aside its uniquely individual nature and affirmed its disposition to be ordered in the collective manner as well. What appeared, that is, from this current of thought was the clear possibility of identifying property both on the level of the factual and on the level of the collective. One sort of property emerged structured indeed in that manner: collective property, understood as a way of holding land on a level that surpassed the individual, based on the objective exigencies of that imperishable reality that is the earth, an ownership within which the position of the single person never succeeded in isolating itself from the intricate organism in which he took his life.

Another fact emerged: it was impossible to arrive at an efficacious understanding of the phenomenon by means of any attempt at qualification that started from the point of view of Roman community. The Roman concept of community was coherent, but it had been reduced by individualistic terms to coownership of shares, that is, to ideal entities that were nevertheless absolutely clearly defined as subject to precise acts of alienation on the part of the single coowners. A complex situation that could not be reduced to a merely patrimonial level, in which community and single members were thought of in an inseparable, indissoluble, and symbiotic relationship, stood in total opposition to this definition.

A *condominium iuris germanici* thus came to be defined in opposition to the privatistic *communio pro indiviso* in which the several tenants stood as titular proprietors of shares of an ideal portion of a patrimony that was subject to absolute liberty of disposition. It stood in contrast also to the idea of the property of the corporation as totally separate and independent of the position of the single members. This *condominium iuris germanici* proposed a relation of unity to plurality in the context of collectivity as a sort of organic connection that did not permit the conceptual detachment of the juridical personality from the person of the participants, but that instead understood both persons as indissolubly and vitally linked.

There is no doubt that a *condominium iuris germanici* was an imaginary figure for anyone who intended to measure it rigorously against the cultural history of the whole of Western experience. But it is equally clear that the figure took on a concreteness in the function that was assigned to it in the culture of late nineteenth-century jurisprudence. *Condominium iuris germanici* is here in fact only a means of giving definition to an opposition: it was valid as a *non-Roman* joint ownership, as a structure liberated from overly rigid individualistic premises. It was more plastic, more open to facts and to their variety, and it was typified by an articulation that was not only patrimonial and was therefore not susceptible to mercenary acts.

The person who was most sensitive to these questions was Filomusi Guelfi. In him the great lesson of the Germanists was translated into the only coherent attempt that Italy had seen to get free of the conditionings of the Romanists and to embark on an autonomous path, one which he followed to the end without hesitation and without regrets. The historian of jurisprudence who looks today at Filomusi's course outlines or the later editions of the *Enciclopedia giuridica*[18] cannot help being struck by his singularly free and open treatment of the problem. This is even more evident when his writings are compared with the more usual courses on landholding rights, in which monotonous conclusions are repeated without imagination or a sense of culture.

Filomusi's reading of German authors and his passion for Germanistic studies had a liberating effect on him. What he took from his beloved Gierke was that it was possible not to identify property as a relation of dominium, as a moral and political supremacy over an object. The Roman hypostasis was embodied in this supremacy: it was an ethico-political notion that could be reduced to a *naked* right; it could see its dimension of enjoyment frustrated and still conserve intact its juridical importance, since the latter was totally concentrated in the extra-economic content of *meum esse*. It was a notion that, in virtue of its elasticity, could even be totally deprived of that content *pro tempore*. Property—a fundamental relation of a subject to goods or holdings—could instead be understood in such a way that its economic embodiment could be held to be unrenounceable. That is, it could be a concept standing outside the ethical dimension and enclosed entirely within the realm of economic relations. It could be found, in particular conditions, wherever a mechanism for the utilization of goods or holdings could be found. In other words, enjoyment could by itself constitute a fact that defined property.

It followed for Filomusi Guelfi that if property was tied to particular economic facts, in relation to that complex economic fact which is the thing, one could have more than one ownership in the same thing, according to the circumstances. Here the Roman, and universally recognized, principle of the impossibility—primarily a logical impossibility—of more than one *dominium* pertaining together over the same goods or holdings showed itself to be absurd.

Filomusi fully exploited the enormous dialectical opportunity offered by Germanistic thought, and he thus arrived at a demythicization of the classical construction of landholding rights and at a relativization of the so-called logic of the classicists, a logic that declared its validity and therefore offered itself as indisputable only within a system founded on particular premises. When these premises had been made subject to historical processes, the interpreter reacquired his liberty of action, and "illogical" notions, like that of divided property and collective property, recovered an intrinsic absolute validity, leaving only the problem of their coherence with one or another positive situation.

For Filomusi and his school, following Gierke's example, the complex articulation of collective property was a concrete instance of "property divided according to its usefulness," suspended between the plurality of joint owners and beneficial owners, the *condomini-utenti,* and the unity of the corporation. The situation of the *condomino-utente* became concrete for that reason in the form of a distributive right to the holding and thus constituted a full participation in the sphere of land ownership.[19]

Anyone who has had experience with the principal tenets of the prevailing civil doctrine on property can see the unusual character of the system Filomusi arrived at. He had the merit of proposing a solution that attempted to construct an organizational category that was fully consonant with the tenets of the Germanic tradition and that used materials proper and congenial to that tradition. Further, it was still a minimal schema, one that lent itself to functioning as a convenient framework for that extreme variety of landholding arrangements which constituted the *genus* of collective property. It was therefore a schema valid both for collective domains and for the rights of usage.

Filomusi's views had one disadvantage if they were meant to be a proposal for positive law: they were learned and well thought-out and logically and culturally well founded. But they appeared to be totally foreign to the legislative system that was prevalent in Italy—indeed, to be polemically opposed to it. Perhaps this mattered little to Filomusi, who started from a pluralistic orientation and who tended to consider the vitality of a juridical order in very different terms from those of its crystallization in legislation and its manifestation in official programs.[20]

This aspect of the question mattered very much to Giacomo Venezian, however. Venezian made a choice in his treatise on usufruct that was exactly opposed to Filomusi's, and he tried to harmonize collective property with the normative system of Italy.

Was this a denial of the insights and the ingenious and courageous ideas expressed in his Camerino lecture of 1887? Certainly not: Venezian's full sympathy for collective landholding structures remains in his later work, as does his open evaluation of them, his increasingly keen interest in Germanistic doctrine and its conclusions, and his anti-individualistic orientation. Still, we see more here of the devotee of *ius positum* and we see a tendency to reconcile the institution of the *Gesamteigentum* with the systematic lines of the positive order of the state. In Venezian's view, in fact, the principles of that institution

> are broad enough so that the economic phenomenon that is designated by this name . . . can find recognition and protection in it. The juridical form that it takes on and that permits it to obtain the protection of the law is that of the property of a moral entity.[21]

This is Venezian's solution in a nutshell: he reduces[22] the complex reality of the collective domains and the rights of usage to the unified notion of the property of a *universitas*, and he sees the subjective situation of the *condomini-utenti* in rights of a purely personal nature. This was a solution that was suggested in the pages of the Camerino lecture; but—since that lecture was wide open to philosophical, sociological, and historical influences—there it was overshadowed by the wealth of problematic considerations that he raised.

In 1895 Venezian's position had not changed, but his discourse could not but reflect the difference in its setting. The unbridled style expected in an inaugural lecture gave way to the more disciplined organization proper to a *Trattato del diritto civile italiano*, which included discussions of institutions such as usufruct, use, and habitation that take up fifty-five articles of the civil Code then in force.

There was another circumstance that had some weight. The essay was written in the spring of 1894, and it was subject to the determining influence of three events. Venezian does not fail to note them: the approval by the Chamber of the Tittoni bill on the organization of the collective domains in the territories of the former Pontifical State (April 1894), the presentation to the Senate (18 February 1893) of the Lacava bill on the *demani* in southern Italy, and the Chamber's consideration (session of 16 March 1894) of the Rinaldi bill on agricultural associations. In all these three events all collective property was restricted to the property of a moral entity.[23]

It seemed to Venezian that this could be the way to safeguard the original characteristics of the phenomenon and, at the same time, to avoid making of them an institution *extra legem*. Collective property signified a structure in which the goods or holdings were not subject to "the power of mobile individual will" but to "a given purpose."[24] It was a structure that the several participants could neither divide nor alienate because it had to serve also, and especially, others who were not the present members of the corporation. If this was so, the schema of property separate from and independent of the moral entity seemed to be the system most congenial to tradition and at the same time in accord with the rules of codified law. Within it the situation of the single members

> does not have the character of a landholding right, does not put the single members in a relation of direct power over the goods of the collectivity, but exclusively in correlation with the collectivity, which has the obligation to continue to use the property for their benefit.[25]

Perhaps the orientation that Venezian felt obliged to give to his juridical construction diminished the problem. Perhaps, on the other hand, there reappeared the principle of the "eurythmy of the legislative edifice" or the principle of the "systematic spirit," which were rejected as belittling methodological canons in the Camerino lecture of 1887. Or perhaps, as it was later noted,[26] Venezian betrayed the richness of causal motives and the plasticity of situations that the Germanists had pointed to in the plasticity of collective structures. However, he found a way to give them a juridical value—not theoretically, on an alternative plane, but practically and within the Italian order, even though he thereby put aside the pluralistic enthusiasms of Filomusi.[27]

      There is no doubt that the problem of the jurists' attempts to arrive at a construction of "collective property" merits a broader and a more thorough treatment. I reserve the possibility of taking up the question again on another occasion.

Notes

Foreword

1. In addition to Grossi's *Un altro modo di possedere* this series includes some of the best scholarship being produced among the younger generation of historians of law: Mario Sbriccoli, *Crimen Laesae Maiestatis. Il problema del reato politico alle soglie della scienza penalistica moderna* (1974); Pietro Costa, *Il progetto giuridico. Ricerche sulla giurisprudenza del liberalismo classico,* vol. 1: *Da Hobbes a Bentham* (1974); Maurizio Fioravanti, *Giuristi e costituzione politica nell'ottocento tedesco* (1979). Those works, as well as *Quaderni Fiorentini,* are published by Giuffrè of Milan.

2. Thus far eight volumes of *Quaderni* have appeared. The editorial statement is in the first volume of *Quaderni* (1972): 1–4; and additional remarks in volume 2 of *Quaderni* (1973): 1–4.

3. *Ricerche sulle obbligazioni pecunarie nel diritto comune* (Milan: Giuffrè, 1960); *'Locatio ad Longum Tempus': Locazione e rapporti reali di godimento nella problematica dell' diritto comune* (1963); *"Usus Facti—*La nozione di proprietà nella inaugurazione dell' età nuova," *Quaderni Fiorentini,* 1 (1972): 287–355; "La proprietà nel sistema privatistico della Seconda Scolastica," in *La Seconda Scolastica nella formazione del diritto privato moderno* (Milan: Giuffrè, 1973), pp. 117–222. *Le situazione reali* was published by Cedam of Padova.

4. On these themes, see Grossi's "Tradizioni e modelli nella sistemazione post-unitaria della proprietà," *Quaderni Fiorentini,* 5/6 (1976–77): 201–338.

5. See the reviews of Giovanni Tarello, *Rivista di diritto civile* 23 (1977): 344–48; Francesco De Sanctis, *Rivista trimestrale di diritto e procedura civile,* 32 (1978): 1315–21; Riccardo Faucci, *Pensiero Politico,* 12 (1979): 460–67; Stefano Borsacchi, *Rivista di diritto agrario* 58 (1979): 103–17; Luigi Capogrossi, *Studi Storici* 20 (1979): 431–37. The only English review of which I am aware is my own in *The American Journal of Legal History* 22 (1978): 343–46.

6. Grossi's reply was given during a round table conference devoted to his

book. The proceedings of the conference, which occurred on 17 December 1977 in Rome, were published in *Nuovo diritto agrario* 5 (1978): 451–71. The quotation is found on p. 470.

Introduction

1. Jean-Baptiste-Victor Proudhon (Chanans 1758–Dijon 1838) was first justice of the peace in his native city, then a member of the Tribunal of the department of the Doubs, over which he presided at the second session. From 1796 he was professor of legislation at the departmental Central School, and after 1806 he held the first chair of civil law at the University of Dijon. The *Traité du domaine de propriété ou de la distinction des biens considérés principalement par rapport au domaine privé* was first published at Dijon in 1839 by Victor Lagier, libraire-éditeur, but, as his son C. Proudhon attests in his *avis au lecteur,* the text had been completed some time before. The date indicated in the text, 1835, is thus an approximate but plausible date for the composition of the work.

2. The italics are mine.

3. Proudhon, *Traité du domaine de propriété,* pp. 57, 58, 59, 62.

4. Crawford Brough Macpherson, *Libertà e proprietà alle origini del pensiero borghese: La teoria dell'individualismo possessivo da Hobbes a Locke,* trans. S. Borutti (Milan, 1973), pp. 229 ff. [*The Political Theory of Possessive Individualism: Hobbes to Locke* (Oxford, 1962)]. Also useful is the perspicacious analysis of Pietro Costa, *Il progetto giuridico: Ricerche sulla giurisprudenza del liberalismo classico* (Milan, 1974), vol. 1.

5. Dino Fiorot, *La filosofia politica dei fisiocrati* (Padua, 1954), pp. 67 ff. and also Giovanni Rebuffa, "Fisiocrazia, ordine naturale, diritti individuali," *Materiali per una storia della cultura giuridica,* ed. Giovanni Tarello (Bologna, 1971), vol. 1.

6. See Stefano Rodotà, "Note intorno all'articolo 544 del Code civil," *Scritti per il XL della morte di P. E. Bensa* (Milan, 1969); André Jean Arnaud, *Essai d'analyse structurale du Code Civil français: la règle du jeu dans la paix bourgeoise* (Paris, 1973). Also useful among general critical overviews of the *Code civil* is G. Tarello, "'Code civil' e regole del gioco borghese," *Sociologia del diritto* 1 (1974).

7. It is perhaps unnecessary to specify that I refer to the eloquently programmatic title of the famous essay by Mercier de la Rivière, *L'ordre naturel et essentiel des sociétés politiques* (Paris, 1767).

8. Gioele Solari, *Filosofia del diritto privato,* I: *Individualismo e diritto privato* (Turin, 1911) gives an intelligent and accurate treatment of this question, but see also the more recent study of André Jean Arnaud, *Les origines doctrinales du Code civil français* (Paris, 1969), reviewed by G. Tarello in *Quaderni fiorentini per la storia del pensiero giuridico moderno* 1 (1972): 379 ff. See also the University of Genoa course outline of Giovanni Tarello, *Le ideologie della codificazione nel secolo XVIII* (Genoa, 1971).

9. The volume appeared in the *Biblioteca antropologico-giuridica* (Turin, 1890) and had been announced the previous year in the *Archivio di psichiatria, scienze penali ed antropologia criminale* 10 (1889): 382, which gives us an indication of the author's methodological tendencies. D'Aguanno had previously published two

247 Notes to pages 4–7

rather biased essays, *Sulla ricerca genetica del diritto di proprietà: Saggio, Archivio giuridico* 41 (1888) and "Origine del diritto di successione. I: Sul fondamento scientifico del diritto di successione," *Rivista di filosofia scientifica* 7 (1888). For further discussion of D'Aguanno, see chapter 7.

10. "Property, as well as to physical well-being and development, aspires strongly to psychic and moral well-being and development. . . . In concert with the psychic faculties, the moral faculties also unfold with the material comforts of life. Of this we have proof in all the history of property, which is at the same time the history of the civilizing of man. And it is truly natural that it should be thus. He who has naught is by necessity selfish" (D'Aguanno, *La genesi e l'evoluzione del diritto civile,* p. 339).

11. These are the scholars whose works D'Aguanno seems to draw on and who he cites in his *Sulla ricerca genetica.*

12. D'Aguanno, *La genesi e l'evoluzione del diritto civile,* p. 339.

13. This literature is fairly abundant in Italy after the 1880s and finds its chief spokesman in Enrico Cimbali, *La proprietà e i suoi limiti nella legislazione civile italiana,* Archivio giuridico 24 (1880): 125 ff. It includes many noted authors: see Giovanni Lomonaco, "I temperamenti della proprietà prediale," appendix 3 to vol. 6 of François Laurent, *Principii di diritto civile,* trans. G. Trono and A. Marghieri (Naples, 1883) [*Principes de droit Civil* (3rd ed.; Bruxelles, 1878]; Ferdinando Bianchi, *I limiti legali della proprietà nel diritto civile* (Macerata, 1885).

14. The problem of collective property had already been approached, for example, by the great southern Italian doctrine of the sixteenth to the eighteenth centuries. There, it had had two specific and opposed dimensions, one metahistorical and one practical (see chapter 7, pp. 146 ff.). It was however, the first time that the problem came to be examined in the nineteenth century in rigorously historico-juridical terms and as a contribution to the theory of property. In general, though, and without contradicting the affirmation that we make in the text, Paul Viollet's remark is accurate ("La communauté des moulins et des fours au Moyen Age: à l'occasion d'un récent article de M. Thévenin," *Revue historique* 32 [1886]: 98): "As with any profound and powerful idea, the theory of the primitive community is an ancient one. Those who have contributed most greatly to bring it to general attention, to clarify it, and to propagate it, did not know, when they began their studies, the works of all those who had come before them. This theory was not *found* one day; it had merely been *rediscovered* after some time."

15. There were, indeed, some socialists, for example, in Italy, and not only juridical socialists.

16. The opening, development, and rapid closing of the debate can be seen in the continuity of the work of a great historian of jurisprudence, Pietro Bonfante. We find tangible traces of this by comparing the first edition of his study, *Res mancipi e nec mancipi* (Rome, 1888) with the second edition, or, to be more accurate, with Bonfante's recasting of the essay for insertion in the second volume of his *Scritti giuridici varî* (Milan, 1916) vol. 2. The shrewd reader will be quick to realize that not only does the Bonfante of 1916 no longer show the youthful ardors of 1888, but also that a whole cultural climate has faded and the enthusiasm for certain anthropological and comparative research has disappeared.

17. This is the scornful and ironical term used by supporters of the individualistic theses in the course of the controversy.

18. See the discussion (chapter 9, pp. 228 ff.) of the "conservative" character of the Hon. Tittoni's decision in favor of collective property.

19. An overview that gives particular attention to labor and peasant struggles can be found in Leo Vallani, "L'Italia dal 1876 al 1915, II: La lotta sociale e l'avvento della democrazia," *Storia d'Italia*, general ed. Nino Valeri (Turin, 1965) vol. 4; and in Giorgio Candeloro, *Storia dell'Italia moderna*, vol. 6: *Lo sviluppo del capitalismo e del movimento operaio* (Milan, 1970). More specific studies emphasizing the social picture can be found in Gino Luzzatto, *L'economia italiana dal 1861 al 1914*, vol. 1: *1861–1894* (Milan, 1963) and in Emilio Sereni, *Il capitalismo nelle campagne 1860–1900* (Turin, 1968).

20. On Italian positivism, with some reference to the jurists, see Lodovico Limentani, "Il positivismo italiano," *La filosofia contemporanea in Italia dal 1874 al 1920*, ed. L. Limentani et al. (Naples, 1928) and G. Tarozzi, "Considerazioni sintetiche sul positivismo italiano nel secolo XIX," *Archivio di storia della filosofia italiana* 4 (1935).

21. Georg Ludwig von Maurer, *Einleitung zur Geschichte der Mark-, Hof-, Dorf- und Stadtverfassung und der öffentlichen Gewalt* (Munich, 1854) and *Geschichte der Markenverfassung in Deutschland* (Erlangen, 1856). On Maurer and particularly on his investigations on the *Mark* and on its influence on European culture of the century, see K. Dickopf, "Georg Ludwig von Maurer. Ein Nachwort," which follows the offset reprint edition of the *Einleitung* (Aalen, 1966), p. 382 but particularly pp. 387 ff.

22. Georg Waitz, *Deutsche Verfassungsgeschichte*, 1 B. (Kiel, 1844).

23. Friedrich Thudichum, *Die Gau- und Markverfassung in Deutschland* (Giessen, 1860) and *Der altdeutsche Staat* (Giessen, 1862). For a retrospective appraisal of these theories, see Karl Siegfried Bader, *Dorfgenossenschaft und Dorfgemeinde* (Cologne, 1962), in his *Studien zur Rechtsgeschichte des mittelalterlichen Dorfes* vol. 2), inserted in a broad historical and juridical reconstruction of the reality of the medieval village.

24. It should not be necessary to repeat that the present volume is dedicated to the reconstruction of a specific debate, and not to the nineteenth-century elaborations of ancient and medieval communitarian forms. For this reason, the extraordinarily dense, rich Germanistic literature—more or less apologetic, more or less fantastic—that scholars throughout the century devoted to the reconstruction of paleogermanic land organizations will not be treated in these pages, as it lies outside the context of the debate.

25. Bökendorf (Paderborn) 1792–Hannover 1866.

26. In "La famille patriarcale," now in *Études sur l'histoire du droit* (Paris, 1889), pp. 465 ff., Maine defines Haxthausen as the first traveler who had really penetrated the structure of Slavic society, recognizes his own debt to him, and states that his books, which appeared from 1847 to 1853, produced in Europe the effect of a revelation, enriching enormously the cultural patrimony of the times. (For a justification of the use of the French translation of Maine, see chapter 1, n. 14.)

27. Among many possibilities, particularly on the German experience, see Haxthausen, *Über die Agrarverfassung in Norddeutschland und deren Conflicte in der gegenwärtigen Zeit* (Berlin, 1829) and *Die ländliche Verfassung in den einzelnen Provinzen der preussischen Monarchie* (Köningsberg, 1839). On the Russian experience see *Etudes sur la situation intérieure, la vie nationale et les institutions rurales de la Russie* (Hanover, 1847–53), published at the same time in German as *Studien über die innern Zustände, das Volksleben, und insbesondere die ländlichen Einrichtungen Russlands* (Hanover, 1847–53); *Transkaukasia. Andeutungen über das Familien- und Gemeindeleben und die socialen Verhältnisse einiger Völker zwischen dem Schwarzen und Kaspischen Meere* (Leipzig, 1956); *De l'abolition par voie législative du partage égal et temporaire des terres dans les communes russes* (Paris, 1858).

28. On the ingenuity of this "discovery" and this "revelation," see Friedrich Engels, "Le condizioni sociali in Russia," in Karl Marx, Friedrich Engels, *India, Cina, Russia,* trans. B. Maffi (Milan, 1960), pp. 224 ff.

29. See above, n. 26.

30. There are many possible citations here. Of particular importance and usefulness among the writings of explorers are the reports of David Livingstone, such as *A Popular Account of Missionary Travels and Researches in South Africa* (London, 1861) and David and Charles Livingstone, *Narrative of an Expedition to the Zambesi and its Tributaries; and of the Discovery of the Lakes Shiva and Nyassa, 1858–1864* (London, 1865). Among the works of travelers, Anatole Leroy-Beaulieu, *L'empire des Tsars et les Russes* (Paris, 1881), of which the first volume treats "Le pays et les habitants," the second, "Les institutions," and the third, "La religion." Leroy-Beaulieu was also engaged in popularizing in the West Russian publications on the subject of collectivist organizations, as in his "Le socialisme agraire et le régime de la propriété," *Revue des deux mondes,* March 1879. Among the writings of colonial functionaries related to our theme are the works of Sir Alfred Lyall (1835–1911), lieutenant governor of the United Provinces of India, who made conspicuous contributions to official investigations on the complicated question of Indian custom, and whose two collections of *Asiatic Studies, religious and social* (London, 1882 and 1899) should be cited. These studies enjoyed wide circulation and great success and were translated for publication by the *Bibliothèque de l'histoire du droit et des institutions* under the title, *Etudes sur les moeurs religieuses et sociales de l'Extrême Orient* (Paris, 1885, 1907, 1908).

31. On the great problem of the enclosure of the open fields, which dominates the entire first half of the English nineteenth century, we refer to the synthesis of Jonathan David Chambers and Gordon Edmund Mingay, *The Agricultural Revolution (1750–1880)* (London, 1966), pp. 77 ff. There is information on the literature of the subject in W. H. Chaloner, "Bibliography of Recent Works on Enclosure, the Open Fields, and Related Topics," *Agricultural History Review* 2 (1954).

32. See H. S. Maine, *Village Communities in the East and West* (3rd ed.; London, 1876), lecture 3, pp. 83 ff.

33. See chapter 8.

34. See *Report of Her Majesty's Commissioners of Inquiry into the Condition of*

the Crofters and Cottars in the Highlands and Islands of Scotland (1884). Detailed references to the inquiry can be found in the report based on the results of the inquiry in E. de Laveleye, "La propriété primitive dans les Townships écossais," *Séances et travaux de l'Académie des Sciences morales et politiques (Institut de France)—Compte-rendu* 124 (1885, deuxième semestre), passim.

35. *Systems of Land Tenure in Various Countries. A Series of Essays published under the sanction of the Cobden Club* (London, 1870). This is a broad series of investigations relative to Ireland, England, India, Belgium, Holland, Prussia, France, Russia, and the United States. The most useful are those of J. Faucher, "Russian agrarian legislation of 1861" and of R. B. D. Morier, "The agrarian legislation of Prussia during the present century." The essay on "Land systems of Belgium and Holland" was written by Emile de Laveleye.

36. Giuseppe Cocchiara, *Popolo e letteratura in Italia* (Turin, 1959), pp. 293 ff.

37. See Sebastiano Timpanaro, *Classicismo e illuminismo nell'Ottocento* (Pisa, 1965), particularly the essay "Carlo Cattaneo e Graziadio Ascoli," I: "Le idee linguistiche ed etnografiche di Carlo Cattaneo" and appendix 2, "A proposito di un inedito del Cattaneo sulla poesia dialettale."

38. This is the thesis regarding Cattaneo of an interesting essay by Norberto Bobbio, "Della sfortuna del pensiero di Carlo Cattaneo nella cultura italiana," now published in his *Una filosofia militante. Studi su Carlo Cattaneo* (Turin, 1971).

39. This is, in substance, the impression given by a letter taken from the *Recueil d'études sociales à la mémoire de Frédfic Le Play* (Paris, 1956).

40. Abundant indications of this can be seen in Alessandro Levi, *Il positivismo politico di Carlo Cattaneo* (Bari, 1928) and the more recent Bobbio, *Una filosofia militante: Studi su Carlo Cattaneo*.

41. Frédéric Le Play, *Les ouvriers éuropéens: Etudes sur les travaux, la vie domestique et la condition morale des populations ouvrières de l'Europe, précédées d'un exposé de la méthode d'observation* (Paris, 1855).

42. F. Le Play, *Les ouvriers des deux mondes: Etudes sur les travaux, la vie domestique et la condition morale des populations ouvrières des diverses contrées et sur les rapports qui les unissent aux autres classes* (Paris, 1857–62). See particularly in vol. 1 (Paris, 1857) the monograph on "Paysans en communauté du Lavedan (Hautes-Pyrénées, France) (Propriétaires-ouvriers dans le système du travail sans engagements), d'après les renseignements recueillis sur les lieux en août 1856" and, in vol. 4 (Paris, 1862), the monograph of L. Donnat, "Paysans en communauté du Ning-Po-Fou (province de Tché-kian' Chine) (propriétaires ouvriers dans le système du travail sans engagements) d'après les faits observés sur les lieux de 1842 à 1846 par Puang-Tching-Yong l'un des membres de la famille recueillis et coordonnés en mars 1861."

43. Carlo Cattaneo, "Su la bonificazione del Piano di Magadino a nome della Società promotrice. Primo rapporto," in *Scritti economici*, ed. A. Bertolino (Florence, 1956) 3:187–88.

44. C. Cattaneo, "Dell'India antica e moderna," in *Opere di Giandomenico Romagnosi, di Carlo Cattaneo, Giuseppe Ferrari*, ed. Ernesto Sestan (Milan, 1957): "They divided the land and the people into many communes of no fewer

than one hundred souls and no more than two thousand. They intended that the commune be jointly responsible for the land tax. . . . Thus property was bound to the commune" (p. 798); "Its social principle is the caste; its administrative principle is an agriculture on behalf of the common good: the individual is always absorbed in the vast vortex of an existence that does not belong to him. He is not by himself conscious of his liberty, and hardly conscious of his desires . . ." (p. 824).

45. This will be the aim of Fustel de Coulanges, as we will see later.

46. One example picked out among thousands is the rigidly evolutionistic passage dedicated to property to Gerolamo Boccardo, *La sociologia nella storia, nella scienza, nella religione e nel cosmo*, in *Biblioteca dell'economista*, third series, vol. 8, part one (Turin, 1881), particularly p. xcvii.

47. It should hardly be necessary to specify, once and for all, that when "individual property" and "collective property" are referred to during the course of this work without additional adjectives, it is to be understood that the terms necessarily refer to the system of ownership that was the most important historically and on an economic plane, which was that of land, and in particular of agricultural land.

Chapter One

1. Since his singular life drew particular meaning from a singular experience as a scholar, it is appropriate to recall some of the facts of Maine's biography. He was born in 1822, studied at Cambridge, and from 1847 was Regius Professor of Civil Law at Trinity Hall, Cambridge. In 1854 he became a reader at Middle Temple, one of the Inns of Court of London, where he practiced as a lawyer. In 1856 he published his first noteworthy work, "Roman Law and Legal Education," and dedicated himself to the preparation of *Ancient Law*, which appeared in 1861. The following year he accepted the governmental office of legal member attached to the council of the governor general of India, to which he joined the office of vice-chancellor of the University of Calcutta. On his return to England in 1869 he taught jurisprudence—in substance, comparative law—at Oxford, and the first fruit of his teaching was the study on *Village-Communities in the East and West*, published in 1871. From 1871 he was also a member of the secretary of state's Council of India. The *Lectures on the Early History of Institutions* appeared in 1875, continuing in the area of paleo-Irish juridical sources the research initiated with *Ancient Law*. In 1877 he left his chair at Oxford to become master of his old college at Cambridge, Trinity Hall, and in 1887 he accepted the chair of international law at Cambridge, in which he succeeded Sir William Harcourt. He died soon after at Cannes on 3 February 1888. Further biographical data and information on his other publications, not mentioned here because they are not pertinent to our interests, can be found in Mountstuart Elphinstone Grant Duff, *Sir Henry Maine: A Brief Memoir of his Life* (London, 1892) and in Leslie Stephen, "Maine Sir Henry James Sumner," *Dictionary of National Biography*, ed. Sidney Lee (London, 1909), vol. 12. A detailed dating of his works, useful data, and commentary can be found in John Wyon Burrow, *Evolution and Society: A Study in Victorian Social Theory* (London, 1966).

2. Maine's thesis held up solidly for the entire nineteenth century. To measure the extent of his influence, see George Lawrence Gomme, *The Village Community, With Special Reference to the Origin and Form of its Survivals in Britain* (London, 1890). Toward the end of this period, interpretations of the Indian village communities appeared which were completely opposed to his: see Baden Henry Baden-Powell, *The Indian Village Community Examined with Reference to the Physical, Ethnographic, and Historical Conditions of the Provinces Chiefly on the basis of the Revenue-Settlement Records and District Manuals* (London, New York, Bombay, 1896). See also in this connection the interesting notes of G. Borsa, "La proprietà della terra in India sotto il dominio inglese," *Nuova rivista storica* 50 (1966): 328 ff. and particularly 334.

3. Icilio Vanni, *Gli studî di Henry Sumner Maine e le dottrine della filosofia del diritto* (Verona, 1892). The same year saw a contribution of the Romanist Silvio Perozzi that was based nearly entirely on Vanni's essay and that first appeared in Orlandi's *Archivio di diritto pubblico*, "Gli studi di H. Sumner Maine e la filosofia del diritto. A proposito di una recente pubblicazione," now in Perozzi, *Scritti giuridici*, ed. U. Brasiello (Milan, 1948) vol. 3: *Famiglia, Successione, Procedure e Scritti vari*, pp. 707 ff. As far as I know, there has not yet been a satisfactory historiographical examination of Maine, although his works continue to be cited and lesser works on him can be found scattered through Anglo-Saxon and other sociological, anthropological, historical, and juridical literatures. For Maine's place in the great cultural currents of the last century, the interpretations of Frederick Pollock and Paul Vinogradoff (see note 4), although not recent, are still valid. A general and evaluative picture of Maine's contribution to English culture of the end of the century can be found in Morgan Owen Evans, *Theories and Criticisms of Sir Henry Maine* (London, 1896), of which pp. 32 ff. discuss the origins and history of property.

4. Frederick Pollock, "Sir Henry Maine and his Work," in his *Oxford Lectures and other Discourses* (London, 1890), pp. 153, 158–59 (the lecture on Maine was written in 1888); Paul Vinogradoff, "The Teaching of Sir Henry Maine," now in *The Collected Papers of Paul Vinogradoff* (Oxford, 1928), vol. 2, p. 180. This paper, which was originally written as an inaugural lecture at Oxford, was first published in *The Law Quarterly Review* (1904).

5. "During the last five-and-twenty years German enquirers have been busy with the early history and gradual development of European ownership, ownership, that is to say, of land. But the Historical Method in their hands has not yet been quickened and corrected by the Comparative Method." (Maine, "The effects of observation of India on Modern European Thought," now in appendix to *Village-Communities in the East and West* [3rd ed.; London, 1876], pp. 223–24. The essay constituted a Rede Lecture for the year 1875 at Cambridge.)

6. This is clearly seen and summarized in Walter Wilhelm's excellent *Metodologia giuridica nel secolo XIX*, trans. P. L. Lucchini (Milan, 1974), pp. 28 ff., but particularly p. 34 and p. 38 [*Zur juristischen Methodenlehre im 19. Jahrhundert* (Frankfurt am Main, 1958)]. See also Aldo Mazzacane, *Savigny e la storiografia giuridica tra storia e sistema* (Naples, 1974), passim.

7. Pollock, *Oxford Lectures*, p. 159; Vinogradoff, "The Teaching of Sir Henry Maine," p. 185.

8. This methodological figure is stated in *Ancient Law:* "These rudimentary ideas are to the jurist what the primary crusts of the earth are to the geologist. They contain, potentially, all the forms in which law has subsequently exhibited itself" (*Ancient Law: Its Connection with the Early History of Society and its Relation to Modern Ideas* [4th ed.; London, 1870], p. 3). Durieu de Leyritz, the French translator of Maine's *Lectures on the Early History of Institutions*, speaks, in his excellent introduction to the translation, of "juridical paleontology" and states that "the law demands its Cuvier" (*Etudes sur l'histoire des institutions primitives*, trans. J. Durieu de Leyritz [Paris, 1880], p. xvi).

9. This explains Maine's nonchalance in taking as a source both the learned essay of Maurer, a historian by profession, and the essay of Morier in the Cobden Club's survey of land tenure systems. As an English diplomat, chargé d'affaires at Darmstadt, Morier spoke from first-hand knowledge, but certainly not as a historian, of the situation of land tenure in Germany. (Robert Burnett David Morier, "The agrarian legislation of Prussia during the present century," *Systems of land tenure in various countries* [London, 1870]). See also Maine, *Village-Communities in the East and West*, pp. 78 ff.

10. See the perspicacious remarks of Vanni, *Gli studî di Henry Sumner Maine*, p. 89.

11. Maine, *Dissertations on Early Law and Custom* (London, 1883), pp. 192–93.

12. "That wonderful terminology which is, as it were, the Short-hand of jurisprudence" (Maine, "Roman Law and Legal Education," now in appendix to *Village-Communities in the East and West*, p. 366). The essay was first published in *Cambridge Essays* in 1856 and thus dates from the creative, constructive moment in Maine's intellectual development when he was preparing *Ancient Law*.

13. As early as the preface to the first edition of *Ancient Law*, Maine confessed that much of his research would never have been accomplished "if there had not existed a body of law, like that of the Romans, bearing in its earlier portions the traces of the most remote antiquity and supplying from its later rules the staple of the civil institutions by which modern society is even now controlled."

14. Ibid., p. 266. Maine always held Haxthausen in high esteem and always admitted his debt to him for information on the structure of Slavic, and particularly Russian, society. See Maine, "La famille patriarcale," *Etudes sur l'histoire du droit* (Paris, 1889), pp. 465–66. (The citation is taken from the French translation rather than from the original English text as it appeared in the *Quarterly Review* of January, 1886 because—as the translator states—the French text had been divested of its polemical cast on Maine's authorization. Certain ambiguities in the original text were eliminated, along with the polemical response to the McLennan brothers' provocatory affirmations, and the resulting format was better founded scientifically.) On Haxthausen, see the introduction, particularly n. 27.

15. This is already fully apparent in *Ancient Law*, as a reading of the first chapter suffices to persuade us, but it is particularly true in *Village-Communities in the East and West*, which as we know appeared ten years later. The introduction to the first edition of this study is most interesting, among other reasons, for an understanding of the role that the high civil servants in the English colonial administration in India played among Maine's sources.

16. I refer to the *Lectures on the Early History of Institutions*, published in

1875, in which Maine utilizes and exploits with historical and comparative method the ancient Irish juridical sources, which the Irish government had begun to collect and translate (see *Ancient Laws and Institutes of Ireland [Hiberniae leges et institutiones antiquae]* [Dublin, 1866, 1869, 1873]). Interesting observations on Maine's view of ancient Gaelic juridic civilization were made by a noted French Celtist, Henry d'Arbois de Jubainville, who participated himself in the great debate on the origins of property, in his introduction to the French translation of Maine's *Lectures, Etudes sur l'histoire des institutions*.

17. Henry d'Arbois de Jubainville, *Introduction à l'étude de la littérature celtique* (Paris, 1883), p. 36.

18. Speaking of attitudes based in natural law and transplanted to scientific observation, Maine states: "It still possesses singular fascination for the looser thinkers of every country, and is no doubt the parent, more or less remote, of almost all the prepossessions which impede the employment of the Historical Method of inquiry." Further: "It gave birth, or intense stimulus, to the vices of mental habit all but universal at the time, disdain of positive law, impatience of experience, and the preference of *à priori* to all other reasoning" (*Ancient Law,* pp. 89 and 91–92).

19. Ibid., p. 251.

20. Ibid. In fact, Maine defines him as "a faithful index of the average opinions of his day."

21. Ibid., p. 257.

22. "The sentiment in which this doctrine originated is absolutely irreconcilable with that infrequency and uncertainty of proprietary rights which distinguish the beginnings of civilisation. Its true basis seems to be, not an instinctive bias towards the institution of Property, but a presumption, arising out of the long continuance of that institution, that *everything ought to have an owner*" (ibid., pp. 256–67).

23. "I venture to state my opinion that the popular impression in reference to the part played by Occupancy in the first stages of civilization directly reverses the truth." And he continues: "Occupancy is the advised assumption of physical possession; and the notion that an act of this description confers a title to 'res nullius,' so far from being characteristic of very early societies, is in all probability the growth of a refined jurisprudence and of a settled condition of the laws" (ibid., p. 256).

24. "Occupancy is pre-eminently interesting on the score of the service it has been made to perform for speculative jurisprudence, in furnishing a supposed explanation of the origin of private property" (ibid., p. 250).

25. "It is each Individual who for himself subscribes the Social Compact. . . . It is an Individual who, in the picture drawn by Blackstone, 'is in the occupation of a determined spot of ground for rest, for shade, or the like'" (ibid., p. 257).

26. Ibid., p. 258.

27. Maine, *Lectures on the Early History of Institutions,* p. 21. The entire first lecture of this collection is worth skimming. It is dedicated to defining the "New Materials for the Early History of Institutions" represented by the ancient Irish law sources. His conclusion was "that these Brehon law-tracts enable us to connect the races at the eastern and western extremities of a later Aryan world, the Hindoos and the Irish" (p. 21).

28. See particularly Maine, *Village-Communities in the East and West*, lecture 1, "The East and the Study of Jurisprudence," especially p. 13.

29. Maine, "La famille patriarcale," p. 466.

30. Maine, *Ancient Law*, pp. 258 ff.; *Dissertations on Early Law and Custom*, chapter 11, "Classifications of Legal Rules."

31. His conclusion is that "the Roman distinction between the Law of Persons and the Law of Things . . . is entirely artificial," and he continues, "that the separation of the Law of Persons from that of Things has no meaning in the infancy of law, that the rules belonging to the two departments are inextricably mingled together, and that the distinctions of the later jurists are appropriate only to the later jurisprudence" (*Ancient Law*, pp. 258–89).

32. "The life of each citizen is not regarded as limited by birth and death; it is but a continuation of the existence of his forefathers, and it will be prolonged in the existence of his descendants" (ibid.).

33. On the subject of the relationship between the primitive subject and nature, I refer the reader to my own course outline, *Le situazioni reali nell'esperienza giuridica medievale* (Padua, 1968), pp. 42 ff.

34. In the Italian literature on Maine there is an older work on his conception of progress: Gino Dallari, "Di una legge del progresso giuridico formulato da Henry Sumner Maine," *Studi Senesi* 22 (1905). See also B. Smith, "Maine's Concept of Progress," *Journal of the History of Ideas* 24 (1963): 407. The relation between evolutionism and historicism in Maine would be worth a painstaking investigation. It would undoubtedly share in that eclecticism that is the most characteristic trait of a good part of the philosophical culture of the nineteenth century and that Maine certainly does not contradict. The biographical summary of E. A. Hoebel, "Maine, Henry Sumner" in the *International Encyclopedia of the Social Sciences* (New York, 1968) vol. 9, hinges on the theory familiar in Maine of the development from status to contract. See also Wolfgang Friedmann, *Legal Theory* (5th ed.; New York, 1967), pp. 214 ff.

35. In a somewhat one-sided interpretation, Vanni, *Gli studî di Henry Sumner Maine*, pp. 87 ff., insists even more than is appropriate on the connection in Maine's thought between private property and progress, but there is no doubt that he regarded the individualization of property sympathetically.

36. Maine, *Ancient Law*, pp. 259–60.

37. Ibid., p. 261.

38. Grossi, *Le situazioni reali nell'esperienza giuridica medievale*, pp. 183 ff.

39. Maine, "The Effects of Observation of India," p. 227.

40. They will be discussed during the course of this work.

41. Maine, *Village-Communities in the East and West*, p. 10, but particularly p. 77.

42. Ibid., p. 12.

43. "It does not appear to me a hazardous proposition that the Indian and the ancient European systems of enjoyment and tillage by men grouped in village-communities are in all essential particulars identical. There are differences of detail between them" (ibid., p. 103).

44. Ibid., p. 10.

45. Ibid., pp. 78 ff.

46. See Maine, *Ancient Law*, pp. 265 ff.; *Village-Communities in the East and*

West, lecture 1, passim; *Lectures on the Early History of Institutions*, the whole of chapter 4, "The Tribe and the Land." This last chapter is completely imbued with the idea of the historical priority of collective property and with that of individual property as the fruit of a gradual process.

47. Maine, *Ancient Law*, p. 269.

48. The investigations of the German school discussed collective property, and in England, economists, historians, and agronomists took up the topic, which was reinforced by the polemics and the inquiry concerning the enclosure of the open fields. Maine was aware of all of these scholars and of the data they had published or that they were to publish. See *Village-Communities in the East and West*, pp. 82 ff.

49. Maine's thesis as it related to North American realities was soon to be tested by Herbert B. Adams, *The Germanic Origins of New England Towns* (Baltimore, 1882).

50. Maine, *Village-Communities in the East and West*, pp. 87–88.

Chapter Two

1. Emile-Louis-Victor de Laveleye was born in Bruges in 1822. After philosophical studies at the University of Louvain, he went in 1842 to the University of Ghent, where he began his study of law and embarked on a close intellectual exchange with the philosopher, François Huet. He frequented liberal progressive circles that gravitated around and contributed to the revue *La Flandre Libérale*, founded in 1847. He accepted the Liberal Party candidacy in Ghent for the elections of 1861, but was not elected. In 1864 he was named professor of political economy and industrial economy at the University of Liège. He died in 1892 at Doyon (Namur), after having dedicated his last years to long peregrinations in and out of Europe, as well as to his customary studies. More ample information on his life and works can be found in Eugène Goblet D'Alviella, "Notice sur Emile-Louis-Victor de Laveleye," *Annuaire de l'Académie royale des Sciences, des Lettres et des Beaux-Arts de Belgique (1895)* (Brussels, 1895); Ernest Mahaim, "Emile de Laveleye," in *Liber memorialis. L'Université de Liège de 1867 à 1935* (Liège, 1936), 1:672 ff.; P. Lambert, "Laveleye (Emile-Louis-Victor de)" in *Biographie nationale publiée par l'Académie royale des Sciences, des Lettres et des Beaux-Arts de Belgique*, (Brussels, 1968), 34-supplement 6 (2). This entry is reproduced as an autonomous essay in English in *History of Political Economy* 2 (1970): 263 ff. Of particular interest are several commemorative articles published in contemporary reviews. See among French publications, articles by E. Mahaim in the *Revue d'économie politique* 6 (1892): 93 ff. and G. Picot, "Notice sur M. de Laveleye correspondant de l'Institut," *Séances et Travaux de l'Académie des Sciences morales et politiques (Institut de France)—Compte rendu* 138 (1892, deuxième semestre): 799 ff. In the Italian reviews there are articles by A. Loria, "Emile de Laveleye," *Nuova Antologia*, 1 February 1892, now in Achille Loria, *Verso la giustizia sociale (Idee, battaglie ed apostoli)* (2d ed.; Milan, 1908), by A. Errera in *Rassegna di scienze sociali e politiche* 10 (1892), by F. S. Nitti in *La scuola positiva* 2 (1892).

2. His principal works were: *De la propriété et de ses formes primitives* (Paris, 1874), which synthesizes preceding minor works; *Le socialisme contemporain*

(Brussels, 1881); "Land System of Belgium and Holland" in *Systems of Land Tenure in Various Countries: A series of essays published under the sanction of the Cobden Club* (London, 1870); "La propriété collective du sol en différents pays," *Revue de Belgique,* October–November 1885 and March 1886; "La propriété primitive dans les Townships écossais," in *Séances et Travaux de l'Académie des Sciences morales et politiques (Institut de France)—Compte rendu* 124 (1885, deuxième semestre); plus many scattered articles, particularly in the *Revue des deux mondes,* in the *Revue de Belgique,* and in the *Fortnightly Review.* One can for the most part find these collected in his *Essais et études— première série (1861–1875)* (Paris, 1894), —*deuxième série (1875–1882)* (Ghent-Paris, 1895), and —*troisième série (1883–1892)* (Ghent-Paris, 1897). That the theme of forms of property was a constant preoccupation can also be seen in his travel notes collected in *La péninsule des Balkans* (Brussels, 1885), one of the best examples of an abundant literature on travels in the nineteenth century.

3. Proudhon's volume is a typical example of this literature (see introduction, n. 1).

4. An example of this can be seen in Friedrich Engels, *The Origin of Family, Private Property, and the State* (New York, 1942). Even though Engels treats the same problems ten years after Laveleye, he does not once cite his work.

5. A second and a third edition of his *De la propriété* followed the first edition of 1874 within several years, and the fourth edition, which appeared in 1891, was completely revised and notably enlarged, taking into account the literature on the subject which had appeared in the meantime.

6. The work was translated into English (*Primitive Property,* trans. G. R. L. Marriott [London, 1878]), into German (*Das Ureigenthum,* trans. K. Bücher [Leipzig, 1879]), and also into Danish and Russian.

7. The next chapter will be devoted to this debate.

8. See "Les formes primitives de la propriété. I: Les communautés de village," *Revue des deux mondes,* July 1872; "II: La marke germanique et l'origine de l'inégalité," ibid., August 1872; "III: Les communautés de famille et le bail héréditaire," ibid., September, 1872. The three articles, in their deliberate reference to *Village-Communities in the East and West* and to the fifth edition of *Ancient Law* bear witness not only to the enormous influence of Maine on Laveleye but also to the Belgian economist's strong desire to continue the English jurist's work. It is interesting to note that John Stuart Mill gave admiring approval to the three articles cited here, as shown in a letter he sent to Laveleye dated 17 November 1872, which appears in the preface to *De la propriété,* p. xii, n. 1.

9. Let me refer again to the text of Proudhon with which I began (Introduction, n. 1) and to which it would be easy to add many others.

10. It should be unnecessary to say that we refer to Adolphe Thiers's well-known *De la propriété* (Paris, 1848), written toward the end of that year at the urgent invitation of the Institut. The work was to a certain extent the manifesto of the counterrevolution in France and the most illustrious—or at least the best known—of those occasional works that Joseph Ferrari would soon qualify as works of "salaried philosophers" (see Joseph Ferrari, *Les philosophes salariés* [Paris, 1849]). Thiers's program was stated openly in his *avant-propos:* it is an energetic defense of "the most natural, the most evident, the most universally

recognized ideas" (p. 1) and of the facts that are "the simplest, the most legitimate, the most inevitable, the least susceptible to contestation and demonstration" (p. 2) and that aberrant doctrines sought to demolish in the minds of "the
multitude, moved, bewildered, and suffering" (p. 3). In this guise of defender of
the evident, the author throws a lifeline to society: "I work not for myself, but for
society in peril" (p. 4). For a first attempt to place Thiers within the history of the
social thought of the century in France, see the brief and scattered references to
him in Maxime Leroy, *Histoire des idées sociales en France* (Paris, 1946–54) 3:
D'Auguste Comte à P. J. Proudhon (1954), passim.

11. Biographical information can be found in Goblet D'Alviella's diligent
"Notice," pp. 47 ff.

12. It is difficult and perhaps fruitless to try to apply rigid classifications to a
polyvalent personality like Laveleye. Certainly political economy was what he
taught and many of his interests turned in that direction. Many inquiries and
collections of data relating to the agrarian economy of different countries also
stand out in his work, giving proof of his preference for investigation that was
solidly based in statistical data and technical concepts. His mentor, François
Huet, always considered him an economist, as seen in the two significant letters of
3 March and 30 May 1857 cited in Goblet D'Alviella, "Notice," p. 66.

13. Laveleye, *De la propriété*, Préface, p. v.

14. Ibid., p. viii.

15. The first edition of *Le socialisme contemporain* dates from 1881.

16. Ibid., Préface, p. xxv.

17. "Europe, prey to class and racial struggle, is in danger of falling into chaos"
(*De la propriété*, Préface, p. iv).

18. "The hostility between classes will endanger liberty everywhere, and the
more property becomes concentrated and the contrast between rich and poor
becomes marked, the more society will be threatened with profound revolution"
(ibid., p. xi).

19. "We thought that we had difficulties of only a political order to resolve, and
it is the social question which rises before us with all of its obscurities and its
abysses" (ibid., p. iv). The new schools of economic thought in Germany also
provided considerable stimulus to Laveleye. He followed them with attention and
showed particular interest in the theories of the *Sociale Frage* and the work of
Adolph Wagner.

20. "Democracy seems to produce nothing but conflicts, disorders, and anar-
chy" (ibid., p. iv); "Democracy leads us to the abyss" (ibid., p. v).

21. Ibid., pp. x–xi.

22. "Modern democracies will escape the destiny of ancient democracies only if
they adopt laws that effect the redistribution of property among a great number of
hands and that would establish a broad equality of condition" (ibid., p. xi); "Our
European societies, in which democracy and inequality develop together" (ibid.,
p. xxiv).

23. Proof of this profoundly felt spiritual search can be found in his anguished
conversion from Catholicism to Protestantism. He contemplated conversion over
a long period of time: although evident signs of it appear in his will, written in

1867, it was not until 1878 that he officially asked to be admitted to the Evangelical Church in Liège (see Goblet D'Alviella, "Notice," pp. 77 and 90).

24. "The egalitarian ideas of the Gospel must penetrate our institutions and our laws. This is a point that François Huet emphasized with admirable clarity in his too little-known book, *Le Christianisme social*" (*De la propriété*, p. xvi). Note also that the volume is dedicated to Huet, together with John Stuart Mill. François Huet (Villeau 1814–Paris 1869) was a complex figure. He attempted to reach a compromise between revolution and Catholicism based on a rediscovery of the values of primitive Christianity, and his *Le règne social du Christianisme* (Paris, 1853) had made a profound impression on Laveleye. Concerning Huet, see Laveleye's own pages on him in *Le socialisme contemporain*, pp. 296 ff. Also useful among the analyses of his near contemporaries is Francesco Saverio Nitti, *Il socialismo cattolico* (2d ed., Turin, 1891), pp. 288 ff. and, among more recent works, Rudolf Rezsöhazy, *Origines et formation du catholicisme social en Belgique, 1842–1909* (Louvain, 1958). Biographical data can be found in the *Biographie nationale publiée par l'Académie royale des Sciences, des Lettres et des Beaux-Arts de Belgique* (Brussels, 1886–87), vol. 9, in the entry under his name.

25. The date is specified by the author in his preface: "If at this moment (1874) the Assembly at Versailles is opposed to the establishment of the Republic, it is not because of an exclusive attachment to the monarchical form, but because it fears that democracy triumphant would soon lead to demands based in an egalitarian spirit" (*De la propriété*, p. x). His customary sensitivity to questions pertaining to the whole of society can be seen here, as well as his customary realistic—even crude—diagnosis of a ruling class looking out for its own interests.

26. The passage cited above, n. 22, contains a truly programmatic declaration.

27. Ibid., p. xvii.

28. Laveleye always regarded the so-called *Kathedersozialisten* with admiration but also with a trace of diffidence. In the preface to his *De la propriété* he is governed by his usual fear of socialism when he states bitterly that "it penetrates the working masses with its ideas and even, more seriously, professors of political economy become *Catheder Socialisten*" (p. xi). At nearly the same time, in a letter dated 6 December 1873, and published by his biographer, Goblet D'Alviella ("Notice," p. 219), he calls himself "nearly socialist" and announces that he had "in publication a volume which will give such a color to my name that you will find I have compromised myself too much" (referring undoubtedly to *De la propriété*). We have here another and later proof of the tensions that divided Laveleye between the fear of the collapse of an order to which he felt he belonged and intellectual sympathies for culturally fresh and vital movements. As an economist he was in fact close to the *Kathedersozialisten*. He participated in the meetings to promote the movement at Eisenach (as he reported in the Italian *Giornale degli economisti*), he assumed doctrinal positions close to it in substance (see the essay, "Les tendances nouvelles de l'économie politique," *Revue des deux mondes*, 15 July 1875), and he claimed that the circle of young men who gathered around Huet had anticipated its principle tenets. Speaking of this group in the *Revue de Belgique*, 15 April 1879, p. 377 he declares: "We did not shrink from the boldest solutions. It is interesting to note that already at that time we had arrived at the

principle solutions of *Katheder* socialism, now adopted with some variations by the professors of political economy of Germany." Laveleye's judgment of the validity of the movement can be seen in his *Le socialisme contemporain*, pp. 311 ff., where his last chapter is dedicated to "Les socialistes de la chaire." On his relations with *Kathedersozialismus*, see also some mention in Lambert, "Laveleye (Emile-Louis-Victor de)," col. 534 ff.

29. "I have attempted to write only a historical essay in this volume," Laveleye stated in his preface to *De la propriété* (p. xxii), but he was quick to add that "knowledge of primitive forms of property could be of immediate interest to new colonies that dispose of immense territories such as Australia and the United States." And his long preface ends with an ingenuous and rhetorical apostrophe to the "citizens of America and Australia" to put into practice the conclusions of his work.

30. Loria, "Emile de Laveleye," p. 137.

31. It may at this point appear insufficiently evident to qualify Laveleye's analysis as "historicist." The following pages contain a fuller justification of the term.

32. These are the two great currents of thought to which Laveleye is indebted and whose teachings mark his entire work. His abundant citations of works in these two schools show this affiliation clearly.

33. Laveleye, *De la propriété*, p. 111.

34. Laveleye, *Le socialisme contemporain*, p. xxiii.

35. "Property today has been stripped of any social character: completely different from what it was originally, nothing collective is left in it. A privilege without obligations, without hindrance, without reservations, it seems to have no other aim but that of assuring the well-being of the individual. That is how it is conceived and how it is defined" (*De la propriété*, p. xv).

36. Laveleye, "La propriété primitive dans les Townships écossais," p. 375.

37. It is easy to follow the distortion of the subjective situation of the proprietor in juridical thought and indeed in theological and philosophical thought when one investigates the genesis of the modern notion of property. May I refer to my own essays: P. Grossi, "La proprietà nel sistema privatistico della Seconda Scolastica," in *La Seconda Scolastica nella formazione del diritto privato moderno* (Milan, 1973); "Usus facti—La nozione di proprietà nell'inaugurazione dell'età nuova," in *Quaderni fiorentini per la storia del pensiero giuridico moderno* 1 (1972).

38. Laveleye, *De la propriété*, p. xv.

39. "And one is given to think that in the future a greater place will be given to the collective element" (ibid., p. xv).

40. This is how his biographer, Goblet D'Alviella, defines him in his "Notice," p. 97. In his study on property, what is more, Laveleye thinks always of agrarian property as the fundamental proprietary category. It is above all the agrarian economist that speaks in him, and it is the peasant and pastoral world that he examines and in which he finds hope for the future. In a polemic with Friedrich List, who had sustained that agricultural populations were inferior to manufacturing peoples, he replied: "The people of agricultors will have a higher chance for

morality, for happiness, for health, for well-being, for real power, than the people of manufacturers'' (ibid., p. 96).

41. Laveleye, *De la propriété,* p. 4: ''When the jurists attempt to explain the origin of this right, they go back to what one calls the state of nature, and they derive absolute individual property, quiritarian *dominium,* from it directly. Thus they ignore that law of gradual development that can be found everywhere in history, and they place themselves in opposition with facts that today are recognized and verified. It is only by a series of successive progressions and in a relatively recent epoch that individual ownership applied to land has been constituted.''

42. Ibid., p. xviii.

43. Ibid., p. xiii.

44. Ibid.

45. Ibid., p. xxii.

46. ''If property is indispensable to liberty, does it not follow that since all men have the right to be free, all have also the right to be proprietors?'' (ibid., p. xxi).

47. ''The famous jurisconsult of the Second Empire, Troplong, in a short work on *La propriété d'après le Code civil,* published in 1848, expresses himself thus to refute the errors of the socialists (p. 12): 'If liberty founds property, equality renders it sacred. All men being equal, hence equally free, each must recognize in others the sovereign independence of the law.' This sonorous phrase makes no sense, or else it means that we must assure to everyone the enjoyment of a property that will be the guarantee of his independence'' (ibid.).

48. Laveleye answers the theory of occupancy with essentially the same arguments as Maine, emphasizing that ''occupancy is a fact that results from chance or from force'' (ibid., p. 383). Locke's theory of work is treated to three pages of calm but close examination: ''If work were the only legitimate source of property, we would have to conclude that a society in which so many workers live in misery and so many idle men live in opulence is contrary to all laws and violates the basis of property'' (ibid., p. 386). Note how Laveleye appeals to the most basic good sense, denying that the doctrine is founded even minimally on ethical evidence. Note also, on the same level, how Thiers is ridiculed bitterly and some of his obvious contradictions are noted without mercy (ibid., p. 386, n. 1). On the theory of contract, see p. 387.

49. Ibid., p. xii.

50. Ibid., p. 77.

51. A glance at the subjects listed in the index to the volume gives a good idea of how Laveleye was led to less-frequented paths in juridical historiography. Some of the more indicative are: the village community in Russia; the village community in Java and India; agrarian communities among the Arabs; the history of landed property in England and in China; the family community among the southern Slavs; the *Allmenden* of Switzerland; state agrarian ownership and the reign of property in India; and agrarian land in Egypt and Turkey. This direction is accentuated in the fourth edition, completely revised by the author. There we find new headings including: the *allmaenningar* in Scandinavia and in Finland; primitive property in Scotland and in the United States; primitive property among the Celts in Ireland and the Gauls; archaic property in the Punjab; archaic property in Japan; primitive

property among the aborigines of America; landed property in Denmark; and primitive property among diverse peoples. Clearly, he attempted to construct his own interpretation with materials that were not those of the Romanistic tradition.

52. In 1845 he was in Italy; in 1847, in Austria and in Germany; in '67 he was in Hungary; in '69, in Spain, Portugal, and in Egypt; in '77 he went to Sweden; in '84, to Scotland; in '83 he visited the Danubian states and the Balkans (see Goblet D'Alviella, "Notice," pp. 189 ff.). Often his analyses are based on direct observation *in loco* (see, for example, his explicit statement regarding the *Allmend* of *De la propriété*, p. 267, n. 1).

53. The chapter on the village community in Russia is constructed with the particular aid of Le Play's investigations (Frédéric Le Play, *Les ouvriers européens: Etudes sur les travaux, la vie domestique et la condition morale des populations ouvrières de l'Europe* (Paris, 1855).

54. Fustel de Coulanges, "Le problème des origines de la propriété," *Revue des questions historiques* 23 (1889): 411.

55. Laveleye, *De la propriété*, p. 381.

56. Ibid., pp. 71 ff.

57. Ibid., pp. 9 ff.

58. Ibid., pp. 49 ff.

59. Ibid., pp. 267 ff.

60. Ibid., pp. 201 ff.

62. Ibid., p. 299.

63. Ibid., p. 301.

64. On Paul Leroy-Beaulieu, see chapter 8, p. 193.

65. Paul Leroy-Beaulieu, *Le collectivisme, Examen critique du nouveau socialisme* (Paris, 1884), p. 86.

66. Ibid., p. 136: "Let us leave the idyll which is met only in poetry and return to prose, to the allmend as it is, with its cramped proportions and its limited influence. The enthusiastic description of the happiness of the Swiss peasant resembles reality about as much as the shepherds of Theocritus or the Coridon and the Alexis of Virgil resemble real Greek or Roman shepherds."

67. Giacomo Venezian, "Reliquie della proprietà collettiva in Italia," now in *Opere giuridiche* (Rome, 1920) vol. 2: *Studi sui diritti reali e sulle trascrizioni, le successioni, la famiglia.*

68. Laveleye, *De la propriété*, p. 302.

69. The preparation and the publication of his long work, *Das deutsche Genossenschaftsrecht*, occupied Gierke for a span of fifty years: the first volume appeared in 1868, the second in 1873, the third in 1881, and the fourth in 1913, all in Berlin.

70. A. Heusler, "Die Rechtsverhältnisse am Gemeinland in Unterwalden," in *Zeitschrift für schweizerisches Recht* 10 (1862).

71. Laveleye, *De la propriété*, p. 116. Laveleye used the German translation of Maxim Kovalevski, *Umriss einer Geschichte der Zerstückelung der Feldgemeinschaft im Kanton Waadt* (Zurich, 1877). For the chapter on the *Allmenden*, aside from Heusler's work, he relied on August von Miaskowski, *Die Verfassung der Land-, Alpen- und Forst- Wirtschaft der deutschen Schweiz*

(Basel, 1878) and *Die schweizerische Allmend in ihrer geschichtlichen Entwicklung vom XIII. Jahrhundert bis zur Gegenwart* (Leipzig, 1879).

72. The full majesty of Gierke's reconstruction of medieval associative law appears to have influenced only the later period of the dispute, and particularly the jurists. For example, its influence can be seen in the university courses on landholding rights of Francesco Filomusi Guelfi (see chapter 10, pp. 237 ff.).

Chapter Three

1. Joseph Alois Schumpeter, *Storia dell'analisi economica*, trans. P. Sylos Labini and L. Occhionero (Turin, 1959), vol. 2, pp. 564 ff.

2. Erwin Nasse (1829–90), a distinguished economist and specialist in financial law, was a professor first at the University of Rostock and, from 1860, at the University of Bonn.

3. Erwin Nasse, *Ueber die mittelalterliche Feldgemeinschaft und die Einhegungen des sechszehnten Jahrhunderts in England* (Bonn, 1869). This short work aroused considerable interest (see, for example, the essay by Georg Hanssen, "Die mittelalterliche Feldgemeinschaft in England nach Nasse, im Zusammenhalt mit der skandinavisch-germanischen," in *Agrarhistorische Abhandlungen* [Leipzig, 1880], vol. 1, pp. 484 ff.) and was translated into English, *On the Agricultural Community of the Middle Ages and Inclosures of the Sixteenth Century*, trans. H. A. Ouvry (London, 1871), published in second edition a year later.

4. Wilhelm Roscher, *Economia dell'agricoltura e delle materie prime*, trans. L. Luzzatti ("Biblioteca dell'Economista" Turin, 1876), 1^3, pp. 71 ff. On Roscher and his methodology, see the penetrating analysis by M. Weber, "Roschers historische Methode," in *Gesammelte Aufsätze für Wissenschaftslehre* (Tübingen, 1968).

5. Adolph Wagner, *Die Abschaffung des privaten Grundeigenthums* (Leipzig, 1870).

6. On Wagner (1835–1917), who was for a long period following 1870 professor of political economy at the University of Berlin, see Erich Thier, *Rodbertus, Lassalle, Adolph Wagner. Ein Beitrag zur Theorie und Geschichte des deutschen Staatssozialismus* (Jena, 1930) and W. Vleugels, "Adolph Wagner—Gedenkworte zur hundersten Wiederkehr des Geburtstages eines deutschen Socialisten," *Schmollers Jahrbuch für Gestzgebung, Verwaltung und Volkswirtschaft im Deutschen Reiche* 59 (1935): 129 ff.

7. Wagner's short work is divided into three essays: "Das Grundeigenthum vor dem socialdemokratischen Arbeitercongress in Basel," "Das privateigenthum am Grund und Boden in Seiner gesellschaftlich notwendigen und berechtigten Entwicklung," "Das Gemeineigenthum am Grund und Boden nach russischen Erfahrungen." He relies heavily on Maurer's and Waitz's works, as well as on Haxthausen's essays.

8. The work of Albert E. F. Schäffle (Nürtingen 1831–Stuttgart 1903) should be noted in this connection. He was inspired by a moderate "collectivism" and he influenced several of the participants in the coming debate. He is honored, for example, with a full and respectful citation by the Hon. Tommaso Tittoni in his

report of 20 February 1893 (see chapter 9, pp. 228 ff.) in the course of an ample and interesting debate in the Italian Parliament. Among Schäffle's works, see his well-known pamphlet, *Die Quintessenz des Socialismus* (Gotha, 1875), first published in the *Deutsche Blätter* the previous year, and his imposing *Struttura e vita del corpo sociale,* trans. L. Eusebio ("Biblioteca dell'economista" Turin, 1881), 7³, parts 1 and 2 [*Bau und Leben des socialen Körpers* (Tübingen, 1875–81)].

9. Paul Viollet, "Caractère collectif des premières propriétés immobilières," *Bibliothèque de l'Ecole des Chartes* 33 (1872): 455 ff.

10. Viollet so informs his readers (see n. 1 following the title). He states that after he had submitted the first two chapters of his work to the editors, he read the first part of a study by Emile de Laveleye in the *Revue des deux mondes* and he found there a point of view and conclusions so similar to his own that he had doubts about the wisdom of publishing his study. Later, during the course of a heated exchange with Fustel de Coulanges about his debt to Henry Sumner Maine, Viollet claimed that he came to know Maine's work only in 1872, as he was preparing the second part of his essay and, for this reason, had cited him only in that second part. Viollet repeated on this occasion his affirmations concerning his debt to Laveleye. See "Observations de M. Paul Viollet," *Revue critique d'histoire et de littérature,* N. S. 22 (1885): 269, in response to a reply of Fustel to Viollet's critical review of Fustel's "Recherches sur quelques problèmes d'histoire" and of his "Etude sur le titre de la Loi salique de migrantibus."

11. Paul Viollet (Tours 1840–Paris 1914) held the chair of history of civil law and canon law at the Ecole des Chartes from 1890, after long years as archivist and librarian at the Faculty of Jurisprudence at Paris. See P. Fournier, "Paul Viollet," *Nouvelle revue historique du droit français et étranger* 38–39 (1914–15), a bombastic but not totally worthless tribute.

12. See Viollet, "Caractère collectif," p. 457 for his use of Livingstone's report of his travels.

13. E. Gibelin, *Etudes sur le droit civil des Hindous—Recherches de législation comparée sur les lois de l'Inde, les lois d'Athènes et de Rome et les coutumes des Germains* (Pondicherry, 1846–47), cited by Viollet in "Caractère collectif," p. 458. Gibelin was attorney general of the French colony at Pondicherry.

14. Ibid., p. 461. Here Viollet cites Eugène Robe, *Les lois de la propriété immobilière en Algérie* (Algiers, 1864).

15. Viollet also cites the investigations of Le Play, on whom see the introduction, pp. 19 ff.

16. Viollet, "Caractère collectif," p. 463, citing W. Roscher, "Ueber die Frage: Haben unsere deutschen Vorfahren zu Tacitus Zeit ihre Landwirtschaft nach dem Dreifelderssysteme getrieben?" in *Berichte ueber die Verhandlunger der K. Saechs. Gesell. der Wiss. zu Leipzig,* Phil. Hist. Klasse, 10 (1858).

17. Viollet, "Caractère collectif," p. 503.

18. Ibid., p. 481.

19. I refer particularly to Caesar *De bello gallico* 4.1; 2.22; Tacitus *Germania* 26; Horace *Carmina* 3.24.9 ff., which provide the overworked phrases on which they exercised their interpretive zeal.

20. Auguste Geffroy (1820–95) was professor in the faculty of letters at Bordeaux and Paris, and later director of the Ecole Française at Rome.

21. Auguste Geffroy, *Rome et les barbares—Etudes sur la Germanie de Tacite* (Paris, 1874), particularly pp. 176 ff.

22. Essential information can be gotten on the singular personality and many works—soon outdated—of Henry George from C. A. Barker, "George, Henry," *International Encyclopedia of the Social Sciences* (New York, 1968), vol. 6.

23. Henry George, *Progress and Poverty: An inquiry into the Cause of Industrial Depressions and of Increase of Want with Increase of Wealth: The Remedy* (San Francisco, 1879), book 7, chapter 4.

24. The Italian translation, *Progresso e povertà*, trans. L. Eusebio ("Biblioteca dell'Economista" Turin, 1890), 3, 9[3] was in circulation from 1888 as a prepublication extract.

25. George's book was reviewed by the "collectivist" Emile de Laveleye, "La propriété terrienne et le pauperisme," *Revue scientifique de la France et de l'étranger* 18[2] (1880): 708 ff.

26. The original title of Morgan's work is *Ancient Society; or, Researches in the Lines of Human Progress from Savagery, Through Barbarism to Civilization* (New York, 1878). For the place of Morgan in cultural thought, see B. J. Stern, "Lewis Henry Morgan: Social Evolutionist" and "Lewis Henry Morgan: American Ethnologist," now in *Historical Sociology: The Selected Papers of Bernhard J. Stern* (New York, 1959) and L. A. White, "Lewis Henry Morgan: Pioneer in the Theory of Social Evolution," in *An Introduction to the History of Sociology*, ed. H. E. Barnes (Chicago, 1954), particularly pp. 145 ff.

27. It should be unnecessary to recall that Friedrich Engels's *The Origin of the Family, Private Property, and the State* bears the subtitle, *In the Light of the Researches of Lewis H. Morgan*. On Marx's and Engels's reading of Morgan, see the informative introduction by Fausto Codino to the Italian translation, *L'origine della famiglia, della proprietà privata e dello Stato*, trans. D. Della Terza (Rome, 1963), passim.

28. Lewis H. Morgan, *La Società antica—Le linee del progresso umano dallo stato selvaggio alla civiltà*, trans. A. Casiccia and L. Trevisan (Milan, 1978), part 4, chapters 1 and 2.

29. See the following chapter.

30. See chapter 8, p. 193.

31. See chapter 6, p. 110.

32. See chapter 6, p. 110.

33. See chapter 3, pp. 76 ff., nn. 20, 21.

34. *Séances et Travaux de l'Académie des Sciences morales et politiques (Institut de France)—Compte rendu* 123 (1885, premier semestre): 705 ff.

35. Ibid., 124 (1885, deuxième semestre).

36. Ibid., 126 (1886, deuxième semestre). (Laveleye's article was published in the *Revue de Belgique* of 1886.)

37. Ibid., 123 (1885, premier semestre): 642 ff.

38. Ibid., 124 (1886, deuxième semestre). Geffroy's speech can be found on pp. 66 ff.; Fustel's reply on pp. 81 ff.; Glasson's comments on pp. 87 ff.; Fustel's reply on pp. 118 ff.; Aucoc's remarks on pp. 129 ff.; Fustel's reply on pp. 141 ff.; Ravaisson's remarks on pp. 147 ff.

39. Ibid., 125 (1886, premier semestre). The "Rapport" is signed by Baudrillart,

Block, Courcelle-Seneuil, Franck, and Passy.

40. Ibid., pp. 513 ff. The discussion of the "Rapport" was evidently impassioned and general. Participants included Aucoc, Baudrillart, Courcelle-Seneuil, Desjardins, Franck, Glasson, Janet, Paul Leroy-Beaulieu, Levasseur, Passy, and Picot.

41. Ibid. The heated discussion can be found in 126 (1886, deuxième semestre): 129 ff.

42. It was Fustel in particular who invoked the asceptic neutrality of both historical investigations and historiographic conclusions.

Chapter Four

1. Recent scholarship has provided reassessments of Fustel de Coulanges to replace Paul Guiraud's apologetic *Fustel de Coulanges* (Paris, 1896) and the saccharine and largely uncritical Jean M. Tourneur-Aumont, *Fustel de Coulanges 1830–1889* (Paris, 1931). A satisfactory bibliography can be found in Jane Herrick, *The Historical Thought of Fustel de Coulanges* (Washington, 1954). On Fustel's contribution to the problem of the origins of property, see A. Galatello Adamo, "Sui caratteri originari della proprietà: esiti ed equivoci nell'opera di Numa Denis Fustel de Coulanges," *Quaderni fiorentini* 5–6 (1976–77).

2. As we have seen (chapter 3, n. 34), this was the title of the paper that Fustel delivered before the Académie des Sciences morales et politiques of Paris, subsequently published in Fustel de Coulanges, *Recherches sur quelques problèmes d'histoire* (Paris, 1885).

3. Fustel often repeated this idea. One example may suffice: "I do not want to combat the theory. . . . I want to discuss not the theory itself, but this covering of erudition that has been given to it" ("Le problème des origines de la propriété foncière," *Revue des questions historiques* 23 [1889], now in *Questions historiques*, ed. Camille Jullian [Paris, 1893], p. 20).

4. Fustel de Coulanges, "De la manière d'écrire l'histoire en France et en Allemagne depuis cinquante ans," in *Questions historiques*, pp. 15–16. The essay was first published in the *Revue des deux mondes* of 1 September 1872.

5. Fustel de Coulanges, "Observations sur un ouvrage de M. Emile de Laveleye intitulé 'La propriété collective du sol en divers pays,' " *Séances et travaux de l'Académie des sciences* 124 (1885, deuxième semestre): 276.

6. See below.

7. See below.

8. Rodolphe Dareste de la Chavanne (1824–1911). See chapter 6, p. 110.

9. See Dareste's second article on " 'Recherches sur quelques problèmes d'histoire' par M. Fustel de Coulanges," *Journal des savants*, October 1886, p. 603.

10. See below.

11. Fustel de Coulanges, "Réponse de M. Fustel de Coulanges à l'article de M. Paul Viollet du 9 août," *Revue critique d'histoire et de littérature*, N. S. 22 (1886): 261. Fustel continues, attacking the methods of the "collectivists" as too deductive and insufficiently historicist.

12. Fustel de Coulanges, *Histoire des institutions politiques de l'ancienne France IV: L'Alleu et le domaine rural* (5th ed.; Paris, 1931), p. 172. All citations from this work will be from this edition.

13. See below.

14. This is how Giorgio Pasquali, who was a philologist by profession and by nature, qualified him in his splendid preface to the Italian translation of *La Cité antique: La città antica*, trans. G. Perrotta (Florence, 1924), p. vii.

15. Ibid., p. x.

16. Charles Seignobos (1854–1942), after 1879 professor at the University of Dijon and, after 1890, at the Sorbonne. He was a student of medieval and modern history and for many years directed the *Revue historique*.

17. In his important *Préface* to Tourneur-Aumont, *Fustel de Coulanges*, p. vii, Seignobos intersperses his benevolent assessment of Fustel as his disciple with an analysis of the real motives for Fustel's methodological choices: "The frank sentiments burst out soon after, with an intensity that surprised us, on the occasion of the criticisms directed at the first volume of his *Histoire des institutions de la France*. The indignation that he felt was so keen that it upset his projects and radically changed the character of his works. He had proposed to present the evolution of political regimes of ancient France in a general picture analogous to his *Cité antique:* that was surely the method most in conformity with the character of his mind, which was synthetic and comprehensive. He abandoned this in order to place himself on his opponents' grounds, and from that time on he published only collections of erudite monographs on controversial questions (which he called 'preparatory works'), based in a minute study of texts." See also C. Seignobos, "L'histoire," in *Histoire de la langue et de la littérature françaises des origines à 1900*, published under the direction of L. Petit de Julleville (Paris, 1899) vol. 8: *Dix-neuvième siècle—Période contemporaine (1850–1900)*, p. 282.

18. Fustel de Coulanges, "Le problème des origines de la propriété foncière," p. 55.

19. Ibid., p. 63.

20. Ibid., p. 80. Speaking of Viollet, but also of the "collectivist school" in general, Fustel had said: "The new school proceeds in another manner. It starts from an idea conceived by the mind, for example from the idea that the first property must have been a people's coproperty, then it looks among all the peoples of the world and finds in each of them one or two facts in concordance with that idea" ("Réponse de M. Fustel de Coulanges à l'article de M. Paul Viollet du 9 août," p. 261).

21. "M. Viollet's citations are always exact in the sense that the line that he cites is indeed found at the place he indicates: his inexactitude consists only in the fact that if you read that line in its context, it means exactly the contrary of what M. Viollet has said" (Le problème des origines de la propriété foncière," p. 81).

22. Seignobos himself avows: "The intelligence of Fustel . . . was more at ease in the interpretation of a text than in the observation of social reality" (Preface to Tourneur-Aumont, *Fustel de Coulanges*, pp. ix, x).

23. A. Loria, "Emile de Laveleye," now in his *Verso la giustizia sociale (Idee, battaglie ed apostoli)* (2nd. ed.; Milan, 1908), p. 137.

24. Tourneur-Aumont, *Fustel de Coulanges*, p. 34.

25. This research lay at the base of a course given at the Sorbonne in 1877–78 and was published as "Recherches sur le droit de propriété chez les Grecs," published in *Nouvelles recherches sur quelques problèmes d'histoire* (2d ed.; Paris, 1923).

26. Fustel de Coulanges, "Recherches sur cette question: Les Germains connaissaient-ils la propriété des terres?" See chapter 3, pp. 79 ff.

27. Fustel de Coulanges, "De la marche germanique," in *Recherches sur quelques problèmes d'histoire*.

28. Fustel de Coulanges, "Observations sur un ouvrage de M. Emile de Laveleye." This exchange has already been discussed: see n. 5 of this chapter.

29. I refer to Fustel de Coulanges, "Le problème des origines de la propriété foncière." This essay was—understandably—immediately translated into English: *The Origin of Property in Land*, trans. M. Ashley (London, 1891).

30. Fustel de Coulanges, *L'Alleu et le domaine rural*.

31. See Fustel de Coulanges, *La cité antique; Étude sur le culte, le droit, les institutions de la Grèce et de Rome* (Paris, 1864), book 2, chapter 6, passim.

32. Fustel de Coulanges, "Recherches sur le droit de propriété chez les Grecs," p. 20.

33. The passage that concludes *L'alleu et le domaine rural* illustrates this: "We have observed the nature and the organism of the rural domain from the fourth century to the ninth. The first thing that struck us in this study was the continuity of facts and usages. What the domain was in the fourth century was what it remained in the ninth. It has the same extension, the same limits. It often bears the same name, which is the one given to it by a former Roman proprietor. It is divided in two parts in the same way as before. One man is proprietor of it by virtue of a right of ownership that has not changed. . . . We have been unable to discover one single instance in which a change has been made in the nature of the rural domain. Germanic invasions brought no modification to it." This is a statement that a historian of law—or anyone trained to be dissatisfied with the externals of a question or with neat stylistic formulas—would find superficial, hasty, and nominalistic.

34. Ibid., chapter 1 passim.

35. Ibid., p. 4.

36. Ibid.

37. Ibid., pp. 8–9.

38. Ibid., chapter 2 passim.

39. Ibid., pp. 98 ff.

40. Ibid., p. 113.

41. Ibid., p. 123.

42. Ibid., p. 130: "Therefore the historian must take it as true that the great convulsions of the fifth century and the arrival of new men neither altered nor lessened the right of ownership over the soil. To suppose that the Germans introduced a new way of possessing the land would be to contradict all of the documents." This idea was deeply rooted in Fustel's mind, and he had already stated it clearly as early as 1873: "The codes that were written soon after the invasion of the Franks . . . admit and seem to know only full and absolute ownership, without conditions and without dependence, the ownership that can be transmitted by succession or by sale and that, finally, they found established in the laws of the indigenous population." ("Les origines du régime féodal—La propriété foncière dans l'Empire romain et dans la société mérovingienne," *Revue des deux mondes* 105 (1873).

43. Fustel de Coulanges, *L'alleu et le domaine rural*, p. 171. On the succeeding page, Fustel returns to the charge with his usual arrogance: "I have read *all* of these documents, not once, but several times, not in extracts, but in their continuity and from one end to the other. I can declare that there is not one line in them that mentions a common use of lands or a village community." He has done everything, and it is up to other historians to accept his conclusions, since they come from direct examination of *all* the documents.

44. Ibid., chapter 5: "Est-il vrai que les Francs aient pratiqué la communauté de village?"

45. Ibid., p. 171, n. 1.

46. "This romance that was introduced into history some thirty years ago must be removed from it, at least if one believes as we do that history is a science" (ibid., p. 198).

47. Those who supported the "collectivist" theories appear on Fustel's pages as a herd of mad sheep who follow blindly a first adventurous and imaginative spokesman: "Schroeder has said that there were texts proving the community of the *march* in the seventh century. . . . Then M. Kowaleski copied Schroeder; then M. Dareste copied Kowaleski, then M. Glasson copied M. Dareste" (ibid., p. 192).

48. Ernest Glasson, *Les communaux et la domaine rural à l'époque franque— Réponse à M. Fustel de Coulanges* (Paris, 1890), passim, but particularly pp. 20 ff.

49. Fustel de Coulanges, *L'alleu et le domaine rural*, p. 174.

50. Ibid.

51. Ibid., p. 175.

52. Tourneur-Aumont, *Fustel de Coulanges*, p. 69. See also p. 142, where Tourneur-Aumont states, whether with disarming candor or with well-directed irony, we do not know, that to Fustel "the regime of individual property seemed the true condition of general happiness and, more particularly, of the happiness of the humble."

53. Fustel de Coulanges, "Le problème des origines de la propriété foncière," p. 116.

54. See above, n. 32.

55. Fustel de Coulanges, "M. Emile Belot," *Revue historique* 32 (1886): 402. The investigation to which Fustel refers speaks of the organization of landholding on the North American island of Nantucket following the colonization of the island in the seventeenth century. This work will be discussed in chapter 5, pp. 104 ff.

56. Fustel de Coulanges, "Le problème des origines de la propriété foncière," p. 117.

57. "Land common to all is land without a master" (Fustel de Coulanges, *L'alleu et le domaine rural*, p. 451).

58. Fustel de Coulanges, "Le problème des origines de la propriété foncière," p. 88.

59. This is true not only of Fustel as he was involved in diatribes on the subject of property: verbal intemperance and the frontal attack were Fustel's preferred polemical techniques in other situations as well.

60. See chapter 6.

61. Fustel de Coulanges, "Réponse de M. Fustel de Coulanges," p. 262. Fustel turns around Paul Viollet's admonition: "Let us never isolate; let us always bring things together," which was the statement with which Viollet had concluded his sharp criticism of Fustel and had reiterated his loyalty to the comparatistic methodology of Maine and Laveleye (see Paul Viollet, "Observations," p. 115).

62. An excellent example of this method can be seen in Fustel's criticism of the third volume of Ernest Glasson's *Histoire du droit et des institutions de la France* (Paris, 1889). Fustel had found Glasson's interpretations particularly distasteful, and he examines Glasson's citations one by one in a requisitory developed analytically in twenty-eight points, ending up with a series of indisputable arithmetic data, a procedure which always gives much satisfaction and peace of mind to the bookkeepers of learning. He declares: "M. Glasson's citations amount to a sum of forty-five. Of these forty-five, thirteen are completely extraneous to the thesis he puts forth, and thirty-two argue the contrary of this thesis. Not one contains even an allusion to a regime of community. Therefore, there is not even one exact citation among the forty-five. History is not an art; it is a science, and its first law, as for all sciences, is exactitude. The work of M. Glasson, while it aims to prove the existence of a regime of community, furnishes the most certain proof that this regime did not exist. It gives the counterproof to our researches and confirms them" (*L'alleu et le domaine rural*, p. 197). This is Fustel's usual method, his customary arrogance, his habitual method of making a *tabula rasa* of the adverse documentation, taken up piece by piece and demolished. He shows not one incertitude, not one perplexity: this is total war requiring total victory for Fustel's thesis.

63. In an act of donation to a certain convent, the text speaks of "anales terras, mancipia, prata, pascua, vineas, aquas" (see Fustel de Coulanges, "Le problème des origines de la propriété foncière," pp. 34–35, and *L'alleu et le domaine rural*, pp. 180–81.

64. As noted by Ernest Glasson, *Les communaux et le domaine rural*, p. 82.

65. Fustel de Coulanges, "Le problème des origines de la propriété foncière," p. 35, and *L'alleu et le domaine rural*, p. 181.

66. See, for example, Fustel de Coulanges, "Le problème des origines de la propriété foncière," p. 59, and *L'alleu et le domaine rural*, p. 191.

67. T. Reinach, "Le collectivisme des Grecs de Lipari," *Revue des études grecques* 3 (1890), p. 88.

68. Fustel de Coulanges, "Le problème des origines de la propriété foncière," p. 75.

69. I refer not only to the autonomous essay entitled "De la marche germanique," written about 1885 and inserted in Fustel's *Recherches sur quelques problèmes d'histoire*, but also to discussion of the *Mark* that crops up in many of the writings that Fustel dedicated to the history of property. In the first of his summarizing works on the question, "Le problème des origines de la propriété foncière," see the pages dedicated to the criticism of Maurer: pp. 368 ff. In the second such work, *"L'alleu et la domaine rural*, he declares: "Furthermore, the word 'march' is not there" (p. 187); "not one word of the march" (p. 194); chapter 8, number 3, particularly p. 269; "In the documents of the seventh, of the eighth, and of the first part of the ninth century, we encounter the word march fifty-one times. Not once does it apply to a common land; not once is the idea of community

tied to it; always, on the contrary, it applies to a parcel of land that is described there as land under private ownership." Fustel is summarized here: his cult of formal exactitude and of arithemetical minutia—which serve very well to enchant and conquer the reader—and the absolute quality of his conclusions—which are at least as decisive as those of the "collectivists."

70. Glasson notes this same conclusion in his *Les communaux et le domaine rural.*

71. See above, n. 33.

72. Fustel de Coulanges, "Le problème des origines de la propriété foncière," p. 115.

73. Feuter notes that Fustel's formation was not juridical. (See Eduard Feuter, *Storia della storiografia moderna,* trans. A. Pinelli (Naples, 1944), vol. 2, p. 272.

74. Calixte Accarias (1831–1903) taught Roman law at the faculty of jurisprudence of Paris and, after 1890, was a *conseiller* at the Cour de Cassation. He was the author of a *Précis de droit romain* published between 1869 and 1883, a work remarkable for the agility and concision of its presentation as well as for the accuracy and appropriateness of its documentation. It has rightly been defined "the Baudry-Lacantinerie of Roman law" (André Jean Arnaud, *Les juristes face à la société du XIXe siècle à nos jours* [Paris, 1975], p. 114).

75. Fustel de Coulanges, *L'alleu et le domaine rural,* p. 194. The citation refers to the papers of the abbey of Saint Gall of 890, published in *Urkundenbuch der Abtei Sanct-Gallen,* ed. H. Wartmann (Zürich, 1863–82) vol. 2, number 680.

76. See P. Grossi, "Naturalismo e formalismo nella systematica medievale delle situazioni reali," *Jus* 18 (1967) and *Le situazioni reali nell'esperienza giuridica medievale* (Padua, 1968).

77. See chapter 10, pp. 239 ff.

78. A historian of jurisprudence, or a historian aware of the socioeconomic dimension, could not help but be astonished by the formalistic vision that underlies the following assertion: "The great convulsions of the fifth century and the arrival of new men neither altered nor lessened the right of ownership over the soil. . . . This truth is of a great importance. It is placed at the beginning of our studies of the feudal world, and we must not lose it from sight. It is in fact on the unshakable foundation of a right to full and complete ownership that feudal society will later be built" (*L'alleu et le domaine rural,* p. 130). It should hardly be necessary to say that a juridical structure like that of feudalism cannot avoid being articulated according to a proprietarian organization. But, by the same token, it cannot avoid being a product of a custom that tends toward the exploitation of different socioeconomic aspects of property, or at least particular and fractionary elements of property, more than a synthetic, global, totally complete power. This is what makes the common mind think it inherent to the nature of property to be split up.

79. Emile de Laveleye, *De la propriété et de ses formes primitives* (4th ed.; Paris, 1891), p. 82, n. 1. Here Laveleye states that "M. Fustel de Coulanges has contested on several occasions the notion that passages in Tacitus and Caesar state the existence among the Germanic people of a regime of collective ownership of land, with a periodic redistribution of the land. I would agree without restriction to the translation and to the commentaries on the text that Fustel

makes, but a jurist would never consider as private or individual the share attributed to one person in an annual redistribution of a territory belonging to a community or to a group of men.''

80. Fustel often states that ''it is never to a village community that land is given or sold'' (*L'alleu et le domaine rural*, p. 173), but he does not take into account the fact that even a flourishing village community would by its very socio-juridical structure necessarily seem like an immobile, somnolent, economic entity. A private holding or even an ecclesiastical institution would show many more visible signs of economic exchange, of occasions in which its name would appear in a document of sale, purchase, donation, or simple concession. The village community was a reality that went far back in time and that by its static nature lived in an economic atmosphere of rarefied consistency.

81. One dimension that has an extensive place in Fustel's personality is his nationalism, and it contributed to any total explanation of his position in the dispute on property. For him, the ''collectivist'' doctrine was wrong—it was not its most important negative aspect nor its least—because it was in part German in origin and because it preferred Germanic norms to those that had come out of the Latin tradition. Fustel's resentment of the Germans comes out of the resounding defeat of France in 1870 and out of France's deeply resented loss of Alsace and Lorraine. For an expression of this sentiment, see Fustel's ''De la manière d'écrire l'histoire en France et en Allemagne depuis cinquante ans,'' an essay which he wrote and published immediately thereafter in the *Revue des deux mondes* in 1872. See also his article on ''Les origines du régime féodal,'' particularly p. 446. This article is more specifically related to the theme that interests us, and was also written and published immediately in the *Revue des deux mondes* of 1873. Fustel's anti-German sentiments should also be taken into account for a dispassioned examination of his monumental *Histoire des institutions politiques de l'Ancienne France*. Even the most enthusiastic admirer of this authentic masterpiece of human intelligence must admit, with Lazare de Gérin-Ricard, that ''the *Histoire des Institutions de la France* is a reaction against the partiality of the Germanists who had written before Fustel'' (Lazare de Gérin-Ricard, *L'Histoire des Institutions Politiques de Fustel de Coulanges* [Paris, 1936], p. 29). (This evaluation is all the more remarkable because Gérin-Ricard does not examine Fustel's work critically.) Maine had already pointed out the one-sidedness of French historiography after 1870, and that it was incapable of an objective and close examination of theses coming out of the German tradition (see Maine, ''La famille patriarcale,'' now in *Etudes sur l'histoire du droit* [Paris, 1889], p. 450). On the anti-German ideology of Fustel, see also the more recent comments of Arnaldo Momigliano, ''La citta antica di Fustel de Coulanges,'' *Rivista storica italiana* 82 (1970): 85 ff.

82. Fustel de Coulanges, ''Le problème des origines de la propriété foncière,'' p. 116.

83. In his inaugural discourse before the Académie Française, René Clair declared: ''In the history of your Company, there are few members who have had as little title to the honor as this producer of shadows who brings you no other baggage than illusions'' (See *Le Monde*, 11 May 1962, p. 11). Jacques de Lacretelle picks up the term, *montreur d'ombres*, in his formal *Réponse* (ibid.).

84. Even the scholar most sympathetic to Fustel and to his work would find it difficult to swallow some of his totally arbitrary interpretations. On these occasions one can see him intent "on torturing the sense or attenuating the significance of the texts," and his own statements can be adopted as "the most characteristic examples of the subjective criticism against which he rightly protested" (Gabriel Monod, "Fustel de Coulanges," now in his *Portraits et souvenirs* (Paris, 1897), pp. 145–46.

Chapter Five

1. Frederic Seebohm, *The English Village Community Examined in its Relation to the Manorial and Tribal Systems and to the Common or Open Field System of Husbandry—An Essay in Economic History* (Port Washington, N.Y., 1971, reprint edition of London, 1883). Frederic Seebohm (1833–1912) represents in English historiography the antiromantic and anti-Germanic reaction that Fustel de Coulanges exemplifies in France. In Seebohm's partisan interpretation, the village communities originated in the advent of serfdom and can be seen in communities of serfs, whom the *dominus fundi* found it convenient to gather within homogeneous structures strongly bound by a sense of solidarity. They have to be understood within the so-called manorial system and offer proof of nothing but collective servile duties owed, standing in contrast to the individual proprietorship of the lord. The elimination of such communities is seen for that reason as an important stage in social emancipation. Seebohm's succeeding works included studies on *The Tribal system in Wales* (London, 1895) and *Tribal Custom in Anglo-Saxon Law* (London, 1902), in which he makes use of his early preparation in jurisprudence, for he had even practiced law.

2. Lothar Dargun, "Ursprung end Entwicklungsgeschichte des Eigenthums," in *Zeitschrift für vergleichende Rechtswissenschaft* 5 (1884). For an idea of the reservations Laveleye's work inspired in certain schools of German juridical culture, see J. Kohler's review of the German translation of *De la propriété, Das Ureigenthum*, trans. K. Bücher (Leipzig, 1879), in *Kritische Vierteljahresschrift für Gesetzgebung und Rechtswissenschaft* 23 (1881): 24 ff. The reviewer is particularly critical of Laveleye's attempt to use a wide array of historical and comparative materials in order to construct a new theoretical base for the consideration of property.

3. Denman Waldo Ross, *The Early History of Land-holding among the Germans* (New York, 1971, reprint edition of Boston, 1883). In his preface Ross states that he began his research on the subject in 1875. Denman Waldo Ross (1853–1935) was a singular figure in the North American cultural scene whose career spanned two centuries. The essay that interests us here was, in fact, his doctoral thesis in 1880, and belongs to the first phase of his intellectual development, when Ross was involved in historical studies. At the death of his father in 1884 Ross felt himself free to follow his own intellectual vocation and dedicated considerable effort to the study and collection of works of art. On his preparation for the 1883 volume and on his views on primitive landholding, see Theodore Sizer, "Ross Denman Waldo" in *Dictionary of American Biography,* ed. Harris Elwood Starr (New York, 1944), vol. 21, supplement 1, p. 641.

4. See Ross, *The Early History of Land-holding*, n. 144, in which he outlines

Fustel's argument at some length. This mention stands out in a rather meager critical apparatus (for example, he refers only once to Viollet, in n. 168).

5. Ibid., pp. 39–41, 56–57, 61–64, 65 for the most significantly polemical pages. The clearest statement of Ross's position can be found on p. 40.

6. "The chief error of the advocates of a primitive communism is that they argue community of land wherever they find undivided land, or land held in undivided shares. The argument is surely inconclusive" (ibid., p. 61).

7. Georges Platon, in his review of Ross's book in the *Revue historique* 27 (1885), speaks of "half proofs" and says that "the argumentation is most insufficient," noting the almost complete lack of discussion of the adverse thesis and the adversaries' documentation. Although we have already referred to it, let us recall the confirmation of Maine's theses that found expression at this same time in North American historical circles in the person of Herbert B. Adams and his school. In his interesting *New Methods of Study in History* (Baltimore, 1884), Adams discusses the methods used to gather data on various New England localities, the results of which are summarized in his *The Germanic Origin of New-England Towns* (Baltimore, 1882), published in the Johns Hopkins University series of studies in history and politics.

8. Emile Belot was born in Montoire in 1829. He was a pupil of Chéruel at the Ecole Normale, and professor of history in secondary institutions at Strasbourg, Versailles, and Paris before he went to the Faculty of Letters at Lyon. He died at Lyon in 1886.

9. Emile Belot, "Nantucket. Etude sur les diverses sortes de propriété," in *Annuaire de la Faculté des Lettres de Lyon* 2 (1884).

10. Ibid., pp. 117 ff.

11. Ibid., pp. 117–18.

12. Belot himself informs us that these settlers had simply reproduced on Nantucket the ancient customs of their Scottish progenitors from Lauder, which customs, if Maine can be believed, constitute the relics of archaic forms that are tied to the customs of primordial Germanic culture.

13. "The two modes of ownership were practiced simultaneously. . . . No inflexible tradition, no preconceived system, no socialist thought, no instinctive sentiment of the supposed rights of man obtained to produce these natural effects" (ibid., p. 132).

14. Laveleye is defined as the author of an "interesting book rich in curious documents" (ibid., p. 109), an implicitly negative judgment that seems to relegate him to a place among the collectors of anecdotes and curiosities.

15. Belot tries with some success to exploit the enormous gap that exists between the socialistic and visionary schemes for a new society and the archaic structuring of long-established village communities that hark back to an immemorial tradition: "The peasants who lived for several generations grouped around the head of the family or his elected successor were pious, submissive to the authority of the master of the house, and very attached to local traditions and to local experience. It is that spirit of piety, of respect and love for the family and for the Church that made pastoral and agricultural communities live and prosper in the hamlets and villages. Do the socialists want to revive these patriarchal, rural, and religious mores?" (ibid., p. 180).

16. "There is a socialism of the chair that tries to give a reasonable form to that which basically does not depend on reason, and to bring science in agreement with the confused aspirations of the multitude. This socialism appears to us to be a well-meaning illusion in which certain generous spirits take pleasure. We have tried to combat it only in order to reestablish the historical veracity of several questions, a veracity that in our opinion has been falsified by latter-day concerns that not even men dedicated to the impartial study of the past can always avoid" (ibid., p. 180).

17. Belot states in his conclusion: "The verities that stand out from this description of the inside history of Nantucket would perhaps justify three sorts of criticism, addressed to the partisans of the reestablishment of agrarian communism. It would seem that their theories contain philosophical errors, historical errors, and contradictions" (ibid., p. 172). The text goes on to ask what is the essence of property, answering that: "It is the mark that man has put on things, the transformation that his labor, his intelligence, and his courage have made them undergo. . . . It is in general what the genius or the strength of man adds to nature as he leaves his mark in the exterior world" (ibid., p. 173). Anyone familiar with the literature on the subject in the area of political science of the age of the bourgeoisie after Locke will recognize here arguments and teachings that were used all too often. Certainly, no one would be surprised by his conclusions, in which he solemnly declares that individual property is in conformity with human nature (ibid., p. 175).

18. Ibid., pp. 179–80.

19. "The historical system that supposes tribal ownership to be anterior to individual ownership has become one of the forms of the modern theory of socialism" (ibid., p. 109).

20. Ibid., pp. 130–31.

Chapter Six

1. This passage has already been cited as an example of Fustel's attitude toward his adversaries (see chapter 4, n. 47). Fustel de Coulanges, *Histoire des Institutions politiques de l'ancienne France* (5th ed.; Paris, 1931), vol. 4: *L'alleu et le domaine rural*, p. 141. Let us note once and for all that neither Fustel nor the other participants in this debate made use of specific works of Friedrich Engels, like his *Zur Urgeschichte der Deutschen,* which first appeared in 1881–82 or his *Die Mark,* which dates from 1882. (Both can now be found in *Marx-Engels Werke* Berlin, 1962, vol. 19, pp. 425 ff. and 317 ff., respectively.) The singular historiographical contributions of Engels, like that of the American, Morgan, found no echo within the sphere of this debate, but were reflected in some writers of clear socialist observance, for example, in Paul Lafargue, *L'origine e l'evoluzione della proprietà,* trans. G. Capponi-Trenca (Palermo, 1896) [*La propriété, origine et évolution; thèse communiste* (Paris, 1895)].

2. One example of these is L. Rioult de Neuville, "Les origines de la propriété suivant M. Emile de Laveleye," *Revue des questions historiques* 26 (1891), an essay inspired by the publication of the fourth edition of Laveleye's *De la propriété* in that year. The author is not an orthodox Fustelian, and indeed agrees more with Laveleye than with Fustel on the exegesis of texts of Caesar and

Tacitus. He is hostile to Laveleye's work because it is full of "pernicious" ideas: "The communist ideas of M. de Laveleye do not therefore threaten to invade the domain of facts. They nevertheless offer a very serious danger.... They will perhaps exercise a dangerous seduction over the minds of a fairly large number of men among politicians, journalists, public functionaries, and legislators. In representing the right to landed property as an injustice, in denouncing its origin as a usurpation, one can fear that they will provoke more than one iniquitous decision, more than one denial of manifest justice. It is infinitely regrettable that the author has employed his extensive knowledge and his real talent to support such ill-founded doctrines, the only effect of which can be a maleficent influence" (p. 227). It is evident that the author has formed his own model of property along rigorously individualistic lines and that he measures, judges, absolves, and condemns according to that standard. His procedure is open and openly based in ideology.

3. On Viollet, see chapter 3, nn. 9, 10, 11.

4. Georges Platon (Pujols-sur-Dordogne 1859–Bordeaux 1916) fulfilled the modest functions of librarian of the faculty of jurisprudence at the University of Bordeaux from 1885 to the date of his death. I have been unable to discover more about him than can be found in the brief references in the *Rapport du Conseil de l'Université (de Bordeaux)—Comptes rendus des travaux des Facultés de Droit, de Médecine et de Pharmacie, des Sciences et des lettres,* Année scolaire 1916–17 (Bordeaux, 1916–17), p. 11 and pp. 37–38. He was the author of a long essay of some merit, "Le droit de propriété dans la société franque et en Germanie," *Revue d'économie politique* 1 (1887), 2 (1888), and 4 (1890).

5. Marcel Thévenin (Pau 1844–Paris 1924), after beginning his juridical studies at Aix and at Paris, concentrated in historical studies in Berlin and Göttingen, where he worked in the *seminarium* of the great historian of Germanic law, Georg Waitz. His professional life centered in the Ecole pratique des Hautes Etudes in Paris, where he was first *répétiteur d'histoire,* then *directeur-adjoint* and finally *directeur d'études.* There is a good critical discussion of his work in E. Parrot, "Marcel Thévenin," *Revue historique de droit français et étranger,* s. 4, 4 (1925): 709 ff. Among other works, Thévenin wrote an essay remarkable for its correct use of historico-juridical techniques, his "Etudes sur la propriété au Moyen Age—Les 'communia,'" in *Mélanges Renier—Recueil de travaux publiés par l'Ecole pratique des hautes études (section de sciences historiques et philologiques) en mémoire de son Président Léon Renier* (Paris, 1887). We should also note, since we are particularly concerned with the quarrel of this group with Fustel de Coulanges, Thévenin's full review and severe judgment of the first volume of Fustel's *Histoire des institutions de l'ancienne France,* in *Revue de législation ancienne et moderne* 5 (1875): 463 ff.

6. Paul Fournier, "Le dernier livre de M. Fustel de Coulanges," *Revue des questions historiques* 40 (1886): 183 ff.

7. Ernest Glasson (Noyon, Oise 1839–Paris 1907) received his *agrégation* from the faculty of jurisprudence in 1865 and taught first at Nancy and later in Paris. His works are varied and complex and include good Romanistic treatises (among which, his still valid *Etude sur Gaius et sur quelques difficultés relatives aux sources du droit romain* [Paris, 1885]), long tracts on the history of jurisprudence

and on trial law, and intelligent investigations based on civil law and juridical sociology. In the latter he demonstrates a keen sensitivity to the cultural and socioeconomic dimensions of juridical phenomena. He contributed to the debates within the Académie des Sciences morales et politiques that followed Fustel's presentation of his paper on property-holding among the ancient Germans (see chapter 3, n. 34). Also interesting to our purposes are his "Quelques observations sur le nature du droit de propriété à l'époque franque," *Revue critique de législation et de jurisprudence* 36 (1887); *Histoire du droit et des institutions de la France* (Paris, 1887–1903), particularly volumes 2 (1888) and 3 (1889); *Les communaux et le domaine rural à l'époque franque—Réponse à M. Fustel de Coulanges* (Paris, 1890); and an article which simply confirmed previous conclusions, "Communaux et communautés dans l'ancien droit français," *Nouvelle revue historique de droit français et étranger* 15 (1891): 446 ff.

8. Rodolphe Dareste de la Chavanne (Paris 1824–1911) was a typical example of a landed nobility that contributed greatly to French erudition in the nineteenth century. After completing juridical and literary studies, he received his degree as archivist and paleographer from the Ecole des Chartes in 1846, and his doctorate in law and letters in 1850. He practiced as a lawyer before the Conseil d'Etat and the Cour de Cassation and, from 1877, was *conseiller* of the Cour de Cassation. He wrote abundantly on many subjects, but his strongest interest lay in comparative history. His most specific contribution to the debate we are considering was the second of two articles on Fustel's *Recherches sur quelques problèmes d'histoire*, published in *Journal des savants*, October 1886 (see chapter 4, n. 9). (The first of these articles appeared in September 1886, and involved only Roman colonies.) I should also mention here his research on property holding in Algeria and on vestiges of primitive custom among various peoples. To avoid possible confusions, let me also mention his brother, Antoine Elisabeth Cléophas Dareste de la Chavanne (1820–1882), who was also a historian. He held the chair of history at the University of Grenoble, then at the University of Lyon, and was the author of a long work, *Histoire des classes agricoles en France* (Paris, 1854) which merits a modest place among the "preparatory work" to the debate by its explicit debt to German scholarship and by its consideration of collective property. His "Memoires sur les partages des terres que les barbares firent dans les Gaules et sur la propriété commune des Germains" in *Séances et travaux de l'Académie des Sciences morales et politiques—Compte rendu* 42 (1857) is also interesting and shows the influence of Grimm, Haxthausen, and Maurer.

9. Maxim Maximovich Kovalevski (1851–1916) was a jurist by education, a sociologist and ethnologist by vocation, and a keen and profound scholar and investigator of Russian custom. His interest in the problem of the history and the origins of landholding structures was consistent, although it was only one of the interests reflected in his varied and abundant works. He saw society in a dualistic vision embracing both the complex of popular and consuetudinarian institutions and the official and normative tradition that confronted them. See particularly his *Tableau des origines et de l'évolution de la famille et de la propriété* (Stockholm, 1890); the later essay, "Le passage historique de la propriété collective à la propriété individuelle," *Annales de l'institut international de sociologie* 2 (1896); "The Origin and Growth of Village Community in Russia," *The Archeological*

Review 1 (1888); and "Etudes sur le droit coutumier russe. II: De l'appropriation du sol par le travail en Petite Russie et en Ukraine," *Nouvelle revue historique de droit français et étranger* 15 (1891): 480 ff. Any evaluation of Kovalevski's contribution to the debate must necessarily be provisory, since it is based on studies available in Western languages and published in the West during his exile. He went through, however, a first period of intense scientific research that found expression in a good deal of *in loco* notation and in solid attempts at theoretical construction, and that saw publication in works inaccessible to us either because they are written in Russian or because they are difficult to find. An exception to this is one essay that was translated into German, *Umriss einer Geschichte der Zerstückelung der Feldgemeinschaft im Kanton Waadt* (Zurich, 1877). As he tells us in the interesting preface to his *Tableau des origines,* he had published in Russian around 1880 a work on the village community and the causes of its dissolution, as well as articles in Moscow scientific journals that completed and integrated the picture offered in this work. He tells us that in them he discussed the doctrines of Fustel de Coulanges. It is evident that our treatment of him here must inevitably be unsatisfactory because of these lacunae. See Achille Loria, "Massimo Kovalevski," *Rivista italiana di sociologia* 20 (1916). For a synthesis of his thought and a chronological picture of his works, see S. Timasheff, "The Sociological Theories of Maksim M. Kovalevski," in *An Introduction to the History of Sociology,* ed., H. E. Barnes (Chicago, 1948), pp. 441 ff.

10. Marie-Henry d'Arbois de Jubainville (Nancy 1827–Paris 1910), after studies in paleography and law, was first archivist, then the first holder of the chair of Celtic language and literature, instituted for him, at the Collège de France. After 1885 he directed the *Revue celtique.* A satisfactory biographical summary can be found in E. G. Ledos, "Arbois de Jubainville (Marie-Henry)" in *Dictionnaire de biographie française* (Paris, 1939), vol. 3. Two among the many commemorative articles are particularly interesting for their evaluation of his contribution to historical and juridical research: P. Collinet, "M. H. D'Arbois de Jubainville," *Nouvelle revue historique de droit français et étranger* 34 (1910): 399 ff., and Emile Chénon, *Notice nécrologique sur Henry d'Arbois de Jubainville* (Paris, 1912). His contribution to the controversy lies particularly in the essay, "La propriété foncière en Gaule," in *Comptes rendus de l'Académie des Inscriptions et Belles Lettres* (1887) and in the ample volume, *Recherches sur l'origine de la propriété foncière et des noms de lieux habités en France (Période celtique et période romaine)* (Paris, 1890). D'Arbois continued the polemic beyond its chronological limits in the slim pamphlet, published several years after the death of Fustel, *Deux manières d'écrire l'histoire—Critique de Bossuet, d'Augustin Thierry et de Fustel de Coulanges* (Paris, 1896). This work was a discourse on method written by a man known for his historical research, by an esteemed Celtist and an authority on charts and land grants, by one who was irritated and dissatisfied by the methodological carelessness of Fustel. Unfortunately, it was also written by an intellectual not skilled in that sort of discourse and insensitive to philosophy, and the thought reflected in the work is sometimes ingenuous, sometimes downright unpolished, revealing the cultural limitations of its author, who might have avoided venturing into a field so incongenial to his talents. We can agree with Arnaldo Momigliano, "*La citta antica* di Fustel de Coulanges," *Rivista storica italiana* 82 (1970) that the "pamphlet" can be reduced "particularly to the

attack of a *chartiste* on a *normalien*," but I could not qualify it as d'Arbois' "sharpest attack" on Fustel. This can be found in his *Recherches sur l'origine de la propriété foncière*, in which d'Arbois draws both vehemence and pertinence from historically positive data, and thus dismantles the prestidigitations of Fustel.

11. P. Collinet, "M. H. d'Arbois de Jubainville," pp. 400, 402. The purely jurid-iccal writings of d'Arbois also attest to this preparation. See *Recherches sur la minorité et ses effects en droit féodal français depuis l'origine de la féodalité jusqu'à la rédaction officielle des coutumes* (Paris, 1852); *Etudes sur le droit celtique. Le Senchus Mór* (Paris, 1881); *Etudes sur le droit celtique, avec la collaboration de P. Collinet* (Paris, 1895); his course on "La saisie mobilière dans le Senchus Mór," summarized in *Revue générale du droit* 12 (1888): 224 ff.; and *La famille celtique. Etude de droit comparé* (Paris, 1905), in which we see his pronounced taste for comparison. To get an idea of how intrinsically juridical was d'Arbois's style, it is interesting to read his introduction to the J. Durieu de Leyritz transla-tion of Henry Sumner Maine's *Lectures on the Early History of Institutions, Etudes sur l'histoire des institutions primitives* (Paris, 1880).

12. Léon Aucoc (1828–1910) was *auditeur* of the Conseil d'Etat from 1852, *conseiller* from 1869, *président de section* from 1872, and professor of administra-tive law in the Ecole des ponts et chaussées. The author of influential works in administrative history in France, he is included here for his contribution to the controversy within the Académie des Sciences morales et politiques, to which he was elected in 1877, and for his essay on "La question des propriétés primitives," *Revue critique de législation et de jurisprudence* 34 (1885).

13. On Emile de Laveleye, particularly as an economist, see chapter 2, n. 12.

14. Among Lamprecht's many works, see his *Deutsches Wirtschaftsleben im Mittelalter* (Aalen, 1960, offset reprint of the edition of 1885–86). In his 1889 essay on the origins of landholding, Fustel severely criticized the "collectivist" orienta-tion of this work, particularly in volume 1, part 1, chapters 3 and 4. Lamprecht's response has an illuminating title: "M. Fustel de Coulanges économiste," *Le Moyen Age* 2 (1889).

15. Among these specialized historians we should also mention Eugène Gar-sonnet for his *Histoire des locations perpetuelles et des baux à longue durée* (Paris, 1879), pp. 11 ff. and 511 ff. It is doubtful whether the essay of F. Bernard, "L'évolution de la propriété foncière," *Journal des économistes* 35 (1886): 173 ff. should be mentioned here. Aside from his initial declaration of agreement with Laveleye's position, he shows no real cultural connection with the matter of the controversy.

16. As we have noted (n. 14, above), it was not without reason that Lamprecht titled his severe reply to Fustel "M. Fustel de Coulanges économiste." He refers ironically to the cultural dimension lacking in Fustel's arid but clever writings.

17. "All of M. Fustel's system, as we see, rests therefore on a word" (Glasson, *Histoire du droit et des institutions de la France*, vol. 3, p. 70).

18. Ibid., pp. 70–75, and Lamprecht, "M. Fustel de Coulanges économiste," p. 131.

19. The debate between Viollet and Fustel, already noted, is recorded in the *Revue critique d'histoire et de littérature*, N.S. 22 (1886). See in particular p. 115 and p. 262.

20. Paul Fournier, who usually measures his terms carefully, refers to the cen-

tral thesis of Fustel with subtle irony: "One hardly knows whether he should admire more the talent of M. Fustel or the knowledge he expends to serve his thesis" ("Le dernier livre de M. Fustel de Coulanges," p. 197).

21. See especially Glasson and Lamprecht, as cited in n. 18.

22. Glasson, *Les communaux et le domaine rural,* p. 53. Thévenin declares that "the difficult points are not taken up and the few texts cited by the author in his study have almost all been misinterpreted" ("Etudes sur la propriété au Moyen Age," p. 122, n. 2). Kovalevski treats with irony Fustel's "ingenuity" in hermeneutic manipulation and notes regarding Fustel's interpretation of the title *de migrantibus* in the *Lex Salica:* "Fustel de Coulanges has recently given a very ingenious explanation, it is true, but unfortunately it takes into account only part of the text" ("Le passage historique de la propriété collective à la propriété individuelle," p. 210).

23. Glasson states in his preface to this study that he intended not only to respond to Fustel but that "this study was written by right of legitimate defense" (Glasson, *Les communaux et le domaine rural,* preface, p. 1).

24. Published in Paris in 1890.

25. Glasson, *Les communaux et le domaine rural,* p. 20.

26. Ibid., pp. 21, 22.

27. Ibid., passim, but particularly p. 132.

28. Ibid., passim, but particularly p. 181: "If M. Fustel had studied law, he would perhaps respect the texts more and interpret them more accurately."

29. D'Arbois de Jubainville, *Recherches sur l'origine de la propriété foncière, Préface,* p. v.

30. "When M. Fustel de Coulanges is dominated by an idea, that idea... is more powerful than his eminently varied and attentive reading; it has the upper hand of his vigorous memory; it is stronger than his erudition" (ibid., p. xxix). In his essay, *Deux manières d'écrire l'histoire,* p. 259, d'Arbois describes Fustel's historiographic procedures as "consciously or unconsciously putting above the facts one or another preconceived thesis that the facts, carefully chosen and cleverly presented, then seem to demonstrate."

31. "He reasons about shreds of sentences or about isolated words that remain in his memory from his long and perseverant reading; he writes without having a complete text before his eyes, with only fragments present in his mind. These very fragments have been transformed by the unconscious workings of his vigorous intelligence, sometimes to the point where they are unrecognizable. One may admire in him an heir of Montesquieu, but it is difficult to be at once the disciple of this great thinker... and to observe throughout a work of erudition the meticulous rules to which the Benedictines were once subjugated" (ibid., p. xxxi).

32. Ibid., p. xxvi.

33. D'Arbois de Jubainville, "La propriété foncière en Gaule," p. 66. Again in his *Recherches sur l'origine de la propriété fonci*ère, p. 117, d'Arbois reproaches Fustel with interpreting passages of Caesar in ways that depend on a completely modern notion of landholding and that are completely extraneous to the historical reality of Gallic civilization. This is a merciless judgment of a scholar as proud of his historical methodology as was Fustel.

34. Fustel de Coulanges, "Le problème des origines de la propriété foncière," part 5.

35. D'Arbois de Jubainville, *Recherches sur l'origine de la propriété foncière*, p. xxxi.

36. For this reason, d'Arbois praises Fustel's "high literary and philosophical qualities" (*Deux manières d'écrire l'histoire*, p. 74) and ridicules in him the pseudo specialist in charters and land grants and the pseudo jurist (ibid., p. 186).

37. "M. Fustel is acquainted with only two opinions on this grave problem, which are absolutely opposed to each other. Certain scholars take a position in favor of the community of lands, of agrarian communism, including all forests, all pasture lands, and even the arable lands. M. Fustel places himself alone on the other side, with the system of absolute private property carried even to all the forests, the meadows, and the uncultivated lands" (Glasson, *Les communaux et le domaine rural*, p. 77).

38. One example may suffice: Glasson criticizes the exaggerations of Maurer concerning the *Mark* in his *Les communaux et le domaine rural*, pp. 79 ff.

39. Kovalevski, *Tableau des origines et de l'évolution de la famille*, particularly lessons IV and XII, and his "Le passage historique de la propriété collective," passim.

40. Glasson, *Histoire du droit et des institutions de la France*, p. 71.

41. D'Arbois de Jubainville, *Recherches sur l'origine de la propriété*, pp. 99 ff.

42. Thévenin, "Etudes sur la propriété au Moyen Age," pp. 132 and 135.

43. Platon, "Le droit de propriété dans la société franque," (1890) vol. 4, p. 166.

44. See the concluding passages of Aucoc, "La question des propriétés primitives," pp. 119–20.

45. Lamprecht, "M. Fustel de Coulanges économiste," p. 129.

46. Kovalevski's criticisms are particularly well documented in his *Tableau des origines et de l'évolution de la famille*, pp. 48 ff. and in "Le passage historique de la propriété collective," pp. 201 ff.

47. D'Arbois de Jubainville noted in his *Deux manières d'écrire l'histoire*, p. 73, referring to the events of 1870–71, that Fustel "has not profited from the lesson that the events of that memorable year gave to us all."

48. This was true of the greater part of the authors involved in this group.

49. Glasson, *Histoire du droit et des institutions de la France*, vol. 3, p. 74.

50. Lamprecht, "M. Fustel de Coulanges économiste," p. 131.

51. Kovalevski refutes the specious argument that claims that a consuetudinary right did not exist if normative acts or notarial documents do not speak of it. He adds that, with a similar argument, some centuries hence one could claim that the forms of collective landholding now present in the Russian *mir* never had existed: "How can one ask of illiterate peasants of the later Middle Ages inventories of their holdings, inventories that probably never were drawn up, since the word of the elders sufficed to recognize the existence of the custom? What folly to claim that the archives of the lords, where such acts might have been preserved, would have found it wise to keep written proof of the invalidity of feudal rights, an invalidity that came from the very fact of the lord's usurpation of the peasants' land" (Kovalevski, "Le passage historique de la propriété collective," pp. 207–8).

52. That of Bakunin, for example. (See below, chapter 9, pp. 224 ff., for the unusual reference to him made by the Hon. Tommaso Tittoni in his long report of 20 February 1893, on the "Ordinamento dei dominii collettivi nelle Provincie dell'ex-Stato Pontifico.")

53. This is the sense of the "Etudes sur le droit coutumier russe" that Kovalevski published in the *Nouvelle revue historique de droit français et étranger* 14 (1890), as if to publicize the phenomenon to Western culture. A first more general essay was followed by a second that was both more specific and more interesting to us, subtitled, "De l'appropriation du sol par le travail en Petite Russie et en Ukraine." This article could be considered an accurate survey of the various landholding situations—many of them true and proper forms of collective property—that existed under Russian consuetudinary law at the end of the nineteenth century, particularly in the areas that were more authentically tied to Russian tradition and less exposed to Western influence. But the theme was developed in many of Kovalevski's works. See Rodolphe Dareste de la Chavanne's review of Kovalevski's book on the Caucasian people of the Ossieti, *Sovremenniy Obitchay i Drevniy Zacone* (Moscow, 1886) (Coutume contemporaine et loi primitive), in *Journal des savants,* March and May 1887.

54. A good example of this can be seen in the essay of Emile de Laveleye that we have cited so many times, "La propriété primitive dans les Townships écossais," *Séances et travaux de l'Académie des Sciences morales et politiques—Compte rendu* 124 (1885, deuxième semestre). In this essay Laveleye responds to Fustel's sharp objections and to a polemical discussion of Belot's conclusions. Laveleye relies extensively on the *Report of Her Majesty's Commission of Inquiry into the Condition of the Crofters and Cottars in the Highlands and Islands of Scotland* (1884). (See Introduction, n. 34.)

55. See chapter 3, n. 41.

56. Laveleye wrote a report of this to Italian economists in his "Il congresso dei socialisti della cattedra ad Eisenach (lettera al direttore del *Giornale degli economisti,*" *Giornale degli economisti,* s. 1, November 1875, pp. 81–89.

57. I will have more to say about Vito Cusumano in the following chapter. The popularizing book referred to in the text bears the author's date of Berlin, 6 May 1873. It was first published as "Sulla condizione attuale degli studi economici in Germania," in *Archivio giuridico* 11–12 (1874). It was later published in book form as *Le scuole economiche della Germania in rapporto alla questione sociale* (Naples, 1875).

58. See Francesco Ferrara, "Il germanismo economico in Italia," in *Nuova Antologia,* August 1875, now in his *Opere complete* (Rome, 1970), vol. 10, pp. 555 ff. This polemical essay opposing Cusumano is particularly useful to an understanding of the doctrinal discussion referred to in the text.

59. It would be unjust not to remark on the difference between the "collectivist" enthusiasms of Laveleye, who combined impassioned historiographical reconstructions with equally impassioned proposals for social policy, and the historicist vigilance of d'Arbois, who arrives at the cautious negative conclusion of the nonpresence of individual landed property among the Gauls (see above, n. 33).

Chapter Seven
1. A general introduction that is somewhat imprecise but still useful is Alberto Cencelli Perti, *La proprietà collettiva in Italia. Le origini. Gli avanzi. L'avvenire. A proposito dell'abolizione dei diritti d'uso nelle provincie ex-pontificie* (Rome,

1890). The second and enlarged edition of this work appeared in Milan in 1920 with the author listed as Alberto Cencelli and the title given as *La proprietà collettiva in Italia. Le origini. Gli avanzi. La ricostruzione. I demani collettivi per i contadini.*

2. On the *vagantivo,* see Antonio Mainardi, *Il vagantivo nelle provincie di Venezia e Rovigo* (Florence, 1888).

3. On the pensionatico, see G. Tolomei, *Sul pensionatico ossia sulla servitù di pascolo invernale delle pecore avuto riguardo alle sole provincie venete* (Venezia, 1842), and Andrea Gloria, *Vicende del pensionatico e sua abolizione utile all'agricoltura alla pastorizia e alle pecore montane delle Venete Provincie* (Padua, 1855), later included in his *Della agricoltura nel Padovano. Leggi e cenni storici* (Padua, 1855). See also *Leggi sul pensionatico emanate per le provincie venete dal 1200 a' dì nostri,* edited and furnished with supplementary documentation by Gloria (Padua, 1851).

4. There is a vast and uneven literature on these forms in the Pontifical States. For legislation dissolving them, see Giovanni Curis, *Le leggi sugli usi civici e i dominii collettivi delle provincie ex-pontificie* (Rome, 1908). For the relative jurisprudence, see Giacomo Carretto, "Raccolta della giurisprudenza relativa alle leggi abolitive degli usi civici e sui dominii collettivi nelle provincie ex-pontificie," in *Atti della Commissione per la riforma delle leggi abolitive degli usi civici e sull'ordinamento dei dominii collettivi* (Rome, 1915), vol. 3, pp. 1 ff.

5. In spite of the passage of seventy years, the most informative study remains that of Arrigo Solmi, "Ademprivia. Studi sulla proprietà fondiaria in Sardegna," which originally appeared in *Archivio giuridico* 72–73 (1904), reprinted in his *Studi storici sulla proprietà fondiaria nel medio evo* (Rome, 1937), pp. 229 ff.

6. The literature on the kingdom of Naples is vast, chaotic, and of very variable quality. The historical picture can be seen in Giovanni Italo Cassandro, *Storia delle terre comuni e degli usi civici nell'Italia meridionale* (Bari, 1943). Ample documentation and information on the legislation to abolish and dissolve these arrangements can be found in Romualdo Trifone, *Feudi e demanî. Eversione della feudalità nelle provincie napoletane* (Milan, 1909).

7. One authoritative voice was that of Antonio Salandra, "Sui demanii comunali nelle provincie del Mezzogiorno," now in *Politica e legislazione—Saggi,* ed. Giustino Fortunato (Bari, 1915). This was the text of a report signed by Salandra and dated Rome, December, 1886, as member of the Commissione pe' Demani nel Mezzogiorno.

8. See Alberto Caracciolo, "Il dibattito sul Ministero di Agricoltura, Industria e Commercio nel periodo cavouriano," *Movimento operaio* 8 (July–December, 1956), to which one might add his "I compiti del Ministero di Agricoltura e Commercio da Cavour a Depretis," in Alberto Caracciolo, *Stato e società civile—Problemi dell'unificazione italiana* (Turin, 1968).

9. *Relazione intorno alle condizioni dell'agricoltura in Italia* (Rome, 1877), vol. 3, pp. 264 ff.

10. See particularly *Notizie e studi sull'agricoltura (1876)* (Rome, 1877), pp. 288 ff., 353 ff.; *Notizie e studi sull'agricoltura (1877)* (Rome, 1879), pp. 903 ff., 1005 ff.; and *Notizie intorno alle condizioni dell'agricoltura negli anni 1878–1879* (Rome, 1882), vol. 3, pp. 230 ff., 446 ff.

11. This expression is typical of Stefano Jacini.

12. See chapter 8, pp. 174 ff.

13. The essential data on the complex events involving the *partecipanze* in Emilia-Romagna in the second half of the nineteenth century can be found in Oreste Regnoli, *Sullo scioglimento delle partecipanze. Memoria per il Municipio di Medicina ai Ministri di Grazia e Giustizia e dell'Interno* (Bologna, 1882), re-printed in his *Scritti editi ed inediti di diritto civile* (Bologna, 1900), particularly pp. 366 ff. This study gives useful data but, since it was born of a particular occasion, it is exaggeratedly partisan. The collection of data published by the Ministry of Agriculture, *Notizie e studi sulla agricoltura—Notizie sulle par-ticipanze, comunanze e università rurali esistenti nelle provincie ex-pontificie e dell'Emilia* (Rome, 1892) is most useful. Data on the *partecipanze* can be found on pp. 2 ff.

14. Regnoli, *Sullo scioglimento delle partecipanze*, pp. 366 ff. The prefect applied two opinions of the Consiglio di Stato on the matter, dating from 1862 and 1864. See Gino Marchi, "Natura giuridica, vigilanza e tutela amministrativa dei dominii collettivi nell'ordinamento della legge 4 agosto 1894, n. 397," *Rivista di diritto pubblico* 8 (1916): 182.

15. Regnoli, *Sullo scioglimento*, p. 383. First Regnoli declares (p. 353) that "the incompatibility in general of the *Partecipanze* with the public law in force [in the kingdom of Italy] is evident." Then he notes that the profound diversity of the organizational schemes of the *partecipanze*, as compared to those schemes com-mon in the unified state, "not only is a perturbing element in the juridical order, but also in the economic, as the one that takes away from useful commerce vast territories, maintaining a sort of mortmain in defiance of the most elementary and most certain principles of public economy, and further, perturbs moral order and public tranquility" (p. 353). He concludes, "that the suppression of the *Par-tecipanze* is demanded by the spirit, the principles, and the dispositions of the legislation in force in Italy; that the said suppression is likewise demanded by our public law and by reasons of public order" (p. 358). It is evident that *interest rei publicae* in its entirety challenges the indisputable schema of quiritarian property—the foundation of the new civil Code, guarantee of progress and cham-pion of liberty—or at least it is proposed as alternative to it. On Regnoli's work as a jurist, see Gian Pietro Chironi, "La formazione del Codice civile italiano e i lavori di Oreste Regnoli," now in his *Studi e questioni di diritto civile* (Turin, 1914), vol. 1.

16. See chapter 7, pp. 145 ff.

17. The stages in this polemic were: a first essay by Giacomo Cassani, *Le partecipanze di Cento e Pieve. Brano di storia del diritto medio-evale* (Bologna, 1877); an answer by Antonio Mangilli in a pamphlet published anonymously, *Le due Partecipanze di Cento e Pieve nei loro rapporti giuridico-sociali colle istitu-zioni politiche e colla civiltà odierna. Appunto di un non-partecipante* (Cento, 1877); Cassani's answer to this in a *Risposta all'anonimo autore delle 'Due par-tecipanze di Cento e Pieve.' Appendice al volumetto 'Le Partecipanze di Cento e Pieve'* (Bologna, 1877); and the counterreply of Mangilli, *L'Autore degli 'Appunti sulle Partecipanze di Cento e Pieve' al Signor Cav. Prof. Don Giacomo Cassani* (Cento, 1877). Cassani puts an end to the polemic with a small volume, *Sul-l'origine ed essenza giuridica delle Partecipanze di Cento e Pieve—Brano di storia*

del diritto medioevale (Bologna, 1878). Antonio Mangilli was a lawyer and deputy to the national Parliament from Cento. Giacomo Cassani was for many years professor of the history of jurisprudence and Canon law at the University of Bologna. A list of his other works concerning the *partecipanze,* collective property, and juridico-agrarian history in Emilia can be found in *Bibliografia del diritto agrario intermedio,* eds. Piero Fiorelli, Mario Bandini, Paolo Grossi (Milan, 1962), *sub voce.*

18. I will return to this literature from and about southern Italy and to the authors cited. I can anticipate to say that I refer, among the large number of works that Antonio Rinaldi dedicated to the problems of the "public lands" and the "social question" (terms found in the title of a later major work), to the essays, "Dei demani comunali e degli usi civici," *Archivio giuridico* 18 (1877), and "Delle prove del demanio e degli usi civici," *Archivio giuridico* 20 (1878). I refer also to Luigi Lombardi, *Delle origini e delle vicende degli usi civici nelle provincie napoletane. Studio storico-legale* (Cosenza, 1882).

19. The term is used by Regnoli in *Sullo scioglimento delle partecipanze,* p. 353.

20. In a nearly total dearth of specific historiographical instruments, we must turn to the essay of Norberto Bobbio, "La filosofia del diritto in Italia nella seconda metà del secolo XIX," *Bollettino dell'Istituto di filosofia del diritto della R. Università di Roma* (1942), and to Guido Fassò, *Storia della filosofia del diritto* (Bologna, 1970), vol. 3: *Ottocento e Novecento,* passim. Some general indications can be found in M. Quaranta, "Positivismo ed hegelismo in Italia," in Lodovico Geymonat, *Storia del pensiero filosofico e scientifico* (Milan, 1971), vol. 5, and in Alberto Asor Rosa, "La cultura," in *Storia d'Italia* (Turin, 1975), vol. 4: *Il positivismo,* part 2: "dall'Unità a oggi," pp. 878 ff.

21. Francesco Filomusi Guelfi said, in 1911, remembering his university years in Naples around 1870: "I was a student of B. Spaventa in 1867 and 1868 even though I was not registered in the Faculty of Philosophy but in that of Jurisprudence. In the University of Naples the tradition that juridical studies could not be dissassociated from philosophical studies was still respected. This was the teaching given by G. B. Vico." (See Francesco Filomusi Guelfi, "Della filosofia del diritto in Italia dalla fine del sec. XVIII alla fine del sec. XIX," now in *Lezioni e saggi di filosofia del diritto* [Milan, 1949], p. 146.) Filomusi was perhaps the jurist who testified most fully to this interdisciplinary vocation. A rapid glance at his *Enciclopedia giuridica,* but also at his many admirable university courses (often buried in humble mimeograph copy) gives us an immediate idea of the extent of his culture and of his constant insistence on the confrontation, exploitation, and enrichment of juridical data, using material drawn from the related fields of the philosophical, economic, and sociological sciences. For further discussion of Filomusi Guelfi, see chapter 10, pp. 237 ff.

22. See the description and bibliographical notes in P. Piovani, "Il pensiero idealistico," in *Storia d'Italia,* vol. 5: *I documenti* (Turin, 1973), especially the section dedicated to "La diffusione dello hegelismo nella cultura meridionale." See also Guido Oldrini, *La cultura filosofica napoletana dell'Ottocento* (Rome-Bari, 1973).

23. The review of Laveleye's book is in *Giornale napoletano di filosofia e lettere, scienze morali e politiche* 1 (1875): 399 ff. The "Rassegna" begins in the

following volume, 2 (1875): 114 ff. with a note on "The polemic concerning the social question in Germany—Treitschke and Schmoller." It is interesting to note, in the same volume (pp. 473 ff.), the interest in Vito Cusumano's essay, published that year in book form by Marghieri in Naples in the series, "Biblioteca di scienze giuridiche e sociali." In volume 3 (1876) we note a review of Adolph Wagner's treatise on political economy (pp. 340 ff.) and of Wilhelm Roscher, *Economia dell'agricoltura* (pp. 650 ff.), as well as an ample note on the recent *Inchiesta agraria in Italia* (pp. 644 ff.). See chapter 9, n. 29 for Salandra's role as rapporteur for the Commissione reale dei demani comunali nelle provincie del Mezzogiorno.

24. The essay that opens the first number of the Neapolitan juridical review, *Il Filangieri*, A. Ciccone, "Della nuova scuola economica tedesca e della sua introduzione in Italia," *Il Filangieri* 1 (1876), is devoted to economic aspects of the debate between the new German school and classically oriented currents. Non-juridical reviews, even those destined for a general readership, welcomed articles by jurists or of technical juridical orientation. An example of these in Italy is the *Nuova Antologia;* a French example is the *Revue des deux mondes.*

25. *Archivio giuridico* 11 (1874): 113–37, 240–65, 395–420; 12 (1874): 284–317. As we have already noted (see n. 23), Cusumano gathered his essays from the two volumes of the *Archivio* into a volume, published by the Neapolitan editor, Marghieri. He included a good deal of new material, changed the title slightly, and added an indicative subtitle, *La scuola del libero scambio, i socialisti cattedratici, i conservatori sociali, il socialismo.* As we have already seen, the book immediately caught the attention of Antonio Salandra, but the world of economists—which was singularly disposed to take to its own use cultural stimuli like Cusumano's work—had already reacted immediately after the appearance of the articles in Ellero and Serafini's review, with endless expressions of agreement, polemics, and discussions. Among the many works that should be mentioned here, let us limit ourselves to two by well-known authors. They stood in sharp and evident contrast to each other, and they appeared, one after the other, on the illustrious pages of the *Nuova Antologia.* They are: Francesco Ferrara, "Il germanismo economico in Italia," *Nuova Antologia* 26 (August, 1874), now in his *Opere complete,* vol. 10, and Luigi Luzzatti, "L'economia politica e le scuole germaniche," *Nuova Antologia* 27 (September, 1874). Ferrara says of Cusumano in his article (p. 997): "But the purest and most resolute adept of this school is undoubtedly Cusumano. . . . When he was still very young, my compatriot left Palermo for Pavia, where he was able, I believe, to follow the courses of Cossa, and was soon after sent to Berlin and Vienna for higher study. He has recently returned, after a year or two, a fervent and active apostle of the new economic Faith." There is hardly a mention of Cusumano in G. Majorana, "Gli economisti siciliani," *La riforma sociale* 10 (1900): 76, where the author limits himself to calling him a "follower of that which is called the Historical School." Vito Cusumano was later professor of finance at the University of Palermo.

26. Leo Valiani emphasizes this in his "L'Italia dal 1876 al 1915. II: La lotta sociale e l'avvento della democrazia," in *Storia d'Italia* (2d ed.; Turin, 1965), vol. 4, pp. 462–63, in a comprehensive cultural picture in which he devotes considerable space to new Italian economic thought. The same is true of Arnaldo Salvestrini, *I moderati toscani e la classe dirigente italiana (1859–1876)* (Florence,

1965), pp. 221 ff., but all of chapter 5 on "Il dibattito delle idee e il contrasto degli interessi" is interesting. G. Bosio refers to one aspect of this question in his "La diffusion degli scritti di Marx e di Engels in Italia dal 1871 at 1892," *Società* 7 (1951): 277. On the historians of economic thought, see the recent study by Riccardo Faucci, *Finanza, amministrazione e pensiero economico. Il caso della contabilità di Stato da Cavour al Fascismo* (Turin, 1975), pp. 62–64, which offers an excellent general picture of the science of economics in Italy and of the new Italian economic reviews, and which refers to the *Giornale napoletano di Filosofia e Lettere, Scienze morali e politiche* as the organ of the Comitato napoletano per il progresso degli studi economici (p. 64, n. 6). For other indications of the growing interest in economic thought in Italy, see Giuseppe Are, *Il problema dello sviluppo industriale nell'età della destra* (Pisa, 1965), particularly chapter 4, "La scienza economica davanti ai problemi dello sviluppo," and chapter 7, "Temi e sviluppi del revisionismo economico." See also Are, "Alla ricerca di una filosofia dell'industrializzazione nella cultura e nei programmi politici in Italia (1861–1915)," *Nuova rivista storica* 53 (1969): 44 ff.

27. Cusumano, "Sulla condizione attuale degli studi economici in Germania," p. 254.

28. Ibid., p. 125.

29. Ibid., pp. 128–29. The philosopher of law and historian of economic thought Luigi Miraglia speaks on the subject as a jurist, in almost perfect symmetry to Cusumano, in "La filosofia del diritto di Hegel, di Trendelenburg e di Ahrens e la scienza economica," *Giornale degli economisti* 2 (1875–76). The *Giornale* was founded in 1875.

30. Ferrara, "Il germanismo economico in Italia." On Ferrara as a polemicist, see the recent Riccardo Faucci, "Francesco Ferrara fra politica ed economia," *Giornale degli economisti e annali di economia,* N.S. 34 (1975), particularly pp. 458 ff. This article reproduces the text, with slight variations, of the introduction to volume 8 of the *Opere complete* of Ferrara.

31. Luigi Luzzatti's translation of Roscher, *Economia dell'agricoltura e delle materie prime,* (see also chapter 3, n. 4) opened the third series of the "Biblioteca dell'Economista"—in 1876—directed by Boccardo. Translations of the works of Schäffle, Schönberg, Wagner, and Nasse were to follow, all of which further circulated in Italy the ideas of the Historical School of economics and the ideas of the *Kathedersozialismus.* See Lucio Avagliano, "Il socialismo della cattedra in Italia (1875–1878)," *Rassegna di politica e storia* 11 (1965).

32. See Massimo Severo Giannini, "Profili storici della scienza del diritto amministrativo," now in *Quaderni fiorentini per la storia del pensiero giuridico moderno* 2 (1973).

33. See Emanuele Gianturco, "Gli studi di diritto civile e la questione del metodo in Italia," originally published in *Il Filangieri* 6 (1881) and now in *Opere giuridiche* (Rome, 1947), vol. 1. This provides an interesting contemporary view. A retrospective view, though from a period not far removed, is given in A. Rocco, "La scienza del diritto privato in Italia negli ultimi cinquant'anni," *Rivista del diritto commerciale* 9 (1911): 1.

34. See Bruno Paradisi, "Gli studi di storia del diritto italiano dal 1896 al 1946," now in his *Apologia della storia giuridica* (Bologna, 1973), which provides abun-

dant data and a cogent analysis in a broad consideration of juridical historiography before 1896 and its cultural causes.

35. Bobbio, "La filosofia del diritto in Italia," pp. 109 ff. The meager information given in Guido Fassò, *Storia della filosofia del diritto,* vol. 3, pp. 208–15, 275–78 is quite unsatisfactory.

36. See Igino Petrone, *La fase recentissimo della filosofia del diritto in Germania* (Pisa, 1895), an important event in the development of juridical philosophy in the period following unification and in the crisis concerning positivistic orientations. Icilio Vanni, a person of extreme cultural sensitivity and a true mirror of the scientific anxieties of the time, also deserves mention. See I. Vanni, *I giuristi della scuola storica di Germania nella storia della sociologia e della filosofia positiva* (Milan, 1885).

37. Cusumano, "Sulla condizione attuale degli studi," vol. 12, pp. 299.

38. Cusumano took the trouble to date his essay: the first installment bears the notice Berlin, 6 May 1873 and the second, Pavia, January 1874.

39. Cusumano says, "We allude to the historical researches on community of property in Germany, in Russia, and in America. In recent times Nasse has written on common property in England in the Middle Ages, and Henry Maine, for India. See the article, 'Les communautés de village,' of Emile Laveleye in the *Revue des deux mondes,* July, 1872, and, regarding communism in Russia, the literature cited by Wagner in his short work, *Die Abschaffung,* etc." (ibid., p. 299, n. 7).

40. See, for example, Antonio Salandra's review of *L'ancien droit* in *Archivio giuridico* 12 (1874); his review of *Etudes sur l'ancien droit et la coutume primitive";* the influential reviews of Francesco Scaduto in *Circolo giuridico* 16 (1885): 168 ff.; and those of Augusto Gaudenzi in *Rivista critica delle scienze giuridiche e sociali* 2 (1884): 161–62.

41. As in the review by Antonio Salandra in *Giornale napoletano di filosofia* 1 (1875):399 ff.

42. Pietro Bonfante, *Res mancipi e nec mancipi* (Rome, 1888).

43. Perozzi, "Gli studi di H. Sumner Maine e la filosofia del diritto."

44. Vanni, *Gli studi di Henry Sumner Maine.*

45. Lazzaro Raiberti, who writes a short work, *Dello scioglimento dei condominii nell'agro romano—Studio e proposte* (Rome, 1877), signs himself "ispettore demaniale."

46. Like Vittorio Danielli, "Segretario capo del Municipio di Fossombrone," author of *Le proprietà collettive e gli usi civici d'Italia—Storia legislazione e dottrina con raffronti alle origini e vicende delle Comunanze agrarie della provincia di Pesaro e Urbino* (Pesaro, 1898).

47. Alberto Cencelli Perti was above all an agronomer or an agrticultural technician, as a great part of his publications go to prove. He was later a senator, and the author of several publications on collective property. The publications of the period that interests us are: "Affrancazione dei diritti d'uso nelle provincie ex-pontificie," *Rivista agricola romana,* (1885); *Affrancazioni dei diritti d'uso nelle provincie ex-pontificie—Memoria seconda* (Rome, 1887); *La proprietà collettiva in Italia,* "Il socialismo e la costituzione della proprietà—Demani e terre incolte," *Nuova rassegna* 2 (1894); "Ordinamento dei dominii collettivi nelle provincie ex-pontificie e nell'Emilia," *Nuova rassegna* 2 (1894).

48. I refer to Carlo De Stefani (Padua 1851–Florence 1924), who, from 1885, held the chair of geology and physical geography in the R. Istituto di studi superiori of Florence, and to his studies: "Delle proprietà comuni e dei limiti alle proprietà private in alcune parti dell'Appennino," *Rivista europea* 9 (1878): 115 ff.; "Su resti d'istituzioni comunistiche dell'Appennino centrale," *Archivio per l'antropologia e la etnologia* 14 (1884); "Resti di sistemi agrari della antiche tribù inglesi," ibid., 15 (1885); "Di alcune proprietà collettive nell'Appennino e degli ordinamenti relativi," ibid., 18 (1888). De Stefani was a singular naturalist: he came to the study and teaching of geology after taking his *laurea* in jurisprudence at Pisa and after having taught statistics and political economy at the University of Siena. His curiosity for the history of social and political institutions remained alive during his entire life, and his last work was in fact a historical investigation of the communities of the Garfagnana. He also collaborated in the work of the Agrarian Inquiry, directed by Jacini (see "Monografia agraria sul circondario di Castelnuovo di Garfagnana," in *Atti della Giunta per l'inchiesta agraria* [Rome, 1883], vol. 10). On his complex personality and his work, see G. Stefanini, "Carlo De Stefani," *Bollettino della Società geologica italiana* 44 (1925), and the essay of his student, G. Dainelli, "Carlo De Stefani e la sua opera," in *Memorie geologiche e geografiche* (Florence, 1930), vol. 1: *1929–1930*, pp. 1 ff. Following this essay is an admirable bibliography of De Stefani's works, edited by Dainelli, of which the historical work indicated above is number 461. We still mention De Stefani again when we speak of another jurist "geologist," Tommaso Tittoni, who also was a curious and well-informed student of collective property (see chapter 9, pp. 220 ff.).

49. Girolamo Savoia, author of a book frequently used by specialists, *I demanii comunali—Note e commenti* (Benevento, 1880), was a "consigliere di prefettura," and Lorenzo Filidei, who wrote *Dei demani comunali* (Benevento, 1888), was a "Consigliere delegato della Prefettura di Benevento."

50. For example, Giovanni Raffaglio, to whom we owe the well-known volume, *Diritti promiscui, demani comunali, usi civici* (Milan, 1905).

51. One name among the many that might be mentioned is that of Ettore Ciolfi, the author of a great number of works on the subject, director and founder of the *Rivista universale di giurisprudenze e dottrina*, founded in 1887, who encouraged and welcomed essays and notes from many sources on the theme of the *usi civici* and collective and communal property.

52. I am thinking of the work of the young Guido Cavaglieri, *Il diritto di tutti gli uomini all'effettivo godimento della terra—A proposito di alcuni avanzi di proprietà collettiva nel Polesine—Osservazioni di ordine economico* (Venice, 1893), which, along with other shorter contemporary essays, attests to the author's interest in this vital and much-discussed question. Cavaglieri (Rovigo 1871–Rome 1917) dedicated himself subsequently to sociology and administrative law, and ended his days as professor of administrative law at the University of Rome.

53. The law of 24 June 1888, n. 5489 abolishing civil servitudes in the territories of the former Pontifical State (see chapter 9) inspired many such publications. To cite only the better of these works, see Luigi Frezzini, *Sull'abolizione delle servitù di pascolo legnatico e simili nelle provincie ex-pontificie* (Castelpiano, 1889); Ettore Ciolfi, *L'abolizione dei diritti civici—Appunti critici alla Legge 24 giugno 1888, n. 5489* (Rome, 1889); Cencelli Perti, *La proprietà collettiva in Italia.*

54. This was true of Fezzini's and Cencelli Perti's studies, cited in the preceding note. It was also true for the more modest A. Matozzi, *Diritti civici* (Rome, 1891).

55. The work of Giacomo Venezian is still, more than sixty years after his death, waiting for a historically viable reconstruction. Some works are almost useless: Alfredo Ascoli, "Giacomo Venezian," *Rivista di diritto civile* 8 (1916): 1 ff. is a sonorous and high-flown commemoration that suffers from wartime rhetoric, and Bartolomeo Dusi, "L'opera scientifica di Giacomo Venezian e di Gian Pietro Chironi," *Rivista del diritto commerciale* 20 (1922), part 1: 2 ff. is a listing of Venezian's more important works with notes on their contents in which, for example, only passing mention is made of the Camerino lecture discussed in our text. The presentation of Pietro Bonfante, "Giacomo Venezian," *Rivista del diritto commerciale* 13 (1915) is sketchy. The commemorative publications are not much more helpful: *La R. Università di Macerata per Giacomo Venezian* (Padua, 1933), supplement to the *Annali della R. Università di Macerata* 9, contains two ringing discourses, by Paolo Greco and Francesco Ercole, and *In memoria di Giacomo Venezian* (Messina, 1934) brings together the contributions of illustrious jurists but contributes little of significance for a historical understanding of Venezian's work. There is a little more substance, in spite of the possibilities for distortion inherent in the occasion of commemorative exercises held at the University of Padua in 1916, in the essay of Vittorio Polacco, "Giacomo Venezian," now in his *Opere minori* (Modena, 1929) vol. 2: *Tendenze scientifiche e didattiche della scuola italiana di diritto civile dopo il 1850,* section 1. Two other commemorative articles show more sensitivity to Venezian's message: Giuseppe Brini, "Commemorazione di Giacomo Venezian," in *R. Università di Bologna 1918–19* (Bologna, 1919), also in *Rendiconti delle sessioni della R. Accademia delle Scienze dell'Istituto di Bologna—Classe di Scienze morali (1918–19)* and Antonio Cicu, *In memoria di Giacomo Venezian. Commemorazione tenuta per iniziativa della Facoltà giuridica della R. Università di Macerata il 12 dicembre 1915.* (Macerata, 1916). Useful information on his teaching at Camerino can be found in Mario Chiaudano, "Giacomo Venezian nell'Università di Camerino," in *Università di Camerino—Annuario, 1932–33* (Camerino, 1933). Recently, Natalino Irti, "Le due scuole del diritto agrario," *Rivista di diritto agrario* 54 (1975): 12–14, barely touches on the place of Venezian in the history of agrarian law in Italy. The many apologetic publications celebrating Venezian as patriot, irredentist, and soldier are not even worthy of serious consideration.

56. This was the important inaugural lecture to which we have already referred, "Reliquie della proprietà collettiva in Italia," now in Venezian, *Opere giuridiche* (Rome, 1920), vol. 2: *Studi sui diritti reali e sulle transcrizioni, le successioni, la famiglia.* It was read at the University of Camerino on 20 November 1887.

57. Ibid., p. 6.

58. Ibid.

59. To speak of "relics of collective property in Italy" in 1887 meant aligning onself with a certain position, coming out in favor of a certain juridical and historical view, and against certain officially sanctioned views.

60. On Carle, a historian but above all a philosopher of law, on his historicist allegiances as they combined with positivistic sensitivities, see Gioele Solari, "La vita e il pensiero civile di Giuseppe Carle," in *Memorie della R. Accademia della Scienze di Torino* 66 (1928), part 2.

61. Carle, "Le origini della Proprietà Quiritaria presso le genti del Lazio," in *Atti della R. Accademia delle Scienze di Torino* 22 (1886–87). As the author notes, the essay is extracted from a broader study, *Le origini del diritto romano* (Turin, 1888). Since his text seems unchanged, we will cite from the volume, which is more accessible.

62. Ibid., p. 62.

63. "The truth is that the one theory as well as the other raises great doubts" (ibid., p. 63).

64. Ibid., p. 61.

65. Ibid., p. 62, n. 1.

66. "Therefore it is true that the only historical law relative to the evolution of property that at the current state of studies can be formulated would be that property, being an eminently social institution, had during all times to assume as many forms as there were stages gone through by the social organization" (ibid., p. 64).

67. Ibid., for example, the beginning of paragraph 50.

68. Ibid., p. 64.

69. Ibid., the beginning of paragraph 50.

70. Bonfante, *Res mancipi e nec mancipi*.

71. Bonfante affectionately dedicates his book to Scialoja.

72. For example, see Baldassarre Squitti, *Studio sulle res mancipi e nec mancipi* (Naples, 1885), which still was notably influenced by Maine.

73. It is time that Romanists gave up fantastic elaborations of a fragment of the Digest and got to work on placing Bonfante's protracted career and powerful work in its cultural context, particularly if such an effort escaped the overused and often undocumented cliché of Bonfante's so-called 'naturalism.' One exception is the fine essay of Paolo Frezza, "A proposito della riedizione delle 'Opere' di Pietro Bonfante," *Studia et documenta historiae et juris* 25 (1958), which hides totally respectable considerations and information under an insignificant title. Also valuable is Luigi Capogrossi Colognesi, *La struttura della proprietà e la formazione dei 'iura praediorum' nell'età repubblicana* (Milan, 1969), vol. 1, pp. 88 ff., which discusses Bonfante's information and the place of his *Res mancipi* with sensitivity to culture. Two articles inviting intelligent consideration of Bonfante's works are Mario Bretone, "Il 'naturalismo' del Bonfante e la critical idealistica," *Labeo* 5 (1959): 275 ff., and Franco Casavola, "Cronaca di una Storia del diritto romano," ibid., pp. 305 ff.

74. See, for example, Bonfante, *Res mancipi*, p. 46 or p. 277, n. 1.

75. Bonfante states this explicitly in his preface.

76. Aside from his declarations of intention contained in the preface (ibid., p. 7), see the opening of part 2, chapter 6, section 2, which he dedicates to the "Origine ed evoluzione primitiva delle res mancipi e nec mancipi." He insists on the use of "the method of induction, . . . which must be real induction and not mere historical comparison," and for which "the title of historical induction perhaps might be preferable to the more common denominations of comparative method or historical method" (ibid., p. 265). Perhaps thinking of excesses found in contemporary literature, Bonfante laments that "the abuse of simple comparison generates the suspicion of the best scholars against the method itself" (ibid.).

77. Bonfante's position on the "collectivist" doctrine is clear and firm: "The

theory is too general, but the confutation is also too general" (ibid., p. 268). He criticizes both those who "accept the principle as a postulate" and "those whom it disgusts." The only correct procedure is that of one who opposes collectivist doctrine by "basing himself in the field of history and facts themselves" (ibid.). In rejecting the tendencies to generalize that he saw as dominant in many writers, Bonfante concludes his argument by reaffirming that his one intention was "to gather from history the elements to resolve a question, not to establish a law" (ibid., p. 269).

78. "Individual dominion over a thing is not the only form of ownership, but there exists a collective form as well; however, it must be conceived of in its juridical construction. This first result is certain, and from it, the rational concept of property has truly undergone an extension and a serious alteration" (ibid., p. 267).

79. Ibid., p. 268.

80. "Rather than a mysterious, continuous development of individual property out of the womb of collective property, an eternal and undefined rise of individualism ... one could perhaps note this general phenomenon: that the perennial struggle of the two elements generates a perpetual alternation, according to whether one or the other of the two elements impresses its character more unmistakably on property, which will be collective or social over a broad or narrow category of objects when the social element is prevalent" (ibid.). After making this statement and foreseeing eventual criticism on the part of an evolutionist reader, Bonfante clarifies: "In order to avoid being misunderstood, I will say that this movement of recurrence is not and never would be, in its concrete manifestations, a return to the older conditions" (ibid., p. 269).

81. Ibid., pp. 268–74.

82. Ibid., p. 275.

83. Ibid., pp. 278 ff.

84. See *exempli causa*, ibid., pp. 272–73.

85. Ibid., p. 268 and p. 270, where this is clearly indicated.

86. Ibid. Cf. pp. 271–72 with pp. 274–75.

87. Ibid., p. 267, where he speaks alternately of "common doctrine" and "dominant opinion."

88. See Carle, *Le origini del diritto romano*, p. 63.

89. As, for example, in Padelletti, "Delle professioni di legge nelle carte medievali," *Archivio storico italiano* 20 (1874).

90. Padelletti, *Storia del diritto romano* (Florence, 1878), p. 148.

91. Ibid., p. 147. ("The hypothesis of the community of the soil in the most antique times, in which certainly Germanic echoes were not unknown, was first posed by Niebuhr, followed by Puchta, 2:235 and also by Mommsen, *Römische Geschichte*, book 1, chapter 13; cf. Sumner Maine, *L'ancien droit*, p. 244. However, all information from the ancient writers and the character of laws relating to land exclude this hypothesis.")

92. An example of Padelletti's capricious interpretations is noted in Francesco Calasso, *Medioevo del diritto* (Milan, 1954), p. 405.

93. Aside from the few references in Paradisi, "Gli studi di storia del diritto," pp. 124–25, but particularly n. 38 of p. 124, see A. Coletti, "Brugi Biagio," in *Dizionario biografico degli italiani* (Rome, 1972), vol. 14.

94. Brugi began his career with a number of studies in which he views the jurist and juridical science in close relation to general cultural trends: *Il moderno positivismo e la filosofia dei giureconsulti romani* (Urbino, 1880); "I romanisti della scuola storica e la sociologia contemporanea," *Circolo giuridico* 14 (1883); plus reviews of works by Barsanti, in *Archivio giuridico* 24 (1880), by Vadalà Papale, in *Rivista critica delle scienze giuridiche e sociali* 1 (1883) and in *Archivio giuridico* 31 (1883); by Cimbali, in *Archivio giuridico* 34 (1885); and by Vanni, in *Archivio giuridico* 36 (1886).

95. See Brugi's review of Pio Barsanti, *La socialità del sistema della proprietà privata* (Lucca, 1880), in *Archivio giuridico* 24 (1880): 503.

96. *Archivio giuridico* 37 (1886): 57 ff.

97. Scaevola, 20.1 *Si servitus vindicetur* (8, 5, 20, 1). The problem that Scaevola poses is the following: "quid iuris" if, after a group of proprietors had acquired a piece of woodland adjacent to their own holdings, keeping it "pro indiviso" and enjoying it in common, one of them alienates his own single holding?

98. Schupfer's review is in *Nuova Antologia* 91 (3, 4) (1887): 376 ff.

99. To be fair to Brugi, we must clarify that he had the decency to recognize his mistake concerning method. See Biagio Brugi, "Dei pascoli comuni nel diritto romano, nel diritto germanico, nel diritto italiano," in Federico Gluck, *Commentario alle Pandette* (Milan, 1900), book 8, p. 312.

100. A picture of this is offered by Cassandro, *Storia delle terre comuni*, pp. 18 ff.

101. Brugi's essay, "Studi sulla dottrina romana della proprietà," *Archivio giuridico* 42 (1889) is disappointing, in spite of its title, since it contains only two modest contributions to the question, one on "La occupazione abusiva del suolo pubblico," and the other on "Condizione giuridica dei fiumi."

102. In his review of the French translation of Maine's *Ancient Law* (*Archivio giuridico* 12 [1874]), Salandra had seen in that work a possible salutory influence on Italian juridical science and states: "Several rancid or distorted opinions, taught even now in our schools, might be revised or corrected" (p. 621).

103. See this chapter, pp. 133 ff.

104. Cassandro, *Storia delle terre comuni*, pp. 247 ff., expounds on this doctrinal school.

105. See the works cited in n. 18, this chapter.

106. Nicola Santamaria, *I feudi, il diritto feudale e la loro storia nell'Italia meridionale* (Naples, 1881), particularly chapters 11 and 12.

107. See the works cited in n. 18, this chapter.

108. Cammillo Del Greco, *Dei demanii nelle provincie meridionali d'Italia* (Vasto, 1885).

109. Rinaldi, "Dei demani comunali e degli usi civici," p. 205.

110. Lombardi, *Delle origini e delle vicende degli usi civici*, p. 45. (The citation is to the pagination of the second edition [Naples, 1885] and not of the first edition [Cosenza, 1882], cited in n. 18 of this chapter. The text, in any event, shows no modification from one edition to the other.)

111. These are the well-known "Istruzioni da seguirsi da' Commissari incaricati col decreto de'23 di ottobre del caduto anno 1809 per la divisione de' demanj," fixed by royal decree of 10 March 1810 (found in *Supplemento del Bullettino della Commissione feudale*, n. 6 [Naples, 1829]). Article 11 states: "The customary

rights of the Communes on the domains that formerly were held by the barons and by the Church, or that should on general principles be regarded as more or less extensive remains of the domain that the populations held on the land, or as reserves set aside by the grantor to assure the aforementioned populations the means to subsist, can be reduced to three classes...."

112. Giambattista De Luca, *Theatrum veritatis et justitiae,* book 4: *De servitutibus praedialibus, usufructu et utroque retractu* (Rome, 1669), discourse 42: "De usu lignandi seu pascendi et aquandi competente civibus vel incolis et an per loci dominum prohiberi possit."

113. As we have said, this is a characteristic of all of the local wisdom concerning the *usi civici* and the *dominii collettivi.*

114. Salandra, in his review of Laveleye's work (p. 401), complains that Laveleye did not treat the situation in southern Italy, where "the demesnial institution" was "a most notable and original part of public law in the kingdom of Sicily." He nevertheless recognizes that it would be difficult for a foreigner unfamiliar with the Italian scene to find the documents, particularly since there had been no Italian work in doctrine acceptable not only for its information but also for its critical foundations since Davide Winspeare. Francesco Schupfer, while recognizing the merits of Lombardi's *Delle origini,* in his review of the work (in *Nuova Antologia* 64, no. 34 of series 2, 1882), expresses his dissatisfaction with the historical and juridical bases of this doctrine. A scholar well familiar with southern literature, Giovanni Abignente, in an enthusiastic review of Schupfer's work on the *usi civici* in the community of Apricena (in *Rivista italiana per le scienze giuridiche* 5 [1888]: 99), also summarized what had been written on the subject before. He was obliged to note that there had been only fortunate insights and half-hearted attempts that did not arrive at much, "by lack of historico-juridical culture," both in the older and the more modern authors, citing Lombardi, Rinaldi, and Del Greco. Bonfante makes interesting and acute observations, although of a general nature, on the older Neapolitan doctrine in his *Res mancipi e nec mancipi,* p. 267.

115. Francesco Schupfer notes this honestly, taking the old and the new Neapolitan doctrine as his point of departure when he prepares to study certain *usi civici* of the Capitanata. See Schupfer, "Degli usi civici e altri diritti del comune di Apricena," in *Atti della R. Accademia dei Lincei, Classe di scienze morali, storiche e filologiche,* s. 4, vol. 2 (1886), p. 276.

116. There are excellent passages in Paradisi, "Gli studi di storia del diritto italiano," pp. 110 ff. Although he dedicates a good deal of attention to Pertile and Schupfer, Francesco Calasso, "Il centenario della prima cattedra italiana di storia del diritto," now in *Storicità del diritto* (Milan, 1966), pp. 14 ff. is sonorous but elusive.

117. Antonio Pertile, *Storia del diritto italiano dalla caduta dell'Impero romano alla Codificazione* (Padua, 1874), vol. 4: *Storia del diritto privato,* chapter 5, "Storia delle proprietà fondiaria," particularly pp. 317 ff. There is some contradiction in the mass of data that Pertile offers us; for example, the divergent affirmations on p. 188 and p. 317, which were also noted by Schupfer.

118. See Pertile's later monograph, "I laudi del Cadore," in *Atti del R. Istituto veneto di scienze lettere ed arti,* s. 6, vol. 8 (1888–89), pp. 127 ff.

119. Pertile, *Storia del diritto italiano*, pp. 317–324. Note, among the many notes, the numerous references to the *laudi*, that is, to the pactlike agreements of the various *regole* [agrarian associations]. On certain contradictions in Pertile regarding the origins of individual property, see Schupfer, *L'allodio—Studi sulla proprietà dei secoli barbarici* (Turin, 1886), later reprinted in *Digesto italiano* 2 (Turin, 1893), part 2, p. 16, n. 1.

120. At least volume 4, on private law, was printed at that date. In the second edition (Turin, 1893), volume 4 does not show substantial changes: the literary documentation is augmented to take note of the works of Laveleye, Calisse, Gaudenzi, d'Arbois de Jubainville, and Fustel.

121. Giuseppe Salvioli, "Consortes e colliberti secondo il diritto longobardo-franco. Contribuzione alla storia del diritto di proprietà in Italia," in *Atti e memorie della Deputazione di storia patria per le Provincie modenesi e parmensi,* s. 3, vol. 2 (Modena, 1883), p. 1: "The Longobards carried into Italy the village community, which was based on relations between members of a common descent. When the community lost its intensity, individual property took its place. . . . Germanic communism thus probably had its best days in Italy. It must at first have been extensive, then when the cultivated lands became private property, it remained limited to grazing lands and forests. . . . Violence and abuses were not lacking to transform all the lands to private domains. The members of the ancient consortium disappeared and went to enlarge the ranks of the agricultural common people. . . . Of the ancient agrarian communism only a few traces remained in the *partecipanze*." (See also ibid., conclusion of the final section, "Risultati"). Salvioli returned to the subject nearly ten years later in a review of the work of a Belgian scholar. See Giuseppe Salvioli, "I 'Masuirs' del Belgio e le recenti questioni sull'origine delle proprietà communali in Europa," *La Scuola positiva*, vol. 2 (1892). The volume he was reviewing was Paul Errera, *Les Masuirs—Recherches historiques et juridiques sur quelques vestiges des formes anciennes de la propriété en Belgique* (Bruxelles, 1891). It was a simple collection of acts, dating from 1174 to 1886, concerning the "masuirs," an extended territory, largely woodlands, situated in Belgium in the commune of Chatelineau and administered communally until 1872, the date of a resolution of the General Assembly of the community in favor of a division of the community property. The resulting controversy was extremely interesting, as it turned around the very nature of the holding that up to that time had been administered in common. The same Salvioli wrote an article that deserves only brief mention, "La proprietà fondiaria in Sicilia (una questione storica sugli usi civici)," *La Rivista Popolare* 2 (1894):65 ff.

122. Carlo Calisse, "Le condizioni della proprietà territoriale studiate sui documenti della provincia romana dei secoli VIII, IX, e X," *Archivio della Società romana di storia patria* 7 (1884):329, and 8 (1885).

123. Augusto Gaudenzi, *Sulla proprietà in Italia nella prima metà del Medio Evo—Cenni* (Bologna, 1884), particularly pp. 3ff, pp. 30 ff.

124. Giovanni Tamassia, *Le alienazioni degli immobili e gli eredi secondo gli antichi diritti germanici e specialmente il longobardo* (Milan, 1885), particularly pp. 18 ff.

125. Pasquale Del Giudice, "Sulla questione della proprietà delle terre in Germania secondo Cesare e Tacito," now in *Studi di storia e diritto* (Milan, 1889), p.

244. The essay was written in 1886, however, and the author says that it was occasioned by the paper read by Fustel before the Académie des Sciences morales et politiques in Paris.

126. Schupfer, *L'allodio,* and "Degli usi civici." The latter was a paper read 16 January 1887, which appeared in the acts of the Accademia dei Lincei of 1886, but Schupfer expressed himself clearly on the subject from the moment of his first work, "Degli ordini sociali e del possesso fondiario appo i Longobardi," in *Sitzungsberichte der Kaiserlichen Akademie der Wissenschaften-Philosophisch-historische Klasse* 35 (1860) (pp. 79 ff. of the extract published separately the following year in Vienna).

127. Several years later this orientation entered into the manuals without difficulty. It was fully evident in the new manuals of the history of Italian law by Salvioli and Calisse, which appeared around 1890, and which dedicated a good deal of attention to the history of private law. See Giuseppe Salvioli, *Manuale di storia del diritto italiano delle invasioni germaniche ai nostri giorni* (Turin, 1890), pp. 33 ff., and Carlo Calisse, *Storia del diritto italiano* (Florence, 1891), vol. 3, pp. 188 ff.

128. I refer to Heusler, "Die Rechtsverhältnisse am Gemeinland in Unterwalden," and to August von Miaskowski, *Die schweizerische Allmend in ihrer geschichtlichen Entwicklung vom XIII. Jahrhundert bis zur Gegenwart* (Leipzig, 1879).

129. Schupfer, *L'Allodio,* pp. 14–16.

130. Even if occasionally different tendencies crop up. An example is offered by the review of Schupfer's *L'allodio* by Cesare Nani in *Rivista italiana per le scienze giuridiche* 1 (1886): 446, in which he appeals explicitly to Fustel in order to temper the totally "collectivist" approach of Schupfer (p. 447).

131. Tamassia, *Le alienazioni degli immobili.* At the time Tamassia was twenty-five.

132. On Tamassia's complex intellectual career, see Gian Piero Bognetti, "Nino Tamassia," *Archivio di studi corporativi* 3 (1932). A short and dependable summary can be found in Paradisi, "Gli studi di storia del diritto italiano," pp. 130–35.

133. "It is necessary to strip oneself of every preconceived idea that could disturb the pure examination of the facts, [a thing that] unfortunately sometimes happens among the historians of law. They take as a point of departure for their examinations the concept of property according to Roman law, and not finding the information given by writers on Germanic property in accord with it, they do their best to torture [that data] to reduce it to an affirmation of their opinions" (Tamassia, *Le alienazioni degli immobili,* p. 18).

134. "If one takes as a starting point Roman law, which presents the summit of perfection in juridical thought, the particulars of certain ancient rights cannot be understood appropriately, nor can they be explained according to the real nature of the things. Our late and lamented Padelletti, for example, called the doctrines of Laveleye brilliantly expressed errors, and called primitive forms of property imperfect and barbaric, because he always had before him the Roman idea of property" (ibid.).

135. "More than from some new interpretation or correction of the few sources

that speak of this, we can profit from and use the examples of the various forms of property offered by many peoples in the different degrees of evolution of the institution itself. This is the method of investigation that Maine and Lubbock propose, and historical studies have gained much from it" (Tamassia, *Le alienazioni degli immobili,* pp. 21–22).

136. See ibid., pp. 39 ff. for Tamassia's repetition of Maine's famous argument on the aphorism, *nemo in communione potest invitus detineri* (see chapter 1, p. 44) and for his use of Slavic and Oriental ethno-juridical material collected by Maine and Laveleye.

137. Ibid., p. 19.

138. Ibid. Besides a very full use of the great works in history and economics of Roscher, Hanssen, Inama-Sternegg, see p. 19, n. 1 for his reliance on economic works of a technical nature, such as Fedele Lampertico, *Economia dei popoli e degli stati* (Milan, 1876), vol. 3: *La proprietà,* and Stefano Jacini, *La proprietà fondiaria e le populazioni agricole in Lombardia* (Milan, 1854). He cites lexicons and purely linguistic works so frequently that we forego giving precise examples.

139. Gaudenzi, *Sulla proprietà in Italia,* p. 3. Gaudenzi has just warned his readers of another erroneous intellectual position, that of "supposing that with the same words identical ideas and institutions were always intended." His reading of Maine had evidently been careful, encouraging him toward methodological renewal and liberating his thought.

140. See above, n. 136.

141. Maine, *Ancient Law,* chapter 4.

142. Tamassia devotes eloquent pages to this in *Le alienazioni degli immobili,* pp. 39 ff.

143. Gaudenzi, *Sulla proprietà in Italia,* p. 5. Because of just this conviction, Guadenzi, although he accepts the methodological orientation of Maine, refuses the proposals for a return to the past contained in Laveleye's work.

144. Schupfer, *L'allodio,* p. 14; "Degli usi civici e altri diritti del comune di Apricena," particularly p. 282. Schupfer likes to describe Germanic property-holding as more "human" and, as such, contrasted to "that passed on to us by the tough-minded genius of Rome." He continues to speak in these terms even in the later *Il diritto privato dei popoli germanici con speciale riguardo all'Italia* (Città di Castello, 1907), vol. 2: *Possessi e dominii,* p. 104.

145. Schupfer, *L'allodio,* p. 16, n. 1.

146. Tamassia, *Le alienazioni degli immobili,* p. 19.

147. Spencer states, on the subject of the origins of property: "The desire to appropriate, and to keep that which has been appropriated, lies deep, not in human nature only, but in animal nature: being, indeed, a condition to survival" (*The Principles of Sociology,* ed. Stanislaw Andreski [Hamden, Conn., 1969], part 2, chapter 15, p. 485). Nevertheless, Spencer adhered, as far as agrarian property was concerned, to the thesis of the primitive community of property. The influence of Spencer among Italian jurists of the end of the century is a fact that is well known and well documented, hence we need not go into it here. This was the epoch of "Social Darwinism" and "Social Spencerianism," to use the terms repeated in the title of Vadalà Papale's famous study, published in 1882. Much of the demand for innovation that ran through the thought of the time is translated

into evolutionism of a Spencerian sort. This was true of the ideological matrices of the so-called juridical socialism, that is, of the reformist current within official juridical science. (A growing number of studies on this subject may be found in *Quaderni fiorentini per la storia del pensiero giuridico moderno* 3–4 [1974–75].) Limiting ourselves to the men most interested in our concerns, an explicit adherence to Spencerian evolutionism can be seen in Gaudenzi, *Sulla proprietà in Italia*, p. 4; and Tamassia, *Le alienazioni degli immobili*, contains an explicit tribute to Darwin (p. 29, n. 6).

148. Spencer and Maine both influenced methodological renewal in jurisprudence. They, as well as the Historical School, are the cultural events most important for the development and formulation of juridical science in the latter part of the nineteenth century in Italy. It is understandable that the most vigilant and sensitive philosopher of law in Italy in the early 1890s, Icilio Vanni, dedicated two nearly contemporaneous and culturally sensitive studies to Maine and Spencer. It was a way of paying homage to two men who had inspired the interpretive work of the preceding decade. I refer to his *Gli studi di Henry Sumner Maine*, which we have already discussed, and "Il sistema etico-giuridico di Herbert Spencer," an essay that serves as a preface to the Italian translation of Spencer's *Justice: Being Part IV of The Principles of Ethics* (London, Edinburgh, New York, 1891), *La giustizia* (Città di Castello, 1893).

149. "Communal real property transforms itself into familial. . . . Finally, with the detachment of the individual from the family, there emerges the last form of property, not only private, but likewise individual" (Tamassia, *Le alienazioni degli immobili*, p. 21); "We have begun with the village community. . . . Nevertheless, a little at a time, the possession of the land solidified in each *fara* or family, and beside the ancient community of the village is placed the new community of the family, until this same community ceded its place to individual property" (Schupfer, *L'allodio*, p. 44); "Laveleye is right when he says that it was only a consequence of a last stage in an evolution, sometimes very long, that property became definitively constituted and arrived at being that absolute, sovereign, personal right defined in our code" (Schupfer, "Degli usi civici e altri diritti del comune di Apricena," p. 282).

150. It is useless to repeat myself. See the preceding notes, particularly nn. 133 ff.

151. See Salvioli, "Consortes e colliberti," p. 43. Salvioli was aware of the development of the controversy, and therefore also of the "individualistic" system with Fustel and Seebohm as its spokesmen. Nevertheless, even in his essay on "I 'Masuirs' del Belgio," p. 350, which was published several years after his study of the *colliberti*, he concludes that "one can explain the origin of the communal goods of free populations only if one admits to the existence of a primitive agrarian communism." See also Gaudenzi, *Sulla proprietà in Italia*, p. 30; Tamassia, *Le alienazioni degli immobili*, pp. 34 ff.; Schupfer, *L'allodio*, passim, but particularly p. 92; Schupfer, "Degli usi civici e altri diritti del comune di Apricena," p. 282: "One remnant of the ancient collectivity is the so-called *public* goods and the possessions left in the *common property* of neighbors, even after private property was introduced."

152. Schupfer shows evident pleasure as he contemplates the extraordinary

richness of both the old and the new material: "Now [in 1886] we can, with the aid of richer sources, penetrate even further into the life of these organisms" (L'allodio, p. 26).

153. Ibid., pp. 27 ff. give an example.

154. Codice diplomatico longobardo dal DLXVIII al DCCLXXIV, con note storiche osservazioni e dissertazioni di Carlo Troya (Naples, 1853), vol. 3, document 481.

155. "Fiuvaida, Figuaida ist die versio langobardica für pascua communia" (Heinrich Brunner, Deutsche Rechtsgeschichte, (2d ed.; Leipzig, 1906), vol. 1, p. 283. More generally, see Gian Piero Bognetti, "La proprietà della terra nel passaggio dal mondo antico al medio evo occidentale," in Dopo il primo convegno internazionale di diritto agrario—Valutazioni e prospettive in un incontro di giuristi italiani (Milan, 1956), p. 132; Bognetti, "I beni comunali e l'organizzazione del villaggio nell'Italia superiore fino al Mille," Rivista storica italiana 77 (1965): 382 and passim.

156. Such as Volpe, Hartmann, Dopsch, Schneider. See a first listing in Codice diplomatico longobardo, ed. Luigi Schiaparelli (Rome, 1929), vol. 1, p. 161.

157. In Schiaparelli's reconstruction (ibid., document 49, pp. 161 ff.) the text is given thus: "sorte de terra nostra quem avire visi sumus de fiuvvadia in loco Arena, sicut alii coliverti nostri ... prope terra Stavili."

158. See Cassandro, Storia delle terre comuni, pp. 76–77. Already in 1903 Hartmann had written a short paper to reject Schupfer's interpretation. See Ludo Moritz Hartmann, "Fiuvaida," in Vierteljahrsschrift für social und Wirtschaftsgeschichte 1 (1903), particularly p. 126.

159. Schupfer, L'allodio, pp. 37–38. An identical interpretation is given in Gaudenzi, Sulla proprietà in Italia, p. 33.

160. Cassandro, Storia delle terre comuni, p. 77.

161. We will cite at least one, that of the Neapolitan philosopher of law, Luigi Miraglia, "La storia della proprietà nella filosofia del diritto," in Atti della Accademia Pontaniana 16 (Naples, 1884), a mediocre exposition in which the theories of Maine and Laveleye are accepted.

162. Philosophy of the law is the discipline that he taught in various universities throughout his academic life, until his tragic death in the disastrous earthquake at Messina in 1908.

163. Pietro Cogliolo (1859–1940) was professor of Roman law at Camerino in 1880, at Modena in 1883, at Genoa in 1889, where he remained until 1934. There is a celebrative volume, In memoria di Pietro Cogliolo, in which, among the ridiculous and unpolished discourses cast in the rhetoric of the period, only Giorgio Bo's is somewhat readable.

164. I refer particularly to Cogliolo, La teoria dell'evoluzione darwinistica nel diritto privato (Camerino, 1882), read 21 November 1881, as the inaugural lecture to his course in Roman law at the University of Camerino. This lecture signals the beginning of his reflections on methodology. The young author at first professed a rigorous evolutionism, an exaggerated faith in principles of biology, and a crude conditioning of the juridical dimension by biological data. His successive development leads, for us, particularly to his Studi storici sull'evoluzione del diritto in Italia (Turin, 1884); to his collection of Saggi sopra l'evoluzione del diritto privato

(Turin, 1885); to the notes on "Gli studii sul diritto degli antichi popoli ariani (a proposito dell'opera del Leist, Graeco-italische Rechts Geschichte 1884)," *Archivio giuridico* 34 (1885); and to his *Filosofia del diritto privato* (Florence, 1888).

165. See particularly the essay, "L'evoluzione giuridica" and the author's postscript in *Saggi sopra l'evoluzione del diritto privato*, pp. 25 ff. What is more, Cogliolo, undoubtedly preoccupied that the term "evolution," solidly lodged in his title, might be misunderstood by the reader, felt it necessary to clarify in his preface that "the evolution that gives this book its title means to indicate only the progressive path followed by a thing that rises up and grows: any idea of an exaggerated philosophical orientation which this word might make one suspect does not correspond to the nature of this work." This is poor jurist's philosophy, that contains many good intentions and little rigor.

166. Cogliolo, *Filosofia del diritto privato*, p. 151.

167. Ibid., p. 188.

168. I have attempted above, in the pages dedicated to Maine, to make clear the mixture of evolutionistic and historicist elements in this thought.

169. D'Aguanno, "Sulla ricerca genetica del diritto di proprietà," p. 13.

170. Ibid., pp. 18 ff.

171. Ibid., pp. 19 ff.

172. See at the beginning of this essay the frequent recourse to paleoethnological data and the constellation of sonorous adjectives like "neanderthalian" or "quaternarian," with lengthy citations not only to Spencer and to Letourneau, but also to the French anthropologist and paleoethnologist Gabriel de Mortillet, whose schematic systemization of prehistoric epochs influenced a good part of European culture.

173. The entire text is of great interest and can be found in Cogliolo, *Filosofia del diritto privato*, pp. 151–52.

174. D'Aguanno, "Sulla ricerca genetica del diritto di proprietà," p. 24.

175. Ibid., p. 13.

176. Guido Padelletti, *Storia del diritto romano*, edited and annotated by Pietro Cogliolo (2d ed.; Florence, 1886), p. 220, note h.

177. The eloquent introduction to the section of the law of things in Cogliolo, *Filosofia del diritto privato*, p. 150 says: "Modern science has confirmed a fact beyond doubt, with many works of research, particularly those comparing different peoples and times. It is, that the first form of property was the common form and that for that reason individual property has not always been known." This could have been written by Maine or Laveleye, and seems to aim at reducing the absolute character of individual property. See also D'Aguanno, "Sulla ricerca genetica," pp. 13 ff.

178. Cogliolo, *Saggi sopra l'evoluzione del diritto privato*, pp. 14–16 and 108–9; *Filosofia del diritto privato*, pp. 150, 152–54; D'Aguanno, "Sulla ricerca genetica," passim.

179. See n. 176. Cogliolo edited and annotated the second edition of Padelletti's *Storia* after the author's untimely death.

180. Cogliolo, *Filosofia del diritto privato*, pp. 152–53.

181. See Cogliolo's praise of Laveleye and Maine who, according to him, had

the merit of making "complete and precise" concepts that before were "mistily fantastic," in *Saggi sopra l'evoluzione del diritto privato*, pp. 10, 14. See also his appreciation of Maine, who, in his use of the comparative method, seemed "the most felicitous example of a similar attempt," in his "Gli studi sul diritto degli antichi popoli ariani," p. 512. See finally Cogliolo, *Filosofia del diritto privato*, pp. 153, 163, 168, 193, to remain within the area of law relating to land. As for D'Aguanno, he cites Laveleye and Maine at every turn.

182. See chapter 2, p. 69. See note 55, above, for bibliographical data on Venezian.

183. Venezian took his *laurea* in 1882, the year of the publication of Regnoli's memorial to the Ministry of Grace and Justice, written in support of the city of Medicina, which concluded a long series of written defenses.

184. On Venezian's knowledge of the German language and German and Austrian juridical literature, see Polacco, "Giacomo Venezian," p. 68. The first volume of Venezian's lengthy study, *Dell'usufrutto, dell'uso e dell'abitazione* (Naples), was to appear in 1895 and, according to indications in the text (p. 194), it fell within the scope of Pasquale Fiore, *Il diritto civile italiano* (Naples, 1886–99).

185. Polacco, "Giacomo Venezian," p. 74.

186. Venezian was in Camerino from the academic year 1885–86 as *professore incaricato* in civil law and Roman law. From 1886–87 he was *straordinario* in Roman law and *incaricato* in history of Roman law and the civil code. In 1887–88 he was made *professore ordinario* when he was given the chair of Roman and civil law (see Chiaudano, "Giacomo Venezian nella Università di Camerino," pp. 88–89). In 1889 he married Emma De Sanctis, of a Camerino family of ancient and noble lineage.

187. Antonio Cicu, "In memoria di Giacomo Venezian," p. 12 mentions Venezian's explorations in the Sibilline Mountains.

188. I will speak at length later of Zucconi (see chapter 9, pp. 203 ff.). Without anticipating too much, suffice it to say that Giovanni Zucconi was deputy to the national Parliament for the district of Camerino, and, as such, he watched over the interests of the members of the collectives of the Marche. Venezian was unreserved in his praise of Zucconi in the inaugural lecture that interests us here (see "Reliquie," p. 29).

189. Already in a short article on criminal anthropology that he wrote while he was a student, Venezian expressed his gratitude to his teacher, Enrico Ferri, for his training "to the positive method even in criminology" (Polacco, "Giacomo Venezian," p. 73), and he always considered himself dedicated to a method of solid positive analysis. Perhaps his passion for research in the field of agrarian law arises from this attitude, since it is a law that arises from the furrows of the soil and that is written in them as in geology (ibid., pp. 74–75). Perhaps also his constant insistence—noted by all of his critics—on investigations into economic and social structures and into the economic foundations of juridical institutions come from that same attitude. The remarks on this question of Paolo Greco and Francesco Ercole (*La R. Università di Macerata per Giacomo Venezian*, respectively, p. 27 and p. 36) are interesting. Venezian's talented student at Messina and close friend, Francesco Ferrara, also frequently remarked on the

solidity of Venezian's preparation in economics (see Ferrara, "L'usufrutto dell'azienda," in *In memoria di Giacomo Venezian*, p. 161, and "Un secolo di vita del diritto civile," now in his *Scritti giuridici* [Milan, 1954], vol. 3, p. 284). Pietro Bonfante is one among others who note that "for his treatment of usufruct he even travels to observe in place and from real life certain original forms" (in *Idea nazionale*, 26 November 1915).

190. See Venezian, *Dell'usufrutto*, vol. 1, chapter 3 of book 1, devoted to "Gli usi pubblici e gli usi collettivi" [public and collective customary rights], pp. 153–224.

191. Venezian was to return to the theme of his inaugural lecture at Camerino in a group of essays at the end of his career. See "Del disegno di legge sugli usi civici e sui domini collettivi," written in 1910, and "Necessità e criteri di una legislazione sugli usi civici per le varie regioni d'Italia," written in 1911, now in *Opere giuridiche*, vol. 2, pp. 319 ff. See also "Sull'acquisto delle servitù civiche" and "Sul possesso di fatto di usi civici," ibid., pp. 482 ff. Of great interest is the memoir, written in 1906, "Circa il disegno di legge sulla colonizzazione italiana," ibid. pp. 281 ff., particularly pp. 290 ff., in which he speaks of the work in Parliament of Zucconi, Tittoni, and Salandra, a subject to which we shall return.

192. See Venezian, "Lezioni di legislazione rurale dettate nella R. Università di Messina nell'a. a. 1898–99," collected and mimeographed through the efforts of Giulio Basile. This course treats collective property in Italy fully, and we shall return to it later.

193. See Venezian, "Reliquie," p. 6 for the eloquent declarations that I have cited above, p. 134.

194. At the beginning of his inaugural lecture, Venezian serenely describes the complexities of the movement, the polemics, and the discussions regarding individual property. Foreseeing clearly what might come, he says: "Individual property, held to be the highest expression and the necessary completion of liberty, is today under discussion. And as the economic abstraction is justly condemned, which claimed to reach harmony with the cooperation of all of the egoistic efforts, as it is impossible to think of an indefinite development of the individualistic principle, bolstered by property, without foreseeing a moment at which all social ties would be broken and the struggle for existence, contained by the law, would be transformed into a savage war of all against all, those who are impatient or violent demand the suppression of individual property; the moderates want to see it surrounded by limits and guarantees; the optimists expect that it will find mitigating factors from within itself and will find the recognition of its duties in the necessity of its existence. Some declare that by the natural force of things social property will be constituted to stand beside individual property; others insist that this come through intelligent and conscious will" (ibid., p. 4).

195. Ibid., p. 29.

196. Venezian declares that the efforts to liquidate and redistribute collective holdings were vain in a passage of splendidly unprejudiced analysis and firm understanding. He sees the political, social, and administrative factors involved as these: "The political factors: the interest of an oppressive government in keeping alive hatred and antagonism between the classes of society, using the arm of the demesnial question; the social factors: the substitution of the *homines novi* for the

ancient nobility, of the bourgeois *nouveaux riches,* more determined and tenacious in defending the interests that they had formerly combatted and that had become theirs; the administrative factors: the ineptitude and the ignorance of the functionaries charged with the application of the laws and the formation of a patronage system and of local tyrannies" ("Reliquie," p. 17).

197. Ibid., p. 27.

198. Ibid., p. 28.

199. Ibid., p. 29.

200. See Venezian, *Lezioni di legislazione rurale,* p. 11.

201. I will anticipate in only one instance: see ibid., p. 94.

202. Venezian, "Reliquie," p. 28.

203. Ibid.

204. Ibid., p. 5.

205. Ibid. These terms are given as they appear in Venezian's transcription.

206. Ibid., p. 4.

207. Ibid., pp. 7 ff.

208. Obviously, I refer to the well-known study of E. Betti, "Falsa impostazione della questione storica dipendente da erronea diagnosi giuridica," in *Studi in onore di Vincenzo Arangio Ruiz* (Naples, 1953), vol. 4.

209. Venezian, "Reliquie," p. 6.

210. Ibid., p. 8.

211. Ibid., p. 19.

212. Ibid., p. 27.

213. "Compared to private law, forced into the logical categories of Roman jurisprudence, it is not recognizing them that would have been impossible, but understanding them" (ibid., p. 14).

214. Ibid., p. 12.

215. In other regions, for example, in particular sectors of the Alpine chain, the phenomenon of collective property assumed the particular form of common property among coheirs in consortium which Giangastone Bolla described in his "Le comunioni familiari ereditarie dei territori alpini e la legge 16 giugno 1927 sul riordinamento degli usi civici," written in 1947; in his "Per la tutela e il progresso della proprietà comune dei montanari nel quadro della Costituzione italiana" (1948); in his "Terre civiche e proprietà comuni di consorti coeredi regolate dal Laudo" (1951); and in his "Famiglia e proprietà terriera nelle regioni di montagna ed in particolare nella Valle d'Ampezzo" (1951), now all in his *Scritti di diritto agrario* (Milan, 1963).

216. Venezian, "Reliquie," pp. 10–12.

217. Francesco Filomusi Guelfi, "Diritti Reali—Appunti sulle lezioni raccolti per cura di E. Piola Caselli e G. Briolini" (mimeographed course notes for the academic year 1888–89, University of Rome), pp. 108 ff.; "Trattato dei diritti reali—Lezioni redatte per cura degli studenti A. Matozzi, C. Mapei, E. Nannini" (mimeographed course notes for the academic year 1891–92, University of Rome), pp. 219 ff.; "Diritti reali—Appunti sulle leżioni di diritto civile raccolti per cura di G. Manganelli" (mimeographed course notes for the academic year 1894–95, University of Rome, pp. 242 ff. The course offered during the academic year

1888–89, according to Filomusi himself, would seem to be, if not his first such course—he offered a course in real law in 1885–86—at least the first such course to be consolidated into a published summary, albeit only in mimeographed form (see Filomusi Guelfi, *Diritti reali—Esposizione pel corso 1901–02* [Rome, 1902], p. 131).

218. The signs are not lacking. One indication is the review that L. Cantarelli devotes to Francesco Fisichella, *Sul fondamento del diritto di proprietà* (Catania, 1881) in *Rivista delle scienze giuridiche e sociali* 1 (1883): 194, a review that was in agreement with Schupfer's views. Fisichella's approach was founded on and articulated according to antiquated patterns. It arrived at the definition of property as the "practical respect of the personal selfness of each person, in itself, in its attributes, in its relations, in its end, and in its activity" (p. 89). Cantarelli objected that this was "an *a priori* theory of property [that] I cannot believe capable of practical results. According to me, it would, on the contrary, be useful to examine the different forms in which property has manifested itself in different historical times. From this historical study it would probably appear that it 'responded to the sentiments and to the necessities of men during the centuries in which it was prevalent' (Laveleye, part 22)." Laveleye's lesson in historiography shows here its most striking fruits. For another example, see the study of G. Capone, "Saggio di ricerche sulle vicende della proprietà e sulla origine del possesso in Roma," *Archivio giuridico* 50, 51 (1893). This study was written—I believe it was his only publication—by a young man killed prematurely, in fact, before the appearance of this essay (see the note of the editors of the review at the head of the essay). For this reason, it has a provisory and "green" quality, but it is indicative of how the "collectivist" notions had taken root in a talented young man.

219. Nicola Coviello, "Delle cosiddette servitù irregolari nel diritto civile italiano," *Archivio giuridico* 41 (1888).

220. Gian Pietro Chironi, *Istituzioni di diritto civile italiano* (Turin, 1888). I pick out Chironi because the young Sardinian civilist (he was born at Nuoro in 1856) had demonstrated in a monographic study, *Il darwinismo nel diritto* (Siena, 1882) and in his inaugural lectures at Siena and Turin, *Il diritto civile nella sua ultima evoluzione* (Siena, 1882) and *Sociologia e diritto civile* (Turin, 1885) not only an acute sensitivity to the problem of the methodological renewal of the working instruments of the jurist, but also a cultural open-mindedness in perfect harmony with the demands of the times.

221. Emanuele Gianturco, "Dei diritti reali, Lezioni di diritto civile, raccolte dal prof. Michele De Palo" (Naples, 1892), now in *Opere giuridiche* (Rome, 1947), vol. 1. The same considerations that we have offered for Chironi are valid for Gianturco. See his inaugural lecture at Naples, *L'individualismo e il socialismo nel diritto contrattuale* (Naples, 1891), or even his first study on methodology, "Gli studi di diritto civile e la questione del metodo in Italia," *Il Filangieri* 6 (1881).

222. Cimbali, "La proprietà e i suoi limiti nella legislazione civile italiana," p. 125.

223. Ibid.

224. Ibid., p. 132.

Chapter Eight

1. Fedele Lampertico, *Economia dei popoli e degli Stati* (Milan, 1876), vol. 3: *La proprietà*.

2. "Laveleye has greatly clarified how the notion of property, as we now imagine it, is not as it was originally imagined, but is instead as it came to be developed along with the progression of civilization. Property first manifests itself in collective form" (ibid., p. 34).

3. "I agree with Laveleye that property, far from presenting in every age that one form that today we are accustomed to imagining as the prevalent, or indeed as the essential, has developed successively" (ibid., p. 35).

4. Ibid.

5. Achille Loria, *La rendita fondiaria e la sua elisione naturale* (Milano, 1880), pp. 15 ff.

6. Salvatore Cognetti de Martiis, *Le forme primitive nella evoluzione economica* (Turin, 1881). Salvatore Cognetti de Martiis (d. 1901) first felt profound sympathy for the lessons of the Historical School, as we can see in his youthful essay, *Delle attinenze tra l'economia sociale e la storia* (Florence, 1865). He later inclined toward positivistic naturalism. See Pasquale Jannaccone, *Salvatore Cognetti de Martiis*, in "Biblioteca dell'Economista," series 4, vol. 5, part 2 (Turin, 1901), pp. clxxxiii ff., and Giovanni Carano Donvito, *Economisti di Puglia* (Florence, 1956), pp. 401 ff., reproduced from an article published in *Rivista di politica economica* 31 (1941).

7. See Cognetti de Martiis, *Le forme primitive*, introduction.

8. Ibid., p. 150.

9. Cognetti cites the volume of essays that I have cited several times, *Systems of land tenure in various countries*, edited by the Cobden Club (2nd ed.; London, 1870).

10. See Alberto Caracciolo, *L'inchiesta agraria Jacini* (Turin, 1973), pp. 33 ff.; Domenico Novacco, "L'inchiesta Jacini," in *Storia del Parlamento italiano*, gen. ed. Niccolò Rodolico (Palermo, 1963), vol. 17, passim.

11. "Relazione finale sui risultati dell'Inchiesta agraria," in *Atti della Giunta per l'Inchiesta agraria e sulle condizioni della classe agricola* (Rome, 1881–86), vol. 15, (1886). On the final report by Jacini, see Caracciolo, *L'inchiesta agraria Jacini*, pp. 90 ff.

12. Jacini was dominated by the idea—which was common among economists, jurists, and politicians—that the only situation that merited regulation was individual property, and that the existence of rival landholding situations ought to be reduced to a minimum. As a result, he disapproved generally of all forms of community holding and he showed a clear preference for dissolution of such structures according to article 681 C. C. 1865, limited only by the economic feasibility of the division (ibid., pp. 101–2, where a group of historical institutions are qualified simply as "anachronisms").

13. See, for example, the minutes of the meeting of 9 March 1884, and the speeches of the commissioners Nobili Vitelleschi and Damiani (*Atti della Giunta*, vol. 15).

14. The term *agiatissimi proprietari* is used by the commissioner Agostino

Bertani. See Caracciolo, *L'inchiesta agraria Jacini,* p. 34 and p. 51, n. 41 (for his citation of Bertani).

15. There is now a good biographical and bibliographical treatment of Agostino Bertani, B. Di Porto, "Bertani Agostino," in *Dizionario biografico degli italiani* (Rome, 1967), vol. 9. Some interesting scraps of information on his work for the Inquiry can be found in the older and apologetic work of Jesse White Mario, *Agostino Bertani e i suoi tempi* (Florence, 1888), vol. 2, chapter 23, pp. 396 ff. The Bertani papers in the Museo storico del Risorgimento in Milan do not seem to be very relevant to his work within the Inquiry (see *Le carte di Agostino Bertani,* ed. Leopoldo Marchetti [Milan, 1962]). A global assessment of Bertani's work with the Giunta can be seen in Caraccioli, *L'inchiesta agraria Jacini,* passim, but one should keep in mind the critical observations of Luigi Cortesi, "Agostino Bertani e l'inchiesta agraria Jacini," in *Società* 15 (1959).

16. I know of no study that treats the work of Ghino Valenti (1852–1921) on a historiographical level. In order to know something about him we must even today refer to the commemorative publications. One that is valuable is Pietro Bonfante, "Ghino Valenti," *Rivista d'Italia* 24 (1921), part 1, pp. 348 ff. See also G. Rocca, "Un economista agrario: Ghino Valenti," *La riforma sociale* 32 (1921), and Filippo Virgilii, "Ghino Valenti nella vita e nella scienza," *Studi senesi* 30 (1921). Valenti's own full introduction to his collected *Studi di politica agraria* (Rome, 1914) may be useful, as it is in many respects a sort of cultural autobiography, or at least an interesting backward glance that gives full indications of the genesis of many of his works.

17. The official rapporteur for the entire fifth district—comprising not only the territories of Perugia, Ascoli Piceno, Ancona, Macerata, and Pesaro, but also those of Rome and Grossetto—was senator Francesco Nobili Vitelleschi. Given the vast extent of the territory, he was authorized to assume special collaborators for each zone. For the Marche, Valenti, as we know, carried on this valuable work. (See Valenti, *Studi di politica agraria,* introduction, p. ix, n. 1.) Senator Nobili Vitelleschi's official recognition of his work can be found in "Relazione del Commissario Marchese Francesco Nobili Vitelleschi, senatore del Regno, sulla Quinta Circoscrizione (Provincie di Roma, Grosseto, Perugia, Ascoli Piceno, Ancona, Macerata e Pesaro)," *Atti della Giunta,* vol. 11, part 1: Provinces of Rome and Grosseto (Rome, 1883), introduction; part 2: Provinces of Perugia, Ascoli Piceno, Ancona, Macerata, and Pesaro (Rome, 1884), introduction.

18. Novacco, "L'inchiesta Jacini," pp. 257–58.

19. This was an old idea of Bertani's. He first raised it when, in 1871–72, he proposed to the Chamber of Deputies an inquiry into "the conditions of the agricultural class and principally of the workers of the soil in Italy." On Bertani's position in the parliamentary debate immediately preceding the launching of the Inquiry and in the sessions of the Giunta, see Caracciolo, *L'inchiesta agraria Jacini,* pp. 24 ff.

20. Bertani, "Proposta di inchiesta parlamentare sulle condizioni attuali della classe agricola e principalmente dei lavoratori della terra in Italia (Discorso pron. il 7 giugno 1872)," in *Scritti e discorsi di Agostino Bertani,* chosen and edited by Jesse White Mario (Florence, 1890), p. 156. The speech is also reproduced in the *Discorsi parlamentari di Agostino Bertani* (Rome, 1913), pp. 188 ff.

21. Caracciolo, *L'inchiesta agraria Jacini,* pp. 29–31.

22. See Bertani, "Proposta di inchiesta parlamentare," p. 160.

23. The observation comes from Luigi Cortese, "Agostino Bertani e l'inchiesta agraria Jacini," pp. 588–89. Cortese concludes his persuasive reassessment of Bertani thus: "Although his vision was insufficiently rationalized and his ideology echoed the deficiencies inherent in democracy in the period of the Risorgimento, he was one who sensed clearly the negative relationship that was being established between the policy of the Italian state and the masses of the people."

24. On the relationship between Bertani and Cattaneo, see Di Porto, "Bertani Agostino," passim. I refer in the text to Carlo Cattaneo, *Opere edite ed inedite,* ed. Agostino Bertani (Florence, 1881–92).

25. *Atti della Giunta,* vol. 10, "Relazione del Commissario Dott. Agostino Bertani, Deputato al Parlamento, sulla ottava circoscrizione (Provincie di Porto Maurizio, Genova e Massa Carrara)" (Rome, 1883), pp. 750 ff. but particularly pp. 755 ff.

26. "Appendice dell'onorevole deputato Agostino Bertani alla Relazione finale sui risultati dell'Inchiesta agraria," in *Atti della Giunta,* 15 (Rome, 1886), p. 115.

27. This emerges clearly (ibid., p. 116) as Bertani states: "How great and how varied is the attention lavished on production, and to how great an extent does it surpass that destined for the agricultural laborers, [who are] left for the most part the mercy of the philanthropy of proprietors and lessors, [who are bound to] the slow progress of the entire agricultural labor force and to the gradual righting of interests that have been wronged or displaced, [who are dependent on] the working out of the laws of compensation and equilibrium that govern moral, physical, and economic facts. But whoever considers the workers of the soil as a separate class, predestined to that office and to those fatiguing labors, forgets that they compose the immense majority of the nation, and that for that reason their interests are the true general interests, while those of the rich and the proprietors, of the industrialists and those in commerce, are particular interests and class interests."

28. His father, Teofilo Valenti (1802–79) was a practicing lawyer and taught civil law at the University of Macerata.

29. See the remarks on this subject in Bonfante, "Ghino Valenti," p. 350, and in Virgilii, "Ghino Valenti nella vita e nella scienza," p. 4.

30. This paper was the *Rassegna Provinciale di Macerata.* It began publication 6 April 1879, and had as a program to "constitute a useful collection of practical studies in which, day by day, the activities and events that make up the life of the Province will be registered" (*Rassegna Provinciale di Macerata,* vol. 1 (1879), p. 2, n. 1). Agriculture had an important place among these events, first, because it was undoubtedly the salient fact of an area like Macerata, at the time totally agricultural, but also since agriculture was a subject dear to the paper's director. It is interesting to note the prominence given to anything regarding the Agrarian Inquiry (see, for example, the anonymous article, "L'inchiesta agraria," ibid., vol. 1. [1879] n. 3 of 20 April 1879) and, among the local news, the great amount of information relating to the work of the subcommittees for the Inquiry at Macerata and in neighboring provinces.

31. These commissions for agriculture had been instituted with the law, L. 23

dicembre 1866, n. 3452. On their activities during their first decades of operation, see P. Corti, "I comizi agrari dopo l'Unità (1866–1891)," *Ricerche di storia sociale e religiosa*, n. 3 (January–June, 1973). The *Rassegna provinciale di Macerata* (vol. 1 [1879], p. 7, n. 1) gives news of the election of Valenti as president of the *Comizio agrario* of Macerata, and the *Rassegna* was always prodigal of news concerning the commissions.

32. Rocca, "Un economista agrario: Ghino Valenti." Valenti himself liked to remember this episode in his intellectual autobiography and mentioned it in the introduction to a late collection of studies, *Studi di politica agraria*, p. ix.

33. Bonfante, "Ghino Valenti," p. 349, rightly insists on the complexity of Valenti's personality, which was made up of a blend of the scientific and the practical.

34. This is true even though statistics would always remain the object of Valenti's research, and one cannot deny him the merit of having founded agrarian statistics in Italy on a solidly scientific base.

35. The official rapporteur, senator Francesco Nobili Vitelleschi, recognized his debt to Valenti in the introductions to books 1 and 2 of volume 11 of the *Atti della Giunta*. Several years later, Valenti gathered the fruit of his labors into a separate volume, destined for the general reader, *L'economia rurale nelle Marche* (Macerata, 1888). For the most part, this work gives the same information and the same data that can be found in the official *Relazione* of the Inquiry for the territories of Ascoli Piceno, Macerata, Ancona, and Pesaro. (The cover of the volume, but not the title page, indicates: I: *L'agricoltura* and announces that a second volume on "La proprietà fondiaria e la classe agricola nelle Marche" is in press. I do not believe that this second volume was ever published.) The complex task of collecting materials was divided between committees and subcommittees. Ghino Valenti was secretary of the subcommittee for Macerata; Giovanni Zucconi was president of the subcommittee for Camerino (see *Atti della Giunta*, vol. 11, book 2, introduction, n. 1). On Zucconi and on future legislation concerning the *servitù di pascolo* in the former Pontifical States, see chapter 9, pp. 203 ff.

36. There is not the slightest doubt that the movement that several years later upset the government's projects for the *servitù di pascolo* in the former Pontifical States—in which movement Zucconi played a prominent role—had its origin in the work done in the Marche for the Inquiry. On the parliamentary itinerary of the Grimaldi bill and the interesting debate in the Chamber, see the whole of the next chapter.

37. *Atti della Giunta*, vol. 11, book 1: Provinces of Rome and Grosseto, pp. 592 ff. offers a largely negative assessment of the "encumbrances on property" and places the servitudes of pasturage, woodcutting, tillage, etc., among them. Book 2: Provinces of Perugia, Ascoli Piceno, Ancona, Macerata, and Pesaro, p. 178, includes the servitudes of pasturage in the province of Perugia under "encumbrances on property." (After reporting both favorable and contrary opinions on the question, the commissioners opt in Salomonic fashion for a fitting reduction of such structures.)

38. *Atti della Giunta*, vol. 11, book 2, chapter 18.

39. Ibid., p. 487.

40. Valenti had already shown that he knew Laveleye's work well in a brief but

tightly written article on collective agrarian organizations in the Marche, published in his *Rassegna* toward the beginning of 1880 and dated Macerata, February 1880. He remained profoundly influenced by Laveleye's thought, and Laveleye could not avoid leading him to Maine. See Valenti, "La proprietà collettiva nell'Appennino marchigiano," in *Rassegna provinciale di Macerata*, vol. 2 (1880), n. 48 of 29 February 1880, and n. 49 of 7 March 1880.

41. *Atti della Giunta*, vol. 11, book 2, p. 487.

42. Ibid., pp. 488 ff. Valenti examines separately the *Consorzio* of the families who lived in Serra S. Abbondio, the *Università* of Frontone and of the twelve families of Chiaserna (Cantiano), various *Comunanze*, among them those of Vestignano (Caldarola), Brunforte (Sarnano), Sassoferrato, Serralta (Sanseverino), Cacciano (Fabriano), and various customary rights.

43. Ibid., pp. 506 ff., where he gives a historical documentation that is exceptional in a work of applied economics.

44. Ibid., pp. 512 ff.

45. Ibid., pp. 495–96.

46. Ibid., pp. 506–7.

47. Ibid., p. 512.

48. Valenti himself tells us of his explorations in the Appennines of the Marche (see "La proprietà collettiva nell'Appennino marchigiano"). Another mention of his investigative excursions for the Inquiry between 1876 and 1880 can be found in Valenti, *L'economia rurale nelle Marche*, p. 5.

49. *Atti della Giunta*, Vol. 11, book 2, p. 513, but also all of section 3, pp. 512–16.

50. Ibid., p. 514.

51. "Thus from the *Comunanza* one passes gradually to the simple right of usage on pasture and woodland, to the servitudes to graze animals and cut wood.... This servitude is evidently connected to, and is nothing other than a trace of, that primitive form of ownership common in other epochs and which, only in some places and because of special conditions of the soil and, consequently, to special needs for working it, has been able to last for so long a time and occasionally, as in the case of our *Comunanze*, has passed through the vicissitudes of the centuries to arrive to our day in its full integrity. And we are reinforced in this belief by the fact that the rights of usage hardly ever are extended to all of the territory of the commune, nor to all of its inhabitants.... The rights of usage take the name of servitudes improperly, and it is an error to consider them as accessory rights that were superimposed on the principal right of the proprietor, while it is more reasonable to believe that the contrary happened. The right of the user represents the primitive natural occupation of the land when the land was res nullius: the right of the proprietor, on the other hand, has feudal origins and represents the usurpation or the protection that in the Middle Ages meant just about the same thing" (Valenti, "La proprietà collettiva nell'Appennino marchigiano," from the second part, *Rassegna* n. 49 of 7 March 1880).

52. Valenti, *Il rimboschimento e la proprietà collettiva nell'Appennino marchigiano* (Macerata, 1887), now in *Studi di politica agraria*, pp. 74–75.

53. Valenti informs his reader in the introduction to his *Studi di politica agraria*,

p. ix, that the writings collected there all were written between 1887 and 1894. An exception to this is the essay, "L'Italia agricola nel Cinquantennio 1862–1912," which was written for the publication of *Cinquanta anni di storia italiana (1860–1910)* (Rome, 1910) by the Accademia dei Lincei. All of the studies, however, had their origin in the enormous amount of work done by Valenti in the context of the Inquiry.

54. Valenti, *Le forme primitive e la teoria economica della proprietà: Saggio* (Rome, 1892). The first phase of Valenti's research seems indeed dominated by this prevalently scientific interest, but one must add that it was to be a continuing interest. See Valenti, *La proprietà della terra e la costituzione economica—Saggi critici intorno al systema di Achille Loria* (Bologna, 1901), and the article from his later years, "La proprietà e l'evoluzione economica," *Rivista d'Italia* (30 June 1918).

55. In his *Il rimboschimento* of 1887, aside from his use of Maine and Laveleye, Valenti relies mainly on Roscher (translated into Italian, as we have seen, in Boccardo's "Biblioteca dell'Economista") and Lampertico. Only in his work of 1892 does he demonstrate full consciousness of all of the ramifications of the literature on the dispute, not only in Italy, but in Europe in general.

56. The Hon. Zucconi would later take pains to praise Valenti's work within the Inquiry in his report of 30 March 1886, on the Grimaldi bill (see *Atti Parlamentari. Camera dei deputati. Legisl. XV, 1a sessione 1882–86. Documenti, Disegni di legge e relazioni, n. 270 A*, p. 12. On this question, see the next chapter.

57. Valenti, *Il rimboschimento*, prefatory letter, p. 3, nn. 1 and 2.

58. See the next chapter.

59. Ibid., p. 91.

60. Valenti, "La proprietà collettiva nell'Appennino marchigiano." The citation comes from the first part, *Rassegna* n. 48 of 29 February 1880.

61. I refer to the listing of Valenti's writings up to 1912 in appendix to his *Studi di politica agraria*. This listing was presumably drawn up by Valenti himself or with his approval, and the article of 1880 does not appear in it.

62. Already in the first study on "La proprietà collettiva nell'Appennino marchigiano," Valenti held the Appennine *Comunanze* worthy of being better known and studied precisely because of their character as alternative to the proprietary structures that were recognized officially and regulated and protected by the law. The "curious" economist placed them in the singular perspective of their diversity, of their belonging to a juridical tradition that was completely different. He states: "Hidden from the eyes of the world and almost completely unknown, there exist in our Appennines since time immemorial institutions that by the special character of their mode of being—poles apart from the economic and juridical theories that generally reign over the rights to ownership today—appear to merit particular consideration."

63. Valenti, *Il rimboschimento*, p. 79.

64. "Our Civil Code, unlike the preceding codes, has a special title concerning community of goods, but does not treat it as a form of property different from the individual, but as a simple modification of the latter, which is the only one to be consecrated in our legislation" (ibid.). It is true that in the civil Code of 1865 a special title, the fourth, in the second book, is reserved for community property. It

follows the title dedicated to the "modifications of property." Furthermore, it is mentioned again in a section that bears the general heading: "Of goods, of property and its modifications." The 1865 Code envisioned the problem of coproperty as the Roman and Romanistic tradition had done, and followed the resolution of the problem of that tradition.

65. Valenti, *Il rimboschimento*, p. 74.

66. The argument recalls Maine even in the choice of specific points to contest, like the conception of the community as a source of discords, and the individualistic vision according to which no one can be constrained to remain *invitus* in a community. These are two points on which the English jurist had insisted particularly.

67. When Valenti speaks of the scholars who had recently contributed to the revival of interest in collective forms of appropriation, he insists on Laveleye's contribution to theory: "Maine was among the first . . . then Laveleye . . . cast great light on this order of unexplored facts, and instituted over them a new theory of property" (*Il rimboschimento*, p. 56).

68. Ibid., p. 82.

69. Valenti was to include himself among those "who do not share that holy horror of collective property that fills many people" (ibid., p. 85). He emphasizes his distance from those fearful individualists, but he also shows political understanding of the problem, and goes on to say that he had taken his place among those who were "free of this preoccupation because profoundly persuaded that one cannot combat the absoluteness of the socialist theories with theories that are not less absolute" (ibid., p. 82). For a clarification of his attitudes toward socialism, see his lengthy dedication to Fedele Lampertico of his *Le forme primitive e la teoria economica della proprietà*, a gesture that can be understood as an act of self-defense against the accusations that Lampertico had made of him.

70. All of the 1887 essay is shaped by the principle that it is necessary to carry out "a beneficent transformation in the conditions of property." Taking "strictly into account the needs and the rights of the populations of the mountains, . . . it is necessary that the question be studied not only from the purely economic point of view, but also and more from the social side" (*Il rimboschimento*, p. 47).

71. Ibid., p. 49.

72. Ibid., p. 80.

73. *Atti della Giunta*, vol. 11, book 2, p. 514.

74. Valenti, *Il rimboschimento*, pp. 82 ff.

75. Ibid., pp. 86–87: "The dissolution of these rights in favor of the users could be judged as an offense to the principle of property, given that property is considered as an inalienable right descended from the heavens on a ray of divine light; given, that is, that no one wants in any way to abandon the overly absolute concept of it held, not so much by the ancient jurisconsults, as by the older philosophers and jurists. If instead property is considered as a social institution, as determined by the contingent economic needs of the people and subordinate to those needs, and as drawing rights and corresponding duties from those needs, it would be difficult, we believe, to demonstrate that the social good would be better served by dissolution of these rights in favor of the proprietors, rather than in favor of the users."

76. Valenti, *Le forme primitive,* p. xvi, from the letter of dedication to Fedele Lampertico.

77. The essay is in fact dated 20 January 1892.

78. Ibid., pp. 4 ff.

79. "It should be considered whether this property that we adore is really a natural product, or whether our fathers have for the most part molded it artificially. Only the primitive form is natural and spontaneous, determined only by economic exigencies and founded on equality of right. Certainly, one cannot say as much for the *dominium quiritarium,* which makes its appearance in history as a privilege of the Roman citizen, nor for feudal property, which is even more clearly a privilege, and not even for modern property, formed by the Napoleonic Code after the Roman type, and which did much to consecrate economically the feudal privileges that the French Revolution had abolished only politically" (ibid., p. viii).

80. "The forms that followed after the primitive and egalitarian form—as differentiated from this first, which was completely founded in economic need—underwent the influence of the political nature of the various peoples, so that they could not be explained only by economic causes; and in that fact lies the superiority of the first form to the following forms" (ibid., pp. 87–88).

81. Ibid., p. viii.

82. "With the current order we have liberated the worker from political servitude, but we have not succeeded in liberating him from economic servitude" (ibid., p. 88).

83. Ibid., pp. 63 ff., but particularly p. 64.

84. "It is said that individual private property is the necessary complement of liberty. And this is true, but this cannot refer to anything other than the ownership of the fruits of labor" (ibid., p. 78), since "the general character of the right that the individual can claim over natural elements of production is that of a personal *right of usage*" (ibid., p. 68).

85. Valenti so states in his lengthy dedication and justification addressed to Senator Lampertico (*Le forme primitive,* p. vii).

86. His considerations of that vestige of collective property widespread in the lower Venetian *terra ferma* known under the name of *vagantivo* provide a good example of this. This collective structure consisted in the right of certain populations to fish or to cut marsh plants in the vast stretches of the tidal *valle* and was viewed with disfavor by writers as an obstacle to a reclamation of the lands. Valenti clarifies: "We say instead: Did the proprietor really have a right to reclaim the land? Had he the right to call his those immense extensions of land, over which the population had from time immemorial exercised a right of usage? Why should greater weight not be given to the sacred title of the laborer, backed by economic need, that alone can justify ownership, rather than to the title based on a concession of a privilege accorded to a single individual? Where is the necessity, the social utility that justifies such a monopoly? . . . We are not [arguing] in favor of the vagantivo, this right proper to a primitive and uncultured population; we merely support the right of the user in preference to that, in our opinion secondary, of one who believes himself invested with the property" (ibid., p. 39).

87. This is Valenti's conclusion expressed in a work dated 1891: "The collective

form of property does not seem *inevitably destined to disappear*... It is not *irreconcilable with the progress of culture*.... *The principle on which collective property is founded is not in antagonism with the one that inspires cooperation*, for the very simple reason that collective property is only a *special aspect of cooperation*, and the *agrarian comunanza*, as it survives today, is a true cooperative association—better, a *perfect* cooperative association. *Cooperation* is not inapplicable to agriculture" (Valenti, "Cooperazione e proprietà collettiva," *Nuova Antologia* 118 [1891], 16 June 1891), p. 322.

88. See particularly Valenti, *L'associazione cooperative. Contributo alla teorica economica della cooperazione* (Modena, 1902), and *Cooperazione rurale* (Florence, 1902).

89. Charles Gide, "De quelques nouvelles doctrines sur la propriété foncière (*Progress and Poverty*, by Henry George)," *Journal des économistes*, 4ᵉ série, 6ᵉ année, 22 (1883).

90. Alfred Fouillée, "Les études récentes sur la propriété," *Revue des deux mondes* 63 (1884). The article was later reprinted in his *La propriété sociale et la démocratie* (Paris, 1884).

91. Paul Leroy-Beaulieu, *Le collectivisme, Examen critique du nouveau socialisme* (Paris, 1884).

92. See the two articles by A. Mangin, "Le socialisme et la propriété devant l'Académie des Sciences morales et politiques," *L'économiste français*, Saturday 19 September and Saturday 26 September 1885, and "Revue de l'Académie des Sciences morales et politiques," *Journal des économistes*, 4ᵉ série, 8ᵉ année, 30 (1885).

93. Fouillée's essay is complex, and merits attention also for its theoretical aspects. He starts from the notion that the social question is knocking at the gates, that "more than ever, social problems demand our attention" (Fouillée, "Les études récentes sur la propriété," p. 762). From there, he gives an acute analysis of the individualistic theory of property as a basic principle that circulates throughout the koine of the modern age. This principle is expressed in the axiom that "the individual thus becomes proprietor of external objects by the same reason that he is proprietor of himself" (ibid.). (See Grossi, "Usus facti. La nozione di proprietà nell'inaugurazione dell'età nuova," *Quaderni fiorentini per la storia del pensiero giuridico moderno* 1 [1972] and Grossi, "La proprietà nel sistema privatistico della Seconda Scolastica," *La Seconda Scolastica nella formazione del diritto privato moderno* [Milan, 1973]. See also Costa, *Il progetto giuridico* [Milan, 1974].) Fouillée reviews critically the traditional postulates of classical individualism. Here, for example, is his reflection on the principle of occupancy, which shows an attentive reading of Maine and a basic agreement with him: "As far as a foundation in nature is concerned, we hold that there are two rival rights. All of the philosophers and the jurists have spoken of one of these, calling it the right of the *first occupant;* the other they have almost neglected. We propose to call this other the right of the last to arrive or of the last occupant" (Fouillée, "Les études récentes," p. 763). Here we see a rethinking of the relation between property and labor and a start at breaking down the connection between "individual effort" and the value of the thing, in the name of a more complex and more comprehensive view of the social dimension of that value (pp. 766–67).

94. Leroy-Beaulieu attempts to undermine all of the constructions and the documentation pertaining to collectivism by examining them in a continual spirit of derision and with the condescension of one in whom the Truth of economic science has been deposited. See the whole of *Le collectivisme,* chapter 5, "Le collectivisme agraire," in which, with the exception of a few concessions, he attacks Laveleye's theses mercilessly. His argument on the subject of occupancy is clear, and reiterates the classical principle: "The fact of first occupancy constitutes a true right. Not only do history, universal agreement, and a sort of reciprocal avowal require this to be so, but reason itself and equity. Without the right of first occupant and that of voluntary or hereditary transfer, humanity would fall into an indescribable chaos. The right of first occupant represents at once a natural fact, simple possession, and a persistent effort of will, a labor" (ibid., pp. 77–78). Of particular interest for us are chapters 6 ("L'évolution de la propriété primitive. Le mir Russe") and 7 ("La propriété collective à Java"), which can be considered true and proper acts of accusation directed against Laveleye. (Note, on p. 86, the reference to Fustel de Coulanges, "with his learning, so complete and so precise.") A good example of Leroy-Beaulieu's argumentation can be seen in his conclusions regarding the *mir,* where his view of the collective structure typical of the Russian tradition is diametrically opposed to the version— admittedly too chromo-like—that Laveleye provides. He says, "This is what the Russian mir is for those who have studied it closely: a disappointment. It offers no serious social advantages along with its enormous cultural inconveniences. It destroys individual initiative; it closes wealth and ease out of the area in which they could be useful, and turns them uniquely toward lending at interest, toward usury. It stifles the sentiment of thrift and it offers almost no honest and loyal employment to accumulated savings. If one adds that the mir is incompatible with intensive cultivation and widespread, diversified production, one can judge of the merit of this first form of collective property" (ibid., p. 100).

95. Charles Letourneau, *L'évolution de la propriété* (Paris, 1889). This work follows Laveleye closely, showing also the influence of Le Play and Henry George. It makes great use of material taken from voyagers and ethnographers.

96. Napoleone Colajanni, "Di alcuni studii recenti sulla proprietà collettiva," *Giornale degli economisti* 2 (1887): n. 1.

97. "Before such an outpouring of facts, the mellifluent doctrines of Ferrara fall apart completely, and they disappear into the abyss of venerable antiquities" (Loria, *L'economia politica in Italia,* I: *La scuola economica italiana,* p. 94).

98. Carlo Bertagnolli, *L'economia dell'agricoltura in Italia e la sua trasformazione secondo i dati dell'Inchiesta agraria* (Rome, 1886), p. 305.

99. Colajanni, "Di alcuni studii recenti." See also Colajanni, "Di uno studio recentissimo sul collettivismo," *Cuore e critica* 2 (1888), a discussion of the short work of the deputy Francesco Cagnola, *Pensieri sulla ricostituzione delle forme sociali libere nei popoli latini* (Lodi, 1895).

100. Giacomo Luzzatti, "Evoluzione economica e legge del valore," *Ateneo veneto* (April–May 1888).

101. Eugenio Masé-Dari, *L'Economia politica e le riforme nella proprietà della terra* (Turin, 1893). Masé-Dari was a student of Cognetti de Martiis, and the essay constituted the inaugural lecture, given at the University of Turin 15 November 1892, of his noncredit course in economics.

102. Ugo Rabbeno, "Proprietà collettiva," *Il pensiero italiano* 5 (May–August 1892). The essay is particularly devoted to the work of Paul Errera on the *masuirs* (see chapter 7, n. 121), which we have seen to be vestiges of an extremely old collective form of appropriation in Belgium. It also discusses the fourth edition of Laveleye's book and the essay of Giulio Bianchi, *La proprietà fondiaria e le classi rurali nel medio evo e nella età moderna. Studio economico-sociale* (Pisa, 1891).

103. I refer in particular to Francesco Coletti, "Proprietà collettiva ed usi civici. Nota bibliografica," *Rassegna di scienze sociali e politiche* 11 (1893), written on the subject of Guido Cavaglieri, *Il diritto di tutti gli uomini all'effettivo godimento della terra* (Venice, 1893) (see chapter 7, n. 52, above).

104. Among the men directly concerned in the subject that interests us, Francesco Coletti and Enrico Ferri are two who illustrate this polarization. In his "Proprietà collettiva ed usi civici," Coletti polemicizes with Cavaglieri and all the "collectivists" of the controversy. He ridicules "the confusion between the universal collectivist form of property—a form that the school of scientific socialism pines for as superior and more perfect and into which the present form is supposed to evolve—and the little fragments of antique communities that still remain as the ruins of an age that was—or as the artificial reconstructions of the same, which philanthropy excogitates and which sometimes give the idea of erudite or romantic and dramatic reconstructions of some scene from the lives of our distant ancestors" (ibid., pp. 29–30). According to Coletti, the fate that arrived to the historic forms of collective property "reveals how misleading the vespers of a declining age can be, how the increasing pressure of population forces [the introduction of] new crops and the clearing of new land, and calls on the aid of capital, methods, and technical skills that bear no resemblance to those of the remembered institutions" (ibid., p. 35). Enrico Ferri, in a speech in the Chamber of Deputies on a bill for the restructuring and reorganization of collective holdings in the former Pontifical territories (see the next chapter), while he recognized the positive aspects of the bill and saw in it "a graft of collectivism into the individualist world of today," still noted that such initiatives were totally extraneous to an authentically socialist program, and repeated his faith in class struggle and his own aim of a structural mutation in the whole of society. (See *Atti parlamentari. Camera dei Deputati. Legislat. XVIII, 1a sessione. Discussioni, Tornata del 13 marzo 1894*, pp. 716 ff. The speech was also published separately with an indicative title: *Proprietà collettiva e lotta di classe—Discorso del deputato Enrico Ferri* [Rome, 1894]. The citation above is on p. 27.)

Chapter Nine

1. Bernardino Grimaldi (Catanzaro 1841–Rome 1897), who had previously held the post of minister of finance, was minister of agriculture, industry, and commerce from 30 March 1884—when Depretis, in one of the many reshapings of his cabinet, got rid of the incongenial Domenico Berti—to 29 December 1888, a period that nearly coincides with that of the itinerary of the law on the servitudes of pasturage. Information on him can be found in Amedeo Moscati, *Ministri del Regno d'Italia* (Naples, 1955–76), vol. 4: *La Sinistra al Potere*, pp. 402 ff.

2. *Atti parlamentari. Camera dei Deputati. Legislat. XV, 1a sessione 1882–83–84. Documenti. Disegni di legge e relazioni*, n. 270.

3. L. 23 aprile 1865, n. 2282.

4. L. 15 agosto 1867, n. 3910.

5. L. 2 aprile 1882, n. 698.

6. Soon after, the law, L. 7 maggio 1885, n. 3093 would be added to these laws extending the abolition of the pasturage and haying rights to the provinces of Treviso and Venice and to the communes of Favria, Andrate, Chiaverano, and Bollengo, all in the province of Turin.

7. *Atti parl. Cam. dei Dep. Leg. XV, 1a sess. 1882–83–84. Doc. Dis. di legge e rel.*, n. 270, p. 1.

8. Ibid., p. 2.

9. Ibid., p. 6. The minister had already (ibid., p. 5) said with satisfaction of the principle of abolition that "now this reasonable principle molds our legislation."

10. Almost as if to enhance the continuity of the social and economic program that the bill continued, the minister had cited only two documents, the pontifical *Notificazione* of 29 December 1849, on the disfranchisement of servitudes of pasturage in the papal territories and the famous "Voto economico sopra la servitù di pascolo" [Economic opinion on the servitudes of pasturage] addressed to the Sacred Economic Congregation by Paolo Vergani, *Assessor generale* to the minister of finance and commerce. This Opinion was decidedly proabolitionist, and although it was written in the context of the Curia, it is strongly influenced by Enlightenment ideas, as was often the case in pre-Unification Italy of the principates, and it cites abundantly Pietro Verri, Montesquieu, Melchiorre Delfico, Adam Smith, Mirabeau, and writers of the classical school of economics.

11. See Luigi Frezzini, *Sull'abolizione delle servitù di pascolo legnatico e simile* (Castelpiano, 1889) for a detailed examination of the Grimaldi bill, the various proposals that followed it, its entire parliamentary itinerary, of the law L. 24 giugno 1888, and of the executing legislation approved by R. Decreto 29 agosto 1889, n. 6397. There is also information in Gaetano Grisostomi, "I dominii collettivi nelle provincie ex-pontificie e dell'Emilia," *Rivista italiana per le scienze giuridiche* 43 (1907): 71 ff.; Giovanni Curis, *Le leggi sugli usi civici e i dominii collettivi nelle provincie ex-pontificie* (Rome, 1908), and in Giuliana D'Amelio, "L'abolizione degli usi civici nell'Italia centrale dopo l'unità," *Rivista di diritto agrario* 38 (1959): 443 ff.

12. *Camera dei Deputati. Archivio storico, Regno d'Italia. Disegni e proposte di legge*, filza 401 (legislat. XV, sess. unica, dis. 270).

13. *Atti parl. Cam. Dep. Leg. XV, 1a sess. 1882–1886. Doc. Dis. di legge e rel.*, n. 270 A.

14. *Atti parl. Cam. Dep. Leg. XVI, 1a sess. 1886–1887. Doc. Dis. di legge e rel.*, n. 145.

15. The minister declares in the introductory portion of his presentation of the bill to the deputies: "I have held it opportune to propose my original project to you again, introducing into it, however, those among the modifications suggested that I believed to be in harmony with the principles and criteria which in my opinion must mold the law under discussion" (ibid., p. 1).

16. Ibid., p. 3. To these basic concerns, the minister added specious technical juridical arguments, as when he rejected the admission of the users as beneficiaries of a dissolution of servitudes because they could not be qualified as lease-holders under emphyteusis.

17. The new commission was composed of Michele Torraca (president), Cesare Fani (secretary), Augusto Righi, Ruggero Mariotti, Ottavio Serena, Leopoldo Franchetti, Pietro Nocito, Francesco Penserini, and Giovanni Zucconi (rapporteur).

18. *Atti parl. Cam. Dep. Leg. XVI, 1a sess. 1886–1887. Doc. Dis. di legge e rel.,* n. 145 A.

19. Ibid., p. 11.

20. This can be found at the end of the Zucconi report (ibid., p. 14). The substance of the agenda is as follows: "The Chamber is confident that the Government, following appropriate administrative inquiry into the *comunanze, partecipanze,* and rural *università* existing in the provinces of the former Pontifical State and in Emilia, will present a bill bearing on the general norms for the existence, exercise, and, where it shall be indicated, the dissolution of the aforenamed collective domains, compatible with the interests of agriculture, the nature of the soil, and the interests of silviculture."

21. *Atti parl. Cam. Dep. Leg. XVI, 2a sess. 1887. Doc. Dis. di legge e rel.,* n. 8.

22. Ibid., p. 2: "The parliamentary commission has furthermore modified article 3 of the ministerial project, prescribing that the proprietors of the holdings encumbered with servitudes be obliged to give to the *generality of the beneficial owners* an indemnity either in land or in an annual canon, whereas with the ministerial proposal they are obliged to give this indemnity to the *interested communes.* The generality of the users has thus been substituted for the communes involved. This substitution, it seems to me, cannot be accepted. The users are not here considered *uti singuli,* since the property is not devolved on them, but are considered *uti cives;* and in that case it appears to me that the indemnity cannot be given to other than the natural agency that represents them, that is, to the Commune; otherwise the users would have to be constituted into an entity distinct from the Commune. . . . It seems to me that this new entity that would have to be created has no counterpart in our traditions, and where by exception it exists, it has proven such a failure as not to encourage the augmentation of its numbers. Undivided property has always been the cause of obstructions to every agricultural improvement, and the cause of disorders. . . ."

23. Ibid., n. 8A.

24. Ibid., n. 8B.

25. Ibid. "When the Arbitration Commission recognizes that it is indispensable for a population to continue in the exercise of the customary right, and the extent of the land to be ceded in compensation for the dissolution is judged by the Commission insufficient to the population to continue as in the past the exercise of sheep-raising or other activities covered by the servitudes, keeping in mind the conditions particular to the locality, the Arbitration Commission will admit the users to the entire encumbered holding, in exchange for the payment of an annual canon to the proprietor."

26. Both Minister Grimaldi, in his presentation to the Chamber of the law as it was modified by the Senate (session of 27 April 1888, ibid., n. 8B bis) and the rapporteur, the Hon. Zucconi (session of 1 June 1888, ibid., n. 8C), remark on this fact.

27. See Giustino Fortunato, "La question demaniale nelle provincie

napoletane," *Rassegna settimanale* 4 (1879), revised and reprinted (Rome, 1882) and now to be found under the title, "La questione demaniale nell'Italia meridionale" in his *Scritti Varii* (Trani, 1900). Zucconi makes extensive use of the Roman edition of 1882, citing it in his report.

28. Leopoldo Franchetti, *Condizioni politiche e amministrative della Sicilia*, volume 1 of Leopoldo Franchetti and Sidney Sonnino, *La Sicilia nel 1876* (Florence, 1877, reprinted 1925).

29. *Atti della Commissione reale pei demani comunali nelle provincie del Mezzogiorno istituita con R. Decreto 4 maggio 1884*. "Sottocommissione economica. Relazione di L. Franchetti" (Città di Castello, 1885). Franchetti's report was printed along with a report of Antonio Salandra, also for the subcommittee on economics, already noted, and a report of Gaetano Semeraro for the juridical subcommittee. We note that Franchetti uses and cites the researches of Maurer and Maine in his report.

30. *Atti parl. Cam. Dep. Leg. XV, 1a sess. 1882–1886. Doc. Dis. di legge e rel.*, n. 270A (the Zucconi report of 20 March 1886, on the first Grimaldi bill), p. 5, nn. 1 and 2; p. 7, n. 1; p. 10, n. 1. These citations are repeated in Zucconi's report of 18 June 1887, on the second Grimaldi bill.

31. Pasquale Villari, *Le Lettere meridionali ed altri scritti sulla questione sociale in Italia* (Florence, 1878).

32. Giovanni Zucconi (Cingoli 1845–Camerino 1894) is to my mind a figure who has been unjustly forgotten. Information on him can be found in the listings of Telesforo Sarti, *Il Parlamento subalpino e nazionale. Profili e cenni biografici di tutti i deputati e senatori eletti e creati dal 1848 al 1890* (Terni, 1890), *sub voce*, and in Alberto Malatesta, *Ministri, deputati senatori dal 1848 al 1922* (Rome, 1941), vol. 3, *sub voce*, which contains, however, many serious inexactitudes. Further information is available in some of the commemorative writings: *Comemorazione funebre del deputato Giovanni Zucconi* (Rome, 1894), which records the ceremonies in the Chamber of Deputies 8 December 1894; Aristide Conti, "Giovanni Zucconi," in *L'Appennino. Gazzetta camerinese* for 10 December 1894; B. Gasparri, *In memoria di Giovanni Zucconi* (Camerino, 1906).

33. To be sure, Zucconi was born in Cingoli, but since he spent nearly the whole of his life at Camerino and considered himself a citizen of that city, I too consider him as from Camerino.

34. "I have for many years been interested in this question, not only for professional reasons, but also for the love that I bear several of these villages, for whom these servitudes and these terrains constitute their wealth and the basis of their subsistence. In this way, I have been able to verify that some of these *università* are extremely well administered" (*Atti parl. Cam. Dep. Leg. XVI, 2a sess. Discussioni*, 15 December 1887, p. 498).

35. It is sufficient to read these same parliamentary reports to note the innumerable times that Zucconi indulges in local references or in sociological observations on the customs of the Piceno mountain folk. He always invites understanding and respect for the apparently abnormal character of their associative life.

36. Even today in the older holdings of the library of Zucconi's legal office in Camerino, where a nucleus of volumes and other publications that surely belonged to him have been preserved, there is a rich collection of documents written by him in defense of both the sylvan-pastoral communities and the communes.

37. See chapter 8, n. 35.

38. We can see both his culture and his historical and juridical calling, for example in the short publication, *L'avvocatura in Camerino nei secoli passati* (Camerino, 1886), published in celebration of the Marsili-Feliciangeli wedding.

39. He first taught administrative law, then political economy and statistics.

40. His "Lezioni d'economia politica," preserved in manuscript in the Zucconi Archive, show strong evolutionistic influences. The fairly rich collection of material that his heirs maintain in his legal offices in Camerino contains for the most part correspondence received, notes and first drafts relative to the parliamentary debates on the law on the servitudes of pasturage, collections of poetry written by him, and a few miscellaneous clippings of local or biographical interest, from his lifetime or from the period immediately following his death. Because this material is neither organized nor inventoried, I will refer to it generically as the Zucconi Papers. Among them, there is a letter from the economist Eugenio Masé-Dari expressing a positive judgment of his just-cited "Lezioni d'economia politica," an opinion which Zucconi's son had solicited in view of the possible publication of the "Lezioni."

41. Correspondence from Cassani to Zucconi, Zucconi Papers.

42. Correspondence from Ghino Valenti to Zucconi, Zucconi Papers. D'Amelio refers to a disagreement between Valenti and Zucconi on the occasion of the 1887 Congresso degli agricoltori marchegiani in her "L'abolizione degli usi civici nell'Italia centrale," p. 453.

43. His relationship with Giustino Fortunato was one of affectionate friendship, as demonstrated by the "Fortunateide," a curious series of sonnets dedicated to Fortunato and collected in a separate booklet in the Zucconi Papers. Their relations were cemented by ties of common political and intellectual interests. Among the Zucconi Papers there is a letter of Fortunato to Zucconi, dated Naples, 22 January 1890, in which he says, among other things: "I remember the promise that I made to give you three of my studies on the ancient history of my province that might relate to the work that you have at hand, and that I hope you have not yet given to the printers." The three studies that were enclosed with the letter concern "Moti sociali di contadini contro i proprietari in Lucania, 3° secolo av. Cristo," based on a text of Livy; "Moti rurali per il dissodamento de' demanii in Lucania, an. 132 av. Cristo," based on a citation from the Corpus Inscript. Latinarum; and "Il brigantaggio in Lucania, 3° secolo dopo Cristo," on a citation from the Corpus Inscript. Latinarum.

44. This is demonstrated by the rich collection of miscellany found even today in the older collection of the library in Zucconi's legal offices in Camerino. Much of it pertains to economic subjects; it all belonged to Giovanni Zucconi, and most of it the various authors had dedicated to him.

45. This is attested by the presence of Maine (in French translation) and Laveleye among the books in the Zucconi library. The Zucconi Papers also include many of his handwritten notes on Maine and Laveleye, dating from the period when he was preparing his speeches in the Chamber.

46. A good example of this can be found in the beginning of Zucconi's report on the first Grimaldi bill, dated 30 March 1886 (*Atti parl. Cam. Dep. Leg. XV, 1a sess. 1882–1886. Doc. Dis. di legge e rel.*, n. 270A, p. 2). He says: "After . . . both the rulers of the various segments of the divided Italy [before Unification] and the

Italian legislators [after] had enacted provisions directed at totally or in large part destroying the common enjoyment of and the servitudes encumbering rural land-holdings in the different provinces, the opinions of the economists and the states-men on this subject were slowly modified. From an acceptance of the axiom that these institutions, characterized as antiquated residues of the feudal regime, were always and in all times and places harmful to agricultural progress and absolutely unworthy of existing, they changed to a doubt of the validity of the doctrine that so generally and absolutely favored the destruction of popular rights. The many learned investigations carried out in recent times on the origin of these customary rights, and the related studies on the primitive forms of rustic property, the studies of the customs and the current state of property among several peoples of Asia and Europe, particularly in India under the English, in Russia, in Serbia, and in Switzerland, led the historians of the law to conclude that civic popular rights, more than a result of the destruction of feudal holdings, are often instead the vestiges of the primitive agrarian regime, in which enjoyment of the land and the exercise of the right to ownership over it was exercised in collective form by the components of the tribe or by the inhabitants of the villages. The writings of Sumner Maine, of Laveleye, of Roscher, of Rosa, and of many others threw great light on facts previously unknown to this doctrine. As in all the forms of evolution, so in the evolution of landed property, individualization came after the complex form of communistic property. Private property succeeds the latter and supplants it slowly, and the collective form remains where by circumstances of climate, soil, and political regime, individual appropriation of the soil is neither useful nor possible."

47. See the text cited in the previous note, in which Zucconi speaks of the need to go beyond an "axiom."

48. Zucconi here pays Gabriele Rosa too much honor. See Gabriele Rosa, *Feudi e comuni* (Brescia,, 1876). Article 13 is dedicated to the "Origine dei fondi co-munali in Italia."

49. Zucconi, *Parere legale sui diritti d'uso civico dei popolani di Fiuminata sui beni ex-camerali* (Camerino, 1884), pp. 13–14.

50. *Atti parl. Cam. Dep. Leg. XV, 1a sess. 1882–1886. Doc. Dis. di leggi e rel.,* n. 270A, pp. 4, 6, 11.

51. Speaking of the tendency that he saw dominant among the commissions of arbitration and in the Courts of Appeals concerning the interpretation of certain of the dispositions of the 1888 law, Zucconi states (*Atti Parl. Cam. Dep. Leg. XVII, 1a sess. Discuss.* 12 March 1891, p. 828): "We must not forget that all of these eminent gentlemen and magistrates have been educated in the school of Roman law, of quiritarian law, which holds individual property as a supreme principle. Individual property is presumed to be free, from which they draw the presupposi-tion that these customary rights, these servitudes are not other than abuses that the populations have introduced or simply tolerated from the proprietors. But this is counter to the fact recognized by studies which have been made recently, which demonstrate clearly to us that these customary rights, these collective domains, are none other than the residue of an ancient communism, of the primitive com-munism. (*Interruption*)—This is now indisputable."

52. "A problem . . . that has more importance than is thought. It has above all

an importance that is, let us say, scientific" (*Atti. parl. Cam. Dep. Leg. XVI, 2a sess. Discuss.* 15 December 1887, p. 495).

53. This is how Zucconi puts it in the report of 30 March 1886, cited many times, p. 2.

54. Ibid., p. 5.

55. Ibid., p. 4.

56. Ibid., p. 3.

57. Ibid., p. 2 (citation of Maine, Laveleye, Nasse, Roscher); pp. 5, 11, 12 (Laveleye); p. 11 (Heusler and the *Report*); p. 3 (Cattaneo); pp. 6, 18 (Cencelli Perti); p. 13 (Cassani); p. 9 (De Luca); pp. 5, 7, 10 (literature on the south); p. 12 (*Acts* of the Agrarian Inquiry and the works of Ghino Valenti).

58. See the conclusions of the report of 30 March 1886 (ibid., p. 7 and 11).

59. "To change, where it is possible, the rights of servitude into collective property" (ibid., p. 14). Also of great interest is the whole of another speech of Zucconi (*Atti parl. Cam. Dep. Leg. XVII, 1a sess. Discuss.* 12 March 1891, pp. 826 ff.). Its context was the discussion of an amendment proposed by the Hon. Tittoni to the bill, "Modificazioni della legge 24 giugno 1888 sull'abolizione delle servitù nelle provincie ex-pontificie." The conclusion is particularly significant (p. 829). In the text of the parliamentary acts, it ends with an invitation to the minister "not only to support this collective property and render it as profitable as possible, but to extend it in Italy." An earlier version, written in Zucconi's hand on the paper of the Chamber of Deputies and conserved in the Zucconi Papers, is much stronger: "Cast away the prejudices of the schools, do not worry if you are called socialists by those doctrinaires who learn everything from books without looking at the reality of facts and of men . . . and you will be easily persuaded that next to individual property one must now place civil and collective property. Fata trahunt—honorable colleagues—and it is only with knowing how to reconcile opposed systems and in becoming cognizant of the needs of the age that governments and parliaments can procure the happiness and the prosperity of humanity."

60. Thus, for example, in the often cited report of 30 March 1886, pp. 4–5.

61. Ibid., p. 4.

62. Ibid.

63. Ibid., p. 5.

64. See his eloquent speech during the debate on the bill modifying the law, L. 24 giugno 1888, in *Atti parl. Cam. Dep. Leg. XVII, 1a sess. Discuss.* 12 March 1891, pp. 828–29.

65. See Conti's commemorative article, "Giovanni Zucconi," passim.

66. Zucconi, *Discorso pronunziato nel 14 novembre 1880 in Camerino al Congresso delle Società Operaie della Provincia di Macerata* (Camerino, 1881).

67. Ibid., pp. 3–4.

68. This met with some extremely harsh reaction on the part of many deputies, as we will see in the next section. This gives further proof that, modest as it was, this measure was unique, foresighted, and courageous.

69. Later, in the context of general debate, the Hon. Franchetti was to denounce vociferously the strong pressures put on the commission by Minister Grimaldi (*Atti parl. Cam. Dep. Leg. XVI, 2a sess. Discuss.* 15 December 1887, p.

507): "I would beg the honorable minister of agriculture and commerce to have pity on this poor commission, dragged from concession to concession. The Commission had made a proposal. . . . The Minister came to meet with the Commission and . . . a new formulation of the article was agreed upon. Now he comes before the Chamber to demand that the Commission take a further step. . . . I beg of the honorable Minister, as long as he has obtained the first concession, not to swallow us up whole, and at least to leave us our feathers."

70. I refer in particular to the speech of Grimaldi during the session of 15 December 1887 (ibid., pp. 500 ff.).

71. Ibid., p. 500.

72. Ibid., pp. 503–4. In support of this, the minister, almost as if to demonstrate that there was a political line of common accord which could not be intermittently followed and denied, recalled to the Commission and to the entire Chamber that the debate on the agrarian question had closed with an invitation to the government "to present a law to suppress all of the ties that encumber property in the diverse parts of Italy, under different names, different forms, and with different effects" (p. 501).

73. Recently quoted by Pietro Rescigno, "Per uno studio sulla proprietà," *Rivista di diritto civile* 18 (1972):9.

74. In the session of 21 January 1888 (*Atti parl. Cam. Dep. Leg. XVI, 2a sess. Discuss.* pp. 610 ff). Giacomo Balestra (Rome 1836–1915), a lawyer, was elected deputy to the fourteenth legislature for the electoral district of Anagni, then, for the fifteenth and sixteenth, for the fourth district of Rome, into which his former district had been absorbed.

75. Ibid., p. 610.

76. Ibid., p. 611.

77. Ibid., p. 616: "Today for the first time I see a proposal that bears the pompous title of abolition of the servitudes of pasturage and that instead does nothing but maintain these servitudes, which everyone must recognize are fatal to the development and the progress of agriculture. If this article 9 were to be maintained as it is proposed, I frankly must declare that I shall vote against the law in the hope that it will be rejected by the Chamber. Then there would remain only the pontifical law of 1849, which is much more liberal than the present, because with that [law] all of the terrains subject to the servitudes of pasturage can be disfranchised unconditionally: with this one, no. Therefore this law is less liberal than the former one." The minister himself had not held back in his praise of the *Notificazione*, adding the text of it as appendix B to his presentation of the first proposal. Balestra's remark in support of the ministerial position was both malicious and provocatory.

78. Andrea Costa appears aloof and perhaps skeptical of these long-standing and marginal collective structures that obviously provided him little material for combat. He limits himself to declaring his support of the users, and his interest in the betterment of their juridical and economic position (ibid., 15 December 1887, p. 492).

79. Francesco Penserini (Macerata Feltria 1834–Florence 1909), deputy from Pesaro-Urbino from 1882.

80. Ibid., 14 December 1887, p. 494.

81. Ibid., p. 503.

82. Edoardo Pantano (Assoro, Enna 1842–Rome 1932), deputy starting with the sixteenth legislature.

83. Ibid., 21 January 1888, p. 619: "When collective property is spoken of, one expects to see anarchic and socialistic theories flying through the air like lightning, but I hardly need to recall to the Chamber how today the defense of collective property has come more through the work of scholars than through the work of revolutionaries, since it is held to be a concept absolutely essential to the development of the agricultural forces of a country and to social harmony."

84. Ibid., pp. 617–18.

85. Ibid., p. 618.

86. Leopoldo Franchetti (Florence 1847–Rome 1917) was deputy starting with the fifteenth legislature for the first electoral district of Perugia and Città di Castello. Some useful information on him can be found in Umberto Zanotti-Bianco, *Saggio storico sulla vita e attività di Leopoldo Franchetti* (Rome, 1950). On his testament, a gesture coherent to an entire lifetime oriented toward philanthropy, see Maghinardo Marchetti, *Un esperimento di grande proprietà trasformata in piccola proprietà coltivatrice. Il testamento Franchetti e la sua attuazione* (Città di Castello, 1935). On his work as promotor and "proprietor-director," along with Sidney Sonnino, of that lively journal, the Florentine *Rassegna settimanale di politica, scienza, lettere ed arti*, that after 1878 grouped many intellectuals and politicians around its directors, see Rosario Villari, "Alle origini del dibattito sulla 'question sociale'" in his *Conservatori e democratici nell'Italia liberale* (Bari, 1964), pp. 41 ff.

87. Parliamentary discussion cited in n. 70, 15 December 1887, pp. 489 ff.

88. Franchetti cites, for example, Ghino Valenti's *Il rimboschimento e la proprietà collettiva nell'Appennino marchigiano*, which appeared in that same year, and invites his fellow deputies to study it attentively (ibid., p. 490).

89. "In the southern provinces we have daily examples of the municipal councils legally stripping the users of the entire administrative organization of which they are the essential element. . . . Now, when the suppression of the customary rights is absolutely necessary, the only way to assure that the class of the population that receives benefit from these organizations loses as little of that benefit as possible, is to give that class of the population special representation" (ibid.).

90. "During the current session, the majority of the Commission has made concessions to the ministerial concept in which I could not follow them; for this reason I am speaking against it" (ibid., p. 490); "I therefore shall vote no" (p. 491).

91. "If it were question—instead of collective rights of a part of the population that is poor, that has no voice in the chapter—if it were a question of personal rights, a way would be found, in such a situation, to resolve the difficulty" (ibid., p. 490).

92. This finds Franchetti in total dissent: "We are not here only to apply the constituted law, but also to create new law when needed in relation to economic conditions and to existent, de facto relationships" (ibid., p. 491). This was a manner of answer to Minister Grimaldi, who had more than once recalled the Chamber to a sense of juridical tradition and to the eurythmy of the legislative system in force.

93. Ibid., p. 491.

94. Not long after, the Hon. Tittoni, speaking on the need to go beyond what had already been accomplished, was to declare: "The law as it was voted was crippled, incomplete. It reflected the contradictory orientations of the government and the commissions; it reflected the improvisational character of amendments introduced into it during the debate in the Chamber but was neither explicated nor coordinated with the rest of the law. It was thus better to foresee the difficulties that its application would bring to light" (see Tittoni, report of 20 February 1893, which will be discussed in detail in the following section).

95. The last subsection of article 9 states: "Against the decision of the commission, it will be possible to appeal to the minister of agriculture, industry and commerce, who, after he has heard the opinion of the cabinet, will take definitive action."

96. The minister of agriculture himself, the Hon. Miceli, so informed the Chamber during the session of 22 May 1890, as he presented his bill, "Modificazioni all'articolo 9 della legge 24 giugno 1888, n. 5489, per l'abolizione della servitù di pascolo ed altre nelle provincie ex ponteficie" (*Atti parl. Cam. Dep. Leg. XVI, 4a sess. 1889–90. Dis. di legge e rel.*, n. 158, p. 2).

97. That this was the policy of the minister and the ministry is demonstrated by the general debate on the budget for agriculture that took place in the Chamber 1 May 1890 (see *Atti parl. Cam. Dep. Leg. XVI, 4a sess. Discuss.* p. 2448). During this debate Minister Miceli, answering a specific question of the Hon. Tittoni, who had asked him to account for the narrow and biased ministerial interpretation, reinforced this interpretation by citing the opinion expressed by the Hon. Balestra as indicative of the sentiments of the Chamber. In other words, he cited the only opinion that had been expressed in the Chamber that was drastically opposed to dissolution in favor of the users. It was an easy matter for the Hon. Tittoni to point out to the minister in the discussion following his presentation how partisan and indeed how isolated Balestra's opinion was, and consequently how inappropriate as a basis for ministerial action (ibid., p. 2450).

98. Article 15 states: "If it is a case of a decision of the Arbitration Commission admitting the users to release of obligations concerning all or part of the encumbered holding, in exchange for payment of an annual canon to the proprietor, the latter can appeal to the minister of agriculture, industry, and commerce, following article 9 of the law, within 30 days of the notification of the decision."

99. Minister Miceli so informs the Chamber of Deputies during the session of 1 May 1890 (*Atti parl.* as cited in note 97).

100. The opinion of the Committee for finance of the Consiglio di Stato, as expressed in its meeting of 28 March 1890, is the only appendix to the bill n. 158 (as cited in n. 96). It is interesting to note that the interpretation of the council was founded almost exclusively on what Minister Grimaldi had had to say during the parliamentary debate. That is, they commit a *petitio principi* when they justify the interpretation of the administrative authority by means of acts and opinions of that same authority.

101. Explicit declarations can be found in speeches by the Hon. Zucconi (*Atti parl. Cam. Dep. Leg. XVI, 4a sess. Discuss.* 1 May 1890, pp. 2448 ff.) and the Hon. Tittoni (*Atti parl. Cam. Dep. Leg. XVII, 1a sess. Discuss.* 12 March 1891, pp. 822 ff.).

102. *Atti parl. Cam. Dep. Leg. XVI, 3a sess. Discuss.* 14 June 1889, pp. 2447 ff.

103. *Atti parl. Cam. Dep. Leg. XVI, 4a sess. Discuss.* 1 May 1890, pp. 2447 ff.

104. It was presented for the first time 22 May 1890, but the Chamber did not have time to discuss it. It was presented the second time 20 January 1891, with some additions.

105. *Atti parl. Cam. Dep. Leg. XVII, 1a sess. 1890–91. Doc. Dis. di legge e rel.,* n. 57A, p. 3.

106. "It seems to me that Minister and Commission both took on too timidly this question of the organization of the users' associations, resolving only one side of the question and avoiding taking it on in its entirety.... This bill has been waiting for three years. . . . I expect from him [that is, from the minister] the formal promise that he will present this bill without delay" (*Atti parl. Cam. Dep. Leg. XVII, 1a sess. Discuss.* 12 March 1891, p. 823).

107. The bill was sponsored by the deputies Tittoni, Zucconi, Garibaldi, Pantano, Pugliese, Fani, Zappi, Colajanni, and Gianforte Suardi.

108. *Atti parl. Cam. Dep. Leg. XVII, 1a sess. 1890–91–92. Doc. Dis. di legge e rel.,* n. 318.

109. This was Tittoni's objective in presenting to the Chamber, in his name and in that of other deputies, the bill on the "Ordinamento dei domini collettivi nelle Provincie dell'ex Stato Pontificio" (4 March 1892). Tittoni remarked that the law of 1888 "did not bother to reorganize the associations that existed, and, giving life to new associations, did not give them the means to live by." He argued that the aim of the new proposal was instead "the recognition of collective property . . . an affirmation of principle that gives legal sanction to the entities that have come up spontaneously" (ibid., p. 2). He cites an interesting case on p. 3: "Recently, for example, the agrarian *università* of Tolfa, in the province of Rome, wrote to me: 'One time they wanted to apply to us the law on the *Opere pie;* another time the prefecture wanted to apply to us the communal and provincial law; now instead they want us to be subject to other special laws: tell us, what law regulates us?' I was obliged to answer: 'No law, because this law to regulate your existence does not exist.' "

110. More than Zucconi, who was old in parliamentary experience although not in years, I am thinking of Napoleone Colajanni, who was among the deputies who proposed this modified bill and who in 1887 had written a well-informed résumé of the problem of collective property for the *Giornale degli economisti* (see n. 96 of the preceding chapter).

111. Some reference can be found in the autobiographical pages that Tittoni wrote not long before his death for the *Nuova Antologia* (1929). See Tittoni, "Ricordi personali di politica interna," now in *Nuovi scritti di politica interna ed estera* (Milan, 1930). There is also some information in Francesco Tommasini, *L'Italia alla vigilia della guerra. La politica estera di Tommaso Tittoni* (Bologna, 1934), vol. 1, pp. 246 ff. and in the anecdotes of Filippo Crispolti, *Politici, guerrieri, poeti, Ricordi personali* (Milan, 1939), who had the advantage of knowing Tittoni personally. Walter Maturi gives interesting biographical notes in his acid but vivacious course at the University of Pisa: see Maturi, *La politica estera italiana da Tittoni a Sonnino* (Pisa, 1942), pp. 7 ff. Among older and occasional writings, there is data in *Numero unico pubblicato dal Comitato degli elettori del*

Collegio di Civitavecchia pel giubileo politico dell'on. Tommaso Tittoni (Civitavecchia, 1913), one part of which, published separately, recalls the story of "I dominii collettivi."

112. Some years before in an article on geology (see Tittoni, "La regione trachitica dell'agro sabatino e cerite—studi geologici," in *Bollettino della Società geologica italiana* 4 [1885]) Tittoni had spoken of "the region where I am accustomed to spending several months of the year," that "solitary and picturesque region that extends from the Lake of Bracciano to Cape Linaro." Later, already in the thick of the parliamentary battle, he felt impelled to explain to his colleagues the reasons for his different point of view: "I speak to you in this way because, living part of the year amid the agricultural population, I know their needs; because even in recent days manifestations of the intense concern and apprehension of the agricultural folk of our province has reached me; because I have received petitions signed by thousands of persons in which they ask me with anxiety whether the application of the law of 24 June 1888 will permit the agricultural workers of the Roman countryside to remain in the villages in which they were born and in which they live, or whether they will be forced to emigrate because there will no longer be land in which they can sow their grain and wood to light their hearthfires" (*Atti parl. Cam. Dep. Leg. XVII, 1a sess. Discuss.* 12 March 1891, p. 824).

113. Tittoni's report of 20 February 1893, was largely based on ideas of "social conservation" and "tradition." See Tittoni's interesting confession concerning the primary importance of order in his "Ricordi personali di politica interna," p. 186.

114. Tittoni himself tells us that geology was "the science that was the great passion of my younger years" (Tittoni, *La geologia dei vulcani romani* (Milan, 1924) p. 5. All of this lecture, given in Rome on April 12, 1924, on the occasion of the fiftieth anniversary of the founding of the Rome chapter of the Alpine Club, is extremely instructive. Tittoni was one of the founders, along with Quintino Sella, also a dedicated student of geology, of the Società geologica italiana (ibid., p. 4). (See the amiable article of another geologist, already known to us, Carlo De Stefani, "Quintino Sella mineralogista e geologo," in *La Nazione* of 29 March 1884). As we have noted, an interest in collective structures and a general interest in agricultural affairs joined Tittoni and De Stefani, who furthermore knew each other (see Tittoni, *La geologia dei vulcani romani,* p. 20).

115. Ibid., pp. 7–8.

116. Tittoni, "Del concetto dello Stato e della sua azione nel campo economico," *L'Ateneo* 1 (November–December 1874, January–February 1875): 318. The article is signed with the pseudonym "Tom."

117. As an older man, Tittoni declared: "For a long time the *Cours de philosophie positive* of Auguste Comte was my philosophical and political Bible ("Ricordi personali," p. 192).

118. This was the little review, *L'Ateneo—Rivista mensile, scientifica e letteraria.* It started up in 1874 and had a very short career, but it gave the young Tittoni, its director and founder (he was nineteen at the time), an occasion to demonstrate his brilliant talents and his broad interests. Specific information on it

can be found in Tittoni, "Ricordi personali," p. 190, n. 2. There is some reference to it in Crispolti, *Politici, guerrieri, poeti,* p. 96.

119. Tittoni, "La giovinezza di John Stuart Mill secondo le sue memorie postume," *L'Ateneo* 1 (1874): p. 59.

120. Tittoni, "Del concetto dello Stato," p. 318, but also p. 314.

121. The article just cited provides and example of this. In it Tittoni gives proof of a broad knowledge of the *Kathedersozialisten,* of the economists of the classical school, and of the complex and varied debate between schools in Italy. Note the reference to Vito Cusumano's monograph (ibid., p. 310), "in which, if the violence of the expressions and the ardor of the neophyte are displeasing, the doctrine and the erudition are admirable," and to the Historical School of law (ibid., p. 314).

122. Tittoni, *La ferrovia Roma-Viterbo* (Rome, 1879).

123. Tittoni, *Osservazioni e reclami del Comizio Agrario contro il regolamento forestale per la Provincia di Roma* (Rome, 1879), a report that treats competently forestry and forestal economics.

124. Tittoni, *La discussione in Parlamento sul bonificamento dell'agro romano* (Rome, 1880), extrated from *La Libertà,* nos. 260–64 of 1879. The tract is a collection of common-sense geo-agronomic considerations arguing against the ill-considered change-over of the *agro romano* to intensive culture. Tittoni's background in agrarian economy and geology is evident. Note the citation of Roscher placed as epigraph to the work and the citations to Spencer.

125. Tittoni, *Il nuovo progetto di legge sull'esercizio della caccia e dell'uccellagione* (Rome, 1880) contains an interesting reference to going beyond the "absolute concept [of property] of the schools of natural law," p. 19.

126. I will cite two of these speeches: *Discorso . . . pronunciato ai suoi elettori a Viterbo nel Teatro dell'Unione il 13 novembre 1887* (Civitavecchia, 1887), published as a supplement to the newspaper, *Il Risorgimento,* and *Discorso pronunciato dall'onorevole deputato Tommaso Tittoni agli elettori del III Collegio di Roma il 27 Gennaio 1889 nella sala comunale di Ronciglione* (Civitavecchia, 1889). The latter, organized into sections according to specific parliamentary measures, is particularly important to our subject. In one section, dedicated to the "Abolizione dei diritti d'uso," Tittoni develops his ideas at considerable length, helping greatly in the interpretation of his actions and speeches in the Chamber.

127. Tittoni tells us of his correspondence with the administration of the *università* of Tolfa, who write to him for juridical advice (see above, n. 109). Another important agrarian *università* not far from Tolfa is that of Allumiere, whose internal affairs Tittoni recounts in detail to the Chamber (*Atti parl. Cam. Dep. Leg. XVII, 1a sess. 1890–91–92. Doc. Dis. di legge e rel.,* n. 318, p. 3). For a concrete example of his particular interest in these collective structures, and for his attempts to find solutions to their problems, see his *Discorso pronunciatio . . . agli elettori del III Collegio di Roma,* p. 9, which speaks of the countryside around Bomarzo.

128. "It is generally said that the rights of usage are harmful to property: it has been written and printed in manuals and tracts that these rights of usage are an obstacle to the progress of agriculture, it has therefore been concluded that they

must be purely and simply suppressed without considering that if they have existed for so many years, if for so many years for good or for ill they have assured existence to the populations, they must contain something that is rational, logical, and natural, and they could not for that reason be annulled with a stroke of the pen" (*Atti parl. Cam. Dep. Leg. XVII, 1a sess. Discuss.* 12 March 1891, p. 824).

129. Tittoni, *Discorso . . . III Collegio di Roma,* p. 6.

130. Thus, in the session of 12 March 1891, during the discussion of the modifications of the law of 1888 (cited above, n. 128).

131. See these writings of Tittoni, all of which have been cited: "La giovinezza di John Stuart Mill," "Del concetto dello Stato," *Discorso . . . ai suoi elettori a Viterbo,* pp. 11–12, *Discorso . . . III Collegio di Roma,* p. 6. The most important is section 3 of his report to the Chamber of 20 February 1893.

132. "An illustrious Belgain thinker, with whom I have had the opportunity to converse several times on these difficult problems, and whose solution torments modern society, Emile de Laveleye" (Tittoni, *Discorso . . . III Collegio di Roma,* p. 7). *Numero unico pubblicato dal Comitato degli elettori,* p. 5 also gives information on his familiarity with Laveleye.

133. Tittoni, "Ricordi personali," p. 191.

134. In his report to the Chamber of 20 February 1893, Tittoni declares that the repugnance toward collective property is only the fruit of ignorance and of prejudice, accumulated during the last hundred years. Speaking of the process of revising the old theories on property, Tittoni says: "The reaction against the individualism of eighteenth-century metaphysics which, if not the inspiration, was certainly one cause of the French Revolution, and the reaction against the economic theory of property of the school of Manchester, which found valid support among the jurists who were fond of the formula of quiritarian law of the Romans, took definitive form in the second half of the present century" (p. 14). Already before,in the speech that I have cited often of the session of 12 March 1891, on the occasion of the discussion of the modifications to the law of 1888, he had clearly expressed his opinion: "The law of 24 June 1888, as it was originally conceived and presented, answered to a theoretical and partisan concept proper to an economic school that had its advantages and its reason for being, but that now is being eclipsed; a school that, on a basis of general, rigid, and inflexible laws, wanted to regulate all the phenomena of economics; a school that claimed to apply its dogmas implacably in all cases and in all circumstances, without ever considering the lessons of experience" (p. 824). See also his youthful articles in *L'Ateneo,* ["Del concetto dello Stato," "La giovinezza di John Stuart Mill"], and the important *Discorso . . . III Collegio di Roma,* p. 6.

135. In the report of 20 February 1893, Tittoni calls on "the force of tradition" and "popular tendencies" as a source of resistance to the senseless and doctrinaire policy of abolishing customary rights. Let us not forget that Tittoni had read and admired the great masters of the German Historical School during his studies in jurisprudence in Rome.

136. "I will limit myself to recalling the vestiges [of collective property] which in many countries of Europe have challenged the work of demolition, first of feudalism, then of the Revolution, and finally of the doctrinaire tendencies of modern constitutions" (ibid., p. 14). It is clear that here feudalism is seen in its

aspect of an attempted appropriation on the part of the lords of the rights of the collectivity.

137. Ibid., p. 20.

138. The incubus of the "return" to the past, on the other hand, makes those who were definitively conquered by evolutionistic canons ill at ease. See Enrico Ferri, *Socialismo e Scienza positiva (Darwin, Spencer, Marx)* (Rome, 1894), particularly the chapter eloquently entitled, "La legge di regressione apparente e la proprietà collettiva," pp. 97 ff.

139. Tittoni, report of 20 February 1893, pp. 9 ff.

140. Ibid., p. 14 ("The collective form was the first that human societies knew").

141. Ibid.

142. "The two forms, the individual and the collective, are always found together in the evolution of property. Property presents two aspects, one individual and one social. He who sees but one is nearsighted. . . . Therefore the classical economists are in error . . . and the socialists are equally in error" (ibid., p. 16). It is interesting to note here that even in official treatments of civil law the two aspects, or moments, of property, the social and the individual, are frequently spoken of, but in a completely different manner. For the reigning doctrine, the influence of the social moment meant only to hypothesize a series of limitations on the liberty of the *dominus* and, consequently, to suppose the interference of the state in a sphere reserved to that *dominus*. That is, we remain in what can be defined as variations on the theme of individual property. The prevalence of the social moment in Tittoni meant instead a property intrinsically different from the schema of individual property, in which the protagonist is a collectivity and in which the subjective situation of the single *condomini* remained at a lower level of protection. We will have the opportunity to return more fully to the attitudes that prevailed in civil law in Italy before Unification in a study in volumes 5 and 6 of *Quaderni fiorentini per la storia del pensiero giuridico moderno* on the problematics of property in modern times. For further discussion of the question, see chapter 10, pp. 234 ff.

143. "The characteristic physiognomy of collectivity has always remained as Caesar and Tacitus sculpted it with phrases of rare and admirable efficacity" (ibid., p. 15).

144. *Atti parl. Cam. Dep. Leg. XVII, 1a sess. 1890–91–92. Doc. Dis. di legge e rel.*, n. 318, p. 4.

145. Two remarks should be made in connection with this bibliography. First, that it is not only ample, but extremely varied, and includes sociologists, economists, and jurists as well as philosophers and historians. All of the breadth of nineteenth-century thought on the origin and historical forms of property is collected here. Second, we find cited here authors who are generally ignored, such as Engels and Morgan, which gives us an indication of how at ease in cultural matters Tittoni felt.

146. Report of 20 February 1893, p. 14, but see also p. 16. Already in his *Discorso . . . III Collegio di Roma*, p. 6, Tittoni had declared: "No question better than this one can lend itself to the application of the various economic doctrines on the social question, and in fact we see here the clash between the absolute

theories of the classical school—which preferred uniformity, whereas in the body social all is variety; which sought simple formulas, whereas in life all is multiform and complex—and the system of the positive school, for which a principle is worth less than alleviating a source of misery and for which a theory, no matter how beautiful it might be, must bow unhesitatingly before the needs of special cases.''

147. *Atti parl. Cam. Dep. Leg. XVI, 3a sess. Discuss.* 12 June 1889, p. 2449; ibid., *Leg. XVII, 1a sess. Discuss.* 12 March 1891, p. 824.

148. Gino Luzzato, *L'economia italiana dal 1861 al 1914* (Milan, 1963), vol. 1: *1861–1894*, pp. 269 ff.

149. See the speech during the session of 12 June 1889, cited in n. 147.

150. Report of 20 February 1893, p. 15.

151. Ibid., p. 17.

152. Ibid., p. 15. After citing Laveleye at length, Tittoni indulges himself in sentimental statements that reek of rhetoric.

153. ''If there is, honorable colleagues, a bill that has a social character, I dare say even more than those that the Parliament has already voted or that it is to examine, it is this one that we present'' (*Atti parl. Cam. Dep. Leg. XVII, 1a sess. 1890–91–92. Doc. Dis. di legge e rel.,* n. 318, p. 4.

154. This is the central theme of both the presentation of the bill n. 318 (cited in the preceding note; see particularly p. 4) and of the report of 20 February 1893, particularly p. 17.

155. The bill openly declares this goal. See Tittoni's affirmation in his presentation of the bill to the Chamber 4 March 1892 (cited in n. 153): ''It is a proposal that aims, along with other provisions that may be created in the near future, above all at restricting the number of migrant and day workers, who are the element within which many of the disturbances and uprisings come to maturity, and at substituting them, where it is possible, with the collective and cooperative form of property, in which we see the most secure bulwark against those disturbances and uprisings.'' See also the report of 20 February 1893, p. 17, where Tittoni insists on the same idea.

156. This is the sense of Tittoni's polemical speech during the session of 12 March 1891 (see note 147, p. 824). His quarrel was with those ''deputies who declare themselves socialists'' and who ''make their socialism consist only in the enunciation of vague and nebulous theories for which it is impossible to see practical application.''

157. ''Proposal of evolution, not of revolution, because it grafts the modern principle of cooperation on the age-old trunk of the *comunanze* that sprouted in the Middle Ages; because it takes into account traditions and progress and harmonizes them together successfully; because it recognizes and promotes collective property without harming or diminishing the rights of individual property'' (presentation of bill n. 318, see n. 153, p. 4).

158. Tittoni refers to a ''Disegno di legge sui demani'' signed Lucio that appeared in *Critica sociale* 3 (1893): 9.

159. Report of 20 February 1893, pp. 18 ff.

160. Ibid., p. 20. After he bitterly criticizes the nearsightedness of the ruling bourgeois class and the capitalistic social order that it had produced, founded uniquely on wealth and thus on the dominance of the rich over the poor, Tittoni

affirms: "This is how *class struggle* arose, which one school today brutally promotes as its program, offering it in opposition to the program of social peace. Thus the workers' unions multiply, as do the societies of resistance and the *fasci*, all associations to which Laveleye's judgment can be applied: 'The new associations that arise lack tradition; they lack a juridical principle, and they are therefore nothing more than combative associations for fighting against capital.'"

161. *Discorso . . . III Collegio di Roma*, p. 9.

162. Tittoni speaks of this in the section of the report of 20 February 1893 that is particularly dedicated to the problem of the juridical structure of collective property, where he follows the theoretical constructions of Andreas Heusler (p. 24).

163. Report of 20 February 1893, p. 29.

164. There is no thorough historical and juridical study of the various bills that followed each other after 1894, nor of the work of the related parliamentary and ministerial commissions, but the material would be of great interest to the historian of jurisprudence. The following works offer limited data and details, but are not satisfactory as total reconstructions: Lorenzo Ratto, *Le leggi sugli usi e demanii civici* (Rome, 1909), pp. 207 ff.; Giovanni Raffaglio, *Diritti promiscui, demani comunali, usi civici* (2d ed., 1915), pp. 123 ff.; Giovanni Curis, *Usi civici, proprietà collettive e latifondi nell'Italia centrale e nell'Emilia* (Naples, 1917), pp. 972 ff.; Gino Marchi, "Natura giuridica, vigilanza e tutela amministrativa dei dominii collettivi," pp. 172 ff.; Romualdo Trifone, *Gli usi civici* (Milan, 1963), pp. 27–55. There are useful references in the last part of the work by Carlo Calisse, *Gli usi civici nella provincia di Roma* (Prato, 1906), pp. 111 ff.

Chapter Ten

1. See Francesco Filomusi Guelfi, "Trattato dei diritti reali, Lezioni red. per cura degli studenti A. Matozzi, C. Mapei, E. Nannini (dispense a. s. 1891–92)," p. 235, on the impropriety of this terminology, which goes back to the Middle Ages.

2. Gustavo Bonelli, "I concetti di comunione e di personalità nella teorica delle società commerciali," *Rivista di diritto commerciale* 1 (1903), part 1:297.

3. Bonelli states: "If we wish to be exact, we must reserve the name of property to the connection of absolute and exclusive dependence between the thing and the individual" (ibid.).

4. Salvatore Romano, "Sulla nozione di proprietà," in *Istituto di diritto agrario internazionale e comparato—Firenze—Atti della Prima Assemblea—Firenze, 4–8 aprile 1960*, vol. 2 (Milan, 1962), pp. 633, 641.

5. This current of thought was largely uniform, but one should at least indicate the thought of Salvatore Pugliatti, who, in "La proprietà e le proprietà," in his *La proprietà nel nuovo diritto* (Milan, 1954), pp. 156 ff., shows a complete freedom from the prevailing clichés. Among several specialists in public law I should cite the course outline of Massimo Severo Giannini, *I beni pubblici* (Rome, 1963) and the broad study of Sabino Cassese, *I beni pubblici—Circolazione e tutela* (Milan, 1969), vol. 1, pp. 147 ff.

6. The terms *dominio solitario* and *rapporto giuridico puro* are from Enrico Finzi, "Le moderne trasformazioni del diritto di proprietà," *Archivio giuridico* 90 (1923): 59.

7. For the history of theoretics, see P. Grossi, "La proprietà nel sistema

privatistico della Seconda Scolastica," in *La Seconda Scolastica nella formazione del diritto privato moderno* (Milan, 1973).

8. With a sincerity equal to his ingenuity, Bonelli, after beating his breast over the common but—for him—erroneous qualification of collective landholding structures as property, complains that "the moral sciences, and especially ours, are too immersed in the profane; they have too many roots in life as it is lived by the people, and thus they are too available to everyone to be able to keep to a rigorously technical use of words" (Bonelli, "I concetti di comunione," p. 297).

9. See Enrico Finzi, "Le moderne transformazioni," pp. 56 ff. This essay was the discourse to inaugurate the academic year of the R. Istituto di Scienze Sociali "Cesare Alfieri," 12 November 1922.

10. See Carlo Manenti, "Concetto della *Communio* relativamente alle cose private, alle cose pubbliche ed alle *communes omnium,*" *Il Filangieri* 19 (1894). He expresses the discomfort we speak of and arrives at an interpretation of *communio* as "something substantially different from property" (p. 504).

11. Silvio Perozzi, "Saggio critico sulla teoria della comproprietà," *Il Filangieri* 15 (1890), now in his *Scritti giuridici,* ed. Ugo Brasiello (Milan, 1948), vol. 1: *Proprietà e possesso,* p. 439.

12. Ibid., p. 554. An example of Byzantine construction is offered in Bonelli, "I concetti di comunione," pp. 297 ff. Starting from his individualistic premises, Bonelli arrives at the coherent conclusion that "whoever renders a thing *common ceases to be its proprietor*" (p. 298), and that "the communist [community member] does not conserve *ownership of the thing* either in whole or in part" (p. 299), and is however obliged to say that "ownership of things, for the period that [they] are under] community . . . is *in suspense*" (p. 300).

13. The clearest expression of this tendency in Italian doctrine is in Umberto Navarrini and his school (see Navarrini, "Società di commercio e proprietà in mano comune [Zur gesammten Hand]," *Il diritto commerciale* 19 [1901], col. 665 ff., and G. Egidi, "Sulla struttura giuridica delle società commerciali," *Archivio giuridico* 68 [1902]). Egidi insists on the need "to liberate the mind pervaded by common juridical notions" and states that anyone who will "make a comparison between the various concepts of the two laws [the Roman and the German] will not take long to realize that Romanistic concepts are the fruit of a long, elaborate, and difficult construction, and that the Germanic ideas are instead simple, primitive, and perfectly in tune with particular contingencies, with facts" (pp. 245–46).

14. To limit ourselves to the first courses on landholding rights, see Filomusi Guelfi, "Diritti reali—Appunti sulle lezioni racc. per cura di E. Piola Caselli e E. Briolini (dispense lit. a. s. 1888–89)" pp. 48–125, and "Trattato dei diritti reali," (1891–92), pp. 225–29. Gaetano Grisostomi, a pupil of Filomusi, carried on his conclusions concerning the juridical structure of collective property. See Grisostomi, "I dominii collettivi nelle provincie ex-pontificie e dell'Emilia," *Rivista italiana per le scienze giuridiche* 42 (1907), 44 (1908), particularly 44 (1908): 146 ff. For his acknowledgment of his debt to Filomusi, see p. 164. Despite its publication date, Grisostomi's work had been written by 1896, with the exception of several additions (see the author's remarks in n. 1 of p. 47 of the first part, vol. 43). For Venezian, see his "Reliquie della proprietà collettiva in Italia," now in *Opere Giuridiche* (Rome, 1920), vol. 2, p. 12 and his *Dell'usufrutto, dell'uso e del-*

l'abitazione (Naples, 1895), pp. 164 ff. When I speak of the school of Venezian, I have in mind particularly Francesco Ferrara, whose cultural attitudes are exemplified in the brief article, "Tracce della comunione di diritto germanico nel diritto italiano," *Rivista di diritto civile* 1 (1909) and later in his lengthy work on *Teoria delle persone giuridiche* (Naples, 1915). Venezian's teaching was also present in the painstaking and intelligent reflections of Enrico Finzi, his student. See his inaugural lecture, "Le moderne trasformazioni del diritto di proprietà," but especially his "Diritto di proprietà e disciplina della produzione," in *Atti del Primo Congresso nazionale di diritto agrario* (Florence, 1935), pp. 158 ff.

15. Oreste Ranelletti, "Concetto, natura e limiti del demanio pubblico—Teoria," *Rivista italiana per le scienze giuridiche* 25–26 (1898).

16. He used extensively the second volume of Otto Gierke, *Das deutsche Genossenschaftsrecht* (Berlin, 1868–1913, offset reprint of the original edition, Graz, 1954), vol. 2: *Geschichte des deutschen Körperschaftsbegriffs*, particularly Gierke's attempt at construction of pp. 136 ff.

17. Johann Kaspar Bluntschli, *Deutsches Privatrecht* (Munich, 1853), vol. 1, sections 58 and 59; Georg Beseler, *System des gemeinen deutschen Privatrechts* (Berlin, 1885), sections 82 and 83; Otto Stobbe, *Handbuch des deutschen Privatrechts* (Berlin, 1885), sections 97 and 98.

18. Until the third edition of the *Enciclopedia* of 1885, one can see the extensive influence of Maine and Laveleye and of the Germans in general. However, it was only with the fourth edition of 1901–4 that we see the wholesale transplantation of the juridical constructions of Germanistic doctrine—already used widely in Filomusi's courses—into the *Enciclopedia*.

19. See Filomusi Guelfi "Diritti reali," pp. 124–25 and his "Trattato dei diritti reali," pp. 226–29.

20. Filomusi declares in an eloquent note ("Trattato dei diritti reali," p. 229, n. 1): "The Romanists are absolutely contrary to such a concept of *divided property* and declare it illogical and absurd. This does not seem to us to be so, but we cannot deny that there is a contrary tendency in modern laws."

21. Venezian, *Dell'usufrutto*, p. 167.

22. Ibid., pp. 212–13.

23. Ibid., p. 168, the lengthy n. 1.

24. Ibid., p. 167.

25. Ibid., pp. 184–85.

26. According to Filomusi's disciple, Grisostomi, "I dominii collettivi," pp. 156 ff.

27. The position of Ranelletti, "Concetto, natura, e limiti del demanio pubblico," pp. 326 ff. of part 2 (vol. 26) is subtler. When confronted with the great variety of juridical situations, he avoids the construction of a unified theory and tends instead to note the peculiarities of the different collective structures.

Index

335